Second Edition

OPPORTUNITIES AND CHALLENGES OF WORKPLACE DIVERSITY

THEORY, CASES, AND EXERCISES

Kathryn A. Cañas
University of Utah

Harris Sondak
University of Utah

Prentice Hall

Boston   Columbus   Indianapolis   New York   San Francisco
Upper Saddle River   Amsterdam   Cape Town   Dubai   London   Madrid
Milan   Munich   Paris   Montreal   Toronto   Delhi   Mexico City   Sao Paulo
Sydney   Hong Kong   Seoul   Singapore   Taipei   Tokyo

For Luke, Rhea, and Neah

Editorial Director: Sally Yagan
Editor in Chief: Eric Svendsen
Acquisitions Editor: Jennifer M. Collins
Editorial Project Manager: Susie Abraham
Editorial Assistant: Meg O'Rourke
Director of Marketing: Patrice Lumumba Jones
Marketing Manager: Nikki Jones
Marketing Assistant: Ian Gold
Senior Managing Editor: Judy Leale
Project Manager: Debbie Ryan
Operations Specialist: Clara Bartunek
Creative Art Director: Jayne Conte

Cover Designer: Axell Designs
Manager, Visual Research: Beth Brenzel
Manager, Rights and Permissions: Zina Arabia
Manager, Cover Visual Research & Permissions: Karen Sanatar
Cover Art: Getty Images, Inc.
Full-Service Project Management: Shiji Shashi/ Integra, Inc.
Composition: Integra Software Services Pvt. Ltd.
Printer/Binder: Bind-Rite
Cover Printer: Bind-Rite
Text Font: 10/12, Times

Credits and acknowledgments borrowed from other sources and reproduced, with permission, in this textbook appear on appropriate page within text.

Cataloging-in-Publication Data for this title can be obtained from the Library of Congress.

10 9 8 7 6 5 4 3 2 1

Prentice Hall
is an imprint of

www.pearsonhighered.com

ISBN 10:   0-13-612517-4
ISBN 13: 978-0-13-612517-4

CONTENTS

PREFACE

DIVERSITY AND THE WORKPLACE: CREATING A DIALOGUE OF OPPORTUNITY

Teaching diversity management—whether to students or managers—is both challenging and rewarding. The topic of diversity management is engaging and dynamic as significant developments emerge daily from well-known organizations such as Abercrombie & Fitch, Coca Cola, the National Football League, and Verizon. While diversity management is a thought-provoking subject, it also poses some challenges for instructors because it is a complex and sometimes paradoxical organizational topic that involves conversations about emotionally charged issues such as racism, sexism, and ageism. Teaching diversity management is rewarding as the classroom has the potential to become a place in which knowledge is constructed through dialogue—through active student engagement, respectful debate, and continuous conversations about both historical and current diversity management business issues and cases. Essential to our purpose is the notion of dialogue as it represents the overarching pedagogical philosophy that frames our motivation for writing this textbook.

New to This Edition

- In Part I, we have updated both of the opening essays and we have added Chapter 3, "Diversity Management as Systemic," in which we describe top-ranked organizations for managing diversity, explicate a best practices integrated model of systemic diversity management, and include a comprehensive essay that highlights how IBM implements diversity management initiatives effectively on a comprehensive, systemic organizational level.
- In Part II, we have incorporated new, timely newspaper articles that begin each of the chapters.
- We are included two new case studies on the topics of race/national origin and the workplace, specifically Abercrombie and Fitch and Denny's Restaurants; one new case study on the GLBT issues and the workplace, "When Steve Becomes Stephanie"; and a new essay on people with disabilities in the workforce, "Counting on Workers with Disabilities."
- We updated the case on age and the workplace (Ford Motor Co.), as well as disabilities and the workplace (IBM, GM, and Cisco).
- In Part III, we have added a new section comprised of mini diversity cases that provide students the opportunity to work in teams and grapple with common yet involved diversity management workplace situations.
- We have enhanced exercises from our first edition and have added new exercises, specifically "Religion and the Workplace: A Brainstorming Activity," "Analyzing Diversity Commitment on Company Web Sites," and "Diversity and Sports: An Examination of the NFL, NASCAR, NHL, PGA, and NBA."

By writing this textbook, we hope to invite and create a dialogue of opportunity about the topic of workplace diversity with scholars, managers, consultants, and students. We, along with a number of diversity practitioners and academics who have contributed to this textbook, engage in dialogue about the intersection of diversity and the workplace. We believe that the most effective method for teaching diversity management is to bring together multiple perspectives, narratives, and voices that unite to cocreate a comprehensive source about the opportunities and challenges of managing diversity. Having a diverse workplace is indeed a business opportunity, but only when its complexities are managed successfully, which requires that they are both acknowledged and understood. Without understanding diversity as a complex phenomenon, it is difficult to gain a comprehensive understanding of what it means to manage a diverse workforce effectively. In essence, we hope to contribute a significant and unique perspective to today's conversation about diversity in the workplace by encouraging and engaging in open dialogue.

As we discuss diversity as an opportunity, we hope to help our readers become more effective and responsible organizational members. The underlying argument supported throughout our discussion is that organizations that manage their diverse workforce effectively will have a competitive advantage over organizations that do not. That is, we believe that managing diversity well will lead to increased organizational performance. A diverse workforce is more likely to gain a competitive advantage when diversity is implemented systemically; diversity must be understood and valued as an essential component of every aspect of the organization rather than incorporated sporadically within it. Organizations that are able to accomplish this will have more opportunity to excel in all areas.

Three-Tiered Structure for Understanding

Our discussion unfolds in three stages: First, we offer a theoretical and pedagogical as well as legal understanding of diversity; second, we provide detailed case studies of U.S. businesses that have both managed and mismanaged diversity; third, we incorporate multiple exercises that help students examine diversity on both personal and organizational levels.

In Part I, "Uncovering the Complexities of Workplace Diversity," our goal is to help explain the complexities of workplace diversity from both managerial and legal perspectives. Managers in today's dynamic workplace need to understand how these two perspectives interact—specifically, how one informs the other in the context of a complex workplace. In the first of the two opening chapters in this part, we examine diversity from a managerial and pedagogical point of view and discuss the following important considerations for understanding diversity in American business: multiple alternative definitions of diversity and important principles to acknowledge when defining diversity; four paradigms or approaches for diversity management; and the strengths and weaknesses of the business case for diversity. In the second chapter, P. Corper James outlines the legal aspects of managing diversity in his explication of the classes of people protected by law, the legal definition of sexual harassment, the Americans with Disabilities Act (ADA), and the Age Discrimination in Employment Act (ADEA). In addition, he offers general legal advice for both managers and employers on the topic of diversity management.

In Part II, "Managing and Mismanaging: Case Studies on American Businesses," we illustrate organizational successes and mistakes of American businesses. This section reflects our belief that understanding diversity is facilitated through detailed examination of real case studies. Our collection of comprehensive case studies focuses on how familiar organizations have grappled with diversity management. Our examples of organizations include Augusta National, Mothers Work, Abercrombie and Fitch, Texaco, Denny's, Ford Motor Company, Tom's of Maine, Cracker Barrel Restaurants, IBM, General Motors, and Cisco; we discuss how these organizations have managed diversity issues related to gender, race and national origin, age, religion and spirituality, sexual identity, and disabilities in the workplace.

In Part III, "Developing Three Essential Skills," our goal is to encourage our readers to examine their own relationship with diversity, assess how organizations manage diversity, and better understand the intersection of diversity and work. These exercises invite students to engage in energized, intelligent dialogue on the many intricacies of diversity in the workplace.

Terms and Concepts that Frame Our Discussion

DIVERSITY   A primary objective of our text is to illuminate the complexities of workforce diversity. We understand *workplace diversity* as a constellation of dynamic and interrelated identity group memberships that operate on both *primary* and *secondary dimensions*[1] as they continuously interact and unite to represent a person in his or her entirety at a particular time in his or her life. These identity group memberships reflect personal characteristics—both visible (e.g., race and gender) and less visible (e.g., religion and marital status)—that differ from whatever is considered the societal norm or standard; as a member of one of these identity groups, an individual is vulnerable to negative employment consequences such as discrimination.

Primary dimensions—those that most profoundly define us—include gender, race and national origin, age, religion and spirituality, sexual identity, and disabilities. Secondary dimensions—often just as important as the primary dimensions but more likely to change—include military experience, parental status, educational background, and social location/economic status. While all dimensions are significant when defining oneself, we choose to focus mostly on the primary dimensions of diversity, although a number of the secondary dimensions are discussed throughout the articles, essays, cases, and exercises.

In addition to understanding diversity as having two interrelated dimensions, we believe that the following five principles are critical to understanding the complexities of diversity: Diversity is expansive but not without boundaries; diversity is fluid; diversity is based on both similarities and differences; diversity is rooted in nonessentialist thought; and diversity is directly related to how one approaches work. In our opening essay we offer a detailed explanation of each of these principles in addition to delineating other definitions of diversity by a variety of diversity scholars.

AFFIRMATIVE ACTION, VALUING DIVERSITY, DIVERSITY MANAGEMENT   Diversity scholars often articulate three stages to understanding how workplace diversity has changed over time: *affirmative action*, *valuing diversity*, and *diversity management* (or *managing diversity*). The phrase "valuing diversity" is a movement beyond the affirmative action position of amending wrongs done in the past to those Americans—most specifically African Americans and women—who have been underrepresented in positions of organizational power. Diversity initiatives that represent the second stage, valuing diversity, are, according to scholar and consultant R. Roosevelt Thomas, "designed to enhance the individual's awareness, understanding and acceptance of differences between people." And, by contrast to diversity management, "valuing differences does not involve the changing of corporate culture and systems."[2]

Diversity management, however, represents a movement beyond valuing diversity and a managerial approach in which diversity is viewed as both a competitive advantage and the right thing to do; diversity is linked to strategic goals and is understood as directly influencing the way employees approach work. Thomas describes this stage as "a holistic approach to creating a corporate environment that allows all kinds of people to reach their full potential in pursuit of corporate objectives."[3] Further, he explains that diversity management approaches diversity from a management perspective, that is, how best to manage the company's human resources given the fact that those resources are now far more diverse than in earlier times. It is not about leveling the playing field to give minorities and women an extra advantage; it is about maximizing the contributions of all employees.[4]

The focus of our text is primarily on the third stage, managing diversity, because we believe it is this framework that American businesses should strive toward. We do not ignore the other stages, however, and we provide discussions of affirmative action and valuing diversity in the opening essays.

DOMINANT AND NONDOMINANT GROUPS   Underlying any discussion of diversity in American business—whether affirmative action, valuing diversity, or diversity management—is the recognition that some groups have had and continue to have more power than others. Those with power represent the *dominant* group and control the construction and dissemination of knowledge, make decisions, and allocate burdens and rewards and thus hold the more influential positions in the workplace. White men have historically held most positions of power in the workplace and thus typically constitute the dominant group in most organizations. In addition, there are groups of people, located on the periphery of power, who have historically been disempowered or *nondominant*. These less powerful groups of people include, but are not limited to, women; people with disabilities; older workers; people of color; people of different ethnicities; and gay, lesbian, bisexual, and transgendered people.

Although less powerful, subordinate groups often possess the ability—especially when working together—to negotiate successfully with the dominant group. And although we focus largely on the nondominant groups of people in our discussion of diversity, we believe white men constitute a critically important component of managing diversity because, as organizational leaders, they often have the ability to make decisions that directly affect the role of diversity in the workplace. Moreover, we often forget that white men are themselves a diverse group—whether, for example, in terms of age, religion, sexual identity, disability, or parental status. Further, unless both the dominant and nondominant groups work together, it is impossible for diversity to become a competitive advantage in the workplace.

PREJUDICE AND DISCRIMINATION   An important objective of this text is to encourage the readers to reflect on the ways in which diversity affects them. While using this textbook, we hope that students will gain a better understanding of how they may be *prejudiced*, often unknowingly, against groups of people they may view as different, seeing them through preconceived notions as lesser or deficient in some way. In addition, we hope that students will understand, specifically from the case study section, that *discrimination*—denying opportunities, resources, or access to a person because of his or her group identity—is, unfortunately, often a business reality. The case studies that illustrate discrimination represent uniquely helpful resources because organizations that have made serious management errors can provide powerful lessons.

STEREOTYPING AND ESSENTIALIZING   Other significant, interrelated concepts that encourage self-reflection include *stereotyping* and *essentializing*. We ask our readers the question: What are the potential effects of stereotyping and essentializing in the workplace? Stereotypes are particularly powerful, as they are formed when we ascribe exaggerated beliefs or generalizations to people based on their group identities rather than seeing each person as an individual (e.g., a professor might expect all athletes to be irresponsible students). Stereotypes are common and often arise from incomplete or incorrect information and restricted experience with a particular group of people.

Just as serious is assuming that a characteristic or set of characteristics is the essence—the essential nature—of all members of a group (e.g., people might expect that women are, by nature, better nurturers than men). Although it may be a human tendency to stereotype or essentialize others, it is important to remember both the inaccuracy of doing so and the potentially devastating effects of these generalizations on individuals' realities in their daily lives.

Instructor's Manual

Because the majority of our textbook is based on teaching diversity through case studies, we have dedicated much of the instructor's manual to the same. To enhance students' learning, each case study is accompanied by a detailed Teaching Note and set of PowerPoint slides. The instructor's manual also includes example syllabi, responses to discussion questions, comprehensive exercise instructions, and suggestions for individual and group assignments.

Acknowledgments

We thank many people for their assistance with this project, which would not have succeeded if not for their contributions. We would like to acknowledge the Pearson/Prentice Hall editorial, production, and permissions team for their professionalism throughout the project. In addition, we extend our appreciation to our research assistants: Nicole Cottelier, Kimberly Neves, and Ellen Donovan. Our deepest appreciation is extended to our families and friends; without them, nothing would have been possible or worthwhile. Dr. Cañas thanks Servando and Carol Cañas, Lance Pearson, Luke Cañas Pearson, Rhea Rose Cañas Pearson, and Susan Cañas Gregoire. Dr. Sondak especially thanks his parents, Fraser Nelson, and Neah Bois.

About the Authors

Dr. Kathryn A. Cañas is a member of the Management Department in the David Eccles School of Business at the University of Utah. Her teaching currently includes courses on diversity management, business communication, and pedagogy; she has taught these subjects to executives, Ph.D. candidates, M.B.A. students, and undergraduates. Her teaching has included courses on rhetorical criticism and theory, advanced public speaking and persuasion, interpersonal communication and coaching, gender communication, managerial writing, and writing for publication.

Dr. Cañas' research investigates best practices for teaching diversity management; communication strategies and models implemented by women—in particular women of color—in the workforce; and the role of dominant work metaphors in constructing and influencing women in organizations. She has presented a number of papers at national and regional conferences; and her professional association memberships include the Academy of Management, the Management Communication Association, and the Association for Business Communication.

Dr. Cañas received her B.A. in English and Communication from Boston College, her M.A. in speech communication from Indiana University, and her Ph.D. in Communication from the University of Utah. For more information, please visit her Web site at www.business.utah.edu/~mgtkc/.

E-mail: *kate.canas@business.utah.edu*

Dr. Harris Sondak is Professor of Business Administration at the David Eccles School of Business at the University of Utah and Adjunct Professor of Business Administration at the Fuqua School of Business at Duke University. His teaching includes courses on groups, negotiations, creating and maintaining business relationships, managing conflict in organizations, competitive strategy, managing diversity, organizational behavior, consulting to nonprofits, philosophy of social science, and business ethics and leadership. He has taught these subjects to executives, Ph.D. candidates, M.B.A. students, and undergraduates from around the world. Dr. Sondak was honored with the Distinguished Teaching Award by the University of Utah.

Dr. Sondak's research investigates the psychology of allocation decisions including two-party and multiparty negotiations, group process and decisions, and procedural justice and ethics. His research has been published in a number of leading academic journals. Dr. Sondak has served as a reviewer, a member of the editorial board, and as the associate editor for scholarly publications.

Dr. Sondak received his B.A. in philosophy from the University of Colorado and his M.S. and PhD in organizational behavior from Northwestern University. He has been a visiting faculty member at the International Institute for Management Development (IMD) in Lausanne, Switzerland; the Graduate School of Business, Stanford University; the Indian School of Business in Hyderabad, India; and the Kellog School of Management, Northwestern University. For more information, please visit his Web site at www.business.utah.edu/~mgths/.

E-mail: *sondak@business.utah.edu*

Notes

1. The concepts of primary and second dimensions of diversity are adapted from Marilyn Loden, *Implementing Diversity* (New York: McGraw-Hill, 1996).
2. R. Roosevelt Thomas, Jr., *Beyond Race and Gender: Unleashing the Power of Your Total Work Force by Managing Diversity* (New York: AMACON, 1991), 169.
3. Ibid., 167.
4. Ibid., 168.

PART ONE

Uncovering the Complexities of Workplace Diversity

In this part, "Uncovering the Complexities of Workplace Diversity," our goal is to explore the complexities of workplace diversity from both managerial and legal perspectives. In Chapter 1, "Diversity in the Workplace: A Theoretical and Pedagogical Perspective," we examine diversity from a managerial point of view and discuss the following important considerations for understanding diversity in American business: the changing U.S. demography; multiple alternative definitions of diversity and important principles to acknowledge when defining diversity; four paradigms or approaches for diversity management; and the complexities of the business case for diversity.

In Chapter 2, "Diversity in the Workplace: A Legal Perspective," P. Corper James outlines the legal aspects of managing diversity in his explication of the classes of people protected by law, the legal definitions of sexual harassment, the Americans with Disabilities Act (ADA), and the Age Discrimination in Employment Act (ADEA). In addition, he offers general legal advice for both managers and employers on the topic of diversity management.

In Chapter 3, we grapple with the question, What constitutes effective diversity management? In particular, we highlight exemplary organizations for managing diversity, articulate a systemic approach to managing diversity, and include a case study, "Diversity as Strategy," that explicates how IBM manages diversity using an integrated, systemic approach.

CHAPTER 1

Diversity in the Workplace: A Theoretical and Pedagogical Perspective

Diversity education is big business. In corporate America and higher education, diversity training has become a multibillion-dollar industry, with a wide variety of diversity summits, workshops, toolkits, books, training videos, e-learning programs, executive coaching sessions, and leadership academies.

With what might seem like an excess of diversity management tools, the importance of managing workplace diversity can easily be reduced to an overhyped workplace trend. The belief that diversity management is nothing more than a transitory phenomenon may in fact represent an organizational ideology that educators are forced to confront when teaching about workplace diversity in both business and academics. It is this misperception combined with other challenges related to diversity education that help to underscore the importance of our goal of creating a pedagogical approach that will allow students and managers to examine more effectively and therefore understand better the complexities of diversity and managing diversity in organizations.

In this essay we examine what it means to teach diversity management, analyze the opportunities and challenges related to teaching diversity management, and present an innovative pedagogical approach that we believe will facilitate the teaching of diversity management. The motivation behind understanding how to manage workforce diversity is twofold: it is the right and ethical thing to do and it can enhance an organization's competitive advantage. The issue is not whether the workforce is or is not diverse; diversity is a business reality, is here to stay, and ought to be embraced. The issue, then, is whether organizations lack the knowledge to unleash the power of their diverse employees through effective diversity management and, if so, how to correct this problem.

Although we illuminate some of the limitations of diversity management education, we uphold a prodiversity position, support organizations that invest in diversity management initiatives as a way to empower employees, and agree that "[O]rganizations that invest their resources in taking advantage of the opportunities that diversity offers should outperform those that fail to make such investments."[1] Our position about diversity in general is that diversity can become an exciting business opportunity, but only when it is managed effectively at all levels of an organization and understood in terms of both its advantages and disadvantages. To explain this position, we first define what it means to manage diversity.

Dr. Kathryn A. Cañas and Dr. Harris Sondak, The University of Utah

DIVERSITY MANAGEMENT

Diversity management is an organizational commitment and systemic approach that moves beyond compliance with legal requirements and statements that simply express the organization's claims to value diversity. We describe effective diversity management as systemic because its dimensions are incorporated throughout the inner workings of a business and linked to strategic business goals. As Michàlle Barak suggests, diversity management is "the voluntary organizational actions that are designed to create through deliberate policies and programs greater inclusion of employees from various backgrounds into the formal and informal organizational structures."[2] Diversity management is distinct from equal opportunity legislation and affirmative action programs because it "is proactive and aimed at creating an organization in which all members can contribute and achieve to their full potential."[3] The purpose of such organizational actions and policies is to incorporate diversity into the main work of the organization so that diverse perspectives influence processes such as decision making, problem solving, and marketing; company image; methods of communication; and product design, as well as have a direct impact on the organization's mission, values, and goals.

A required component of an effective diversity management policy is a steadfast commitment from organizational leadership. Business leaders play a crucial role in how diversity is perceived and implemented in their organizations, and without authentic commitment from the executive ranks, diversity will remain a stagnant or even festering organizational issue. Leaders must be able to express clearly how diversity is defined and what role diversity plays in their corporate culture; they must commit themselves to recruiting and retaining diverse employees, incorporating diverse perspectives into the main work of the organization, implementing supplier diversity initiatives, linking diversity to financial success, and using some type of metrics for measuring the successes (or failures) of their diversity initiatives. Further, it is also necessary for leaders to understand that although diversity challenges may arise, they cannot be ignored but rather recognized and resolved.

Because of the comprehensive nature of diversity management, teaching its complexities is no easy task, and it is not surprising that implementing an effective approach to teaching this topic poses pedagogical challenges for both educators and students. Diversity management is not all about difficulties, however, as we describe a few of the opportunities related to teaching about diversity in organizations.

OPPORTUNITIES OF TEACHING DIVERSITY MANAGEMENT

The enthusiasm surrounding the issue of diversity in organizations in both business and academia is palpable. This enthusiasm encourages lively discussion about thought-provoking, progressive classroom topics as students see familiar businesses embrace diversity and publicly declare their allegiance to promoting diversity as an organizational strategy.

American Express, for example, maintains that "the connection between the diversity of our workforce and our overall performance quality is clearly valued."[4] Marriott International enthusi-astically describes its commitment to diversity as "absolute" and asserts that diversity "is more than a goal . . . it's our business. From our global workforce to our suppliers, owners and fran-chisees, and customers and communities, we thrive on the differences that give our company its strength and competitive edge."[5] Boldly claiming that "diversity is who we are," Starbucks Coffee Company describes diversity as "a way of life" and "the core of our culture and a foundation for the way we conduct business."[6] Verizon boasts that "[W]e have made diversity an integral part of our business, from workforce development and supplier relationships to economic development, marketing, and philanthropy."[7] Businesses such as these do more than just post their diversity missions on posters, pamphlets, and Web sites; by contrast, they are committed to giving diversity a legitimate voice in executive decision-making processes by creating positions such as Chief Diversity Officer; Senior Vice President of External Affairs and Global Diversity Officer; and Vice President of Workplace Culture, Diversity, and Compliance.

Like businesses, many universities value diversity, often promoting diversity as a critical component of their success and identity as an organization. Reflecting this trend, the University of North Carolina describes diversity as a "key component" in its "academic plan" and its "pursuit of excellence."[8] In addition to universities at large, business schools are independently communicating their value of diversity. The Kellogg School of Management at Northwestern University highlights specific dimensions of diversity in its diversity philosophy, and it works to solidify its commitment by offering the graduate elective Managing Workforce Diversity. Similarly, Rutgers Business School offers the graduate elective Managing Organizational Diversity within the concentration of Management and Global Business. On an undergraduate level, examples include the business schools at the University of California, the University of Connecticut, the University of Illinois, and the University of Utah, which all offer diversity management courses. Mirroring corporate America, universities are also moving toward implementing executive positions such as Chief Diversity Officer and Associate Vice President for Diversity.

Student enthusiasm for learning about diversity management comes from their own experiences in relation to the reality of today's diverse workforce. Leaders of businesses and universities have realized that although there may be differing opinions about diversity management, one aspect of diversity cannot be disputed: The American workforce and classroom are becoming increasingly heterogeneous. Students, many of whom are taking classes in addition to working in either part-time or full-time jobs, see the emergence of diversity issues—such as the prevalence of older workers in the workforce, employees who want to express themselves spiritually during work hours, or the formation of employee resource groups—in the organizations in which they work. Further, students become increasingly engaged as they realize that the dynamic workforce demographics do not simply represent a more diverse workforce but also highlight some unexpected realities within these demographic trends.

One demographic that students may be familiar with is the record numbers of women and minorities entering the U.S. workforce. According to the U.S. Bureau of Labor Statistics, women now account for 46 percent of all full-time and part-time workers. While this fact may be obvious to students, not as obvious is the fact that despite their increased numbers in the workforce, women and minorities still receive a disproportionately low share of the rewards allocated by U.S. businesses. For example, women occupy only about 8 percent of executive vice president positions (and above) at Fortune 500 companies.[9] In addition, African Americans and Latinos represent approximately 25 percent of the U.S. population yet hold fewer than 5 percent of senior-management positions.[10] In response to these demographics, we ask our students to grapple with the following question: Why is the increasing profusion of diverse workers not being matched by similarly expanded opportunities in the executive suites?

Perhaps more interesting for students to discover is that in some cases efforts to increase opportunities have been associated with actual declines. The number of people with disabilities entering the workforce, for example, seems to have decreased overall in the last decade, despite the passage of the Americans with Disabilities Act (ADA) in 1990, which was supposed to provide better access for them.[11] Furthermore, various minority groups continue to suffer discrimination beyond restricted access to employment or low pay. In the case of gay and lesbian workers, nearly two out of five say they consistently face some form of hostility or harassment on the job.[12] And despite the fact that 95 percent of Americans say they believe in God, and 48 percent say they talk about their religious faith at work, the EEOC reports a 29 percent spike since 1992 in the number of religion-based discrimination charges.[13] In light of statistics such as these, we ask students to contemplate why these workplace inconsistencies occur.

When teaching students about diversity management, the pedagogical opportunities are based in the students' own experiences as they are witnesses to diversity's dominant presence and dynamic quality in the workplace and classroom. While diversity represents a significant and obvious component of today's workforce, diversity management is a somewhat nascent organizational concept; because of this, teaching about managing diversity can pose some pedagogical challenges.

CHALLENGES OF TEACHING DIVERSITY MANAGEMENT

Although there is a clear movement in corporate America and academia to embrace diversity, not so clear is the public acknowledgment and dialogue about the challenges associated with diversity management education. Students need to realize that diversity management is a sometimes difficult process with often uncertain results; even skilled managers with the best intentions can fail to anticipate and resolve the problems that managing diversity presents. The diversity paradox represents the potential challenges or inconsistencies that diversity may raise. An illustration of such a challenge is that while diversity is a proven source of creativity and innovation in organizations, it is also a cause of misunderstanding and conflict.[14]

As students grapple with the idea that sometimes diversity within an organization can be paradoxical, they begin to understand the complexity of diversity management. An organization that illuminates a diversity paradox is Xerox. Xerox, a progressive leader in diversity management, has won a long string of diversity-related awards and has been rated as one of the Top 10 companies in hiring minorities, women, people with disabilities, and gay and lesbian employees by *Fortune*, *Forbes*, *Working Mother*, *Latino Style*, and *Enable Magazine*.[15] Xerox's approach to managing diversity has been clear and consistent; Chairman and Chief Executive Officer Anne M. Mulcahy states: "diversity breeds creativity. Maybe it's because people with different backgrounds challenge each other's underlying assumptions, freeing everybody from convention and orthodoxy."[16] Nonetheless, diversity management at Xerox has had its problems. Not only was evidence found that suggested the clear lack of promotional opportunity and equal pay for African Americans, but Xerox employees "fashioned a workplace display of African American dolls with nooses around their necks, igniting a lawsuit against the company in 2002."[17] Although Xerox has been a model of diversity management for over 40 years, it represents a diversity paradox as it recently was charged with blatant, systemic discrimination of African Americans.

For the diversity management educator, illuminating problematic aspects of diversity is just as important as illuminating diversity's strengths. Another challenge facing the diversity educator is effectively teaching the business case for diversity. Despite the organizational intricacies of having and managing a diverse workforce, many business leaders and educators unconditionally embrace the main premise of the business case for diversity: having a diverse workforce will improve financial performance. The business case for diversity is, in effect, "a management-focused, economic argument to promote corporate investments in workforce diversification. The business case links investments in organizational diversity initiatives to improvements in productivity and profitability."[18] The business case for diversity asserts that a diverse workforce creates a competitive advantage by decreasing overall costs while enhancing creativity, problem solving capability, recruitment and marketing strategies, overall productivity, leadership effectiveness, global relations, and organizational flexibility.[19] The business case discourse is powerful and pervasive as it has spread not only within the United States, but also globally throughout the United Kingdom, Australia, Canada, the Netherlands, South Africa, and Scandinavia.[20]

Nonetheless, it is the diversity educator's responsibility to illuminate that although the business case argument may well be appealing on an ideological level and represents a popular position on workforce diversity, it fails to take into account the challenges associated with a diverse workforce such as the potential of more conflict and misunderstanding because of people's differences. While some researchers have discussed the flaws of the business case,[21] this cautionary conversation goes mostly unrecognized in diversity training programs and college courses. Popular books that are used in both training and college courses, for example, often dedicate very little discussion to the lack of research supporting the business case for diversity.[22] We believe that failing to recognize the problematic nature of diversity and taking the business case for diversity for granted, however, leaves students and managers less well equipped than necessary to handle the potential challenges, pitfalls, and paradoxes associated with diversity.

We believe that when teaching about diversity management, the pedagogical framework must take into account real complexities and challenges that diversity may present. We have developed a three-phase pedagogical framework to help diversity educators navigate diversity's complexities and create a more accurate and therefore more useful conversation about diversity and diversity management. The first phase is to grapple with the definition of diversity. As diversity educators and students alike often ask the question, "What is diversity?" educators should encourage a conversation about definitions that illuminate diversity's complexities. The second phase facilitates an understanding of diversity management from an organizational leadership perspective. In the third phase, diversity educators should present in detail the arguments of the business case for diversity and encourage an examination of the validity of the assumptions supporting these arguments.

We believe that the pedagogical framework presented here facilitates a method through which diversity educators can begin a more accurate and helpful conversation about diversity management in business and academia. The main goal of this three-phase framework is to make teaching more effective—to create a more meaningful, honest, and dynamic dialogue about diversity in the workplace. We first begin with a detailed explication of phase one: defining diversity.

DEFINING DIVERSITY

When teaching students and managers about managing diversity, it is important to know what diversity means. Diversity educators should explain the various ways in which diversity is defined by scholars, practitioners, and organizations as a way to illuminate the breadth of interpretations and then to encourage students to determine what they view as the most representative or useful definition. In this section, after we present some of these definitions—by examining their weaknesses and highlighting their strengths—we present principles that will enhance a more comprehensive understanding of diversity.

Society for Human Resource Management

The Society for Human Resource Management (SHRM), a leading professional association, recognizes that although diversity "is often used to refer to differences based on ethnicity, gender, age, religion, disability, national origin and sexual orientation," it also encompasses an "infinite range" of "unique characteristics and experiences, including communication styles, physical character such as height and weight, and speed of learning and comprehension."[23]

Marilyn Loden

Marilyn Loden, a nationally recognized organizational change consultant, emphasizes the importance of an all-encompassing definition of diversity, because, as she believes, when any group—white men, for example—is excluded, managing diversity may create division rather than inclusion. To "avoid widescale opposition," corporations should define diversity such that "everyone's diversity is valued."[24] Because of this need for widespread endorsement from organizational members, Loden views diversity as "important human characteristics that impact individuals' values, opportunities, and perceptions of self and others at work."[25] Loden's widely embraced model of diversity, as represented in Figure 1-1, explicates diversity as having both primary and secondary dimensions.

Loden's primary dimensions of diversity are "interlocking segments of a sphere" that represent the core of each individual's identity while the secondary dimensions are "more mutable, less visible to others around us, and more variable."[26] Loden explains that because the secondary dimensions are more dynamic, their power is "less constant" and "more individualized than is

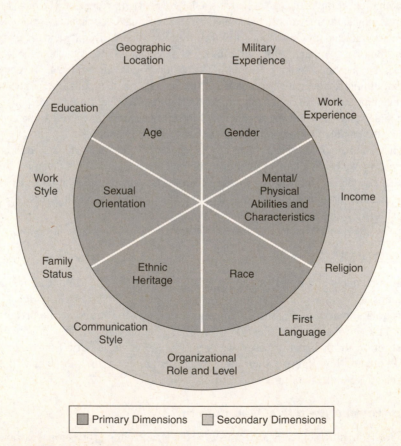

FIGURE 1-1 The Diversity Wheel
Loden Associates designs innovative models such as the diversity wheel to facilitate understanding of a broad range of primary and secondary dimensions of diversity.   *Source:* From *Implementing Diversity* © 1996. Irwin Professional Publishing.

true for the core dimensions."[27] In effect, the dimensions work in tandem to give definition to people's lives "by contributing to a synergistic, integrated whole—the diverse person."[28]

Anita Rowe and Lee Gardenswartz

Anita Rowe and Lee Gardenswartz, human resource experts on managing workforce diversity, embrace Loden's definition of diversity but add two additional dimensions as represented in Figure 1-2—one, personality, in the center and the other, organizational membership, on the periphery. According to Rowe and Gardenswartz, at the center of the diversity model is "personality" which is "the innately unique aspect" that "permeates all other layers" and unites them.[29] The next layer is "internal dimensions" (Loden's primary dimensions) which is then followed by "external dimensions" (Loden's secondary dimensions).[30] The outermost layer consists of organizational characteristics such as union affiliation, management status, and work content or professional field. In sum, these four layers of diversity come together to form one's "diversity filter."[31]

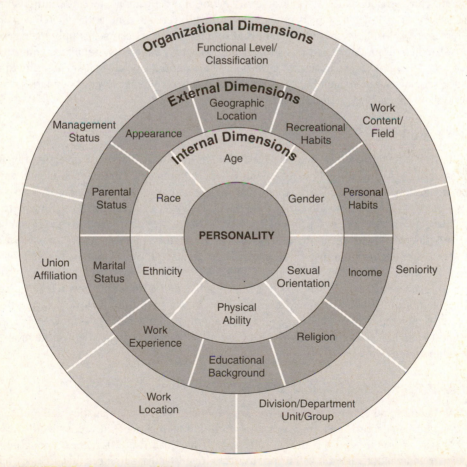

FIGURE 1-2   Four Layers of Diversity

Internal Dimension and External Dimensions are adapted from Marilyn Loden and Judy Rosener, *Workforce America!* (Business One Irwin., 1991). *Source:* From *Diverse Teams at Work.* Gardenswartz & Rowe (Irwin, 1995).

R. Roosevelt Thomas, Jr.

The definition of diversity articulated by R. Roosevelt Thomas, Jr., CEO of R. Thomas & Associates, Inc. and founder and president of the American Institute for Managing Diversity, emphasizes the relationship between diversity and individuals' similarities rather than their differences. Thomas maintains that diversity is "any mixture of items characterized by differences and similarities"[32] and explains that when business leaders make decisions, they must deal with both differences and similarities among members of their workforce simultaneously. In addition, Thomas emphasizes that diversity must be viewed as inclusive insofar as "if you are concerned about racism, you include all races; if you're concerned about gender, you include both genders; or if you're concerned about age issues, you include all age groups."[33]

Some diversity scholars would argue that the strength of these definitions, as presented by SHRM's Diversity Forum, Loden, Rowe and Gardenswartz, and Thomas, is their inclusiveness—the way in which they tend to make room for all members of an organization within the framework of diversity. Diversity, in this sense, becomes broad and all-encompassing. Yet we believe that by not creating boundaries of what diversity is not in organizations, these definitions imply that all organizational members are diverse. This assumption creates a situation whereby diversity management risks losing its special meaning and significance as it becomes simply management in general. When discussing definitions such as these, diversity educators should encourage a dialogue on the strengths and weaknesses of all-inclusive definitions of diversity. They should also introduce scholars who, through their definitions of diversity, attempt to put boundaries around the meaning of diversity in organizations.

Myrtle P. Bell

Myrtle P. Bell directly addresses the issue of the expansion of the notion of diversity. For Bell, the areas of diversity include only race, ethnicity, sex, religion, age, physical and mental ability, sexual orientation, work and family status, and weight and appearance. She emphasizes these specific areas of difference because they "are based on power or dominance relations between groups, particularly 'identity groups,' which are the collectivities people use to categorize themselves and others."[34] In addition, these areas are "often readily apparent, strong sources of personal identity, and stem from historical disparities in treatment, opportunities, and outcomes." Further, she explains that while other areas of difference are indeed important because they affect "people's organizational experiences," such as values and attitudes, "they are rarely readily apparent or strong sources of personal identity and generally do not stem from historical disparities in treatment, opportunities, or outcomes."[35] The strength of this definition is how Bell creates meaningful boundaries when defining diversity, specifically in the context of power relations and historical inequities.

David A. Thomas and Robin J. Ely

David A. Thomas and Robin J. Ely focus on how diversity affects work as they define diversity as "the varied perspectives and approaches to work that members of different identity groups bring."[36] Diversity is thus "not simply a reflection of the cosmetic differences among people, such as race and gender; rather, it is the various backgrounds and experiences that create people's identities and outlooks."[37] Further, the authors explain how diverse groups bring not only their "insider information" but also "different, important, and competitively relevant knowledge and perspectives about how to actually do work," for example, how to set and achieve goals, design organizational processes, frame tasks, communicate, and work effectively in teams.[38] If an organization truly embraces the value of diversity, it will allow diverse employees to challenge basic assumptions about an organization's inner workings. This freedom will enable employees to "identify more fully with the work they do," thereby "setting in motion a virtuous circle."[39] The significance of this definition is how the authors frame diversity in terms of how it affects the way that employees approach and do work—that employees' diversity directly impacts the very essence of their organizations.

Michàlle E. Mor Barak

Michàlle E. Mor Barak extends the discussion of diversity across national and cultural boundaries. With diversity having different interpretations in different countries, she admits that "generating a definition of workforce diversity that will be relevant in different countries and applicable in various cultural and national contexts proves to be a challenge."[40] Thus, she maintains that workforce diversity refers to "the division of the workforce into distinction categories that (a) have a perceived commonality within a given cultural or national context, and that (b) impact potentially harmful or beneficial employment outcomes such as job opportunities, treatment in the workplace, and promotion prospects—irrespective of job-related skills and qualifications."[41] Barak argues that this definition works in the global context for two main reasons. First, "it provides a broad umbrella that includes any distinction categories that may be relevant to specific cultural or national environments" without imposing the categories onto the culture but rather allowing the categories to emerge from within the specific culture. Second, it works because it highlights the significance of the "consequences of the distinction categories," thus overcoming "the limitation of the broad definitions that include benign and inconsequential characteristics in their diversity categories."[42]

Four Principles for an Improved Definition of Diversity

When teaching about diversity, diversity educators should encourage students to reflect on the usefulness of various definitions and should remind students that an organization's definition of diversity represents the beginning, foundational steps for how the organization will manage diversity. Reflecting on and building upon the various definitions we have reviewed here, we rely on the following principles when defining and discussing diversity: (1) diversity is expansive but not without boundaries; (2) diversity is fluid and dynamic; (3) diversity is based on both differences and similarities; (4) diversity is rooted in nonessentialist thought; and (5) diversity is directly related to how one approaches work.

DIVERSITY IS EXPANSIVE BUT NOT WITHOUT BOUNDARIES   The principle that diversity is expansive but has boundaries challenges two commonly held, contrary assumptions about diversity. Too narrow is the assumption that diversity is limited to one's obvious demographic characteristics such as gender and skin color. We include other dimensions of diversity in our conception, including as diverse, for example, single parents and people who embrace spirituality. If these less easily observed dimensions are omitted, distinctions among people may be so broad that important conceptions of core identity are ignored. Too broad, however, is the way in which some definitions extend diversity to the individual level of personality and organizational position. When organizations are described as having nearly unlimited layers of diversity—for example, including an employee's functional area, formal division, or work location—diversity gets overextended so that almost any imaginable organizational or social structure and context are considered diverse. We think that understanding an individual's experience is important, but that is true for management in general, not just for managing diversity. It seems to us that if the concept of diversity were to include every characteristic of every individual in any workplace, it would lack both clarity and usefulness and so we tie the notion of diversity to the people and groups of people who work in organizations. Our goal is to help students and managers develop the ability to distinguish between more or less diverse organizations and groups.

DIVERSITY IS FLUID   Often overlooked in diversity management education is diversity's characteristic of fluidity. Although diversity affiliations are often portrayed as absolute and clearly distinct, they are, we believe, fluid, continuous, and indefinite. Consider race, for example. The Census Bureau identifies race as a "socio-political" construct rather than a biological one. Thus, it should not be surprising that people's conception of race is complex and variable. About six percent of Americans say that they do not belong to any of the races identified by the Census Bureau, and more than two percent say they belong to at least two races simultaneously.[43] As organizational scholar Deborah R. Litvin explains, "The categories constructed through the discourse of workforce diversity as natural and obvious are hard-pressed to accommodate the complexity of real people."[44]

In addition, the lines of diversity overlap, as most individuals associate themselves with a number of social category dimensions. An example we use in class is a disabled woman of Christian Lebanese descent who might define herself in terms of various constellations of gender, religion, national origin, or disability. Also, we remind students that employees often move in and out of diversity categories—a single parent may get married, a man assumed to be straight may come out as gay, an able-bodied employee may have an accident and become disabled, or an employee may newly require a flexible schedule to care for an ailing parent.

DIVERSITY IS BASED ON BOTH DIFFERENCES AND SIMILARITIES   Diversity's dynamic quality is often ignored because of our tendency to define ourselves in terms of differences. Thus, we believe that organizations should reconceptualize diversity so that it is understood in terms of both differences and similarities. In this approach to diversity, affiliations will no longer represent rigid categories; individuals will view themselves as having qualities in common rather than narrowly defining themselves in terms of how they differ, and the advantages of diversity can be realized while its potential disadvantages can be avoided or minimized.[45]

Furthermore, we encourage students and managers to consider that not only do people identify with multiple dimensions of diversity simultaneously, but the combinations of their multiple demographic categories influence group processes and outcomes. Demographic category memberships may be aligned by individuals or not; when they are, they create deeper divisions within groups than when they are not. Thus, when a number of dimensions of diversity align they can create strong "faultlines" in a group.[46] For example, consider the workgroup represented in Table 1-1. In Panel A, the group is divided along categories of sex, race, age, and function, so that a strong faultline separates the men from the women (also the whites from the Asians, the young from the midcareer, and the finance analysts from the marketers). In Panel B, however, no strong subgroups are likely to form, because the dimensions of diversity are aligned neither with each other nor with functional areas. The strength of faultlines, and not just the amount of diversity in a group, may affect group morale, conflict, and performance.[47]

DIVERSITY IS ROOTED IN NONESSENTIALIST THOUGHT   When defining diversity in terms of specific categories like race or age, it is easy to fall into the trap of essentialist thinking. Categorizing people or inviting them to categorize themselves can lead to essentializing

TABLE 1-1	Examples of Strong and Weak Faultlines			

A: Strong Faultline

Group Member	Sex	Race	Age	Functional Expertise
1	Male	White	26	Finance
2	Male	White	30	Finance
3	Male	White	27	Finance
4	Female	Asian	47	Marketing
5	Female	Asian	53	Marketing

B: Weak Faultline

Group Member	Sex	Race	Age	Functional Expertise
1	Male	White	53	Finance
2	Male	White	30	Marketing
3	Male	Asian	27	Finance
4	Female	White	47	Marketing
5	Female	Asian	26	Finance

them—making the assumption that a characteristic, or set of characteristics, is the essential nature of all members of a group. Essentialism, as discussed by Litvin, is damaging because it "encourages individuals to immediately attribute their colleagues' thoughts and behaviors to their demographic category membership."[48] Students and managers need to understand this danger so they can avoid it.

An example of essentialist thinking is presuming that because someone is a woman, it is in her nature to want children. Although it may be true that most women have at least one child,[49] it is not the case that maternal desires are necessarily part of what it means to be a woman. Other examples of essentializing members of particular groups include assumptions such as the following: Asian Americans are strong quantitative thinkers; women use a relationship-based communication style; and men are persuaded by hard facts rather than emotional appeal. Although it is much easier simply to categorize people as members of groups, a nonessentialist framework transcends such generalizations while encouraging us to see the specific character of each individual.

DIVERSITY IS DIRECTLY RELATED TO HOW ONE EXPERIENCES WORK   In discussions of workplace diversity, diversity should be examined in the context of how it informs the way in which one approaches his or her job. Unfortunately, however, diversity is often incorporated superficially in organizations, for instance, being simply mentioned in a mission statement or articulated as a value and pursued only in terms of numbers of diverse employees. It should, by contrast, be considered in terms of its direct relationship with how employees perceive and perform their work and interact with both their colleagues and those outside their organizations. As explained by Thomas and Ely, companies that effectively manage diversity have developed "an outlook on diversity that enables them to incorporate employees' perspectives into the main work of the organization and to enhance work by rethinking primary tasks and redefining markets, products, strategies, missions, business practices, and even cultures."[50]

In sum, these five principles will help students and managers understand the complexities of diversity and how important it is for an organization's definition of diversity to capture these complexities. We point out that diversity educators and organizational leaders might struggle not only to define diversity but also to formulate an approach to direct and shape their philosophy on diversity. What follows next is a discussion of leadership-based approaches to managing diversity that will help students to determine the level of effectiveness at which organizations are managing diversity.

UNDERSTANDING LEADERSHIP-BASED ORGANIZATIONAL PARADIGMS FOR MANAGING DIVERSITY

Organizational leaders have embraced various paradigms, or approaches, to understanding and managing diversity.[51] These diversity management paradigms can serve as conceptual categories to help students and managers diagnose the status and effectiveness of an organization in terms of diversity management. These paradigms include: resistance, discrimination-and-fairness, access-and-legitimacy, and integration-and-learning. When discussing these paradigms we ask the students to examine the strengths and weaknesses of each diversity management approach. We suggest that working in tandem with these paradigms are the rhetorics of resistance, affirmative action, valuing diversity, and diversity management. The rhetoric that represents each of the approaches is developed primarily by the language used by leaders within organizations and functions to constitute and reconstitute the characteristics within each of the paradigms.

Although these paradigms developed, in turn, prior to the Civil Rights era (resistance paradigm) to the present day (integration-and-learning paradigm), we make it clear to our students that their history should not be seen as a continuous trend toward improved diversity management in American business. To assume that one approach has built on another and that progress has been made through this development does not account for the diversity inconsistencies that often exist in today's workplace. For example, paradigms may coexist in organizations (such as Xerox) so that progressive organizations that incorporate diversity management systemically (integration-and-learning paradigm) may still contain pockets of serious refusal or defiance (resistance paradigm) against diversity management. Thus, although we discuss the following approaches as they appeared chronologically, we take time to explain that their manifestations in real organizations do not always follow such a clear, progressive trajectory.

Resistance Paradigm

The resistance paradigm is based on the rejection and evasion of diversity and diversity-promoting initiatives. Although this perspective was more commonly expressed in the United States prior to the civil rights movement, it continued into the 1970s and beyond. For many years, management in a number of industries and occupations consisted of largely homogeneous groups of white men; diversity remained misunderstood and unappreciated.[52] Much of the workforce was made up of immigrants and/or ethnic minorities, but in an effort to maintain privilege, established majorities both among managers and blue-collar workers resisted changes in workplace demographic diversity—particularly in terms of color of skin and gender—because of outright prejudice or because they believed that minority groups might gain power and influence.[53]

RHETORIC OF RESISTANCE   As the resistance paradigm considers diversity as more of a threat than an opportunity, the discourse of resistance takes the form, for example, of "defiant assertions that changes are inefficient or unacceptable to shareholders because they increase costs and reduce profits."[54] A powerful example of this kind of argument that we use in the classroom is the case of Cracker Barrel Restaurants and its founder Dan Evins. Cracker Barrel was accused of blatantly discriminating against gays and lesbians working in its restaurants. Reflecting the rhetoric of resistance, Cracker Barrel and its leadership maintained that because Cracker Barrel was "founded upon a concept of traditional American values" it was deemed "inconsistent with our concept and values and . . . with those of our customer base, to continue to employ individuals . . . whose sexual preferences fail to demonstrate normal heterosexual values which have been the foundation of families in our society."[55] Although this example of resistance happened in 1991, students are still surprised, and some shocked, that this level of blatant discrimination was and continues to be legal in some states.

Discrimination-and-Fairness Paradigm

The discrimination-and-fairness paradigm, often adopted in the late 1960s and 1970s, is based on accommodating the legal responsibilities of diversity, often in terms of federal mandates. The underlying philosophy of this paradigm is described by Thomas and Ely as follows: "Prejudice has kept members of certain demographic groups out of organizations" and "[a]s a matter of fairness and to comply with federal mandates, we need to work toward restructuring the makeup of our organizations to let it more closely reflect that of society."[56] The appeal of this approach is that it makes efforts to recruit and, to some extent, to retain diverse employees, but this approach treats all people within a given social demographic category as the same. In other words, the paradigm's weakness is that it does not "allow employees to draw on their personal assets and perspectives to do their work more effectively."[57] Unsurprisingly, organizations that embrace this paradigm have no real strategy for managing diversity, since they believe that the minority view should "conform to the expectations of the organization's existing culture."[58]

RHETORIC OF AFFIRMATIVE ACTION   Because the discrimination-and-fairness paradigm is reflected in the rhetoric of affirmative action, we use this discussion to teach about this emotionally charged, often misunderstood topic. We explain that the intentions behind affirmative action were sound as it was grounded in moral and social responsibility, with the goal of amending wrongs done in the past to those Americans—minorities and women in particular—who were underrepresented in positions of organizational and political power. The phrase "affirmative action" was first used in 1961 when President John F. Kennedy issued Executive Order 10925 which created the Committee on Equal Employment Opportunity and mandated that federal funds be used to take affirmative action to ensure that hiring and employment practices were free of racial bias. Then, in 1965, President Lyndon Johnson issued Executive Order 11246 requiring federal contractors to take affirmative action to ensure that employees are treated during employment without regard to their race, creed, color, or national origin. In 1967 Johnson expanded the Order to include affirmative action requirements to benefit women.

Although affirmative action was created as a temporary remedy to equalize discrimination that had persisted despite constitutional promises, it became, for many, synonymous with language such as "preferential treatment" and "quotas," which worked quickly to dishonor the policy's fundamental purpose. Affirmative action has been strongly challenged in both political and judicial contexts. An example is the historic 2003 case involving the University of Michigan's admissions policies, whereby the Supreme Court upheld the University's law school affirmative action policy—to continue to consider race as one element when selecting their students. In this situation, the Court found that "diversity is a compelling interest in higher education, and that race is one of a number of factors that can be taken into account to achieve the educational benefits that flow from a diverse student body."[59] This groundbreaking decision was negated in 2005, however, when the state of Michigan passed an initiative prohibiting preferential treatment based on skin color or gender in public contracting, public employment, and public education.

Access-and-Legitimacy Paradigm

Companies operating from the access-and-legitimacy paradigm, common in the 1980s and early 1990s, emphasize bottom-line reasons for incorporating diversity. In this approach, companies "accept and celebrate differences so they can better serve their diverse pool of customers."[60] The underlying philosophy of this paradigm is that because of diverse demographics in various markets, "new ethnic groups are quickly gaining consumer power" so organizations need "a demographically more diverse workforce to help . . . gain access to these differentiated segments."[61] Employees who are multilingual, for example, will help organizations to understand and serve customers better, thereby gaining legitimacy with them.

This model creates opportunities for people from less-represented groups to enter new positions in business because their diversity is, at least on some levels, valued by the organization. The paradigm's most serious limitation is clear: When a business regards employees' experience as useful only to gain access to narrow markets, those employees are, and are likely to feel, marginalized. In effect, the diverse employees and their work are pigeonholed rather than integrated systemically throughout the organization.

RHETORIC OF VALUING DIVERSITY   The rhetoric of valuing diversity, as used in the access-and-legitimacy paradigm, extends beyond the discourse of affirmative action by embracing "awareness, education, and positive recognition of the differences among people in the workforce."[62] Leaders who use this rhetoric are not just trying to satisfy federal guidelines under antidiscrimination law but rather claim to value the contributions that diverse employees make in an effort to create a profitable or effective organization.

We point to Avon's CEO, Andrea Jung, illustrating how organizations can leverage diversity as a competitive advantage. The once-struggling Avon boasts not only increased profits and innovations but also having more women in management positions than any other Fortune 500 company; in addition, people of color make up a third of Avon's workforce.[63] The company's famous direct-selling method now has a corps of 3.9 million independent sales representatives worldwide, many of whom are women of color selling products to a diverse clientele. Furthermore, Avon has been actively developing Latina-geared cosmetics called *Avon Eres Tu* (Avon Is You) and has launched ad campaigns featuring women of color, including tennis champions Venus and Serena Williams and actress Salma Hayek. John Fleming, regional vice president for Avon West, sums up Avon's diversity philosophy: "Avon is committed to diversity. The marketplace is becoming more and more diverse each year, thus the diversity we see in the marketplace must be reflected in our representative ranks and in our management ranks."[64]

Integration-and-Learning Paradigm

The fourth paradigm, the integration-and-learning paradigm, which largely emerged in the 1990s, reflects characteristics of both the discrimination-and-fairness paradigm and the access-and-legitimacy paradigm but goes beyond them by embracing the business case for diversity and "by concretely connecting diversity to approaches to work."[65] Leaders who adopt this approach recognize that employees frequently make decisions and choices at work that draw upon their identity-group affiliations.[66] Executives actively recruit and retain their diverse workforce, invest in diversity training, and expect that having a diverse workforce and management team will lead to better decisions and an enhanced bottom line.

Organizational leaders who adopt this paradigm are proactive about learning from diversity, encourage people to use their cultural experience at work, fight forms of dominance and subordination based on demographic categories, and ensure that conflicts related to diversity are acknowledged and resolved with sensitivity.[67] When using this approach, leadership "must recognize both the learning opportunities and the challenges that the expression of different perspectives presents for an organization."[68] Not only should leaders understand the challenges, but they must be able to communicate easily and clearly their message about diversity and diversity management within their company. Employees within these organizations should have a clear understanding of the critical and integrative role that diversity plays within the organization.

RHETORIC OF DIVERSITY MANAGEMENT   The integration-and-learning paradigm is reflected in the rhetoric of diversity management. This rhetoric is different from both the rhetoric of affirmative action and the rhetoric of valuing diversity, specifically because it maintains that effective diversity management creates not only a competitive advantage in consumer markets but an environment in which differences are "valued and allowed to influence positively [organizational members'] experience in and contribution to the work of the organization."[69] Diversity management seeks to align the skills and personal experiences of the individual members of the organization with its mission and strategy.

A business example that is representative of this approach is IBM. Former CEO of IBM Louis V. Gerstner's rhetoric of diversity management was the catalyst for IBM's philosophical shift from "minimizing differences to amplifying them and to seizing on the business opportunities they present."[70] Gerstner and IBM's vice president of Global Workforce Diversity, Ted Childs, created eight diversity task forces made up of the following demographic executive-led constituencies: Asians, African Americans, gays/lesbians/bisexuals/transgender (GLBT) individuals, Hispanics, white men, Native Americans, people with disabilities, and women. After receiving feedback from these constituencies, Gerstner allowed diversity perspectives to influence the main work of IBM; by doing this, he encouraged diversity to have systematic influence throughout IBM. IBM indeed looks different today than it did in 1995 at the beginning of Gerstner's tenure, with, for example, a 370 percent increase in the number of female executives worldwide, a 733 percent increase of GLBT executives, and a tripling of the number of executives with disabilities. According to Thomas, IBM succeeded in managing diversity because it had put in place four "pillars of change": IBM demonstrated leadership support, engaged employees as partners, integrated diversity with management practices, and linked diversity goals to business goals.[71]

Although the diversity management model presents a progressive way of understanding diversity in the workplace, one of its underlying assumptions is the validity of the business case for diversity. We believe that the diversity educator should lead an open discussion on why this assumption is potentially problematic. For the past decade, many proponents of the business case for diversity have maintained that a diverse workforce yields a competitive advantage to organizations. The business case is unclear, however, as shown in the academic literature,[72] even though we believe that it is often taught without presenting many qualifications to students. Because of the emotion often associated with diversity issues, this critically important discussion of the weaknesses of the business case for diversity has been inadvertently avoided or actively silenced in diversity education.

UNDERSTANDING THE BUSINESS CASE FOR DIVERSITY

The Business Case for Diversity

Even though there are questions about the soundness of some of the arguments in favor of the business case for diversity, it is important for students to understand the assertions of the case, specifically because organizations are making significant diversity-related decisions (i.e., management, training, and recruiting) based on assumptions about its validity. Those who support the business case for diversity argue that diverse organizations will realize cost savings, recruit the best talent, and have high rates of growth.

COST SAVINGS   The business case suggests that by embracing the value of diversity and diversity management, an organization will reduce costs and create a competitive advantage.[73] For example, if employees believe they are respected, they will stay with the company longer while maintaining strong accountability and productivity. The Society for Human Resource Management (SHRM) reminds us of the commonsense argument that a company's return on investment "is reduced when commitment and productivity are lost because employees feel disregarded, time is wasted with conflicts and misunderstandings, and money is spent on legal fees and settlements."[74] The business case for diversity assumes that managing diversity will lead to lower turnover among women and minorities, higher commitment from them, and fewer lawsuits. Lowering these factors should reduce costs to the company and, in turn, raise profits.

WINNING THE COMPETITION FOR TALENT   An organization with a strong reputation for managing its diverse workforce will be more likely to attract and recruit the most talented workers. It is, therefore, a competitive advantage to be ranked in one of the "top diversity lists"—such as *Fortune's* "Best Companies for Minorities," *DiversityInc's* "Top Companies for Diversity," or *Working Mother's* "The 100 Best Companies for Working Mothers List." In addition, it is now common for talented recruits to "ask about an organization's diversity initiative and factor that into their employment decision."[75]

DRIVING BUSINESS GROWTH   The business case for diversity frames business growth in terms of marketing, creativity and problem solving, and flexibility and global relations. In light of the increasingly global and diverse consumer market, one commonly heard business case argument is that the "cultural understanding" needed to market to specific demographic niches "resides most naturally in marketers with the same cultural background."[76] In fact, some scholars suggest that "[i]n some cases, people from a minority culture are more likely to give patronage to a representative of their own group" and "[f]or at least some products and services, a multicultural sales force may facilitate sales to members of minority culture groups."[77]

The argument of the business case is that when employees feel that their diverse backgrounds and perspectives are recognized and appreciated, the quality of problem solving and creativity is likely to improve. There is evidence to suggest that heterogeneous groups perform well in terms of making well-considered decisions.[78] Researchers have suggested that "minority views can stimulate consideration of nonobvious alternatives in task groups" and that "persistent exposure to minority viewpoints stimulates creative thought processes."[79] According to the business case, diverse workforces have the potential to solve problems better because of several factors: a greater variety of perspectives brought to bear on the issue; a higher level of critical analysis of alternatives; and, because there is a lower probability of groupthink, a higher probability of generating creative solutions.[80]

According to the business case, the skills of flexibility and adaptability that are learned in a diverse workplace will extend generally and enhance the employee's ability to communicate across national and organizational cultures. Thus, diverse companies should be able to compete more successfully in a complex and global economy. Research suggests, for example, that companies with greater diversity make better business partners and merge more smoothly with other companies. The transition is less difficult for diverse companies because they are familiar with accepting the differences among people and within cultures.[81] Scholars argue that this characteristic of adaptability will enhance a company's ability to communicate more effectively when faced with developing and maintaining relations internationally.[82]

Assessing the Business Case for Diversity

We believe that the business case for diversity represents an important yet incomplete step toward understanding the intersection of diversity and the workplace. In an effort to advance the understanding of the principles of diversity management and the integration-and-learning paradigm, we illuminate several assumptions underlying the business case and pose some questions about them. Because organizations are basing their diversity-related decisions on the business case, it is important for diversity educators to review carefully the strengths and weaknesses of the business case for diversity.

A DIVERSE WORKFORCE AND PRODUCTIVITY   Thomas A. Kochan, codirector of the Institute for Work and Employment Research at MIT's Sloan School of Management, and his colleagues maintain that "The diversity industry is built on sand . . . The business case rhetoric for diversity is simply naïve and overdone. There are no strong positive or negative effects of gender or racial diversity on business performance."[83] This statement is based on the findings of a five-year research project led by the Diversity Research Network and published in the journal *Human Resource Management*.[84]

Unfortunately, perhaps, one cannot assume that a diversity program will benefit an organization; in fact, "[p]oorly managed diversity programs can be as harmful as well-run ones can be beneficial."[85] And, adding even more complexity, "[e]ven when diversity is managed well, the results are mixed. The best organizations can overcome the negative consequences of diversity, such as higher turnover and greater conflict in the workplace, but that still does not mean that there are positive outcomes."[86]

MEASURING THE RESULTS OF DIVERSITY EFFORTS   Human resources executives often do not demand documented evidence proving the bottom-line value of diversity initiatives because, in many cases, it is both difficult and costly to obtain. Kochan and his colleagues advise that "[h]uman resource managers and other professionals in charge of diversity efforts should take a more analytical approach in performing their roles. Sophisticated data collection and analyses are needed to understand the consequences of diversity within organizations, and to monitor an organization's process in managing diversity."[87] According to Laura Liswood, senior advisor to Goldman Sachs on diversity issues and a scholar at the University of Maryland's Academy of Leadership, it is difficult to create valid measures of increased organizational performance because of diversity: "There is a connection between diversity and financial success, but typical profit-and-loss systems don't capture the benefits that diversity creates."[88] It is one thing to measure diversity in terms of recruitment, promotion, or turnover rates; but it is entirely different to measure the full strategic or financial impact of diversity initiatives.

SUPPORT OF DIVERSITY INITIATIVES BY DIVERSE EMPLOYEES   Because one of the goals of diversity initiatives is to empower diverse employees, a discussion of resistance by diverse employees is often omitted from discussion of the business case for diversity. It is important to have this discussion nonetheless because, as one study found, "[m]any employees, even women and other minority groups, think corporate diversity programs benefit only black employees."[89] Also intriguing is that, in the same study, African American employees were also critical of corporate diversity efforts.[90] Given these findings, organizations should keep in mind that just because employees may fall into a group affiliation that is considered diverse, they may not support the initiatives that are implemented in support of the business case for diversity.

DIVERSITY TRAINING AND ADDED VALUE   Diversity training programs are sometimes questioned and have even been charged with hampering an organization's efforts to understand diversity and use diversity management as a business advantage.[91] Some diversity training efforts can indeed be counterproductive, specifically with the result being a decrease in the number of women and minorities in managerial positions.[92] According to David Tulin of Tulin and Associates, a diversity-consulting firm in New York City, diversity training may raise expectations by increasing "the minorities' anger and frustration" while increasing "the white males' isolation and exclusionary behavior."[93] Training programs aimed at addressing subtle forms of discrimination and exclusion often do not lead to long-term changes in behaviors.[94] Instead, "group members and leaders must be trained to deal with group process issues, with a focus on communicating and problem-solving in diverse teams."[95]

Despite large investments in diversity training (it is an estimated 8 billion dollar industry), the total number of discrimination charges filed with the EEOC have increased steadily since 1996—hitting a seven-year high in 2002—within the categories of race, sex, national origin, religion, age, and disability.[96] This trend may represent increased dissatisfaction because of organizational failures despite the efforts of managers and consultants, or increased expectations; alternatively, increased awareness of these issues may simply have made it easier to recognize problems and enter complaints. In other words, factors leading to the increase of filings with the EEOC may include real failure, higher expectations, or increased awareness.

DIVERSE EMPLOYEES AND DIVERSE MARKETS   One of the most frequently made business case arguments is that by hiring diverse employees, organizations will be able to capitalize on diverse markets. This claim rests on the assumption that customers desire to be served by those who physically resemble themselves. Evidence to support this argument, however, is lacking. The Diversity Research Network, for example, "finds no consistent evidence that most customers care whether the salespeople who serve them are of the same race or gender."[97] In short, there is no clear proof that diversity causes better market performance. Indeed, the causal relationship between diversity and performance may be the reverse: Better-performing companies may simply attract the best talent among all groups of workers.[98]

WHITE MEN AND DIVERSITY   Some diversity scholars use an expansive definition of diversity so that members of no group—in particular, white men—feel excluded, whereas other scholars fail even to address the relationship between the dominant group (typically, white men) and diversity. Sondra Thiederman, president of Cross-Cultural Communications, a San Diego-based consulting firm for workplace diversity and cross-cultural business practices, believes that one common mistake that diversity advocates make is failing to incorporate white men in their strategies.[99] According to DiversityInc.com, one important role of the diversity manager/trainer is to help the white-male employee understand and embrace the diversity movement by reassuring him that he is not targeted as the enemy; helping him to see his position of privilege; and explaining how diversity is not only a societal value but also a competitive advantage.[100] Another approach is to invite white-male employees to become part of the organization's diverse culture by, for example, participating in a diversity-strategy group, mentoring and coaching people from nondominant groups, or organizing the minority development programs or minority recruitment.[101]

Most discussions of diversity neglect any recognition of the diversity within the "white male" category. When looked at from a nonessentialist perspective, white-male employees might affiliate themselves just as strongly with their religion, sexual identity, parental status, or age, as with their race. For example, a white man may experience discrimination because he is Jewish, gay, a single parent, or an older worker. Lost in the business case rhetoric is a discussion of the multiple layers of diversity within the category "white male," a clear method for making the white male voice legitimate in the conversation about managing diversity, and acknowledgment that white males also represent a protected class under the categories "color of skin" and "race" as defined by the federal government.

CONCLUSION

We believe that a learning opportunity is represented in the pedagogical framework that we have presented in this essay. The first phase—crafting a definition of diversity—invites students and/or managers to grapple with a definition that is inclusive enough to account for diversity's complexities while not being so expansive as to imply that each individual is uniquely "diverse." This phase forces students and/or managers to reflect on the process of defining diversity so that a more representative, meaningful definition can be crafted. The second phase—examining leadership-based paradigms of diversity and the paradigms that support them—helps to create a framework for diagnosing and examining stages of diversity management in organizations. One of the assignments in our class is for the students to write a detailed analysis of a national organization known for its effective or ineffective diversity-management practices through the lens of the diversity-management paradigms. Through this assignment, students discover that many organizations are in the process of transitioning between paradigms, are stuck in a less effective paradigm, or are taking diversity management seriously as they strive toward the integration-and-learning paradigm. After the students examine the organization through the lens of the diversity management paradigms, they are able to diagnose strategies for the organization to implement in order to make diversity management a systemic force and competitive advantage.

The third phase—understanding and assessing the arguments of the business case for diversity—is necessary because these arguments represent the premise on which American businesses make their decision to invest millions of dollars in diversity training and initiatives. The widely believed and taught business case for diversity holds that managing diversity well can lead to improved organizational performance. This relationship may hold true under some conditions, but it is clear that managing diversity poorly can lead to disastrous results. If managers lead a diverse organization poorly, they will engender high levels of interpersonal conflict and low levels of group cohesion, employee morale, and organizational commitment. Carefully examining the weaknesses of the business case for diversity helps to determine where diversity management and management research need to be strengthened. Challenging diversity principles that are often accepted as truth can be controversial. We realize how raising these sensitive issues might make teaching about diversity and diversity management more challenging, yet we encourage diversity educators to take what we believe is a worthwhile and productive pedagogical risk.

Indeed, the U.S. workforce is more diverse than ever before and will become more so with increasing globalization and immigration. There are no easy answers about how to manage effectively in general, let alone managing a diverse workforce effectively. Managers and students should recognize the complexity of this task and embrace it as a learning opportunity for themselves and their organizations. Managing diversity well depends on many of the same skills as managing effectively in general. In this essay, we have argued that students and managers need to understand the complexity of managing diversity, alternative models for thinking about how to do so, and some of the issues that make that task challenging. Management is difficult, fraught with much uncertainty, and recognizing the complexities that increase that uncertainty is important in helping students and managers learn how to recognize effective management.

Discussion Questions

1. What do you believe is the most significant demographic change facing the American workplace? Why?
2. Why is it important for an organization to have a clear definition of diversity?
3. What principles are the most important in defining and understanding diversity?
4. What organizations can you identify that exemplify each of the diversity management paradigms: resistance, discrimination-and-fairness, access-and-legitimacy, and integration-and-learning?
5. Which dimensions of the business case for diversity are the most persuasive? Why?
6. What are the strengths and weaknesses of the business case for diversity?

Notes

1. Thomas Kochan and others, "The Effects of Diversity on Business Performance: Report of the Diversity Research Network," *Human Resource Management* 42 (Spring 2003): 18.
2. Michàlle E. Mor Barak, *Managing Diversity: Toward a Globally Inclusive Workplace* (Thousand Oaks, CA: Sage, 2005), 222.
3. Ibid.
4. American Express, "Diversity: Business Formula for Success," http://www10.americanexpress.com/sif/cda/page/0,1641,13345,00.asp.
5. Marriot International's statement on diversity, http://marriott.com/corporateinfo/culture/Diversity.mi.
6. Starbucks, "Diversity: Diversity Is Who We Are," www.starbucks.com/aboutus/SB-DIVERSITY-FIN.pdf.
7. Verizon, "Making Progress Through Diversity, http://multimedia.verizon.com/diversity.
8. University of North Carolina, http://www.unc.edu/diversity/diversityplan/baselinediversityreport-june07-updated.pdf.
9. Betsy Morris, "How Corporate America Is Betraying Women," *Fortune,* January 10, 2005, 66.
10. Witech-Combs and Harris Interactive, *DiversityInc Factoids & Style Guide*, 27.
11. David C. Stapleton and Richard V. Burkhauser, eds., *The Decline in Employment of People with Disabilities: A Policy Puzzle* (Kalamazoo, MI: W.E. Upjohn Institute Research, 2003).
12. Management Leadership for Tomorrow, *DiversityInc Factoids & Style Guide*, 76.
13. Michelle Conlin, "Religion in the Workplace: The Growing Presence of Spirituality in Corporate America," *Business Week*, November 1, 1999, http://www.businessweek.com/archives/1999/b3653001.arc.htm.

14. Nigel Basset-Jones, "The Paradox of Diversity Management, Creativity, and Innovation," *Creativity and Innovation Management* 14, no. 2 (2005): 169–75.

15. Xerox, "Diversity: Making All the Difference," www.xerox.com/diversity.

16. Ibid.

17. Fay Hansen, "Diversity's Business Case Doesn't Add Up," *Workforce.com*, April 2003, www. workforce.com/archive.

18. Deborah R. Litvin, "Making Space for a Better Case," in *Handbook of Workplace Diversity*, eds. Allison Konrad, Pushkala Prasad, and Judith Pringle (London: Sage, 2006), 75.

19. Norma Carr-Ruffino, *Making Diversity Work* (New Jersey: Prentice Hall, 2005); Taylor Cox, *Cultural Diversity in Organizations: Theory, Research, & Practice* (San Francisco, CA: Berrett-Koehler Publishers, 1993); Katharine Esty, Richard Griffin, and Marcie Hirsch, *Workplace Diversity* (Holbrook, MA: Adams Media Corp., 1995); Ellen Kossek, Sharon Lobel, and Jennifer Brown, "Human Resource Strategies to Manage Workforce Diversity: Examining 'The Business Case,' " In Allison Konrad, Pushkala Prasad, and Judith Pringle; Gail Robinson and Kathleen Dechant, "Building a Business Case for Diversity," *Academy of Management Executive* 11, no. 3 (1997): 21–31.

20. Litvin, "Making Space for a Better Case."

21. Kochan and others, "The Effects of Diversity on Business Performance"; Carol Kulik and Loriann Roberson, "Diversity Initiative Effectiveness: What Organizations Can (and Cannot) Expect From Diversity Recruitment, Diversity Training, and Formal Mentoring Programs," in *Diversity at Work*, ed. Arthur Brief (New York: Cambridge University Press, 2008), 265–317; Stella Nkomo and Taylor Cox, "Diverse Identities in Organizations," in *Handbook of Organizational Studies,* eds. Stewart Clegg, Cynthia Hardy, and Walter Nord (London, Sage: 1996); Anne Tsui and Barbara Gutek, *Demographic Differences In Organizations: Current Research and Future Directions* (Lanham, MD: Lexington Press, 1999).

22. Carr-Ruffino, *Diversity Success Strategies* (Boston, MA: Butterworth-Heinemann, 1999); Esty, Griffin, and Hirsch, *Workplace Diversity*; Carol Harvey and June Allard, *Understanding and Managing Diversity: Readings, Cases, and Exercises* (Upper Saddle River, NJ: Pearson Prentice Hall, 2005); Frederick Miller and Judy Katz, *The Inclusion Breakthrough: Unleashing the Real Power of Diversity* (San Franssiso, CA: Berrett Koehler, 2002); Kim Olver and Sylvester Baugh, *Leveraging Diversity at Work* (Country Club Hills, IL: Inside Out Press, 2006); Sondra Thiederman, *Making Diversity Work* (New York: Kaplan, 2008).

23. SHRM's definition of diversity is available at www.shrm.org/diversity/definingdiversity.asp.

24. Marilyn Loden, *Implementing Diversity* (New York: McGraw-Hill, 1996), 13.

25. Ibid., 14.

26. Ibid., 15.

27. Ibid., 15.

28. Ibid., 16.

29. Lee Gardenswartz and Anita Rowe, *Diverse Teams at Work: Capitalizing on the Power of Diversity* (New York: McGraw-Hill, 1994), 32.

30. Ibid., 32.

31. Ibid., 32.

32. R. Roosevelt Thomas, Jr. *Redefining Diversity* (New York: AMACOM, 1996), 5. See also, R. Thomas Jr., *Beyond Race and Gender: Unleashing the Power of Your Total Work Force by Managing Diversity* (New York: AMACOM, 1991).

33. R. Thomas, Jr., *Redefining Diversity*, 7–8.

34. Myrtle Bell, *Diversity in Organizations* (Mason, OH: Thomson Higher Education, 2007), 4.

35. Ibid., 4.

36. David A. Thomas and Robyn J. Ely, "Making Difference Matter: A New Paradigm for Managing Diversity," *Harvard Business Review on Managing Diversity* (Boston, MA: Harvard Business School Publishing Corp., 2001): 36.

37. Kali Saposnick, "Managing Diversity as a Key Organizational Resource: An Interview with David Thomas," *Leverage Points*, no. 37, Pegasus Communications (2003), www.Pegasuscom.com/levpoints/thomasint.html.

38. Thomas and Ely, "Making Difference Matter," 36–37.

39. Ibid.

40. Barak, *Managing Diversity*, 131.

41. Ibid., 132.

42. Ibid.

43. U.S. 2000 Census Bureau, http://www.census.gov/prod/cen2000/dp1/2kh00.pdf.

44. Deborah R. Litvin, "The Discourse of Diversity: From Biology to Management," *Discourse and Organization* 4, no. 2 (1997): 202.

45. Jeffrey T. Polzer, Laurie P. Milton, and William B. Swann, Jr., "Capitalizing on Diversity: Interpersonal Congruence in Small Work Groups," *Administrative Science Quarterly* 47 (June 2002): 296–325.

46. Dora C. Lau and Keith J. Murnighham, "Demographic Diversity and Faultlines: The Compositional Dynamics of Organizational Groups," *Academy of Management Review* 23 (1998): 325–40.

47. Sherry M. B. Thatcher, Karen A. Jehn, and Elaine Zannuto, "Cracks in Diversity Research: The Effects of Diversity Faultlines on Conflict and Performance," *Group Decision and Negotiation* 12 (2003): 217–41.

48. Litvin, "The Discourse of Diversity," 204, 207.

49. Barbara Downs, "Fertility of American Women: June 2002," *Current Population Reports*, October 2003, 20-548, http://www.census.gov/prod/2003pubs/p20-548.pdf.

50. Thomas and Ely, "Making Difference Matter," 48.

51. Ibid.

52. Parshotam Dass and Barbara Parker, "Strategies for Managing Human Resource Diversity: From Resistance to Learning," *Academy of Management Executive* 13 (1999): 68–80.

53. Ibid.

54. Ibid., 70.

55. John Howard, "The Cracker Barrel Restaurants," in *Opportunities and Challenges of Workplace Diversity: Theory, Cases, and Exercises*, eds. Kathryn A. Cañas and Harris Sondak (New Jersey: Prentice Hall, 2006), 178.

56. Thomas and Ely, "Making Difference Matter," 38.

57. Ibid.

58. Saposnick, "Managing Diversity as a Key Organizational Resource," www.pegasuscom.com/levpoints/thomasint.html.

59. "Chronology of Key Rulings in the University of Michigan Affirmative Action Lawsuits and Other Higher Education Affirmative Action Suits," http://www.vpcomm.umich.edu/admissions/faqs/chronology.html.

60. Saposnick, "Managing Diversity as a Key Organizational Resource," www.pegasuscom.com/levpoints/thomasint.html.

61. Thomas and Ely, "Making Difference Matter," 44.

62. SHRM Diversity Forum, "How is a Diversity Initiative Different from My Organization's Affirmative Action Plan?" SHRMOnline, http://www.shrm.org/diversity/diversityvsaffirmaction.asp.

63. Linda Bean, "Avon: Diversity Key to Rebuilding an Ailing Brand," *DiversityInc.com*, December 6, 2004, www.diversityinc.com/members/10704.cfm.

64. "110 Years of Direct Selling Success," MinorityCareer.com: Online Employment Opportunities Resource, http://minoritycareer.com/features2.html.

65. Thomas and Ely, "Making Difference Matter," 37.

66. Ibid.

67. Ibid.

68. Ibid., 52.

69. Saposnick, "Managing Diversity as a Key Organizational Resource," www.pegasuscom.com/levpoints/thomasint.html.

70. David A. Thomas, "Diversity as Strategy," *Harvard Business Review*, September 2004, 100.

71. David A. Thomas, "Diversity as Strategy."

72. Kochan and others, "The Effects of Diversity on Business Performance."

73. Peter Wright, Stephen Ferris, Janine Hiller, and Mark Kroll, "Competitiveness through Management of Diversity: Effects on Stock Price Valuation," *Academy of Management Journal* 38 (1995): 272–87.

74. SHRM Diversity Forum, "What is the 'Business Case' for Diversity?" SHRMOnline, http://shrm.org/diversity.businesscase.asp.

75. Carr-Ruffino, *Diversity Success Strategies*, 11. See also, Carr-Ruffino, *Making Diversity Work*.

76. Gail Robinson and Kathleen Dechant, "Building a Business Case for Diversity," *Academy of Management Executive* 11, no. 3 (1997): 233.

77. Cox and Blake, "Managing Cultural Diversity: Implications for Organizational Competitiveness," *Academy of Management Executive* 5, no. 3 (1991): 47.

78. Poppy McLeod and Stephen Lobel, "The Effects of Ethnic Diversity on Idea Generation in Small Groups," *Academy of Management Best Paper Proceedings*, 1992, 227–31; Warren Watson, Kamalesh Kumar, and Larry Michaelsen, "Cultural Diversity's Impact on Interaction Process and Performance: Comparing Homogeneous and Diverse Task Groups," *Academy of Management Journal* 36 (1993): 590–602.

79. Cox and Blake, "Managing Cultural Diversity: Implications for Organizational Competiti-venss," *Academy of Management Executive* 5, no. 3 (1991): 47.

80. Carr-Ruffino, *Diversity Success Strategies*.

81. Sherry Kuczynski, "If Diversity, then Higher Profits?" *HRMagazine* 44, no. 13 (1999): 69.

82. Robinson and Dechant, "Building a Business Case for Diversity"; Carr-Ruffino, *Diversity Success Strategies*.

83. Hansen, "Diversity's Business Case Doesn't Add Up," www.workforce.com/archive/feature/23/42/49/index.php.

84. Kochan and others, "The Effects of Diversity on Business Performance."

85. Kuczynski, "If Diversity, Then Higher Profits?" 69.

86. Hansen, "Diversity's Business Case Doesn't Add Up," www.workforce.com/archive/feature/23/42/49/index.php.

87. Kochan and others, "The Effects of Diversity on Business Performance."

88. Hansen, "Diversity's Business Case Doesn't Add Up," www.workforce.com/archive/feature/23/42/49/index.php.

89. Martha Frase-Blunt, "Thwarting the Diversity Backlash," *HR Magazine* 48, no. 6 (June 2003): 137.

90. Ibid.

91. Shari Caudron, "Training Can Damage Diversity Efforts," *Personnel Journal* 72 (April 1993): 50–62; Patricia Nemetz and Sandra Christensen, "The Challenge of Cultural Diversity: Harnessing a Diversity of Views to Understand Multiculturalism," *Academy of Management Review* 21 (April 1996): 434–62.

92. Shankar Vedantam, "Required Diversity Training Fails: Women, Minorities Still Shut Our of Managerial Posts," January 21, 2008, http://www.signonsandiego.com/uniontrib/20080121/news_1n21diverse.html.

93. Caudron, "Training Can Damage Diversity Efforts."

94. Kochan and others, "The Effects of Diversity on Business Performance."

95. Hansen, "Diversity's Business Case Doesn't Add Up," www.workforce.com/archive/feature/23/42/49/index.php.

96. Ibid.

97. Kochan and others, "The Effects of Diversity on Business Performance."

98. Kuczynski, "If Diversity, Then Higher Profits?"

99. Frase-Blunt, "Thwarting the Diversity Backlash."

100. Jordan Pine, "Getting White Men to Buy In: Corporate America's Biggest Challenge," *DiversityInc.com*, December 11, 2001, www.diversityinc.com/members/1939.cfm.

101. Yoji Cole, "White Men Can Be Diversity Leaders, Too," *DiversityInc.com*, October 11, 2002, http://www.diversityinc.com/members/3657.cfm.

CHAPTER 2

Diversity in the Workplace: A Legal Perspective

Some might argue that "diversity in the workplace" is a concept created by the federal legislature. Whether the American workplace would have evolved to its current level of diversity without government intervention is an interesting question, but there is no doubt that federal laws prohibiting discrimination and harassment in the workplace based on certain characteristics at least aided some of the social change that has occurred in this country over the past half century. In fact, until the federal government required businesses and organizations to become more diverse by enacting legislation—including executive orders, laws, and judicial decisions—prohibiting employment discrimination and harassment, there was almost no incentive to hire a diverse staff. The first federal laws regarding employment pertained to labor unions and child labor, but over time as labor unions became less common, federal laws were enacted by the legislature to protect employees in the workplace. After reading this chapter, readers should have a comprehensive understanding of U.S. legislation related to diversity in organizations. Imagine if these laws requiring fair workplace treatment had never been passed. Would our society have changed and become more inclusive the way it has on its own?

Workplace discrimination and harassment law has evolved to include prohibitions against various types of conduct based on certain characteristics. In the nearly 50 years since the enactment of the prohibition of unlawful discrimination, common beliefs surrounding discrimination law have emerged. Whereas most people in today's society are aware that certain forms of discrimination and harassment in the workplace violate the law, they are often surprised to find that many types of discrimination and harassment—while impolite, boorish, or crude—are not illegal, and that in many cases an employee has no legal recourse for being mistreated.

Many parts of the law are simple and easy to understand. For example, a person cannot be treated differently or poorly in the workplace based on his or her age, as long as the employee is over 40. The analysis for such an "age-based" claim is not much more complicated than that. However, many parts of discrimination and harassment law are very difficult to digest and comprehend.

For example, not only was the Americans with Disabilities Act (ADA) of 1990 difficult for employers and employees to understand, but very few attorneys could explain all its nuances; the

P. Corper James, J.D., Mabey Wright & James, Salt Lake City, Utah

federal courts have struggled for years to determine the ADA's proper scope and interpret its difficult language. The federal legislature's response to the confusion, at least in part, was to pass the Americans with Disabilities Act and Amendments Act (ADAAA) of 2008, but it will still take years to determine the scope of the acts. For that reason, in this essay I spend more time on some issues than on others. The cases chosen as examples for this essay are often the seminal cases in each category but are sometimes just among the most interesting. The cases represent, in some way, the foundation of some particular piece of the law and sometimes the surprising and interesting claims and findings that result. In addition, I have also included a brief outline for cases and federal acts, called "historical perspective," to give the reader a better framework of the evolution of the law when applicable to the larger protected class categories.

The demographics of the American workforce, and how an employer can run his or her business, changed with the passage of Title VII of the Civil Rights Act of 1964, which prohibits discrimination on the basis of race, color, religion, sex, or national origin in employment-related matters.[1] Title VII is the most sweeping and important civil rights legislation ever enacted in this country. The act applies to employers with 15 or more employees, because, it is assumed, that companies of that size are likely to engage in interstate commerce and therefore be subject to federal regulation due to the Commerce Clause of the United States Constitution. The Commerce Clause states that the Federal Government can regulate interstate commerce. Therefore, if an employer has more than 15 employees, it likely engages in interstate commerce and is therefore compelled to comply with Title VII and other federal employment laws.

With the passage of Title VII, the U.S. Congress intended to eliminate both employment discrimination as well as the broader economic and social effects of discrimination. However, gathering enough votes to pass Title VII was a difficult task. The notes and legislative history of the act show that it was "sold" to skeptical members of Congress and the public as a sound economic policy, not as an important social or moral policy. According to congressional leaders at the time, "The failure of our society to extend job opportunities to the Negro is an economic waste. The purchasing power of the country is not being fully developed."[2]

Title VII outlaws discrimination in hiring, promoting, and the general treatment of employees. In addition, the law has since been expanded to include protection for vendors and patrons of businesses. When Title VII was first proposed, it included protection against discrimination based on race, national origin, color of skin, and religion. It did not originally include protection against gender-based discrimination.

In an attempt to kill Title VII, Representative Howard W. Smith from Virginia included a ban on gender discrimination. Smith assumed that the inclusion would encourage fellow representatives to oppose the legislation. Congress passed Title VII despite the amendment, and gender became a part of the law. Women's groups such as the National Women's Party had unsuccessfully lobbied for the inclusion of gender in Title VII, and Smith, in an attempt to kill the law, ironically accomplished what they could not.

ADMINISTRATION OF THE LAW

Title VII is administered by the Equal Employment Opportunity Commission (EEOC), an independent executive agency consisting of five presidentially appointed members who serve five-year terms. Violations of Title VII are brought to the EEOC through agency investigation and individual complaints. A complaint or "charge" must be filed with the EEOC within 180 days after the occurrence of the alleged unlawful employment practice, unless there is a state or local organization operating under a similar state or local statute, in which case the claim can be placed with that organization.

If the claim is filed with a state or local agency, an EEOC claim may be filed up to 300 days after the alleged discrimination occurs, or 30 days after the local proceedings end, whichever occurs first. The investigating organization determines whether the charge has merit, or is "meritorious." If the charge is deemed meritorious, the EEOC attempts conciliation with the offending organization. If the charge is deemed nonmeritorious or no conciliation has been reached within 180 days, the EEOC notifies the person who filed the complaint in a "right to sue" letter. The charging party then has 90 days after receiving the letter to bring a civil action in federal court under Title VII.

AMENDMENTS TO TITLE VII

Title VII was expanded in 1967 with the Age Discrimination in Employment Act (ADEA), 29 United States Code, Sections 621–634; in 1974 with the Vietnam Veterans Readjustment Assistance Act of 1974, 38 United States Code, Section 2011; in 1978 with the Pregnancy Discrimination Act; and in 1990 with the ADA, 42 United States Code, Section 12101. The ADA was amended by the ADA Amendments Act of 2008.

Today there are eight "protected classes." The protected classes comprise characteristics for which the United States Supreme Court and the United States Congress have determined employees have suffered a disproportionate share of discrimination as a result of that characteristic. An employee who is able to demonstrate discrimination or harassment as a result of some protected class is therefore entitled to bring a federal lawsuit against an employer. However, before an individual may file a lawsuit in federal court, he or she must first file a claim with the EEOC.

THE PROTECTED CLASSES

Race

Title VII does not specifically define race, and distinguishing among races is a difficult task. In general, people choose their race based on the categories found on federal or state employment applications. Some of the general categories are familiar to most Americans: Caucasian/White, Asian, African American/Black, Pacific Islander/Native Hawaiian, American Indian/Alaskan Native. For the purposes of Title VII and employment discrimination, an employer may not treat an employee or applicant differently or poorly on the basis of race, generally based on those federal categories.

Historical Perspective

- *Dred Scott v. Sandford*[3] (1857): United States Supreme Court decides 7–2 that African descendants are not and cannot be citizens of the United States even if they live in nonslave states.
- **Emancipation Proclamation/Thirteenth Amendment** (1863/1868): Effectively abolishes slavery in the United States.
- **Fourteenth Amendment to the United States Constitution** (1868): Post–Civil War amendment overturns Dred Scott allowing African descendants full citizenship.
- *Plessy v. Ferguson*[4] (1896): Declares "separate but equal" public accommodations for blacks and whites constitutional.
- **Executive Order 8802** (1941): Prohibits discrimination based on race for federal employers, primarily national defense; represents the first workplace antidiscrimination law in the United States.

- *Brown v. Board of Education*[5] (1954): Overturns "separate but equal" doctrine and declares that all public accommodations—including schools and trains—must be accessible to all people regardless of race.
- **Title VII of the Civil Rights Act of 1964**: Prohibits discrimination and ultimately harassment in the workplace on the basis of race, color, national origin, gender, and religion.
- *Loving v. Virginia*[6] (1967): Decriminalizes mixed-race marriage.
- *Griggs v. Duke Power Co.* (1971): Creates "disparate impact" theory (even where an employer is not motivated by discriminatory intent, Title VII prohibits an employer from using a facially neutral employment practice that has an unjustified adverse impact on members of a protected class) for race cases.

Griggs v. Duke Power Co.

An early case entitled *Griggs v. Duke Power Co.*[7] illustrates how Title VII can be applied in the workplace. It also illustrates how employers may try to circumvent the act. In *Griggs*, a North Carolina power company required employees to have a high school diploma or to pass a standardized general intelligence test as a condition of employment or transfer to jobs that were categorized as more than general labor. Traditionally, African American employees were not promoted beyond the general labor class of jobs. The company argued that the intelligence test was required for all employees regardless of race and therefore the company's policy did not violate Title VII. The United States Supreme Court determined that even though the test requirements were neutral on their face in terms of race, the requirements were not related to a "legitimate business purpose" and had an unfair or "disparate" impact on African Americans. In essence, the court held that the power company was unable to demonstrate how compliance with the requirements translated to successful performance of the jobs. As a result, the court ruled that the requirements were a violation of Title VII.

National Origin

National origin is a large and somewhat general category that includes a person's country of birth, ethnicity, ancestry, or culture. Although race and national origin may seem to be the same, they are in fact different. There are many people of the same race but from different cultures, ethnicities, and countries. For example, not all Americans are Caucasians, and not all Hispanics were born in Mexico. An employer cannot treat an employee or applicant differently or poorly based on his or her country of birth, ethnicity, ancestry, or culture.

Fragante v. Honolulu

In *Fragante v. Honolulu*,[8] a Filipino applicant was rejected despite good qualifications and scores on a preemployment exam. The applicant spoke English with a thick Filipino accent. The position required the clerk to deal with 330 angry, English-speaking customers per day by telephone. The applicant sued claiming national origin discrimination. The federal appeals court ultimately held that the requirement that clerks be able to communicate effectively in English was necessary to the job and thus was a bona fide occupational qualification that satisfied a legitimate business purpose under Title VII. Therefore, the city's rejection of the applicant was not a violation of Title VII.

Color of Skin

Color of skin can be distinguished from race and national origin. Two people may be from the same country and of the same race, but may still have different colors of skin. Title VII makes it illegal for an employer to treat an employee or applicant differently or poorly based on his or her color of skin—regardless of the color. Some people struggle with this category because this classification does not apply to only one color of skin; it applies to all colors of skin.

Equal Employment Opportunity Commission v. Trailways, Inc.

In *Equal Employment Opportunity Commission v. Trailways, Inc.*,[9] an African American employee filed a discrimination charge with the EEOC based on color of skin and race alleging that his employer's prohibition of beards had a disparate impact on African Americans who suffer from a disease known as pseudofolliculitis barbae (PFB). For people with PFB, shaving can cause serious physical consequences including infection and facial scarring. The EEOC found for the employee and brought the lawsuit against the company claiming that PFB is a condition unique to African Americans and based on their color of skin, and that therefore the company's policy had a disparate impact on African American employees. The court found for the EEOC and held that the evidence demonstrated that the 25 percent of the male African American workforce who suffer from the condition were effectively excluded from the company's job market as a class because of their color of skin and this racial trait.

Religion

Religion could be considered the first protected class given the role religious freedom played in the early stages of the founding of the United States. According to Title VII, the religion category includes all aspects of religious observance and practice, as well as belief. Title VII defines belief broadly to include almost any belief system, or lack of belief in any particular traditional belief system, including agnosticism and atheism. In the employment context, an employer may not treat an employee or applicant differently or poorly because of his or her beliefs. In addition, the act requires that an employer accommodate an employee's or applicant's observance of his or her religious beliefs when reasonable. An accommodation is reasonable when it does not cause undue hardship on the employer's business.

Historical Perspective

- **Establishment Clause of the First Amendment of the United States Constitution**: Dictates that Congress shall make no law respecting the establishment of a religion. The clause prohibits: (1) the establishment of a national religion by Congress, or (2) the preference of one religion over another or the support of a religious idea with no identifiable secular purpose.
- **Free Exercise Clause of the First Amendment of the United States Constitution**: Establishes that Congress can make no law prohibiting the free practice of religion.
- **Title VII of the Civil Rights Act of 1964**: Prohibits discrimination and ultimately harassment in the workplace on the basis of race, color, national origin, gender, and religion.
- ***Corporation of the Presiding Bishopric of the Church of Jesus Christ of Latter-Day Saints v. Amos*** (1987): Creates exemption from Title VII for religious organizations in dealing with employees.
- ***Board of Education of Kiryas Joel Village School District v. Grumet***[10] (1994): Clarifies the concept that government should not prefer one religion to another, or religion to irreligion.

Corporation of the Presiding Bishopric of the Church of Jesus Christ of Latter-Day Saints v. Amos

In *Corporation of the Presiding Bishopric of the Church of Jesus Christ of Latter-Day Saints v Amos,*[11] two individuals fired from their jobs with church-owned corporations for failure to live by certain church standards brought an action for religious discrimination. In *Amos,* the United States Supreme Court upheld a provision exempting religious organizations from Title VII's prohibition against discrimination in employment on the basis of religion. The holding of the *Amos* case means that churches can discriminate on the basis of religion in favor of their own members.

Age

The Age Discrimination in Employment Act (ADEA) of 1967 prohibits employers from discriminating against employees based on age. The act applies only to workers age 40 and over. The ADEA's protections apply to both employees and job applicants. Under the ADEA, it is unlawful to discriminate against a person because of his/her age with respect to any term, condition, or privilege of employment, including hiring, firing, promotion, layoff, compensation, benefits, job assignments, and training. Further, it is illegal to retaliate against an individual for opposing employment practices that discriminate based on age or for filing an age-discrimination charge, testifying, or participating in any way in an investigation, proceeding, or litigation under the ADEA. The ADEA applies to employers with 20 or more employees, including state and local governments; employment agencies and labor organizations; and the federal government.

Historical Perspective

- **Age Discrimination in Employment Act of 1967**: Adds age (workers 40 and over) as a protected class to Title VII.
- **Older Workers Benefit Protection Act of 1990**: Primarily intended to amend the ADEA to clarify the protections given to older individuals in regard to employee benefit plans.
- *General Dynamics Land Systems, Inc. V. Cline* (2004): Reinforces the principle that the age-based protected class applies only to people over 40. Any age claim filed by an employee under 40 will be dismissed.

General Dynamics Land Systems, Inc. v. Cline

In *General Dynamics Land Systems, Inc. v. Cline,*[12] the United States Supreme Court upheld an amended collective bargaining agreement that eliminated the company's obligation to provide health benefits to retired employees, except for current workers at least 50 years old. Workers under 40 sued under Title VII. The court held that workers under 40 did not have a claim, holding that Title VII is not designed to stop an employer from favoring an older employee over a younger one.

Veterans

In the employment context, this protection applies only to Vietnam veterans and disabled veterans.[13] The statutes that have been enacted likely protect only those two groups of veterans, since those groups have had the most difficulty assimilating into the workforce. Of course, in the future the courts could expand the class to include a wider scope of veterans. There are certain veterans' preference laws, and other protections that apply to all veterans, but for the purposes of discrimination and harassment, the class extends only to those two groups of veterans.

Historical Perspective

- **Vietnam Veterans' Readjustment Assistance Act of 1974**: The act is a direct response to the difficulty Vietnam veterans face in obtaining and retaining jobs.
- Since 1990 several pieces of legislation—with the goal of expanding the scope of the 1974 Act to other veterans, particularly Gulf War and Iraq War veterans—have failed.
- **Additions to FMLA** (2008): FMLA is expanded to include additional time off protections for Iraq War veterans and families dealing with injured veterans or veterans called to duty.

United States v. Board of Trustees of Illinois State University

In *United States v. Board of Trustees of Illinois State University,*[14] the federal court held that a hiring program adopted to circumvent a lawful veterans' preference program violated Title VII. Under the program, veterans were given preference points on an employment exam that allowed many to be hired. The majority of the veterans who applied for and received jobs were white males. The university attempted to alter the system to promote the hiring of more women and minorities. The federal court held that the university's attempt to alter the system amounted to discrimination against white males and that the veterans' preference was lawful. This case illustrates a virtual exception to Title VII. In this case, despite the fact that the veterans' preference law created a disparate impact on women and minorities, the court held that that preference was lawful.

Disability

In 1990, the Americans with Disabilities Act (ADA) became the single most important employment law of its generation. The ADA includes protection from discrimination based on a disability as well as requirements for employers and those offering other public facilities regarding access and accommodations for disabled employees, vendors, and patrons. The ADA prohibits private employers, state and local governments, employment agencies, and labor unions from discriminating against qualified individuals with disabilities in job application procedures, hiring, firing, advancement, compensation, job training, and other terms, conditions, and privileges of employment. The ADA covers employers with 15 or more employees, including state and local governments. It also applies to employment agencies and to labor organizations.

The ADA Amendments Act of 2008 (ADAAA), a federal act that was passed to expand the scope of those who are considered disabled, retains the ADA's basic definition of "disability" as a physical or mental impairment that substantially limits one or more major life activities, a record of such an impairment, or being regarded as having such an impairment. "Impairment" is defined as a diagnosable physiological, mental, or psychological disorder or condition. "Substantially limits" is defined as limited more than the average person based on the nature and severity of the condition, and the duration of the condition.

The ADAAA explicitly overturned two controversial Supreme Court decisions: *Sutton v. United Air Lines*, and *Toyota Motor Mfg., KY, Inc. v. Williams* that interpreted the ADA in a way that made it difficult to prove that an impairment is a "disability." In light of this, the ADAAA broadens the scope of coverage under both the ADA and Section 503 of the Rehabilitation Act. The statute contains a nonexhaustive list of "major life activities" that adds additional activities to those currently listed in the ADA and Section 503 regulations, and a nonexhaustive list of "major bodily functions." The list of major life activities now includes, but is not limited to, caring for oneself, performing manual tasks, seeing, hearing, eating, sleeping, walking, standing, lifting, bending, speaking, breathing, learning, reading, concentrating, thinking, communicating, and working. Major bodily functions include, but are not limited to, functions of the immune system; normal cell growth; and digestive, bowel, bladder, neurological, brain, respiratory, circulatory, endocrine, and reproductive functions.

If an employee is substantially limited in one or more of the major life activities, he or she may qualify as disabled. If the employee qualifies as disabled, he or she is eligible for protection under the three primary functions of the ADA: disability discrimination, reasonable accommodation, and access.

DISABILITY DISCRIMINATION   The definition of discrimination based on disability is broader in scope than the other protected classes. An employee has a claim for discrimination if he or she (1) has a current disability, (2) has a record or history of a disability, or (3) is regarded as or perceived to be disabled. For example, an employee may be subjected to discrimination for a medical condition that he or she used to suffer from but has successfully treated or overcome. Mental and emotional disabilities and other medical conditions that are associated with social taboos generally fall into this category. Likewise, an employee may suffer discrimination based on a perceived disability. As with other protected classes, an employer may not discriminate against an employee, applicant, vendor, or patron based on a disability.

REASONABLE ACCOMMODATION   If an individual is able to perform the essential functions of his or her job, with or without an accommodation, but there are barriers owing to disability, the employee may request an accommodation from his or her employer. Accommodations provided by employers range from a customized piece of equipment such as telecommunications devices for the deaf (TDD) or Braille machines, to raised or lowered desks, flexible schedules, or similar accommodations. An accommodation can come in any form as long as it is reasonable and not unduly burdensome for the employer. Unduly burdensome accommodations include those that are very costly and/or fundamentally alter the nature or operation of the employer's business. An employer may also deny an accommodation request that is a direct threat to the safety and health of employees.

All businesses should have a comprehensive procedure in place for dealing with accommodation requests. Employers should also beware that owing to the broad scope of disability discrimination, it is never appropriate for them to approach an employee about a perceived disability or unilaterally to recommend some type of accommodation. Individuals with disabilities must be the ones who request accommodations. Once an employee requests an accommodation or identifies that he or she is having difficulty performing the functions of the job owing to some medical condition, the ADA requires the employer to try to accommodate that employee.

ACCESS   The ADA drastically altered the American business landscape with new accessibility requirements far broader than those imposed by the Rehabilitation Act of 1973. The ADA includes strict requirements for businesses, universities, sports stadiums, and virtually any other public place with regard to ramps, door width, parking, and accessible restrooms and facilities. The ADA takes the original economic philosophy of Title VII—particularly that the purchasing power of a large group of Americans is not being utilized—and extends it from the workplace to the marketplace, capitalizing on the "purchasing power" of disabled persons.

Historical Perspective

- **Rehabilitation Act of 1973**: Provides discrimination protection on the basis of disability in some federal and state jobs; requires access in some federal and state buildings.
- **American's with Disabilities Act of 1990**: Requires all public accommodations to be accessible, adds disability as a protected class to Title VII, and sets forth rules for reasonable accommodations for disabled employees.
- *Lanman v. Johnson County* (2004): Creates a harassment or "hostile work environment" claim for employees who qualify as disabled.
- **ADAAA of 2008**: Increases the scope of who may qualify as disabled.

Lanman v. Johnson County

In *Lanman v. Johnson County,*[15] decided in December 2004, a deputy sheriff sued the employing county alleging there was a hostile work environment in violation of the ADA after she had been called "crazy" and "nuts" and been asked "are you off your medication" and several other questions regarding her mental health. The court ruled that although an action could be brought under the ADA, the jokes and comments directed toward her did not fit within the "perceived disability" category of the ADA, since the comments were more likely a sign of personality conflicts and simple rude behavior and not evidence that her employer regarded her as "substantially limited in one or more major life activities." Simply rude or boorish behavior, while obviously not recommended in the workplace, is not illegal.

PGA Tour, Inc. v. Martin

In *PGA Tour, Inc. v. Martin,*[16] the United States Supreme Court ruled that allowing golfer Casey Martin to ride in a golf cart owing to his disability was a reasonable accommodation, since it did not fundamentally alter the nature of the event. The Court's analysis included a discussion about the nature of the competition and the potential advantage gained by a cart user.

Toyota Motor Manufacturing, Kentucky, Inc. v. Williams

In *Toyota Motor Manufacturing, Kentucky, Inc. v. Williams,*[17] the United States Supreme Court held that an assembly-line worker was not substantially limited in the major life activity of performing manual tasks owing to her carpal tunnel syndrome. Although her condition affected her ability to do her job, it did not restrict her from engaging in activities that are central to most people's daily lives, and therefore she did not qualify as disabled. To some people's surprise, this case makes clear that although an employee may be unable to do a particular job, that inability does not necessarily mean that he or she is substantially limited in any major life activity.

Sex/Gender

This category includes protection based on being male or female; in addition, it protects against pregnancy discrimination and sexual harassment.

GENDER DISCRIMINATION   Women scored their first victory against workplace discrimination with the passage of the Equal Pay Act of 1963, a year before the passage of Title VII. However, the Equal Pay Act turned out to be a small victory, since most claims won by women or men were limited in terms of how a claim was filed and how much a victorious employee could recover. Both of those issues were addressed in two subsequent acts. The Civil Rights Act of 1991 allowed a victorious claimant to a trial by jury in a Title VII case and emotional distress damages. The Lilly Ledbetter Fair Pay Act of 2009 extended the statute of limitations for filing an equal pay complaint to each instance of improper conduct by the employer.

PREGNANCY DISCRIMINATION   Pregnancy discrimination was added in 1978 and protects women from being treated differently or poorly based on pregnancy, childbirth, or related medical conditions. In essence, an employer must treat a pregnant woman like anyone else who may need temporary accommodations for medical reasons.

SEXUAL HARASSMENT   Sexual harassment evolved as a subcategory of gender discrimination. Prohibitions against sexual harassment, and the ADA, have had the greatest impact on the American workplace. Sexual harassment comes in two forms: quid pro quo and hostile work environment.

Quid Pro Quo Sexual Harassment   Quid pro quo is a Latin term that means "this for that." Quid pro quo sexual harassment occurs when a supervisor promises or confers benefits in return for sexual favors, or when a supervisor adversely affects an employee's status based on the employee's rejection of the sexual advances. For a situation to constitute quid pro quo sexual harassment, the perpetrator must maintain a position of power over the victim, and the victim must suffer some tangible employment action as a result of the harassment. An employer cannot promote, or demote, an employee based on his or her acceptance or rejection of sexual advances. Conditioning employment status on the acceptance of sexual advances is a violation of Title VII.

Hostile Work Environment Sexual Harassment   Hostile work environment sexual harassment has less to do with job status and more to do with the job environment. An employee may make a claim for hostile work environment based on sexual jokes, comments, e-mails, or pictures in the workplace. Because hostile work environment sexual harassment is about the work environment, the relative employment positions of the perpetrator and victim are irrelevant. A supervisor can harass a subordinate, a subordinate can harass a supervisor, and coworkers of equal status can harass each other. In fact, since the focus of these claims is on the environment, a visitor, vendor, or patron of a business can assert a harassment claim if he or she is subjected to a hostile work environment. To prevail on a sexual harassment claim, a claimant must demonstrate each of the following:

1. *He or she has been subjected to conduct that is sexual in nature.* Employers who are trying to prevent this kind of conduct should not have difficulty defining "sexual in nature." Common sense dictates the difference between a sexual and a nonsexual pat on the back or comment about a coworker's appearance. Items or conduct of a sexual nature found in the workplace can be visual, physical, or verbal. Examples of visual materials might include photographs, calendars, e-mails, Web sites, and gestures that are sexual in nature. Examples of physical conduct include any touching, petting, patting, or grabbing that is sexual in nature. Examples of verbal conduct include jokes, comments, and stories that are sexual in nature. Cautious employers will attempt to keep any items or conduct that might be construed as sexual in nature out of the workplace.

2. *The sexual conduct must be severe and/or pervasive.* The law states that the sexual conduct must alter the work environment to the point that the victim can no longer remain

in the workplace. Pervasive conduct is ongoing, widespread, or repetitive to the point that is has created a hostile environment. The mildest sexual jokes and comments can become pervasive over time to create a hostile work environment. In contrast, one incident can constitute hostile work environment harassment if it is severe enough. To be considered substantially severe, one incident almost always has to include sexual touching of some type. Regardless of the conduct, if it is relatively minor and has not altered the environment to the point that the victim can no longer come to work, the conduct will not rise to the level of sexual harassment.

3. *The sexual conduct must be unwelcome and/or unwanted.* Sexual conduct is not inherently unlawful. In fact, it is unlawful only when it is unwelcome or unwanted. The problem, of course, is that supervisors and coworkers often do not know when someone is going to be offended by a joke or comment. To prevail, a claimant must have in some way demonstrated his or her disapproval of the sexual conduct. A claimant may manifest unwelcomeness in a variety of ways, including telling the joke teller that his or her jokes are offensive, not participating, walking away, or reporting the conduct to a supervisor. The best rule to adopt is that since it is impossible to know how someone will react to sexual conduct, it is better to prohibit the conduct in the workplace altogether.

Gender is no longer relevant to sexual harassment insofar as anyone can harass or be harassed. According to the law, a man can sexually harass another man just as he can sexually harass a woman. Likewise, a woman can sexually harass a man or another woman.

When discussing sexual harassment, or any kind of harassment including racial, religious, or any other unlawful discrimination based on a protected class, it is important to remember that a party's intent is irrelevant. It is never an adequate defense to say "I was trying to be funny" or "I was trying to be friendly." The only relevant factor is how the affected person perceives the joke or comment. Since it is impossible to predict how people will respond to sexual or racial jokes or comments, such topics are better left out of the workplace.

Historical Perspective

- **Nineteenth Amendment to the United States Constitution** (1920): Grants women the right to vote.
- **Equal Pay Act of 1963:** Requires equal pay for equal work, and renders gender irrelevant in terms of pay.
- **Title VII of the Civil Rights Act of 1964**: Prohibits workplace discrimination based on gender but does not specifically set forth a claim for sexual harassment.
- **Pregnancy Discrimination Act** (1978): Requires that a woman be treated the same as a man out of work temporarily.
- **The Civil Rights Act of 1991**: Allows a claimant to a trial by jury in a Title VII case and emotional distress damages.
- *Ellison v. Brady* (1991): Creates "reasonable woman" standard for analysis of sexual harassment claims.
- **Family and Medical Leave Act** (1993): Has an unintended negative impact on women since it replaces most maternity policies and is generally unpaid leave.
- *Burlington Industries, Inc. v. Ellerth* (1998): Clarifies the existence of an independent "hostile work environment" sexual harassment claim.
- *Oncale v. Sundowner Offshore Services, Inc.* (1998): Renders gender irrelevant to a sexual harassment claim.
- **The Lilly Ledbetter Fair Pay Act of 2009**: Strengthens the Equal Pay Act by extending.

Burlington Industries, Inc. v. Ellerth

In *Burlington Industries, Inc. v. Ellerth,*[18] the United States Supreme Court distinguished between "quid pro quo" and "hostile work environment" sexual harassment when it ruled that a female employee who had been subject to a supervisor's sexual advances even though no tangible employment action had yet resulted may still have a hostile work environment claim. In today's workplace most supervisors are aware that soliciting sexual favors in exchange for job status is inappropriate and illegal, therefore making hostile environment cases much more prevalent.

Ellison v. Brady

In *Ellison v. Brady,*[19] a federal appeals court established a "reasonable woman" standard, stating that the focus should be on the perspective of the victim. In *Ellison,* an employee was frightened by her coworker's subtle advances and strange love notes. The court held that a reasonable woman could have had a similar reaction and found that her perception was therefore reasonable. Other courts have extended the standard of reasonableness to all parties, male or female, claiming sexual harassment. Courts now generally call the standard the "reasonable person, similarly situated" standard. The standard evaluates the reasonableness of a person's claim based on who the claimant is, and how other, similarly situated people might react in the same situation. Thus, the standard prevents any outrageous, bad-faith claims from progressing in the courts.

Oncale v. Sundowner Offshore Services, Inc.

In *Oncale v. Sundowner Offshore Services, Inc.,*[20] the United States Supreme Court stated that same-gender sexual harassment qualifies under Title VII. In *Oncale,* a heterosexual male employee worked on an all-male crew on an oil platform in the Gulf of Mexico. The employee was subjected to humiliating sex-related actions by several male coworkers. The court held that the gender of the harassers and the harassed was irrelevant under Title VII and that the employee could bring an action under Title VII.

Sexual Orientation

At the time of writing this chapter, sexual orientation is not yet a federally protected class under Title VII. However, in the early summer of 2009 President Barack Obama extended benefits to some gay federal employees, and based on case law and trends such as an increasing number of jurisdictions recognizing and legalizing gay marriage and/or civil unions, it is very possible that sexual orientation will emerge in the next few years as an additional protected class under Title VII. Several states, and numerous municipalities, corporations, universities, and other organizations in the United States not only recognize equal benefits for same-sex couples, but many also include sexual orientation as a protected class in their state and city law, or corporation, university, and organization policy. This classification in particular has rapidly changed over the past several years and appears to be headed for protected status.

Historical Perspective

- *Bowers v. Hardwick*[21] (1986): United States Supreme Court upholds a Georgia statute criminalizing sodomy (oral and anal sex) between consenting adults.
- *Lawrence v. Texas*[22] (2003): United States Supreme Court directly overturns *Bowers*, holding that such laws are unconstitutional.
- **Vermont Legislature** in 2009 becomes the first to legalize gay marriage through statute. To that point, only state courts had found laws prohibiting gay marriage to be unconstitutional. Vermont is the first legislature to enact law legalizing the practice.
- **President Barack Obama** in 2009 extends domestic partner benefits to some federal employees, citing that gay federal employees have long been denied basic employment rights.

In sum, any other classifications such as marital status, political affiliation, and weight are not protected classes. This means that an employer may discriminate against employees based on political affiliation, and the employees have no recourse in a federal or state court. Of course, such behavior by the employer will nevertheless likely affect the business negatively, such as through bad publicity or by word of mouth.

ADVICE FOR MANAGERS

Have a Title VII Policy and Procedure

Employers have a relatively simple and powerful defense against any Title VII claim. Developing a thorough, well-articulated equal opportunity policy, in conjunction with a complaint and investigation procedure, is the most important step a company can take to protect itself from any Title VII charge. The company or organization should require supervisors to adhere strictly to its policies and procedures and provide periodic training for supervisors and subordinates. A company's ability to demonstrate that it has a policy that it follows and that it trains employees regularly will protect employers from losing most Title VII cases.

Be Clear about the "Legitimate Business Purpose" Concept

Of course, nothing can prevent an employee from making an internal complaint or filing a complaint with the EEOC. Almost every company with more than 15 employees will at some point be asked to respond to a charge of unlawful discrimination or harassment. A company's first defense is that the company has a policy in place, the company followed the policy, and the employees were aware of the policy. A company may also defend itself with the "legitimate business purpose" concept. A company can do almost anything, including discriminate based on a protected class, if it can show it did so for a legitimate business purpose or out of business necessity.

For example, a construction company will not be required to hire a disabled person who cannot lift more than 25 pounds if the essential functions of the job include regularly lifting more than 25 pounds. In such a case the company is discriminating by not hiring the applicant based on his or her disability; however, the company has a legitimate business purpose for doing so. But again, companies must beware: What constitutes a "legitimate business purpose" and "essential functions of the job" are hotly contested issues. A company can get itself into trouble with definitions that are either too broad or too narrow in scope.

Develop Objective Job Criteria

Perhaps most important, a company can act in accord with the intent and language of Title VII by making all its hiring and firing decisions based on objective job criteria. How an employee performs his or her job should be the only factor in determining that employee's status. Companies should be blind to race, religion, gender, disability, or any other protected category. New hires, promotions, demotions, and terminations should be made without regard to any of the characteristics identified in the protected classes.

Do Not Retaliate

Title VII includes a provision that protects any employee from retaliation for lodging a complaint of discrimination or harassment. An employee cannot be demoted or terminated for filing a complaint or lawsuit. To be protected, the employee need not prevail on his or her complaint but rather must demonstrate a reasonable, good-faith belief that the complaint was valid. Under this provision, a company can find itself in trouble even if it wins a discrimination or harassment claim. Imagine a scenario in which an employee complains that he or she is being sexually harassed. The company immediately responds by investigating the claim, disciplining the alleged harassers, and preventing another such incident. Or, imagine that the company conducts an investigation and finds that the allegations are not serious enough to warrant any action or discipline. In other words, in either case, the company does exactly what it is supposed to do. However, another problem arises if the complaint creates hard feelings that lead to a negative reaction. Imagine that one of the alleged harassers is a supervisor and that this person is so upset about the complaint that he or she scales back the complaining employee's job duties until the employee is fired six weeks later. Under these circumstances, the company may have a hard time defending itself against a retaliation claim.

ADVICE FOR EMPLOYEES

Follow Policies and Procedures

Employees have rights under Title VII, but they also have responsibilities. To prevail on a legal complaint or charge of discrimination or harassment, an employee must show that he or she at least generally followed all policies and procedures. This principle is important for two reasons. First, part of any analysis into a discrimination or harassment complaint is determining whether the employee followed the company's complaint procedure. Second, being a cooperative and productive employee makes it difficult for an employer to demonstrate a legitimate, nondiscriminatory reason for any discriminatory conduct.

Most companies have written policies and procedures in an employee handbook or other official company documents. Most employees also receive policy and procedure information and training at an orientation. If employees perform their job and follow any complaint guidelines, they increase their chances with any charge or complaint.

Behave Reasonably

Employees have a simple way to avoid being the subject of a Title VII allegation and to respond appropriately to unwanted conduct: Behave reasonably and professionally. It is not that difficult to determine when jokes or comments contain content that is "sexual in nature." Likewise, employees engaging in conversations pertaining to protected class issues should be respectful. Title VII is not intended to be a code of conduct that prohibits certain topics of discussion; it is intended to prevent members of protected classes from being treated differently or poorly based on protected-class status in the employment context. Realistically, employees will engage in personal conversations with each other on a wide variety of topics.

Although many lawyers would recommend to their corporate clients that all issues subject to Title VII protections not be discussed at all in the workplace, such a hope is, of course, not realistic; what managers should insist on, however, is that all organizational members be respectful in their discourse and avoid jokes, derogatory terms, and stereotypes. Likewise, an employee who is offended by a joke, comment, or other conduct should immediately report it to a supervisor or speak to the instigator. A little common sense and consideration is the best approach to any difficult workplace scenario.

A WORD ABOUT AFFIRMATIVE ACTION

Affirmative action is not a component of Title VII and does not generally affect the private sector. It does, however, affect government organizations and universities. One could argue that Title VII and affirmative action are opposites. Traditionally, affirmative action included preferences and quotas in interviewing and hiring, whereas Title VII outlawed differentiating between those who are part of a protected class and those who are not. By 2005 the two were more in harmony. Affirmative action currently requires government employers and state actors to actively recruit and reach out to minority candidates but does not allow quotas or preferences.[23]

THE FUTURE OF TITLE VII

There are many examples in the media of businesses and organizations that seem to struggle with managing a diverse workforce and have repeatedly dealt with Title VII claims; there are also many organizations that are flourishing under the law. However, the companies or organizations involved are not necessarily obvious ones.

For example, the Oakland Raiders football team is known for its commitment to excellence, rabid fans, and colorful collection of players. Not as well known, however, is that for more than 40 years, the Oakland Raiders have pioneered workplace diversity. The Raiders were the first to draft an African American quarterback in the first round of the amateur draft (Eldridge Dickey); the first to employ a Hispanic American quarterback (Tom Flores); and the first to hire a Hispanic American head coach (Tom Flores). Further, the team was the first in the NFL in the modern era to hire an African American head coach (Art Shell) and the first to boast a female chief executive officer (Amy Trask). The Raiders were also the first U.S. sports franchise to launch a separate alternative-language (Spanish) Web site and have since added German- and Mandarin-language sections to its Web site for its German and Chinese fans. The Raiders lead by example in the National Football League, and thousands of other organizations do likewise in their own business sectors.

The Raiders' approach is smart and effective because the American workplace is going to become only more diverse as the country's demographics continue to change. It is more important than ever for employers to understand when their or their employees' conduct is unlawful and how to protect themselves from the unwanted cost and scrutiny of a Title VII lawsuit. Accomplishing these goals is challenging, in part because employment discrimination law is fluid. Not only do the relevance and application of the various protected classes change over time, the categories themselves change.

For example, prior to September 11, 2001, the protection against discrimination based on Middle Eastern or Muslim national origin or religion was rarely an issue. In the post 9/11 world, national origin litigation has become more prevalent, and relevant, as people of Middle Eastern descent have lately been discriminated against more frequently. However Title VII changes in the future, it will continue to be an important law that protects employees from discriminatory workplace conduct and therefore fosters workplace diversity.

Federal Acts Relating to Workplace Diversity

Emancipation Proclamation (1863)

Issued by President Abraham Lincoln; freed the slaves in those territories still rebelling against the Union; allowed blacks the opportunity to work for wages.

Executive Order 8802 (1941)

Signed by President Franklin D. Roosevelt on the eve of World War II; prohibits government contractors from engaging in employment discrimination based on race, color, or national origin.

Equal Pay Act of 1963

Requires that men and women be given equal pay for equal work in the same establishment. Although the jobs need not be identical, they must be substantially equal; it is job content, not job titles, that determines whether jobs are substantially equal.

Title VII of the Civil Rights Act of 1964

Prohibits employment discrimination based on race, color, religion, gender, or national origin. Enforced by the Commerce Clause of the U.S. Constitution and limited to employers with 15 or more employees, state or federal employers, or companies receiving state or federal money.

Executive Orders for Affirmative Action (EO 11246 in 1965 and 11375 in 1967)

Issued by President Lyndon Johnson; requires government contractors to "take affirmative action" toward prospective minority employees in all aspects of hiring and employment. Contractors must take specific measures to ensure equality in hiring and must document these efforts. Amended in 1967 to cover discrimination on the basis of gender.

The Age Discrimination in Employment Act (ADEA) of 1967

Incorporated as part of Title VII; protects individuals who are 40 or older from employment discrimination based on age. The ADEA's protections apply to both employees and job applicants.

Rehabilitation Act of 1973

Prohibits discrimination against qualified individuals with disabilities who work in the federal government.

Vietnam Veterans Readjustment Assistance Act of 1974

Requires covered federal government contractors and subcontractors to take affirmative action to employ and advance in employment-specified categories of veterans protected by the Act and prohibits discrimination against such veterans.

(continued)

Pregnancy Discrimination Act of 1978

An amendment to Title VII; maintains that discrimination on the basis of pregnancy, childbirth, or related medical conditions constitutes unlawful sex discrimination. Women who are pregnant or affected by related conditions must be treated in the same manner as other applicants or employees with similar abilities or limitations.

Older Workers Benefit Protection Act of 1990

An amendment to the Age Discrimination in Employment Act of 1967; established to safeguard older workers' employee benefits from age discrimination. Allows reductions in benefits based on age as long as the employer's costs of providing benefits to older workers are the same as their costs for providing benefits to younger workers.

Americans with Disabilities Act of 1990

Prohibits private employers, state and local governments, employment agencies and labor unions from discriminating against qualified individuals with disabilities in job application procedures, hiring, firing, advancement, compensation, and job training. Covers employers with 15 or more employees, including state and local governments; also applies to employment agencies and to labor organizations.

Civil Rights Act of 1991

An amendment to Title VII of the Civil Rights Act of 1964. Provides monetary damages in cases of intentional employment discrimination; allows for jury trials; extends coverage of act to U.S. citizens working abroad for U.S. companies.

Family and Medical Leave Act of 1993

Allows employees to receive up to a total of 12 workweeks of unpaid leave during any 12-month period for one or more of the following reasons: (1) for the birth and care of the newborn child of the employee; (2) for placement with the employee of a son or daughter for adoption or foster care; (3) to care for an immediate family member (spouse, child, or parent) with a serious health condition; or (4) to take medical leave when the employee is unable to work because of a serious health condition.

Lilly Ledbetter Fair Pay Act 2009

Extends the statute of limitations for filing an equal pay complaint to each instance of improper conduct by the employer.

Americans with Disabilities Act Amendments Act 2009

Revises the definition of "disability" to more broadly encompass impairments that substantially limit a major life activity; expands the scope of those who are considered disabled.

Sources: United States Equal Employment Opportunity Commission, www.eeoc.gov; and United States Department of Labor, www.dol.gov.

Discussion Questions

1. Why is it important for managers to understand diversity management from both managerial and legal perspectives?

2. If you were a diversity educator, how would you frame the importance of understanding and abiding by the legal dimensions of diversity within

the larger framework of managing diversity in organizations?

3. Describe the significance of the passage of Title VII of the Civil Rights Act of 1964.

4. Describe the classes protected by the federal government and the related legislation for each. Do you think sexual orientation will become a protected class in the near future?

5. In light of some of the legal cases highlighted in this chapter, response to the following questions:

   • *Griggs v. Duke Power Co.*: What was the power company really trying to do? How can a company demonstrate that employment screening procedures serve legitimate business purposes?

   • *Fragante v. Honolulu*: Under this rule, when can a company discipline, terminate, or refuse to hire an employee?

   • *Corporation of the Presiding Bishopric of the Church of Jesus Christ of Latter-Day Saints v. Amos*: What impact do you think the Court's ruling has had on religious universities such as Brigham Young University or the University of Notre Dame?

   • *General Dynamics Land Systems, Inc. v. Cline*: Do workers who are under the age of 40 have any recourse against age-based discrimination? Should they?

   • *PGA Tour, Inc. v. Martin*: Does a golf cart give a golfer an advantage over competitors who are required to walk?

   • *Oncale v. Sundowner Offshore Services, Inc.*: Does the *Oncale* finding challenge your stereotypes of sexual harassment?

Notes

1. *U.S. Code* 2000 et seq.
2. U.S. *Code Cong. & Admin. News*, 88th Congress, 2nd sess., 1964, 2513–2517.
3. 60 US 393 (1857).
4. 163 US 537 (1896).
5. 347 US 483 (1954).
6. 388 US 1 (1967).
7. 401 U.S. 424 (1971).
8. 888 F. 2d 591 (9th Cir. 1989).
9. 530 F. Supp. 54 (D. Colo. 1981).
10. 512 US 687 (1994).
11. 483 U.S. 327 (1987).
12. 540 U.S. 581 (2004).
13. See Vietnam Era Veterans' Readjustment Assistance Act of 1974, 38 *U.S. Code* 793, 794.
14. 944 F. Supp 714 (C.D. Ill. 1996).
15. 393 F3d 115 (2004).
16. 532 U.S. 661 (2001).
17. 534 U.S. 184 (2002).
18. 524 U.S. 742 (1998).
19. 924 F.2d 872 (9th Cir. 1991).
20. 523 U.S. 75 (1998).
21. *Bowers v. Hardwick* 478 US 186 (1986).
22. *Lawrence v. Texas* 539 US 558 (2003).
23. See *Gratz v. Bollinger*, 539 U.S. 244 (2003).

CHAPTER 3

Diversity Management as Systemic

How do organizations manage diversity effectively? What are some "best practices" for managing diversity? What does it mean to manage diversity systemically? These poignant questions together constitute the framework of this chapter. In this chapter we highlight top-ranked organizations for diversity management, describe a systemic approach to managing diversity, and include an essay that examines IBM's comprehensive diversity management policy.

A number of organizations have been praised in their efforts to manage diversity and have been identified as exemplary organizations in terms of diversity management. Although there are a number of diversity rankings, we have chosen to focus on *DiversityInc*'s 2009 "The Top 50 Companies for Diversity" for a few reasons: First, *DiversityInc*'s methodology for determining the ranking is public knowledge; second, the results of the ranking were recognized by credible media outlets such as the *Wall Street Journal, BusinessWeek,* MSNBC, and CNN; and third, the ranking examines four important areas of diversity—human capital, CEO commitment, corporate communications, and supplier diversity.

The following list of the top-ranking companies briefly outlines their strategic attempts to implement diversity initiatives systemically throughout their organization.

#1: JOHNSON & JOHNSON

- There is strong CEO leadership in diversity management from Chairman and CEO William C. Weldon. He meets regularly with employee-resource groups and has the chief diversity officer report directly to him.
- The organizational culture values diversity with, "more than six percent of the bonuses of [CEO] direct reports are tied to diversity results."[1]
- The company has a diverse board of directors: 9 percent black, 9 percent Asian, 9 percent Latino, and 27 percent female.
- Additional *DiversityInc* rankings: #4: "Top 10 Companies for Recruitment and Retention"; #5: "Top 10 Companies for Asian Americans"; #2: "Top 10 Companies for Executive Women"; #10: "Top 10 Companies for LGBT Employees."

#2: AT&T

- Leadership is directly involved with diversity management; Chairman, CEO, and President Randall Stephenson is a strong promoter of diversity and is chairman of the NAACP

Corporate Centennial Campaign. Stephenson also chairs the company's quarterly internal diversity council meetings.
- The company's workforce is highly diverse: 39 percent are black, Latino, Asian, and American Indian; new hires are 49 percent black, Latino, Asian, and American Indian. Managers reflect diversity with 30 percent of the company's managers being black, Latino, Asian, and American Indian.
- The company is a leader in supplier diversity with "9.6 percent of its total procurement with Tier 1 suppliers who are minority- or women-owned businesses."[2] AT&T also has 16 employees dedicated to its supplier-diversity efforts.
- Additional DiveristyInc rankings: #7: "Top 10 Companies for Recruitment and Retention"; #1: "Top 10 Companies for African Americans"; #8: "Top 10 Companies for LGBT Employees."

#3: ERNST & YOUNG

- A high value is placed on mentoring programs: the Executive Mentoring Program pairs high-potential black, Latino, Asian, and American Indian partners and principals with members of the firm's Americas Executive Board; Learning Partnerships provides black, Latino, Asian, and American Indian professionals access to senior leaders; Pathways to Meaningful Partnership Provides training for women, blacks, Latinos, Asians, and American Indians; and Minority and Women's Leadership Conferences help women and minorities to gain leadership skills.
- Diversity training is mandatory for the whole workforce. The training is held monthly and lasts more than a full day.
- The firm participates in philanthropic activities focused on diversity; 20 percent of the firms' philanthropy goes to multicultural organizations.
- Additional *DiversityInc* rankings: #2: "Top 10 Companies for People with Disabilities"; #1: "Top 10 Companies for LGBT Employees."

#4: MARRIOTT INTERNATIONAL

- CEO leadership makes efforts both internally and externally; Chairman and CEO J.W. (Bill) Marriott is a serving member of the Executive Leadership Cabinet for the Martin Luther King Jr. National Memorial Project Foundation and honorary cochair of the American Foundation for the Blind's Helen Keller Achievement Awards.
- Diversity is highly valued within the organization; CEO Marriott personally signs off on executive's compensation tied to diversity, accounting for "13 percent of the bonuses of his six direct reports."[3]
- The company touts strong workforce diversity; 60.4 percent of the U.S. workforce is black, Latino, Asian, and American Indian.
- Additional *DiversityInc* rankings: #4: "Top 10 Companies for Supplier Diversity"; #9: "Top 10 Companies for African Americans"; #10: "Top 10 Companies for Executive Women."

#5: PRICEWATERHOUSECOOPERS

- The firm values "branding its diversity commitment as a key trigger for recruitment, retention, talent development, client acquisition and retention, community development, and supplier diversity."[4] Through internal and external communications, the firm focuses on the importance of diversity in all aspects of business.

- The importance of diversity and work-life balance is stressed through mentoring programs, including the "Full Circle Program," an on-ramping and off-ramping program; Mentor Moms; National Special Needs Caregiver Circle; and a Working Parents microsite, which includes an executive health program and emergency backup childcare centers, among other services.
- PricewaterhouseCoopers achieves demographic diversity through new hires; 31 percent are black, Asian, Latino, and American Indian and 51.6 percent are women.
- Additional *DiversityInc* rankings: #1: "Top 10 Global Diversity Companies"; #3: "Top 10 Companies for LGBT Employees."

#6: SODEXO

- Quickly becoming a leader in diversity management, the company has developed a metrics platform to assess diversity behavior. There are four specific areas: diversity-training metrics; an employee-engagement survey; the Sodexo Diversity Index; and 360-assessments.
- The company has made strong efforts to communicate about diversity externally. Its Web site has a perfect score "for its consistent and very visible diversity message in both words and images."[5]
- An emphasis on diversity is evident through mentoring programs, work-life benefits, and use of employee-resource groups.
- Additional *DiversityInc* rankings: #3: "Top 10 Companies for Recruitment & Retention"; #3: "Top 10 Companies for African Americans"; #2: "Top 10 Companies for Latinos"; #1: "Top 10 Companies for Executive Women"; #9: "Top 10 Companies for People with Disabilities"; #7: "Top 10 Companies for LGBT Employees."

#7: KAISER PERMANENTE

- The company finds success in diversity through leadership encouragement; Chairman and CEO George C. Halvorsen supports diversity and "ties 10 percent of his 10 direct reports' bonuses to diversity goals."[6]
- Diversity is reflected in the company's workforce, with 56.9 percent black, Asian, Latino, and American Indian and 76.4 percent women. This same diversity is found within the highest management with CEO and direct reports being 33.4 percent black, Latino, Asian, and American Indian and 42.9 percent women.
- Additional *DiversityInc* rankings: #5: "Top 10 Companies for People with Disabilities"; #7: "Top 10 Companies for Executive Women"; #1: "Top 10 Companies for Latinos."

#8: MERCK & CO.

- Diversity is not a new concept at Merck & Co; it is the company's seventh year in a row on Diversity Inc's "Top 50 Companies for Diversity."
- Strong leadership advocacy allows Merck & Co to be a "trendsetter in creating an inclusive work force."[7] Chairman, President, and CEO Richard T. Clark signs off on executive compensation tied to diversity and goals and achievements for supplier diversity.
- CEO Clark's 10 direct reports include three blacks, one Asian, one Native American, and two women.

#9: COCA-COLA CO.

- The company's demographics show a commitment to diversity: Coca-Cola's management is 31.8 percent black, Latino, Asian, and American Indian and 47 percent female.

- Employee involvement in diversity is promoted by holding diversity-training programs and talks. Topics include: "The Powerful Mix of Money, Race & Age in the New Century" and "Perpetrators—Bystanders: Is there a Difference?"
- Coca-Cola continues to engage in philanthropic activities focused on diversity; 26 percent of its total philanthropic budget goes to multicultural groups.

#10: IBM CORP.

- Chairman, President, and CEO Samuel Palmisano insists top performance evaluations are only achievable if managers are fostering "teamwork and inclusion among all employees— across locations, cultures, and geographies—and promote IBM's diversity values."[8]
- IBM's 12-member board reflects diversity with two blacks, one Latino, one Asian, and three women members.
- Additional *DiversityInc* rankings: #1: "Top 10 Companies for People with Disabilities"; #2: "Top 10 Companies for Supplier Diversity"; #4: "Top 10 Companies for Asian Americans"; #4: "Top 10 Companies for LGBT Employees"; #2: "Top 10 Global Diversity Companies."

The rest of the "The Top 50 Companies for Diversity" are the following:

#11: Procter & Gamble

#12: Verizon Communications

#13: American Express Co.

#14: Bank of America

#15: JPMorgan Chase

#16: Abbott

#17: Cox Communications

#18: Pepsi Bottling Group

#19: MGM MIRAGE

#20: Novartis Pharmaceuticals Corp.

#21: KPMG

#22: Health Care Service Corp.

#23: Accenture

#24: PepsiCo

#25: Capital One Financial Corp.

#26: Henry Ford Health System

#27: Colgate-Palmolive

#28: Ford Motor Co.

#29: The Walt Disney Co.

#30: Comerica Bank

#31: Wells Fargo & Co.

#32: Blue Cross and Blue Shield of Florida

#33: Deloitte

#34: HSBC—North America

#35: Xerox Corp.

#36: Monsanto Co.

#37: AARP

#38: Time Warner Cable

#39: Starwood Hotels & Resorts Worldwide

#40: Toyota Motor North America

#41: MasterCard Worldwide

#42: Cummins

#43: MetLife

#44: WellPoint

#45: Prudential Financial

#46: SC Johnson

#47: General Mills

#48: Aetna

#49: CSX Corp.

#50: KeyBank

A SYSTEMIC APPROACH TO MANAGING DIVERSITY

The systemic approach to managing diversity (see Figure 3-1) is an expansion of the integration-and-learning diversity management paradigm discussed in detail in Chapter 1.[9] With authentic commitment from leadership, diversity is incorporated throughout the organization; and as a result, diverse employees and diversity initiatives have the ability to influence and affect work outcomes. Diversity, within this framework, operates systemically as it is understood and valued as an essential organizational component rather than as a sporadic organizational strategy.

The purpose of our discussion is to describe a systemic approach to diversity management that consists of six diversity components and associated diversity initiatives. The diversity management components include leadership commitment, organizational communication, recruitment and retention, the incorporation of diversity into the main work of the organization, the linkage of diversity initiatives to business outcomes, and external relationships. Together, they constitute a systemic approach to managing diversity. As a way to further explicate each of the six components of diversity management, we provide examples of ways in which Verizon Communications, a top organization for diversity management, attempts to employ each of these components.

The implementation of this systemic approach of diversity management has the potential for success because it addresses diversity's complexity by operating on three different levels of organizational change: structural, cultural, and behavioral.[10] As the three levels of change work together to transform an organization, they operate "synergistically" as they are "interrelated in a complex and mutually reinforcing manner."[11] As these three levels of change interact with each other, they may overlap, reinforce each other, and at times even contradict each other.

Dr. Kathryn A. Cañas

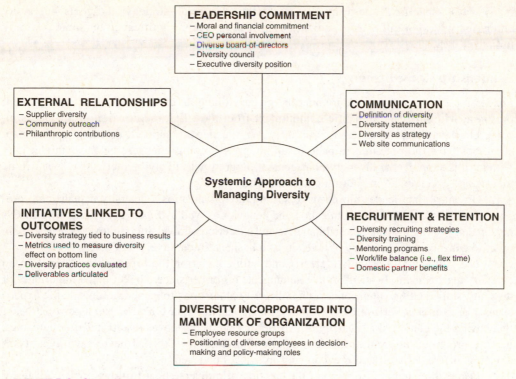

FIGURE 3-1   Systemic Approach to Managing Diversity

Evangelina Holvino, Bernanrdo Ferdman, and Deborah Merrill-Sands explicate the three levels of change. Structural interventions "focus on the formal systems that guide and control the work of the organization."[12] Our approach to managing diversity incorporates multiple diversity initiatives that work to create structural change, for instance, recruitment and retention practices, mentoring programs, work–family balance programs, flexible work schedules, and the integration of women and minorities into executive positions. The second level of organizational change is cultural change which "concerns the basic assumptions, values, beliefs, and ideologies that define an organization's view of itself, its effectiveness, and its environment."[13] Our approach includes multiple diversity initiatives that influence cultural change: leadership commitment, effective organizational communication, clarity about how diversity fits within the organizational strategy, having diverse organizational members in decision-making and policy-making positions, diversity training, and the creation and development of external relationships. Diversity strategies that influence the third level of change, behavioral change, "seek changes in behaviors, attitudes, and perceptions within and between individuals, and within and between work groups, that support or hinder the goals of diversity"[14] and include comprehensive diversity education and training, the creation of employee resource groups, and mentoring programs.

Each of the main diversity management components and the associated diversity initiatives are interrelated in a type of diversity matrix that operates on multiple levels of change. One of the primary challenges for an organization is to determine the most effective combination of diversity initiatives—that operate on all three levels of change—that work together to create a competitive advantage for that particular organizational framework. As organizations differ in so many ways—specifically in terms of organizational cultural, strategy, and goals—diversity emphases will also differ as organizations will place more significance on some diversity initiatives over others.

Leadership Commitment

Leadership commitment is the foundation for developing an effective diversity management program; without firm, authentic commitment from the CEO, the creation of a successful, comprehensive diversity program is unlikely. With leadership support, diversity management strategies have the potential to become an integrated, comprehensive business model; and without this support, the diversity management program will likely be ineffective as it will be viewed and executed as an intermittent management strategy.

Organizational leadership needs to sustain the organization's diversity management program through supportive communication and behavior as well as financial backing. The CEO's personal involvement with the establishment and execution of diversity initiatives is necessary in order to enhance the legitimacy of diversity as a business imperative.

The CEO should articulate clearly and with conviction the organization's position on diversity management. In an effort to communicate his or her sincere belief in the importance of diversity, skilled CEOs often connect their diversity philosophy to personal values or life experiences. For example, Verizon CEO Ivan Seidenberg stated, "I have always had a personal belief that having the benefit of a diversity of experiences and perspectives results in better outcomes. Having grown up in a culturally rich neighborhood in New York, I never saw diversity as anything different than what I grew up with and what I believed in."[15]

Leadership should also support the creation of a diverse board of directors. With fewer women and minorities in top executive positions, organizations may find it challenging to create a diverse board. Nevertheless, a diverse board is a significant symbol of an organization's stance on diversity management. The board of directors at Verizon, a company committed to the value of diversity, consists of eight white men, two white women, and one African American man. Although there is indeed some diversity on Verizon's board, increasing its diversity would send a powerful message to Verizon's employees and stakeholders.

Also indicative of leadership commitment is the creation of and support for a diversity council. Diversity councils serve multiple purposes as the supervisory body for diversity management; they help develop the organization's diversity strategy, check the overall progress of the diversity management program, and set diversity goals. There are two types of diversity councils: internal and external. The councils that operate internally are typically comprised of senior executives, members of employee resource groups, and are led by the CEO. The councils that operate externally are typically comprised of diversity experts from a variety of arenas such as business, government, and academia.

Leadership commitment is also reflective of the creation and support of an executive-level diversity position such as Vice President for Diversity, Director of Diversity, or Chief Diversity Officer. The person who holds this position is responsible for crafting, implementing, and managing the overall diversity strategy and also has a direct line of communication with the CEO or is one report removed from the CEO. Magda N. Yrizarry holds the top diversity position at Verizon as the Vice President of Workplace Culture, Diversity, and Compliance. Yrizarry, who is frequently quoted in diversity-based and mainstream magazines and journals, maintains, "Diversity helps Verizon compete in our increasingly diverse and competitive marketplace. We're focused on maintaining a culture of diversity and inclusion, one that benefits our shareholders and customers.

It also allows us to tap into the creativity and vitality of our workforce and suppliers."[16] An established, executive-level diversity position such as Yrizarry's sends the message that the organization views diversity management as not only the right thing to do but also as a business opportunity—that a long-term investment in a diverse workforce will increase productivity and revenue.

Communication

The overall communication about diversity and diversity management is an essential component of an effective diversity management program. It is the CEO's responsibility to communicate with clarity the organization's position in regard to diversity. Verizon CEO Seidenberg persuasively articulates Verizon's position on diversity: "You have to be clear about your expectations in a big organization like Verizon. So we also manage diversity the way we do anything we truly care about as a business: with disciplined goals, a focus on results, a commitment to operating excellence and a grounding in our corporation's core values and beliefs."[17]

In addition to effective communication from the CEO, it is necessary for an organization to craft a clear definition of diversity. Since there is not a one-size-fits-all definition of diversity for every organization, each organization must craft its own definition. Working in tandem with the organization's definition of diversity is a diversity statement that reflects the organization's position on diversity. This statement should not be hidden in a policies and procedures manual; rather, it should be common knowledge among all employees and easily found on the company Web site. Verizon combines its definition and diversity statement in the following:

> As a company that serves millions of customers, it is imperative that we have an inclusive workforce. The most powerful communications solutions come from the widest range of thoughts and ideas and it is our people who will distinguish us in the marketplace.
>
> Our definition of diversity includes the whole range of human differences, including age, ethnicity, education, sexual orientation, work style, race, gender and more. Over time, we have made diversity an integral part of our business, from work force development and supplier relationships to economic development, marketing and philanthropy.
>
> The diverse minds, experiences, culture and unique perspectives of our employees are what give us our competitive advantage. Diversity and inclusion are a critical link to our customers, communities and shareholders. Verizon firmly believes that embracing and cultivating diversity in our corporate culture is both the right business strategy and the right thing to do.[18]

In addition to having a well-crafted definition of diversity and diversity statement, diversity should be articulated within a strategic framework: How does diversity fit within the larger organizational strategy? Like the diversity statement, the diversity strategy should be communicated within the organization to employees and outside the organization to the public through marketing strategies and via the company Web site. Verizon's diversity strategy is as follows: "The goal of our diversity strategy is to have an aligned and integrated workplace where diversity is transparent, and where Verizon is an inclusive organization that leverages the diversity of employees, customers and suppliers for increased productivity, profitability and an enhanced reputation."[19]

The organization's definition of diversity, diversity statement, and diversity strategy should all be represented and easily accessible on the company Web site. An organization's Web site is a significant communication tool because is acts as a public representation of an organization; and for potential customers or employees, it may be the first step when learning about an organization. The following questions serve as a framework for examining the ways in which an organization communicates about diversity on its Web site:

- Is information about diversity or a link to a diversity section found on the Web site's home page?
- Are the organization's definition of diversity and diversity mission statement clearly articulated on the Web site? Are they easy to locate?
- Is a statement by the CEO reflecting the organization's commitment to diversity posted on the Web site?
- Does the Web site reflect diversity-related issues such as employee resource groups, recruiting strategies, diversity training, supplier diversity, and community relations?
- Are diversity videos—in which the CEO, Director of Diversity, HR Executive, and/or employees discuss the company's commitment to diversity—easily accessible?
- Are current annual diversity reports accessible from the company's Web site?
- Does the Web site contain current information on the company's diversity awards and any diversity-related news?
- Are images on the Web site representative of diversity in terms of the organization's employees and customers?

When examined through the lens of these questions, Verizon's Web site represents and is consistent with its strong value of diversity. Links to multiple aspects of its diversity strategy help to communicate how the value of diversity is integrated throughout the organization. There is one aspect, however, that Verizon could change to create a more diversity-friendly Web site. On Verizon's home page, a visitor must first click the "About Us" link before getting to the link for "Verizon's Diversity Program." Verizon could convey a stronger dedication to diversity as well as facilitate one's ability to locate the diversity information if it were to have a diversity link located on its home page so that its value of diversity is evident instantly and only one click away.

Recruitment and Retention

RECRUITMENT   Recruitment and retention strategies are critical components to both building and managing diversity in organizations. Effective recruiting practices have been described as "the most direct way to transform a corporation's culture and its responsiveness to the market-place."[20] If an organization is struggling to create a more diverse pool of qualified candidates for a particular position, it may want to rethink its recruiting process. Women and racial minorities typically have less access "to informal sources of job information" and therefore tend to rely on "the messages presented in formal job ads as a basis for forming expectations of the job and the organization."[21] In light of this, recruiting through word of mouth and/or the company Web site are not effective strategies for creating a more diverse applicant pool.

Carol Kulik and Loriann Roberson offer three strategies for recruiting a more diverse workforce. They are as follows: (1) the use of recruiting advertising photos or text that highlights the diversity of the organization's workforce; (2) the inclusion of statements that communicate the organization's equal employment opportunity (EEO) or diversity management policies in recruiting materials; and (3) the use of female and racial minority recruiters.[22] Holvino, Ferdman, and Merrill-Sands describe possible changes in current recruitment practices such as "requiring that all interview panels be diverse in their makeup, changing the weight of the interview in the selection process, and reviewing job and job descriptions to focus on requirements as opposed to style preferences."[23]

Another way for organizations to attract diverse candidates is to craft and make public a statement on diversity recruiting. Verizon, for example, articulates a general diversity recruiting philosophy on their Web site: "Verizon wants only to hire the best people and actively recruits employees with diverse styles, backgrounds and skills sets." One way that Verizon accomplishes this is by forming "strategic partnerships with colleges and universities and professional and community-based organizations."[24] After implementing effective recruiting strategies, the second step is for organizations to implement diversity initiatives that enhance the retention of diverse employees.

RETENTION   Four significant retention strategies include diversity training, mentoring, flex time, and domestic partner benefits. Many organizations view diversity training as the cornerstone of their diversity management program.[25] Organizations may incorporate diversity training to accomplish a variety of goals: to create awareness of how people's different identity groups affect who they are on personal and professional levels; to describe diversity's benefits; to explain how managing diversity can become a competitive advantage for their business; to explicate the company's diversity strategy; to teach skills that will increase inclusive language and behavior in the workplace; to distribute information related to the legal dimension of workforce diversity (i.e., information regarding Family and Medical Leave Act, sexual harassment policies, the Americans with Disabilities and Amendments Act, etc.); and to encourage open, honest conversations about issues of diversity.

Organizations have found that diversity training has both advantages and disadvantages. Some of the advantages include raising awareness about indirect discrimination and privilege, providing voice to those who have been historically underrepresented, debunking myths and stereotypes, and sending a message that diversity is an important initiative throughout the organization.[26] The disadvantages of diversity training occur when the training is poorly designed and taught by a diversity educator who does not teach the complexities of diversity and diversity management such as weaknesses of the business case for diversity, potential workplace challenges related to a diverse workforce, and the role of the white male within the framework of diversity management. Further, diversity training can "create additional stereotypes if the content is too simplistic, or it can alienate dominant groups if the process of training is believed to favor some groups at the expense of others."[27]

DiversityInc, in conjunction with consulting groups Global Lead and Guardian Quest, offers ten suggestions for successful diversity training:

- Make it mandatory for the entire workforce, with clear public support from the CEO.
- Hold top managers accountable for measurable training goals.
- Tie the net outcome to the company's overall business direction.
- Offer it frequently, at least once a month.
- Have it last at least one day.
- Design training that enables employees to be more effective in their jobs.
- Add the component of personal leadership.
- Do not talk about theories or use platitudes. Use case studies and facts and figures.
- Make the training hands-on and intellectually stimulating.
- Have formal follow-up.[28]

For Verizon, diversity training is just one aspect of its overall diversity management strategy. Verizon describes diversity training as a "powerful supplement" because it "provides employees with the opportunity to better understand and appreciate issues of human difference and how those issues can inhibit or enhance an individual's and group's contribution to our common goals." Furthermore, Verizon maintains that diversity training "equips employees with the skills they need to take productive action on this understanding and appreciation."[29]

In addition to diversity training, another powerful diversity initiative that helps to retain diverse employees is the implementation of a mentoring program. According to Kulik and Roberson, mentoring programs have two main goals: career development and advancement; and retention.[30] The implementation of effective mentoring programs may be a key diversity initiative for retaining diverse employees since studies have found that women and people of color face barriers when advancing in their career rather than when beginning their career.[31] A lack of mentoring is consistently mentioned by diverse employees as a significant advancement barrier.[32] In fact, a Catalyst survey found that 48 percent of Latinas, black, and Asian women cited "not having an influential mentor or sponsor" as their greatest impediment, while 33 percent cited "lack of role models in my racial/ethnic group."[33] In many cases, mentoring relationships have yielded higher job career satisfaction, larger salaries, and faster promotion rates.[34] In light of the positive employee responses to mentoring programs, it seems reasonable to suggest that mentoring programs would likely encourage and promote the retention of diverse employees.

Due to different retention goals in each organization, the design and implementation of mentoring programs will also differ. Barbara Frankel from *DiversityInc* articulates her view of "best practices" for mentoring programs. In particular, she suggests that the organization implement both formal, structured mentoring programs and informal mentoring networks. In addition, she maintains that organizations should do the following: place an emphasis on cross-cultural mentoring, create metrics for measuring the success or failure of a particular mentoring program, and publicize the success of their mentoring programs. Frankel offers examples of how specific companies, such as Abbott, American Express, IBM, and Rockwell Collins, implement these mentoring best practices.[35]

Like these companies, Verizon also invests in employee development resources—such as mentoring—as a way to retain its diverse employees. Verizon explains that they have developed mentoring and leadership development programs to "ensure that diverse members of our multi-cultural work force are prepared for career advancement." Furthermore, Verizon explains that these employee development resources "have strengthened Verizon's leadership team by developing high quality managers from diverse backgrounds who are prepared to assume new job assignments and additional responsibilities."[36]

WORK-LIFE BALANCE AND DOMESTIC PARTNER BENEFITS   Flex time—when, where, and how organizational members do their work—is a significant diversity initiative. For single parents and women in particular, flexibility during the day and, if necessary, during the arc of their career is critical to creating and maintaining a successful profession. Sylvia Hewlett and Carolyn Luce found that in business sectors, the majority of women they surveyed believe that access to reduced-hour jobs is important.[37] Without a flexible organizational structure, the experience of many women—as they attempt to re-enter the workplace—is often psychologically demeaning as well as financially detrimental, specifically in terms of the loss of earnings: "Across sectors, women lose a staggering 37% of their earning power when they spend three or more years out of the workforce."[38] As a strategy to retain talented women, organizations should create more on-ramps for women to return to the workplace, or negotiate creative work models, like acting as a consultant for a certain period of time rather than as a full-time employee. Creative work models are significance because they allow women to keep their association with their company rather than having to exit completely.

Verizon embraces flexibility through its teleworking options and support of family-friendly policies. For example, Verizon has consistently been ranked high in *Working Mother Magazine's* rankings, specifically in terms of child care, leave policies, flexibility programs, family-friendly programs and policies, and job-guaranteed time off for childbirth or adoption. In addition, Verizon has also been recognized for cutting-edge policies and practices that support African American, Asian, Latina, and Native American women in the workplace.[39]

In addition to flex time and creative work models, another retention strategy is domestic partner benefits. According to SHRM, although only 33 percent of organizations overall offer same-sex domestic partner benefits, an impressive 80 percent of Fortune 100 companies offer these benefits.[40] The companies that offer these benefits understand that treating all employees equally is not only the right thing to do, but also a business advantage insofar as they will enhance employees' sense of job satisfaction and security that may lead to longevity with the company.

Incorporation of Diversity into the Main Work of Organization

We focus on two primary strategies for incorporating diversity into the main work of an organization: the creation and development of employee resource groups and having women and minorities in decision-making and policy-making roles. By implementing these two strategies, diversity has the potential to become deeply embedded within the organization insofar as diversity has the ability to influence how work is done, decisions are made, and products are created. First, we will discuss the diversity initiative, employee resource groups.

An employee resource group is a "company-sanctioned group of employees with similar backgrounds or interests."[41] Employee resource groups are typically created around identity groups such as gender, race, national origin, age, religion, sexual identity, and/or disabilities. Their efficacy is increased, however, when they are created with inclusiveness as a goal insofar as they are "open to anyone interested in participating, whether or not they are a member of the specified group."[42]

Although the purpose of an employee resource group varies depending on the organization, some include the following: to facilitate networking with coworkers and executives; to help employees voice concerns over specific work-related issues; to strategically use members' ideas to enhance the organization's bottom line; to help organizations understand how to market more effectively to diverse customers; to help organizations understand better how to recruit, advance, and retain women and minorities; and to brainstorm product or policy ideas or ways to improve both products or policies. In essence, employee resource groups are helpful to both employee and organization; as employees gain networking and mentoring opportunities, organizations gain new perspectives and viewpoints that can impact the actual work of the organization. In light of this, employee resource groups represent a direct link between diversity and work, and if managed effectively, can represent a direct, positive link between diversity and the bottom line.

Verizon effectively implements the diversity initiative, employee resource groups. Verizon's employee resource groups—Asian Pacific Employees for eXcellence (APEX), Consortium of Information and Telecommunications Executives (CITE), Disabilities Issues Awareness Leaders (DIAL), Gay, Lesbian, Bisexual, and Transgender Employees of Verizon and their Allies (GLOBE), Hispanic Support Organization (HSO), National Jewish Cultural Resource Group (NJCRG), Native American People of Verizon (NAPV), South-Asian Professionals Inspiring Corporate Excellence (SPICE), Veterans Advisory Board of Verizon

(VABVZ), and Women's Association of Verizon Employees (WAVE)—are company supported and employee run and have the purpose of promoting "personal and professional growth of employees, enhance career advancement and provide a stronger sense of community within the company."[43] The specific projects associated with Verizon's employee resource groups include the following: (1) helping the company with marketing, advertising, branding, sales, strategic planning, recruitment, sourcing, employee development, external partnership, and diversity awareness; (2) going into the community and working for humanitarian causes; (3) hosting events that give members and employees the opportunity to network and develop skills, in such areas as career development; and (4) celebrating cultural, educational, and other special events during their groups' history or heritage month.[44]

In addition to employee resource groups, integrating women and minorities in key positions across the corporate structure is another way for diversity to have a direct impact on the work of the organization. Holvino, Ferdman, and Merrill-Sands note that this type of integration is significant because it provides access to decision-making and organizational power. In addition, it "may help reduce stereotyping and prejudice, provide important role models for the incorporation of other groups, and diminish the dynamics of tokenism that often reduce the effectiveness of employees from non-dominant groups."[45]

DiversityInc reports that Verizon is increasing its commitment to hiring people who reflect its customer base. African Americans, Latinos, and Asians are 33.8 percent of the workforce and 41.8 percent of new hires. In addition, African Americans, Latinos, and Asians constitute 35.8 percent of managers and received 38.2 percent of management promotions.[46] Verizon highlights several diverse executives—among them, women, African Americans, Asians, and Indians—in a section on its Web site called "Diversity at the Top."[47]

Linkage of Diversity Initiatives to Organizational Outcomes

Measuring the effect of diversity investments on business performance is a complex, challenging task. The Society for Human Resource Management (SHRM) maintains that "Many companies struggle with effectively measuring the results of diversity initiatives. In part, the challenge is determining what measures will yield useful information. For others, this task is difficult because they do not yet collect the necessary data required to measure diversity."[48] Another obstacle is that because the outcomes of some diversity initiatives are abstract—such as, more effective problem solving, creativity, team work, communication between dominant and nondominant groups, networking among employees, customer service, and recruiting strategies—they are difficult to measure.

Regardless of the challenges of measuring diversity's impact on the organization, gathering data is a critical component of the diversity management process and therefore unavoidable. Collecting and examining such data is important because it will help to link diversity strategies to organizational goals, determine the efficacy of particular diversity initiatives, articulate diversity deliverables, and facilitate support—both moral and financial—for diversity management programs. In essence, through the implementation of diversity metrics such as Diversity Return on Investment (DROI),[49] an organization's diversity management program will gain legitimacy. According to Edward Hubbard, examples of meaningful data include level of participation in the firm's diversity vision formulation; number of diverse employees in formal mentoring programs who get promoted; percentage of diversity objectives aligned with key strategic business objectives that are tied to bonus and compensation systems; representative mix on the board of directors; overall organizational climate and culture ratings and their effects on all represented groups.[50]

Diversity metrics play an important role at Verizon. Taking a hands-on approach to managing the diversity measurement system at Verizon, Seidenberg personally reviews Verizon's diversity scorecard on a quarterly basis which consists of 17 key diversity metrics.[51] As Seidenberg explains, "We review our diversity performance index every quarter and have board-level oversight of our progress."[52] Furthermore, Verizon has a variety of measurements in place that reflect different ways to measure diversity in organizations. One example of this is the *Inclusion Index* which "[m]easures employees' sense of belonging through an index developed by our research team based on responses to our Employee Opinion survey." Another example is the *Diversity Performance Incentive*, which is a measurement that tracks the workforce composition in each line of business, as well as the number of hires and promotions of diverse candidates. Each line of business has a unique goal, depending on their individual unit's composition. A third example is *Supplier Diversity*, which is a "[m]easure derived from the procurement opportunities and developing and advocating a diversified Supplier base."[53]

External Relationships

A systemic approach to management diversity consists of extensive external relationships such as supplier diversity, community outreach programs, and philanthropic contributions such as creating scholarships or supporting diversity-based nonprofit organizations.

One example of how an organization can strengthen its external relationships with women- or minority-owned organizations is by investing in supplier diversity. Supplier diversity is when an organization purchases its goods and services from businesses that are owned by, for example, women, minority groups, people with disabilities, and members of the GLBT community. According to *DiversityInc*, "As corporate America continues to try to find ways to cut costs and faces increasing pressure to make inroads into the fast-growing racial and ethnic markets, supplier diversity has emerged as one of the most viable and measurable methods of accomplishing those goals."[54] Investing in supplier diversity is an important aspect of an organization's overall diversity management program specifically because such suppliers "provide unique insights into emerging markets, build a loyal customer base and, most importantly, create wealth in communities."[55]

One of Verizon's diversity goals is to increase its investment in supplier diversity, maintaining that it "actively seeks and cultivates minority suppliers on an ongoing basis."[56] Impressively, Verizon is a charter member of the elite Billion-Dollar Roundtable, which is a group of select corporations that each spends more than $1 billion annually with minority- and women-owned businesses. In addition, as a strategy to increase the number of minority firms in its supply chain, Verizon supports supplier education and development. In fact, Verizon established supplier development programs for minority suppliers in telecommunications high-tech areas.[57]

Creating relationships with the community is an important dimension of diversity management. Diversity initiatives that focus on improving the community should not be viewed as secondary; they should be implemented with the same dedication as the other components of the systemic diversity management approach.

Verizon has created the Strategic Alliances Group as a way to "advance Verizon's business, regulatory and public policy initiatives through relationships with national third-party organizations that represent general consumer, low-income, seniors, education, African American, Asian American, Hispanic, disabled, minority small business, and small rural constituencies."[58] In addition to the Strategic Alliances Group, Verizon also creates external relationships through the Verizon Foundation which, in 2007, awarded more than $67.4 million in grants to nonprofit agencies in the United States and abroad.[59] Verizon has partnerships with community-based organizations such as the League of Latin American Citizens, Hispanic Association of Colleges and Universities, the Organization of Chinese Americans, and the American Indian College Fund.[60]

In sum, our systemic approach to managing diversity represents the integration of six diversity components that affect structural, cultural, and behavioral levels of change. The main components include leadership commitment, organizational communication, recruitment and retention, the incorporation of diversity into the main work of the organization, the linkage of diversity initiatives to business outcomes, and external relationships. The diversity initiatives that are associated with each of these components work together in such a way that diversity becomes integrated systemically through the organization.

Case Study: Diversity as Strategy

When most of us think of Lou Gerstner and the turnaround of IBM, we see a great business story. A less-told but integral part of that success is a people story—one that has dramatically altered the composition of an already diverse corporation and created millions of dollars in new business.

By the time Gerstner took the helm in 1993, IBM already had a long history of progressive management when it came to civil rights and equal employment. Indeed, few of the company's executives would have identified workforce diversity as an area of strategic focus. But when Gerstner took a look at his senior executive team, he felt it didn't reflect the diversity of the market for talent or IBM's customers and employees. To rectify the imbalance, in 1995 Gerstner launched a diversity task force initiative that became a cornerstone of IBM's HR strategy. The effort continued through Gerstner's tenure and remains today under current CEO Sam Palmisano. Rather than attempt to eliminate discrimination by deliberately ignoring differences among employees, IBM created eight task forces, each focused on a different group such as Asians, gays and lesbians, and women. The goal of the initiative was to uncover and understand differences among the groups and find ways to appeal to a broader set of employees and customers.

The initiative required a lot of work, and it didn't happen overnight—the first task force convened almost two years after Gerstner's arrival. But the IBM of today looks very different from the IBM of 1995. The number of female executives worldwide has increased by 370 percent. The number of ethnic minority executives born in the United States has increased by 233 percent. Fifty-two percent of IBM's Worldwide Management Council (WMC), the top 52 executives who determine corporate strategy, is composed of women, ethnic minorities born in the United States, and non-U.S. citizens. The organization has seen the number of self-identified gay, lesbian, bisexual, and transgender executives increase by 733 percent and the number of executives with disabilities more than triple.

But diversity at IBM is about more than expanding the talent pool. When I asked Gerstner what had driven the success of the task forces, he said, "We made diversity a market-based issue. . . . It's about understanding our markets, which are diverse and multicultural." By deliberately seeking ways to more effectively reach a broader range of customers, IBM has seen significant

Source: David Thomas, *Harvard Business Review* 82, no. 9 (September 2004). *David A. Thomas (dthomas@hbs.edu) is a professor of organizational behavior and human resource management at Harvard Business School in Boston.*

bottom-line results. For example, the work of the women's task force and other constituencies led IBM to establish its Market Development organization, a group focused on growing the market of multicultural and women-owned businesses in the United States. One tactic: partnering with vendors to provide much-needed sales and service support to small and midsize businesses, a niche well populated with minority and female buyers. In 2001, the organization's activities accounted for more than $300 million in revenue compared with $10 million in 1998. Based on a recommendation from the people with disabilities task force, in October 2001 IBM launched an initiative focused on making all of its products more broadly accessible to take advantage of new legislation—an amendment to the federal Rehabilitation Act requiring that government agencies make accessibility a criterion for awarding federal contracts. IBM executives estimate this effort will produce more than a billion dollars in revenue during the next 5–10 years.

Over the past two years, I have interviewed more than 50 IBM employees—ranging from midlevel managers all the way up to Gerstner and Palmisano—about the task force effort and spent a great deal of time with Ted Childs, IBM's vice president of Global Workforce Diversity and Gerstner's primary partner in guiding this change process. What they described was a significant philosophical shift—from a long tradition of minimizing differences to amplifying them and to seizing on the business opportunities they present.

Constructive Disruption

Gerstner knew he needed to signal that diversity was a strategic goal, and he knew that establishing task forces would make a powerful impression on employees. Early in his tenure, Gerstner had convened various task forces to resolve a range of strategic choices and issues. He used the same structure to refine and achieve IBM's diversity-related objectives.

Gerstner and Childs wanted people to understand that this was truly something new. IBM had a long practice of being blind to differences and gathering demographic information only to ensure that hiring and promotion decisions didn't favor any particular group. So this new approach of calling attention to differences, with the hope of learning from them and making improvements to the business, was a radical departure. To effectively deliver the message and signal dramatic change, IBM kicked off the task forces on Bastille Day, July 14, 1995. "We chose Bastille Day . . . because it's considered to be a historic day of social disruption," Childs told me. "We were looking for some constructive disruption."

Each task force comprised 15–20 senior managers, cutting across the company's business units, from one of the following demographic employee constituencies: Asians; blacks (African American and of African decent); gays/lesbians/bisexuals/transgender individuals (GLBT); Hispanics; white men; Native Americans; people with disabilities; and women. To be eligible, members had to meet two criteria: executive rank and member of the constituency. (Three of the groups—people with disabilities, Native Americans, and GLBT—didn't have enough representation in the executive ranks to fill the task forces, so membership also included midlevel managers.) Members were chosen by Ted Childs and Tom Bouchard, then senior vice president of human resources, based on their knowledge of and experiences with the top executive team. In particular, Childs sought executives who had spoken to him or to a colleague in his office about their own experiences and perceptions that diversity was an untapped business resource; he persuaded those individuals to participate by describing the effort as a chance to make a difference and eliminate some of the roadblocks they may have faced in their careers.

Each task force also had two or more executive cochairs who were members of the constituency. For these roles, Childs and Bouchard recruited high-performing, well-respected senior managers and junior executives who were at least at the director level. Each task force was also assigned an executive sponsor from the WMC, who was charged with learning about the relevant constituency's concerns, opportunities, and strategies and with serving as a liaison to top management. The executive sponsors were senior vice presidents, and most reported directly to Gerstner. They were selected by Bouchard and Childs based on their willingness to support the change process and on the potential for synergies within their given business areas.

The first sponsor of the women's task force, for instance, was the senior vice president of sales and marketing worldwide. Childs knew that the company's senior executives believed that potential buyers in many countries outside of the United States wouldn't work with female executives and that this could interfere with women's success in international assignments. By connecting this SVP with the women's task force, Bouchard and Childs hoped these barriers could be better understood—and that opportunities for women to advance in the sales organization might improve. Similarly, the SVP for research and development was asked to sponsor the people with disabilities task force, with the expectation that if he could get closer to the day-to-day experiences of people with disabilities in his own organization, he would gain new insights into the development of accessible products.

Sponsors were not necessarily constituents of their groups. The sponsor for the white men's task force was a woman; the sponsor for the women's task force, a man. Indeed, there was a certain advantage to having sponsors who didn't come from the groups they represented. It meant that they and the task force members would have to learn from their differences. A sponsor would have to dig deep into the issues of the task force to represent its views and interests to other WMC members.

In addition to having a sponsor, cochairs, and members, each task force was assigned one or two HR employees and a senior HR executive for administrative support, as well as a lawyer for legal guidance. The groups also received logistical and research support from Childs's Global Workforce Diversity organization, which was responsible for all of IBM's equal employment and work-life balance programs.

Once the task forces had been set up and launched, Bouchard sent an e-mail to every U.S. employee detailing the task forces and their missions and underscoring how important the initiative was to the company. In his message, he acknowledged IBM's heritage of respecting diversity and defined the new effort in business terms. Here's an excerpt from the e-mail:

> To sustain [IBM's recognition for diversity leadership] and strengthen our competitive edge, we have launched eight executive-led task forces representing the following IBM employee constituencies. . . . We selected these communities because collectively they are IBM, and they reflect the diversity of our marketplace.

He also encouraged employees to respond with specific suggestions for how to make IBM a more inclusive environment. Childs then compiled more than 2,000 responses to the e-mail and channeled them to the appropriate task forces. As a result of these suggestions, the task forces focused on the following areas for evaluation and improvement: communications, staffing, employee benefits, workplace flexibility, training and education, advertising and marketplace opportunities, and external relations.

The initial charge of the task forces was to take six months to research and report back to the CEO and the WMC on four questions: What is necessary for your constituency to feel welcome and valued at IBM? What can the corporation do, in partnership with your group, to maximize your constituency's productivity? What can the corporation do to influence your constituency's buying decisions, so that IBM is seen as a preferred solution provider? And which external organizations should IBM form relationships with to better understand the needs of your constituency?

At first, skepticism prevailed. Here's what one white male executive told me:

> This whole idea of bringing together people in the workplace and letting them form these groups was really repugnant on its face to a lot of people, and of course IBM had been a nonunion company in the United States for a long, long time. I mean, having groups was like letting them into your living room.

And from a black executive:

> I was somewhat skeptical, and there was a level of reluctance in terms of how successful this would ultimately become in IBM, given some of the complex issues around the topic of diversity.

The groups faced other challenges as well. When the women's task force met for the first time, many members were relieved to hear that some of their colleagues were sharing similar struggles to balance work and family; at the same time, some of IBM's women believed strongly that female executives should choose between having children and having a career. The dissenting opinions made it more difficult to present a united front to the rest of senior management and secure support for the group's initiatives.

Task force members also disagreed on tactics. Some within the black task force, for instance, advocated for a conservative approach, fearing that putting a spotlight on the group would be perceived as asking for unearned preferences, and, even worse, might encourage the stereotype that blacks are less capable. But most in the group felt that more aggressive action would be needed to break down the barriers facing blacks at IBM.

In both cases, members engaged in lengthy dialogue to understand various points of view, and, in light of very real deadlines for reporting back, were forced to agree on concrete proposals for accomplishing sometimes competing goals. The women's group concluded that IBM needed to partner with its female employees in making work and family life more compatible. The black group decided it needed to clarify the link between its concerns and those of the company—making it clear that the members were raising business issues and that the task force effort was not intended to favor any group.

During the six months of the initial phase, Childs checked in with each group periodically and held monthly meetings to ensure that each was staying focused. The check-ins were also meant to facilitate information sharing across groups, especially if several were grappling with similar issues. The task forces' work involved collecting data from their constituencies, examining internal archival data to identify personnel trends, and reviewing external data to understand IBM's labor and customer markets. Their most critical task was to interpret the data as a means of identifying solutions and opportunities for IBM. Task forces met several times a month, in subcommittees or in their entirety, and at the end of the research period, Childs met with each group to determine its top issues—or the "vital few." These were defined as the issues and concerns that were of greatest importance to the group and would have the most impact if addressed. Childs and the task force cochairs also realized that not addressing these issues would hamper the credibility of the initiative with frontline employees.

On December 1, 1995, the task forces met to share their initial findings. Again, the date was chosen with the idea of sending a message to employees: It was the 40th anniversary of Rosa

Parks's refusal to give up her seat on a bus in Birmingham, Alabama, to a white passenger. That act, of course, led to her arrest and ignited the Birmingham bus boycotts that ushered in the modern U.S. civil rights movement. Just as the Bastille Day launch signaled a release from old ways of thinking, the timing of this meeting indicated a desire for a radically new approach to diversity.

Several of the task forces shared many of the same issues, such as development and promotion, senior management's communication of its commitment to diversity, and the need to focus on recruiting a diverse pool of employees, especially in engineering and science-related positions. Other concerns were specific to particular groups, including domestic partner benefits (identified by the GLBT task force) and issues of access to buildings and technology (raised by the people with disabilities task force). Overall, the findings made it clear that workforce diversity was the bridge between the workplace and the marketplace—in other words, greater diversity in the workplace could help IBM attract a more diverse customer set. A focus on diversity was, in short, a major business opportunity.

All eight task forces recommended that the company create diversity groups beyond those at the executive level. In response, IBM in 1997 formed employee network groups as a way for others in the company to participate. The network groups today run across constituencies, offering a variety of perspectives on issues that are local or unique to particular units. They offer a forum for employees to interact electronically and in person to discuss issues specific to their constituencies.

Another recommendation, this time put forth by the women's group, aimed to rectify a shortage in the talent pipeline of women in technology, identifying young girls' tendency to opt out of science and math in school as one of the causes. To encourage girls' interest in these disciplines, in 1999 a group of women engineers and scientists in Endicott, New York, ran a pilot "EXITE" (Exploring Interests in Technology and Engineering) camp. The program brought together 30 middle-school girls for a week that summer to learn about science and math in a fun, interactive way from female IBM employees. In 2000, the women's task force replicated the program in five other locations throughout the United States, reaching 400 girls, and in 2001 the program expanded internationally. In 2004, IBM will have a total of 37 EXITE camps worldwide—15 in the United States, one in Canada, eight in Asia Pacific, six in Europe, and seven in Latin America. After the girls attend camp, they are assigned an IBM female scientist or engineer as a mentor for one year.

Since 1999, IBM has reached 3,000 girls through EXITE camps. In 2003 alone, 900 girls attended, and in 2004, 1,100 will have gone through the program. In collaboration with IBM's technology group, the women's task force also created a steering committee focused on retaining women in technology currently at IBM and attracting female scientists from universities.

As for external initiatives that arose from the task forces, IBM's Market Development (MD) unit came directly out of the groups' responses to the third question: What can IBM do to influence your constituency's buying decisions, so that the company is seen as a preferred solution provider? It became clear that IBM wasn't well positioned in relation to the market's fastest-growing entrepreneurial segments—female- and minority-owned businesses. The MD was formed as a unit of the Small and Medium-Sized Business Sales and Marketing organization. Initially, the group helped IBM revamp its communications strategy for reaching female- and minority-owned companies. Its role has since evolved into identifying and supporting sales and marketing strategies aimed at these important segments.

The MD's efforts have directly translated into hundreds of millions of dollars in new revenue. More important to IBM's senior executives, the MD is elevating the company's overall level of cultural competence as it responds to the needs of IBM's diverse customer base. A case in point is advertising, where the MD convened teams from the task forces and the advertising department to create constituency casting guidelines and other communications. These changes have helped ensure appropriate representation of constituencies in all aspects of the company's marketing, with the guidelines forming the basis for ongoing discussions about how to reach and relate effectively to IBM's diverse customer base.

The people with disabilities task force (PWD), which initially focused on compliance with accessibility laws, began in 2001 to think about making the leap from compliance to market initiatives. That same year, Ted Childs arranged for each task force to meet with senior management, including Sam Palmisano, then IBM's president. The PWD task force leaders took the opportunity to point out the tremendous market potential in government contracts if IBM made its products more accessible. Palmisano agreed, and PWD received the green light it needed to advance its projects.

One reason for the increased focus on accessible technology was that in June 2001, the U.S. Congress implemented legislation mandating that all new IT equipment and services purchased by federal agencies must be accessible. This legislation—known as Section 508—makes accessibility a more important decision criterion than price in many bid situations, thus creating an opportunity for accessibility IT leaders to gain market share, charge a price premium, or both, from federal buyers. In addition to legislation, other indicators made it clear that the demand for accessibility was growing: a World Health Organization estimate of more than 750 million disabled people across the globe, with a collective buying power of $461 billion, and an increase in the number of aging baby boomers in need of accessible technology.

IBM believes that business opportunities will grow as countries around the world implement similar legislation. Furthermore, the private-sector opportunity for accessible technology could be far greater than that of the government as companies address a growing aging population. IBM's worldwide Accessibility Centers comprise special teams that evaluate existing or future IBM technologies for their possible use in making products accessible. There are now a total of six IBM Accessibility Centers, in the United States, Europe, and Japan.

Pillars of Change

Any major corporate change will succeed only if a few key factors are in place: strong support from company leaders, an employee base that is fully engaged with the initiative, management practices that are integrated and aligned with the effort, and a strong and well-articulated business case for action. IBM's diversity task forces benefited from all four.

Demonstrate Leadership Support

It's become a cliché to say that leadership matters, but the issue merits discussion here because diversity is one of the areas in which executive leadership is often ineffectual. Executives' espoused beliefs are frequently inconsistent with their behavior, and they typically underestimate how much the corporation really needs to change to achieve its diversity goals. That's because diversity strategies tend to lay out lofty goals without providing the structures to educate senior executives in the specific challenges faced by various constituencies. In addition, these strategies often don't provide models that teach or encourage new behaviors.

IBM has taken several approaches to helping executives deepen their awareness and understanding. To begin with, the structure of the task forces—how they operate and who is on them—immerses executive sponsors in the specific challenges faced by the employee constituency groups. The groups are a formal mechanism for learning, endorsed at the highest levels of the company.

Second, the chief diversity officer, Ted Childs, acts as a partner with the CEO as well as coach and adviser to other executives. In addition to educating them on specific issues, as he did when the company decided to offer domestic partner benefits, Childs also works to ensure that they behave in ways that are consistent with the company's diversity strategy. A senior executive described Childs's role as a coach and teacher:

> I know that he's had a number of conversations with very senior people in the company where he's just sat down with them and said, "Listen, you don't get it, and you need to get it. And I care about you, and I care about this company. I care about the people who are affected by the way you're behaving, and so I owe it to you to tell you that. And here's how you don't get it. Here's what you need to do to change."

And third, Gerstner and later Palmisano not only sanctioned the task force process but actively sought to be role models themselves. A number of the executives I interviewed were struck by Gerstner's interest and active involvement in the development of high-potential minority and female senior managers and junior executives; he took a personal interest in how they were being mentored and what their next jobs would be. He also challenged assumptions about when people could be ready for general management assignments. In one case, Gerstner and his team were discussing the next job for a high-potential female executive. Most felt that she needed a bigger job in her functional area, but Gerstner felt that the proposed job, while involving more responsibility, would add little to the candidate's development. Instead she was given a general management assignment—and the team got a signal from the CEO about his commitment to diversity. His behavior communicated a sense of appreciation and accountability for people development. Indeed, accountability for results became as critical in this domain as it was for all business goals.

Gerstner also modeled desired behaviors in his interactions with his direct reports. One of them told me this story:

> During a board of directors dinner, I had to go to [my daughter's] "back-to-school night," the one night a year when you meet the teachers. I had been at the board meeting that day. I was going to be at the board meeting the next day. But it was the dinner that posed a problem, and I said, "Lou, I'll do whatever you want, but this is the position I am in," and . . . he didn't even blink. He said, "Go to back-to-school night. That is more important." And then . . . he told the board at dinner why I wasn't there and why it was so important . . . to make it possible for working parents to have very big jobs but still be involved parents. He never told me that he told the board. But the board told me the next day. They . . . said, "You should know that Lou not only said where you were but gave a couple minute talk about how important it was for IBM to act in this way."

CEO leadership and modeling didn't stop when Gerstner left. One senior executive who is a more recent arrival to the WMC described how Palmisano communicates the importance of the diversity initiative:

> Executive involvement and buy-in are critical. Sam has played a personal and very important role. He personally asked each task force to come and report its progress and agenda to him. He spent time with the [task force that I sponsor] and had a detailed review of what we are doing on the customer set. What are we focused on

internally? How can he help in his role as CEO? He's really made it clear to the senior-level executives that being good at [leading the diversity initiative] is part of our job.

Engage Employees as Partners

While the six-month task force effort was consistent with IBM's history of promoting equal opportunity, the use of the task force structure to address issues of diversity represented a significant culture shift. IBM was an organization that had discouraged employees from organizing around any interest not specifically defined by the requirements of their jobs. The idea of employees organizing to advocate was anathema. One white male executive said, "Does this mean that we can have a communist cell here? Are we going to have hundreds and hundreds of these?" The skepticism reached up to the highest levels: When Childs first proposed the task force strategy, Gerstner asked him one question: "Why?"

But in the end, IBM's task force structure paved the way for employee buy-in because executives then had to invite constituent groups to partner with them in addressing the diversity challenge. The partnerships worked because three essential components were in place: mutual expectations, mutual influence, and trust.

When the task forces were commissioned, Childs and Gerstner set expectations and made sure that roles and responsibilities were unambiguous. Initially, the task forces' charters were short, only six months (the groups are still active today), and their mission was clear: to explore the issues, opportunities, and strategies affecting their constituencies and customers. Once this work was done, it fell to the corporation's senior executives to respond and to report on the task forces' progress at various junctures to the WMC. Gerstner and Childs followed up with the task force sponsors to ensure that the groups were gathering meaningful information and connecting it to the business.

The task forces' work has evolved to focus on more tactical issues, and the organization has demonstrated its willingness to be influenced, committing significant resources to efforts suggested by the groups. Trust was also built as the task force structure allowed employees more face time with executives—executives they would likely not have had a chance to meet—and provided new opportunities for mentoring. According to one task force participant:

> What got me to trust that this was a real commitment by the WMC was when I saw them ask for our advice, engage us in dialogue, and then take action. They didn't just do whatever we said, but the rationale for actions was always shared. It made me feel like our opinions were respected as businesspeople who bring a particular perspective to business challenges.

The task force structure has been copied on a smaller scale within specific business units. Even without a mandate from corporate brass, most units have created their own diversity councils, offering local support for achieving each unit's specific diversity goals. Here, too, the employee partnership model prevails.

Integrate Diversity with Management Practices

Sustaining change requires that diversity become an integrated part of the company's management practices. This was a priority for Gerstner, who told me:

> If you were to go back and look at 10 years' worth of executive committee discussions, you would find two subjects, and only two, that appeared on every one of the agendas.

One was the financial performance, led by our CFO. The second was a discussion of management changes, promotions, moves, and so on, led by our HR person.

In my interviews, among the most frequently mentioned diversity-related HR practice was the five-minute drill, which began with Gerstner's top team and has cascaded down from the chairman to two levels down from CEO. The five-minute drill takes place during the discussion of management talent at the corporate and business unit levels. During meetings of the senior team, executives are expected at any moment to be able to discuss any high-potential manager. According to interviewees, an explicit effort is made to ensure that minorities and females are discussed along with white males. The result has been to make the executives more accountable for spotting and grooming high-potential minority managers both in their own areas and across the business. Now that it's been made explicit that IBM executives need to watch for female and minority talent, they are more open to considering and promoting these individuals when looking to fill executive jobs.

Managing diversity is also one of the core competencies used to assess managers' performance, and it's included in the mandatory training and orientation of new managers. As one executive responsible for designing parts of this leadership curriculum commented, "We want people to understand that effectively managing and developing a diverse workforce is an integral part of what it means to manage at IBM."

Both Gerstner and Palmisano have been clear that holding managers accountable for diversity-related results is key. Gerstner noted, "We did not set quotas, but we did set goals and made people aware of the people in their units who they needed to be accountable for developing." And Palmisano said, "I reinforce to our executives that this is not HR's responsibility; it is up to us to make sure that we are developing our talent. There is a problem if, at the end of the day, that pool of talent is not diverse."

Link Diversity Goals to Business Goals

From the beginning, Gerstner and Childs insisted that the task force effort create a link between IBM's diversity goals and its business goals—that this would be good business, not good philanthropy. The task force efforts have led to a series of significant accomplishments.

For instance, IBM's efforts to develop the client base among women-owned businesses have quickly expanded to include a focus on Asian, black, Hispanic, mature (senior citizens), and Native American markets. The Market Development organization has grown revenue in the company's Small and Medium-Sized Business Sales and Marketing organization from $10 million in 1998 to hundreds of millions of dollars in 2003.

Another result of the task forces' work has been to create executive partner programs targeting demographic customer segments. In 2001, IBM began assigning executives to develop relationships with the largest women- and minority-owned businesses in the United States. This was important not only because these business sectors are growing fast but because their leaders are often highly visible role models, and their IT needs will grow and become increasingly more sophisticated. Already, these assignments have yielded impressive revenue streams with several of these companies.

The task force effort has also affected IBM's approach to supplier diversity. While the company has for decades fostered relationships with minority-owned businesses as well as businesses owned by the disabled, the work of the task forces has expanded the focus of IBM's supplier diversity program to a broader set of constituencies and provided new insights on the particular challenges each faced. The purpose of the supplier diversity program is to create a level-playing field. It's important to note, though, that procurement contracts are awarded on the merits of the bid—including price and quality—not on the diversity of the vendor. In 2003, IBM did business worth more than $1.5 billion with over 500 diverse suppliers, up from $370 million in 1998.

The cynics have come around. One black executive said, "Yes, I think [the initiative] has been extremely effective if you look at where we started back in the mid-nineties. I can tell you that I was somewhat skeptical [at first]." Another commented on the growing acceptance of the effort across IBM: "You can see that support actually changed over time from 'I'm not sure what this is about' to . . . a complete understanding that diversity and the focus on diversity make good business sense."

Perhaps the best evidence of the task forces' success is that the initiative not only continues but has spread and has had lasting impact. In more than one instance, after an executive became a task force sponsor, his or her division or business unit made significant progress on its own diversity goals. Leaders of some of the task forces described seeing their sponsors grow in their ability to understand, articulate, and take action on the issues identified by their groups. One executive described how the task force sponsor experience had been important for him as a business leader and personally, as well as for IBM:

> There is no doubt that this is critical for how we manage the research organization, because of the need for diverse thought. It has affected me substantially because . . . I became involved with diverse populations outside of IBM that I may well not have been connected with if it hadn't been for my involvement with the task force. I'm on the Gallaudet University [school for the deaf] board. Without the task force, I would have never thought of it. And so this has been a terrific awakening, a personal awakening. . . . Since it's focusing particularly on accessibility, we can help in a lot of ways with technology for accessibility, and Gallaudet turns out to be, for the subset of people who are hearing impaired, a terrific place to prototype solutions in this space.

Such comments were not atypical. In many instances, the sponsorship experience was developmental in important and unexpected ways. Having eight task forces means that in a group of 52 top leaders, there is always a critical mass strategically connected to the issues. Today, more than half of the WMC members have been engaged with the task forces in the role of sponsor or task force leader prior to being promoted to the senior executive level.

For IBM, that makes good business sense. The entire effort was designed to help the company develop deeper insights into its major markets, with a direct tie to two of Gerstner's central dictates. One: IBM needed to get closer to its customers and become more externally focused. Two: It needed to focus on talent—attracting, retaining, developing, and promoting the best people. On both measures, the company has come a long way.

Discussion Questions

1. IBM created eight task forces to enhance diversity within the organization. Which constituencies do these task forces represent? What was the purpose of the task forces? Did they help IBM manage diversity? How?

2. Lou Gerstner said: "We made diversity a market-based issue . . . It's about understanding our markets, which are diverse and multicultural." What implications does this statement have for IBM's marketing strategy?

3. Describe how IBM has focused extensively on people with disabilities both internally with their own employees and externally with their products and customers. What impact has this approach had on IBM?

4. Describe IBM's four "pillars of change." How have these pillars affected IBM and its diverse employees?

Notes

1. DiversityInc.com, The 9th Annual DiversityInc Top 50 Companies for Diversity, Johnson & Johnson, http://www.diversityinc.com/public/5449.cfm.

2. DiversityInc.com, The 9th Annual DiversityInc Top 50 Companies for Diversity, AT&T, http://www.diversityinc.com/public/5505.cfm.

3. DiversityInc.com, The 9th Annual DiversityInc Top 50 Companies for Diversity, Marriott International, http://www.diversityinc.com/public/5508.cfm.

4. DiversityInc.com, The 9th Annual DiversityInc Top 50 Companies for Diversity, PwC, http://www.diversityinc.com/public/5509.cfm.

5. DiversityInc.com, The 9th Annual DiversityInc Top 50 Companies for Diversity, Sodexo, http://www.diversityinc.com/public/5454.cfm.

6. DiversityInc.com, The 9th Annual DiversityInc Top 50 Companies for Diversity, Kaiser Permanente, http://www.diversityinc.com/public/5510.cfm.

7. DiversityInc.com, The 9th Annual DiversityInc Top 50 Companies for Diversity, Merck & Co., http://wwwdiversityinc.com/public/5483.cfm.

8. DiversityInc.com, The 9th Annual DiversityInc Top 50 Companies for Diversity, IBM, http://www.diversityinc.com/public/5511.cfm.

9. David A. Thomas and Robyn J. Ely, "Making Difference Matter: A New Paradigm for Managing Diversity, *Harvard Business Review on Managing Diversity* (Boston, MA: Harvard Business School Publishing Corp., 2001).

10. Belle Rose Ragins, "Diversity, Power, and Mentorship in Organizations: A Cultural, Structural, and Behavioral Perspective," in *Diversity in Organizations: New Perspectives for a Changing Workplace*, eds. Martin M. Chemers, Stuart Oskamp, and Mark A. Costanzo (Thousand Oaks, CA: Sage, 1995), 91–132.

11. Evangelina Holvino, Bernardo M. Ferdman, and Deborah Merrill-Sands, "Creating and Sustaining Diversity and Inclusion in Organizations: Strategies and Approaches," in *The Psychology and Management of Workplace Diversity*, eds. Margaret S. Stockdale and Faye J. Crosby (Malden, MA: Blackwell Publishing, 2004), 250.

12. Ibid., 251.

13. Ibid., 252.

14. Ibid., 253.

15. Barbara Frankel, "How to Make Diversity Management Real," *Diversity Inc*, June 2008, 46.

16. Verizon, "Workforce Development," *Verizon.com*, http://newscenter.verizon.com/kit/diversity/workforce.html.

17. Frankel, "How to Make Diversity Management Real," 45.

18. Verizon, "Making Progress Through Diversity," *Verizon.com*, http://multimedia.verizon.com/diversity/.

19. Verizon, "Diversity Strategy," *Verizon.com*, http://multimedia.verizon.com/diversity/index.asp?PageID=diversity.

20. Yoji Cole, "Recruitment," *DiversityInc Special Issue*, 2006, 43.

21. Carol Kulik and Loriann Roberson, "Diversity Initiative Effectiveness: What Organizations Can

(and Cannot) Expect From Diversity Recruitment, Diversity Training, and Formal Mentoring Programs," in *Diversity at Work*, ed. Arthur Brief (Cambridge: Cambridge University Press, 2008), 270. See also, Katherine Giscombe and Mary Mattis, "Leveling the Playing Field for Women of Color in Corporate Management: Is the Business Case Enough?" *Journal of Business Ethics* 37 (2002): 103–19; Jean Powell Kirnan, John Farley, and Kurt Geisinger, "The Relationship Between Recruiting Source, Applicant Quality, and Hire Performance: An Analysis by Sex, Ethnicity, and Age," *Personnel Psychology* 42 (1989): 293–308.

22. Kulik and Roberson, "Diversity Initiative Effectiveness," 270.
23. Holvino, Ferdman, and Merrill-Sands, "Creating and Sustaining Diversity and Inclusion in Organizations," 251.
24. Verizon, "Recruitment," Verizon.com, http://multimedia.verizon.com/diversity/index.asp?PageID=diversity&SubPageID=recruitment.
25. Kulik and Roberson, "Diversity Initiative Effectiveness," 277.
26. Holvino, Ferdman, and Merrill-Sands, "Creating and Sustaining Diversity and Inclusion in Organizations," 253.
27. Ibid., 255.
28. Peter Ortiz, "Making Diversity Training Pay Off," *DiversityInc Magazine Special Issue,* 2006, 62.
29. Verizon, "Recruitment."
30. Kulik and Roberson, "Diversity Initiative Effectiveness," 284.
31. Claire McCarty Kilian, Dawn Hukai, and C. Elizabeth McCarty, "Building Diversity in the Pipeline to Corporate Leadership," *Journal of Management Development* 24, no. 2 (2005): 155–68.
32. Ibid.
33. Barbara Frankel, "5 Mentoring Best Practices," *DiversityInc*, April 7, 2009, http://www.diversityinc.com/public/5653.cfm. See also, www.catalyst.org.
34. Lillian T. Eby and Angie Lockwood, "Proteges' and Mentors' Reactions to Participating in Formal Mentoring Programs: A Qualitative Investigation," *Journal of Vocational Behavior* 67 (2005): 441–58.

35. Frankel, "5 Mentoring Best Practices."
36. Verizon, "Recruitment."
37. Sylvia Hewlett and Carolyn Buck Luce, "Off-ramps and On-ramps: Keeping Talented Women on the Road to Success," *Harvard Business Review*, March 2005, 41.
38. Ibid., 38.
39. Verizon News Release, "For Eighth Consecutive Year, Verizon Named to Working Mother Magazine's List of 100 Best Companies," Verizon.com, September 23, 2008, http://newscenter.verizon.com/press-releases/verizon/2008/for-eighth-consecutive-year.html.
40. SHRM, "Organizations Providing Same-Sex Domestic Partner Benefits," shrm.org, http://www.shrm.org/Research/Articles/Articles/Pages/MetricoftheMonthOrganizationsProvidingSameSexDomesticPartnerBenefits.aspx. See also, SHRM 2007 Benefits Survey Report, http://www.shrm.org/ and Human Rights Campaign Foundation, "The State of the Workplace for Gay, Lesbian, Bisexual and Transgender Americans," http://www.hrc.org/.
41. Brenda Velez, "Why Your Company Needs Employee Resource Groups," *DiversityInc*, August 28, 2008, http://www.diversityinc.com/members/285.cfm.
42. Ibid.
43. Verizon, "Employee Resource Groups," *Verizon.com*, http://multimedia.verizon.com/diversity/index.asp?PageID=groups.
44. Ibid.
45. Holvino, Ferdman, and Merrill-Sands, "Creating and Sustaining Diversity and Inclusion in Organizations," 250.
46. "DiversityInc Top 50," Verizon Communications, *DiversityInc.com*, http://www.diversityinc.com/public/5477.cfm.
47. Verizon, "Diversity at the Top," http://newscenter.verizon.com/kit/diversity/top.html.
48. SHRM, "Diversity Management Series Part II: Measuring ROI for Diversity Management," *shrm.org*, http://www.shrm.org/Research/Articles/Articles/Pages/Diversity_20Management_20Series_20Part_20II__20Measuring_20ROI_20for_20Diversity_20Management.aspx
49. Edward E. Hubbard, *The Diversity Scorecard: Evaluating the Impact of Diversity on*

Organizational Performance (Burlington, MA: Elsevier Butterworth, 2004). Hubbard has written a number of books on the topic of measuring diversity's organizational effects, for example, *How to Calculate Diversity Return on Investment* and *Measuring Diversity Results*.

50. Ibid.
51. Verizon Communications, "DiversityInc Top 50 Companies for Diversity," *DiversityInc.com*, http://www.diversityinc-digital.com/diversity-incmedia/200806/?pg=52.
52. Frankel, "How to Make Diversity Management Real," 45.
53. Verizon, "Diversity Strategy," http://multimedia. verizon.com/diversity/index.asp?PageID= diversity.

54. Editors of DiversityInc, "Supplier Diversity Basics," *DiversityInc*, August 7, 2006, http:// www.diversityinc.com/members/204.cfm.
55. Ibid.
56. Verizon, "Supplier Diversity," *Verizon.com*, http://multimedia.verizon.com/diversity/index. asp?PageID=diversity&SubPageID=supplier_ diversity.
57. Ibid.
58. Verizon, "Strategic Alliances," *Verizon.com*, http://multimedia.verizon.com/diversity/index. asp?PageID=diversity&SubPageID=alliances.
59. Verizon, "Our Giving," http://multimedia.verizon. com/diversity/index.asp?PageID=diversity&Sub PageID=foundation.
60. Ibid.

PART TWO

Managing and Mismanaging
Case Studies on American Businesses

In this part, "Managing and Mismanaging: Case Studies on American Businesses," we illustrate organizational mistakes and successes of U.S. businesses. This section reflects our belief that understanding diversity is facilitated through detailed examination of case studies.

Our collection of comprehensive case studies focuses on how familiar organizations have grappled with diversity management. In particular, we consider six primary dimensions of diversity and how organizations address them: gender (Augusta National and Mother's Work); race and national origin (Abercrombie & Fitch, Texaco, and Denny's); age (Ford Motor Co.); religion and spirituality (Tom's of Maine); sexual orientation (Cracker Barrel); and disabilities (General Motors, IBM, and Cisco). In addition to these cases, we have included timely newspaper articles and critical essays that further explore the complexities of each of these topics.

CHAPTER 4

Gender

The federal government protects the rights of both men and women in the workplace under the protected class gender. In this chapter the focus is on women in the workplace, specifically because they are increasingly present and visible in the workforce and are often faced with a challenging set of circumstances as they attempt to balance work and family, advance up the corporate ladder, and function successfully in arenas traditionally dominated by men.

Objectives

- To examine the relationship between the women and the workplace.
- To examine the complexities of women's experiences in the workplace.
- To examine why women often choose to leave their careers and how they face a variety of obstacles when attempting to reenter the workplace.
- To examine claims of gender discrimination in both public and private organizations.

Preview Questions

- Do women face special obstacles to advancing their careers?
- What can organizations do to make their female employees more productive at work and more satisfied as members of the organization?
- Are there circumstances under which either public or private organizations should be allowed to discriminate openly against women?

Some Important Dates

1839   Mississippi becomes the first state to grant women the right to hold property in their own name, with their husband's permission.

1869   The first women's suffrage law in the United States is passed in the territory of Wyoming.

1872   Susan B. Anthony is arrested in Rochester, New York, for trying to vote.

1890   Wyoming becomes the first state to grant women the right to vote in all elections.

1900   Every state has passed legislation modeled after New York's Married Women's Property Act (1848), granting married women some control over their property and earnings.

1920   The Nineteenth Amendment to the U.S. Constitution is ratified. It declares: "The right of citizens of the United States to vote shall not be denied or abridged by the United States or by any state on account of sex."

1963   The Equal Pay Act is passed by Congress, promising equitable wages for the same work, regardless of the race, color, religion, national origin, or sex of the worker.

1964   Title VII of the Civil Rights Act passes and includes a prohibition against employment discrimination on the basis of race, color, religion, national origin, or sex.

1969   In *Bowe v. Colgate-Palmolive Company*, 416 F. 2d 711 (7th Cir. 1969), the Seventh Circuit Court of Appeals rules that women meeting the physical requirements can work in many jobs that had previously been for men only.

1974   *Cleveland Board of Education v. LaFleur*, 414 U.S. 632 (1974), determines it is illegal to force pregnant women to take maternity leave on the assumption they are incapable of working in their physical condition.

1978   The Pregnancy Discrimination Act bans employment discrimination against pregnant women.

1981   The U.S. Supreme Court rules that excluding women from the draft is constitutional.

1997   Elaborating on Title IX of the Education Amendments of 1972 to the Civil Rights Act of 1964 (the first comprehensive federal law to prohibit sex discrimination against students and employees of educational institutions), the Supreme Court rules that college athletics programs must actively involve roughly equal numbers of men and women to qualify for federal support.

Obama Signs Equal-Pay Legislation

WASHINGTON—President Obama signed his first bill into law on Thursday, approving equal-pay legislation that he said would "send a clear message that making our economy work means making sure it works for everybody."

Mr. Obama was surrounded by a group of beaming lawmakers, most but not all of them Democrats, in the East Room of the White House as he affixed his signature to the Lilly Ledbetter Fair Pay Act, a law named for an Alabama woman who at the end of a 19-year career as a supervisor in a tire factory complained that she had been paid less than men.

After a Supreme Court ruling against her, Congress approved the legislation that expands workers' rights to sue in this kind of case, relaxing the statute of limitations.

"It is fitting that with the very first bill I sign—the Lilly Ledbetter Fair Pay Act—we are upholding one of this nation's first principles: that we are all created equal and each deserve a chance to pursue our own version of happiness," the president said.

He said he was signing the bill not only in honor of Ms. Ledbetter—who stood behind him, shaking her head and clasping her hands in seeming disbelief—but in honor of his own grandmother, "who worked in a bank all her life, and even after she hit that glass ceiling, kept getting up again" and for his daughters, "because I want them to grow up in a nation that values their contributions, where there are no limits to their dreams."

The ceremony, and a reception afterward in the State Dining Room of the White House, had a celebratory feel. The East Room was packed with advocates for civil rights and workers

(continued)

rights; the legislators, who included House and Senate leaders and two moderate Republicans—Senators Susan Collins and Olympia Snowe, both of Maine—shook Mr. Obama's hand effusively (some, including House Speaker Nancy Pelosi, received presidential pecks on the cheek) as he took the stage. They looked over his shoulder, practically glowing, as Mr. Obama signed his name to the bill, using one pen for each letter.

"I've been practicing signing my name very slowly," Mr. Obama said wryly, looking at a bank of pens before him. He handed the first pen to the bill's chief sponsor, Senator Barbara Mikulski, Democrat of Maryland, and the last to Ms. Ledbetter.

The ceremony also marked First Lady Michelle Obama's policy debut; she spoke afterward in a reception in the State Dining Room, where she called Ms. Ledbetter "one of my favorite people."

Mr. Obama told Ms. Ledbetter's story over and over again during his campaign for the White House; she spoke frequently as an advocate for him during his campaign, and made an appearance at the Democratic National Convention in Denver.

Now 70, Ms. Ledbetter discovered when she was nearing retirement that her male colleagues were earning much more than she was. A jury found her employer, the Goodyear Tire and Rubber Company plant in Gadsden, Ala., guilty of pay discrimination. But in a 5–4 decision, the Supreme Court threw out the case, ruling that she should have filed her suit within 180 days of the date that Goodyear first paid her less than her peers.

Congress tried to pass a law that would have effectively overturned the decision while President George W. Bush was still in office, but the White House opposed the bill; opponents contended it would encourage lawsuits and argued that employees could delay filing their claims in the hope of reaping bigger rewards. But the new Congress passed the bill, which restarts the six-month clock every time the worker receives a paycheck.

Ms. Ledbetter will not see any money as a result of the legislation Mr. Obama signed into law. But what she has gotten, aside from celebrity, is personal satisfaction, as she said in the State Dining Room after the signing ceremony.

"Goodyear will never have to pay me what it cheated me out of," she said. "In fact, I will never see a cent. But with the president's signature today I have an even richer reward."

Source: Sheryl Gay Stolberg, "Obama Signs Equal-Pay Legislation," *New York Times*, January 29, 2009.

ESSAY: OFF-RAMPS AND ON-RAMPS

Keeping Talented Women on the Road to Success

Throughout the past year, a noisy debate has erupted in the media over the meaning of what Lisa Belkin of the *New York Times* has called the "opt-out revolution." Recent articles in the *Wall Street Journal*, the *New York Times*, *Time*, and *Fast Company* all point to a disturbing trend—large numbers of highly qualified women dropping out of mainstream careers. These articles also

Sylvia Ann Hewlett (cwlp@centerforwork-lifepolicy.org) is the founder and president of the Center for Work-Life Policy, a New York–based not-for-profit organization. She also heads up the Gender and Public Policy Program at the School of International and Public Affairs at Columbia University in New York. Her most recent book is *Creating a Life* (Miramax Books, 2002). Carolyn Buck Luce (carolyn.buck-luce@ey.com) is the global managing partner for Ernst & Young's health sciences industry practice in New York. She is the cochair for the Center for Work-Life Policy's Hidden Brain Drain task force.

Sylvia Ann Hewlett and Carolyn Buck Luce, *Harvard Business Review*, March 1, 2005 (HBR OnPoint Enhanced Edition), DOI: 10.1225/9416.

speculate on what might be behind this new brain drain. Are the complex demands of modern child rearing the nub of the problem? Or should one blame the trend on a failure of female ambition?

The facts and figures in these articles are eye-catching: a survey of the class of 1981 at Stanford University showing that 57 percent of women graduates leave the workforce; a survey of three graduating classes at Harvard Business School demonstrating that only 38 percent of women graduates end up in full-time careers; and a broader-gauged study of MBAs showing that one in three white women holding an MBA is not working full-time, compared with one in 20 for men with the same degree.

The stories that enliven these articles are also powerful: Brenda Barnes, the former CEO of PepsiCo, who gave up her megawatt career to spend more time with her three children; Karen Hughes, who resigned from her enormously influential job in the Bush White House to go home to Texas to better look after a needy teenage son; and a raft of less prominent women who also said goodbye to their careers. Lisa Beattie Frelinghuysen, for example—featured in a recent *60 Minutes* segment—was building a very successful career as a lawyer. She'd been president of the law review at Stanford and went to work for a prestigious law firm. She quit after she had her first baby three years later.

These stories certainly resonate, but scratch the surface, and it quickly becomes clear that there is very little in the way of systematic, rigorous data about the seeming exodus. A sector here, a graduating class there, and a flood of anecdotes: No one seems to know the basic facts. Across professions and across sectors, what is the scope of this opt-out phenomenon? What proportion of professional women take off-ramps rather than continue on their chosen career paths? Are they pushed off or pulled? Which sectors of the economy are most severely affected when women leave the workforce? How many years do women tend to spend out of the workforce? When women decide to reenter, what are they looking for? How easy is it to find on-ramps? What policies and practices help women return to work?

Early in 2004, the Center for Work-Life Policy formed a private sector, multiyear task force entitled "The Hidden Brain Drain: Women and Minorities as Unrealized Assets" to answer these and other questions. In the summer of 2004, three member companies of the task force (Ernst & Young, Goldman Sachs, and Lehman Brothers) sponsored a survey specifically designed to investigate the role of off-ramps and on-ramps in the lives of highly qualified women. The survey, conducted by Harris Interactive, comprised a nationally representative group of highly qualified women, defined as those with a graduate degree, a professional degree, or a high-honors undergraduate degree. The sample size was 2,443 women. The survey focused on two age groups: older women aged 41–55 and younger women aged 28–40. We also surveyed a smaller group of highly qualified men (653) to allow us to draw comparisons.

Using the data from the survey, we've created a more comprehensive and nuanced portrait of women's career paths than has been available to date. Even more important, these data suggest actions that companies can take to ensure that female potential does not go unrealized. Given current demographic and labor market trends, it's imperative that employers learn to reverse this brain drain. Indeed, companies that can develop policies and practices to tap into the female talent pool over the long haul will enjoy a substantial competitive advantage.

Women Do Leave

Many women take an off-ramp at some point on their career highway. Nearly four in 10 highly qualified women (37 percent) report that they have left work voluntarily at some point in their careers. Among women who have children, that statistic rises to 43 percent.

Factors other than having children that pull women away from their jobs include the demands of caring for elderly parents or other family members (reported by 24 percent) and personal health issues (9 percent). Not surprisingly, the pull of elder care responsibilities is particularly strong for women in the 41–55 age group—often called the "sandwich" generation, positioned as it is between growing children and aging parents. One in three women in that bracket have left work for some period to spend time caring for family members who are not children. And lurking behind all this is the pervasiveness of a highly traditional division of labor on the home front. In a 2001 survey conducted by the Center for Work-Life Policy, fully 40 percent of highly qualified women with spouses felt that their husbands create more work around the house than they perform.

Alongside these "pull" factors are a series of "push" factors—that is, features of the job or workplace that make women head for the door. Seventeen percent of women say they took an off-ramp, at least in part, because their jobs were not satisfying or meaningful. Overall, under-stimulation and lack of opportunity seem to be larger problems than overwork. Only 6 percent of women stopped working because the work itself was too demanding. In business sectors, the survey results suggest that push factors are particularly powerful—indeed, in these sectors, unlike, say, in medicine or teaching, they outweigh pull factors. Of course, in the hurly-burly world of everyday life, most women are dealing with a combination of push and pull factors—and one often serves to intensify the other. When women feel hemmed in by rigid policies or a glass ceiling, for example, they are much more likely to respond to the pull of family.

It's important to note that, however pulled or pushed, only a relatively privileged group of women have the option of not working. Most women cannot quit their careers unless their spouses earn considerable incomes. Fully 32 percent of the women surveyed cite the fact that their spouses' income "was sufficient for our family to live on one income" as a reason contributing to their decision to off-ramp.

Contrast this with the experience of highly qualified men, only 24 percent of whom have taken off-ramps (with no statistical difference between those who are fathers and those who are not). When men leave the workforce, they do it for different reasons. Child-care and elder-care responsibilities are much less important; only 12 percent of men cite these factors as compared with 44 percent of women. Instead, on the pull side, they cite switching careers (29 percent), obtaining additional training (25 percent), or starting a business (12 percent) as important

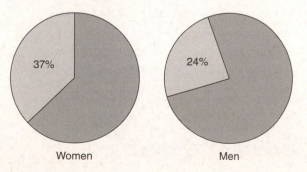

Women   Men

FIGURE 4-1 How Many Opt Out?

In our survey of highly qualified professionals, we asked the question, "Since you first began working, has there ever been a period where you took a voluntary time out from work?" Nearly four in ten women reported that they had—and that statistic rises to 43% among women who have children. By contrast, only 24% of highly qualified men have taken off-ramps (with no statistical difference between those who are fathers and those who are not).

reasons for taking time out. For highly qualified men, off-ramping seems to be about strategic repositioning in their careers—a far cry from the dominant concerns of their female peers.

For many women in our study, the decision to off-ramp is a tough one. These women have invested heavily in their education and training. They have spent years accumulating the skills and credentials necessary for successful careers. Most are not eager to toss that painstaking effort aside.

Lost on Reentry

Among women who take off-ramps, the overwhelming majority have every intention of returning to the workforce—and seemingly little idea of just how difficult that will prove. Women, like lawyer Lisa Beattie Frelinghuysen from the *60 Minutes* segment, who happily give up their careers to have children are the exception rather than the rule. In our research, we find that most highly qualified women who are currently off-ramped (93 percent) want to return to their careers.

Many of these women have financial reasons for wanting to get back to work. Nearly half (46 percent) cite "having their own independent source of income" as an important propelling factor. Women who participated in focus groups conducted as part of our research talked about their discomfort with "dependence." However good their marriages, many disliked needing to ask for money. Not being able to splurge on some small extravagance or make their own philanthropic choices without clearing it with their husbands did not sit well with them. It's also true that

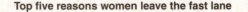

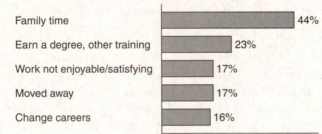

FIGURE 4-2   Why Do They Leave the Fast Lane?
Our survey data show that women and men take off-ramps for dramatically different reasons. While men leave the workforce mainly to reposition themselves for a career change, the majority of women off-ramp to attend to responsibilities at home.

a significant proportion of women currently seeking on-ramps are facing troubling shortfalls in family income: 38 percent cite "household income no longer sufficient for family needs" and 24 percent cite "partner's income no longer sufficient for family needs." Given what has happened to the cost of homes (up 38 percent over the past five years), the cost of college education (up 40 percent over the past decade), and the cost of health insurance (up 49 percent since 2000), it's easy to see why many professional families find it hard to manage on one income.

But financial pressure does not tell the whole story. Many of these women find deep pleasure in their chosen careers and want to reconnect with something they love. Forty-three percent cite the "enjoyment and satisfaction" they derive from their careers as an important reason to return—among teachers this figure rises to 54 percent and among doctors it rises to 70 percent. A further 16 percent want to "regain power and status in their profession." In our focus groups, women talked eloquently about how work gives shape and structure to their lives, boosts confidence and self-esteem, and confers status and standing in their communities. For many off-rampers, their professional identities remain their primary identities, despite the fact that they have taken time out.

Perhaps most interesting, 24 percent of the women currently looking for on-ramps are motivated by "a desire to give something back to society" and are seeking jobs that allow them to contribute to their communities in some way. In our focus groups, off-ramped women talked about how their time at home had changed their aspirations. Whether they had gotten involved in protecting the wetlands, supporting the local library, or rebuilding a playground, they felt newly connected to the importance of what one woman called "the work of care."

Unfortunately, only 74 percent of off-ramped women who want to rejoin the ranks of the employed manage to do so, according to our survey. And among these, only 40 percent return to full-time, professional jobs. Many (24 percent) take part-time jobs, and some (9 percent) become self-employed. The implication is clear: Off-ramps are around every curve in the road, but once a woman has taken one, on-ramps are few and far between—and extremely costly.

The Penalties of Time Out

Women off-ramp for surprisingly short periods of time—on average, 2.2 years. In business sectors, off-rampers average even shorter periods of time out (1.2 years). However, even these relatively short career interruptions entail heavy financial penalties. Our data show that women lose an average of 18 percent of their earning power when they take an off-ramp. In business sectors, penalties are particularly draconian: In these fields, women's earning power dips an average of 28 percent when they take time out. The longer you spend out, the more severe the penalty becomes. Across sectors, women lose a staggering 37 percent of their earning power when they spend three or more years out of the workforce.

Naomi, 34, is a case in point. In an interview, this part-time working mother was open about her anxieties: "Every day, I think about what I am going to do when I want to return to work full-time. I worry about whether I will be employable—will anyone even look at my résumé?" This is despite an MBA and substantial work experience.

Three years ago, Naomi felt she had no choice but to quit her lucrative position in market research. She had just had a child, and returning to full-time work after the standard maternity leave proved to be well-nigh impossible. Her 55-hour week combined with her husband's 80-hour week didn't leave enough time to raise a healthy child—let alone care for a child who was prone to illness, as theirs was. When her employer denied her request to work reduced hours, Naomi quit.

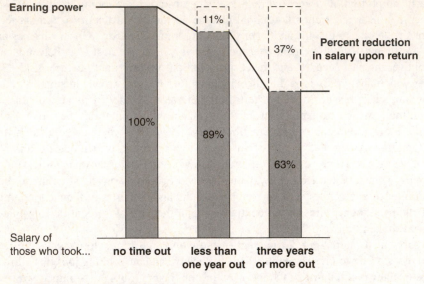

FIGURE 4-3   The High Cost of Time Out
Though the average amount of time that women take off from their careers is surprisingly short (less than three years), the salary penalty for doing so is severe. Women who return to the workforce after time out earn significantly less than their peers who remained in their jobs.

After nine months at home, Naomi did find some flexible work—but it came at a high price. Her new freelance job as a consultant to an advertising agency barely covered the cost of her son's day care. She now earns a third of what she did three years ago. What plagues Naomi the most about her situation is her anxiety about the future. "Will my skills become obsolete? Will I be able to support myself and my son if something should happen to my husband?"

The scholarly literature shows that Naomi's experience is not unusual. Economist Jane Waldfogel has analyzed the pattern of earnings over the life span. When women enter the workforce in their early and mid-twenties they earn nearly as much as men do. For a few years, they almost keep pace. For example, at ages 25–29, they earn 87 percent of the male wage. However, when women start having children, their earnings fall way behind those of men. By the time they reach the 40–44 age group, women earn a mere 71 percent of the male wage. In the words of MIT economist Lester Thurow, "These are the prime years for establishing a successful career. These are the years when hard work has the maximum payoff. They are also the prime years for launching a family. Women who leave the job market during those years may find that they never catch up."

Taking the Scenic Route

A majority (58 percent) of highly qualified women describe their careers as "non-linear"—which is to say, they do not follow the conventional trajectory long established by successful men. That ladder of success features a steep gradient in one's 30s and steady progress thereafter. In contrast, these women report that their "career paths have not followed a progression through the hierarchy of an industry."

Some of this nonlinearity is the result of taking off-ramps. But there are many other ways in which women ease out of the professional fast lane. Our survey reveals that 16 percent of highly qualified women work part-time. Such arrangements are more prevalent in the legal and medical professions, where 23 percent and 20 percent of female professionals, respectively, work less than full-time, than in the business sector, where only 8 percent of women work part-time. Another common work-life strategy is telecommuting; 8 percent of highly qualified women work exclusively from home, and another 25 percent work partly from home.

Looking back over their careers, 36 percent of highly qualified women say they have worked part-time for some period of time as part of a strategy to balance work and personal life. Twenty-five percent say they have reduced the number of work hours within a full-time job, and 16 percent say they have declined a promotion. A significant proportion (38 percent) say they have deliberately chosen a position with fewer responsibilities and lower compensation than they were qualified for, in order to fulfill responsibilities at home.

Downsizing Ambition

Given the tour of women's careers we've just taken, is it any surprise that women find it difficult to claim or sustain ambition? The survey shows that while almost half of the men consider themselves extremely or very ambitious, only about a third of the women do. (The proportion rises among women in business and the professions of law and medicine; there, 43 percent and 51 percent, respectively, consider themselves very ambitious.) In a similar vein, only 15 percent of highly qualified women (and 27 percent in the business sector) single out "a powerful position" as an important career goal; in fact, this goal ranked lowest in women's priorities in every sector we surveyed.

Far more important to these women are other items on the workplace wish list: the ability to associate with people they respect (82 percent), the freedom to "be themselves" at work (79 percent), and the opportunity to be flexible with their schedules (64 percent). Fully 61 percent of women consider it extremely or very important to have the opportunity to collaborate with others and work as part of a team. A majority (56 percent) believe it is very important for them to be able to give back to the community through their work. And 51 percent find "recognition from my company" either extremely or very important.

These top priorities constitute a departure from the traditional male take on ambition. Moreover, further analysis points to a disturbing age gap. In the business sector, 53 percent of younger women (ages 28–40) own up to being very ambitious, as contrasted with only 37 percent of older women. This makes sense in light of Anna Fels's groundbreaking work on women and ambition. In a 2004 HBR article, Fels argues convincingly that ambition stands on two legs— mastery and recognition. To hold onto their dreams, not only must women attain the necessary skills and experience, they must also have their achievements appropriately recognized. To the extent the latter is missing in female careers, ambition is undermined. A vicious cycle emerges: As women's ambitions stall, they are perceived as less committed, they no longer get the best assignments, and this lowers their ambitions further.

In our focus groups, we heard the disappointment—and discouragement—of women who had reached senior levels in corporations only to find the glass ceiling still in place, despite years of diversity initiatives. These women feel that they are languishing and have not been given either the opportunities or the recognition that would allow them to realize their full potential. Many feel handicapped in the attainment of their goals. The result is the vicious cycle that Fels describes: a "downsizing" of women's ambition that becomes a self-fulfilling prophecy. And the discrepancy in ambition levels between men and women has an insidious side effect in that it results in insufficient role models for younger women.

Reversing the Brain Drain

These, then, are the hard facts. With them in hand, we move from anecdotes to data—and, more important, to a different, richer analytical understanding of the problem. In the structural issue of off-ramps and on-ramps, we see the mechanism derailing the careers of highly qualified women and also the focal point for making positive change. What are the implications for corporate America? One thing at least seems clear: Employers can no longer pretend that treating women as "men in skirts" will fix their retention problems. Like it or not, large numbers of highly qualified, committed women need to take time out. The trick is to help them maintain connections that will allow them to come back from that time without being marginalized for the rest of their careers.

Create Reduced-Hour Jobs

The most obvious way to stay connected is to offer women with demanding lives a way to keep a hand in their chosen field, short of full-time involvement. Our survey found that, in business sectors, fully 89 percent of women believe that access to reduced-hour jobs is important. Across all sectors, the figure is 82 percent.

The Johnson & Johnson family of companies has seen the increased loyalty and productivity that can result from such arrangements. We recently held a focus group with 12 part-time managers at these companies and found a level of commitment that was palpable. The women had logged histories with J&J that ranged from 8 to 19 years and spoke of the corporation with great affection. All had a focus on productivity and pushed themselves to deliver at the same level they had achieved before switching to part-time. One woman, a 15-year J&J veteran, was particularly eloquent in her gratitude to the corporation. She had had her first child at age 40 and, like so many new mothers, felt torn apart by the conflicting demands of home and work. In her words, "I thought I only had two choices—work full-time or leave—and I didn't want either. J&J's reduced-hour option has been a savior." All the women in the room were clear on one point: They would have quit had part-time jobs not been available.

At Pfizer, the deal is sweetened further for part-time workers; field sales professionals in the company's Vista Rx division are given access to the same benefits and training as full-time employees but work 60 percent of the hours (with a corresponding difference in base pay). Many opt for a three-day workweek; others structure their working day around children's school hours. These 230 employees—93 percent of whom are working mothers—remain eligible for promotion and may return to full-time status at their discretion.

Provide Flexibility in the Day

Some women don't require reduced work hours; they merely need flexibility in when, where, and how they do their work. Even parents who employ nannies or have children in day care, for example, must make time for teacher conferences, medical appointments, volunteering, child-related errands—not to mention the days the nanny calls in sick or the day care center is closed. Someone caring for an invalid or a fragile elderly person may likewise have many hours of potentially productive time in a day yet not be able to stray far from home.

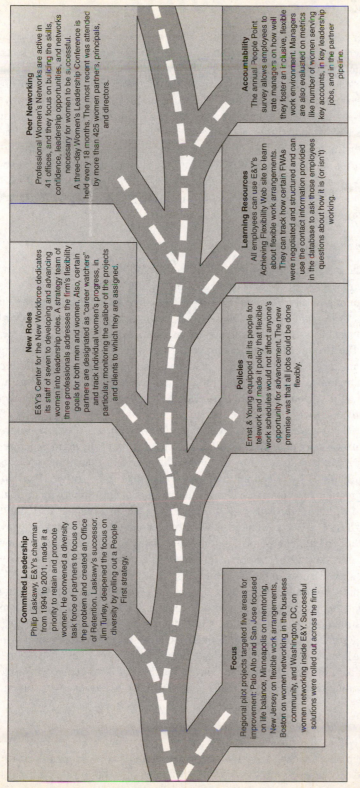

FIGURE 4-4 How Ernst & Young Keeps Women on the Path to Partnership

In the mid-1990s, turnover among female employees at Ernst & Young was much higher than it was among male peers. Company leaders knew something was seriously wrong; for many years, its entering classes of young auditors had been made up of nearly equal numbers of men and women—yet it was still the case that only a tiny percentage of its partnership was female. This was a major problem. Turnover in client-serving roles meant lost continuity on work assignments. And on top of losing talent that the firm had invested in training, E&Y was incurring costs averaging 150% of a departing employee's annual salary just to fill the vacant position.

E&Y set a new course, marked by several important features outlined here. Since E&Y began this work, the percentage of women partners has more than tripled to 12% and the downward trend in retention of women at every level has been reversed. E&Y now has four women on the management board, and many more women are in key operating and client-serving roles. Among its women partners, 10% work on a flexible schedule and more than 20 have been promoted to partner while working a reduced schedule. In 2004, 22% of new partners were women.

Committed Leadership

Philip Laskawy, E&Y's chairman from 1994 to 2001, made it a priority to retain and promote women. He convened a diversity task force of partners to focus on the problem and created an Office of Retention. Laskawy's successor, Jim Turley, deepened the focus on diversity by rolling out a People First strategy.

Focus

Regional pilot projects targeted five areas for improvement: Palo Alto and San Jose focused on life balance, Minneapolis on mentoring, New Jersey on flexible work arrangements, Boston on women networking in the business community, and Washington, DC, on women networking inside E&Y. Successful solutions were rolled out across the firm.

New Roles

E&Y's Center for the New Workforce dedicates its staff of seven to developing and advancing women into leadership roles. A strategy team of three professionals addresses the firm's flexibility goals for both men and women. Also, certain partners are designated as "career watchers" and track individual women's progress, in particular, monitoring the caliber of the projects and clients to which they are assigned.

Policies

Ernst & Young equipped all its people for telework and made it policy that flexible work schedules would not affect anyone's opportunity for advancement. The new premise was that all jobs could be done flexibly.

Peer Networking

Professional Women's Networks are active in 41 offices, and they focus on building the skills, confidence, leadership opportunities, and networks necessary for women to be successful. A three-day Women's Leadership Conference is held every 18 months. The most recent was attended by more than 425 women partners, principals, and directors.

Learning Resources

All employees can use E&Y's Achieving Flexibility Web site to learn about flexible work arrangements. They can track how certain FWAs were negotiated and structured and can use the contact information provided in the database to ask those employees questions about how it is (or isn't) working.

Accountability

The annual People Point survey allows employees to rate managers on how well they foster an inclusive, flexible work environment. Managers are also evaluated on metrics like number of women serving key accounts, in key leadership jobs, and in the partner pipeline.

For these and other reasons, almost two-thirds (64 percent) of the women we surveyed cite flexible work arrangements as being either extremely or very important to them. In fact, by a considerable margin, highly qualified women find flexibility more important than compensation; only 42 percent say that "earning a lot of money" is an important motivator. In our focus groups, we heard women use terms like "nirvana" and "the golden ring" to describe employment arrangements that allow them to flex their workdays, their workweeks, and their careers. A senior employee who recently joined Lehman Brothers' equity division is an example. She had been working at another financial services company when a Lehman recruiter called. "The person who had been in the job previously was working one day a week from home, so they offered that opportunity to me. Though I was content in my current job," she told us, "that intriguing possibility made me reevaluate. In the end, I took the job at Lehman. Working from home one day a week was a huge lure."

Provide Flexibility in the Arc of a Career

Booz Allen Hamilton, the management and technology consulting firm, recognized that it isn't simply a workday, or a workweek, that needs to be made more flexible, it's the entire arc of a career.

Management consulting as a profession loses twice as many women as men in the middle reaches of career ladders. A big part of the problem is that, perhaps more than in any other business sector, it is driven by an up-or-out ethos; client-serving professionals must progress steadily or fall by the wayside. The strongest contenders make partner through a relentless winnowing process. While many firms take care to make the separations as painless as possible (the chaff, after all, tends to land in organizations that might employ their services), there are clear limits to their patience. Typically, if a valued professional is unable to keep pace with the road warrior lifestyle, the best she can hope for is reassignment to a staff job.

Over the past year, Booz Allen has initiated a "ramp up, ramp down" flexible program to allow professionals to balance work and life and still do the client work they find most interesting. The key to the program is Booz Allen's effort to "unbundle" standard consulting projects and identify chunks that can be done by telecommuting or shorts stints in the office. Participating professionals are either regular employees or alumni that sign standard employment contracts and are activated as needed. For the professional, it's a way to take on a manageable amount of the kind of work they do best. For Booz Allen, it's a way to maintain ties to consultants who have already proved their merit in a challenging profession. Since many of these talented women will eventually return to full-time consulting employment, Booz Allen wants to be their employer of choice—and to keep their skills sharp in the meantime.

When asked how the program is being received, DeAnne Aguirre, a vice president at Booz Allen who was involved in its design (and who is also a member of our task force), had an instant reaction: "I think it's instilled new hope—a lot of young women I work with no longer feel that they will have to sacrifice some precious part of themselves." Aguirre explains that trade-offs are inevitable, but at Booz Allen an off-ramping decision doesn't have to be a devastating one anymore. "Flex careers are bound to be slower than conventional ones, but in ten years' time you probably won't remember the precise year you made partner. The point here is to remain on track and vitally connected."

Remove the Stigma

Making flexible arrangements succeed over the long term is hard work. It means crafting an imaginative set of policies, but even more important, it means eliminating the stigma that is often attached to such nonstandard work arrangements. As many as 35 percent of the women we surveyed report various aspects of their organizations' cultures that effectively penalize people who take advantage of work-life policies. Telecommuting appears to be most stigmatized, with 39 percent of women reporting some form of tacit resistance to it, followed by job sharing and part-time work. Of flexible work arrangements in general, 21 percent report that "there is an unspoken rule at my workplace that people who use these options will not be promoted." Parental leave policies get more respect—though even here, 19 percent of women report cultural or attitudinal barriers to taking the time off that they are entitled to. In environments where flexible work arrangements are tacitly deemed illegitimate, many women would rather resign than request them.

Interestingly, when it comes to taking advantage of work-life policies, men encounter even more stigma. For example, 48 percent of the men we surveyed perceived job sharing as illegitimate in their workplace culture—even when it's part of official policy.

Transformation of the corporate culture seems to be a prerequisite for success on the work-life front. Those people at or near the top of an organization need to have that "eureka" moment, when they not only understand the business imperative for imaginative work-life policies but are prepared to embrace them, and in so doing remove the stigma. In the words of Dessa Bokides, treasurer at Pitney Bowes, "Only a leader's devotion to these issues will give others permission to transform conventional career paths."

Stop Burning Bridges

One particularly dramatic finding of our survey deserves special mention: Only 5 percent of highly qualified women looking for on-ramps are interested in rejoining the companies they left. In business sectors, that percentage is zero. If ever there was a danger signal for corporations, this is it.

The finding implies that the vast majority of off-ramped women, at the moment they left their careers, felt ill-used—or at least underutilized and unappreciated—by their employers. We can only speculate as to why this was. In some cases, perhaps, the situation ended badly; a woman, attempting impossible juggling feats, started dropping balls. Or an employer, embittered by the loss of too many "star" women, lets this one go much too easily.

It's understandable for managers to assume that women leave mainly for "pull" reasons and that there's no point in trying to keep them. Indeed, when family overload and the traditional division of labor place unmanageable demands on a working woman, it does appear that quitting has much more to do with what's going on at home than what's going on at work. However, it is important to realize that even when pull factors seem to be dominant, push factors are also in play. Most off-ramping decisions are conditioned by policies, practices, and attitudes at work. Recognition, flexibility, and the opportunity to telecommute—especially when endorsed by the corporate culture—can make a huge difference.

The point is, managers will not stay in a departing employee's good graces unless they take the time to explore the reasons for off-ramping and are able and willing to offer options short of total severance. If a company wants future access to this talent, it will need to go beyond the perfunctory exit interview and, at the very least, impart the message that the door is open. Better still, it will maintain a connection with off-ramped employees through a formal alumni program.

Provide Outlets for Altruism

Imaginative attachment policies notwithstanding, some women have no interest in returning to their old organizations because their desire to work in their former field has waned. Recall the focus group participants who spoke of a deepened desire to give back to the community after taking a hiatus from work. Remember, too, that women in business sectors are pushed offtrack more by dissatisfaction with work than pulled by external demands. Our data suggest that fully 52 percent of women with MBAs in the business sector cite the fact that they do not find their careers "either satisfying or enjoyable" as an important reason for why they left work. Perhaps not surprisingly, then, a majority (54 percent) of the women looking for on-ramps want to change their profession or field. And in most of those cases, it's a woman who formerly worked in the corporate sphere hoping to move into the not-for-profit sector.

Employers would be well advised to recognize and harness the altruism of these women. Supporting female professionals in their advocacy and public service efforts serves to win their energy and loyalty. Companies may also be able to redirect women's desire to give back to the community by asking them to become involved in mentoring and formal women's networks within the company.

Nurture Ambition

Finally, if women are to sustain their passion for work and their competitive edge—whether or not they take formal time out—they must keep ambition alive. Our findings point to an urgent need to implement mentoring and networking programs that help women expand and sustain their professional aspirations. Companies like American Express, GE, Goldman Sachs, Johnson & Johnson, Lehman Brothers, and Time Warner are developing "old girls networks" that build skills, contacts, and confidence. They link women to inside power brokers and to outside business players and effectively inculcate those precious rainmaking skills.

Networks (with fund-raising and friend-raising functions) can enhance client connections. But they also play another, critical role. They provide the infrastructure within which women can earn recognition, as well as a safe platform from which to blow one's own horn without being perceived as too pushy. In the words of Patricia Fili-Krushel, executive vice president of Time Warner, "Company-sponsored women's networks encourage women to cultivate both sides of the power equation. Women hone their own leadership abilities but also learn to use power on behalf of others. Both skill sets help us increase our pipeline of talented women."

Adopt an On-Ramp

As we write this, market and economic factors, both cyclical and structural, are aligned in ways guaranteed to make talent constraints and skill shortages huge issues again. Unemployment is down and labor markets are beginning to tighten, just as the baby-bust generation is about to hit "prime time" and the number of workers between the ages of 35 and 45 is shrinking. Immigration levels are stable, so there's little chance of relief there. Likewise, productivity improvements are flattening. The phenomenon that bailed us out of our last big labor crunch—the entry for the first time of millions of women into the labor force—is not available to us again. Add it all up, and CEOs are back to wondering how they will find enough high-caliber talent to drive growth.

There is a winning strategy. It revolves around the retention and reattachment of highly qualified women. America these days has a large and impressive pool of female talent. Fifty-eight percent of college graduates are now women, and nearly half of all professional and graduate degrees are earned by women. Even more important, the incremental additions to the talent pool will be disproportionately female, according to figures released by the U.S. Department of Education. The number of women with graduate and professional degrees is projected to grow by 16 percent over the next decade, while the number of men with these degrees is projected to grow by a mere 1.3 percent. Companies are beginning to pay attention to these figures. As Melinda Wolfe, head of global leadership and diversity at Goldman Sachs, recently pointed out, "A large part of the potential talent pool consists of females and historically underrepresented groups. With the professional labor market tightening, it is in our direct interest to give serious attention to these matters of retention and reattachment."

In short, the talent is there; the challenge is to create the circumstances that allow businesses to take advantage of it over the long run. To tap this all-important resource, companies must understand the complexities of women's nonlinear careers and be prepared to support rather than punish those who take alternate routes.

Discussion Questions

1. Why do women leave careers after having invested heavily in developing the skills that would help them succeed in those careers?
2. Would men leave their careers if they had a spouse who was earning enough to support their family?
3. What would employers have to do to allow women who leave their jobs to return and catch up to where they would have been had they not left? How would these policies affect those who do not take time off from work?
4. Why do more women professionals work part-time than their counterparts in business?
5. What are the costs and benefits to a company of providing full benefits and training to those employees who work part-time?
6. What risks do they take when employees make use of their companies' work-life policies? Are these risks the same for men and women?
7. Are women more likely to leave a job because it is uninteresting or unenjoyable than men? Why?

The complete statistical findings from this research project, and additional commentary and company examples, are available in an HBR research report entitled "The Hidden Brain Drain: Off-Ramps and On-Ramps in Women's Careers" (see www.womenscareersreport.hbr.org).

Case Study: Augusta National Golf Club

Membership for Women or Staying the Course?

It was early November of 2002, and William Johnson—known to friends and associates as "Hootie"—chairman of the venerable Augusta National Golf Club, had just finished his last interview with one of several national news organizations. Speaking candidly about the club's membership policies, Mr. Johnson had requested that his comments not be published until the following week. He also talked about how actions that had taken place over the previous seven or eight months would affect the 2003 Masters Golf Tournament, a competition that many

This case was written by Research Assistants Ray B. Swart, Ashish K. Singh, and Andrew Nelson under the direction of James S. O'Rourke, Concurrent Professor of Management, as the basis for class discussion rather than to illustrate either effective or ineffective handling of an administrative situation.

Eugene D. Fanning Center for Business Communication, Mendoza College of Business, University of Notre Dame.

people regard as the most prestigious golf event in North America, but one that was now shrouded in controversy.

The First Six Months

On Sunday, April 14, 2002, golfing phenomenon Tiger Woods had won the Masters Golf Tournament for the third time, having previously finished first in 1997 and 2001. News of his accomplishment—three victories by age 26, and two in a row—made headlines the world over. It was also during the 2002 Masters that Lloyd Ward, the chief executive of the United States Olympic Committee and an African American member of the Augusta National Golf Club, commented to reporters that he was advising the leaders of the club to admit a woman, and to do it soon. Mr. Ward said that he would work from within Augusta to lobby for women, adding, "Inclusion does not just mean people of color."[1] Little did Mr. Ward know (or anyone else for that matter) that his innocuous remarks would be the impetus for even more attention-grabbing headlines in the near future.

Martha Burk, Ph.D., Chair of the National Council of Women's Organizations read Mr. Lloyd's comments and decides to take action. On June 12, Ms. Burk writes a letter to William "Hootie" Johnson, Chairman of Augusta, telling him that "the NCWO knows that Augusta National and the sponsors of the Masters do not want to be viewed as entities that tolerate discrimination against any group, including women." She then urged him to open their membership to women immediately, so that it would not be issue when the tournament [the Masters] is staged next year.[2]

On July 8th, Mr. Johnson wrote Ms. Burk a brief, three sentence response, in essence stating that as a distinctly private club, Augusta cannot talk about its membership practices with those outside the organization, and that he found her letter's references to discrimination, allusions to the sponsors and setting of deadlines to be both offensive and coercive. The next day, Mr. Johnson issues a public press release lashing out at Ms. Burk and the NCWO. In that statement, he said that Augusta "will not be bullied, threatened or intimidated. Our membership alone decides our membership—not any outside group with its own agenda. There may well come a day when women will be invited to join our membership but that timetable will be ours and not at the point of a bayonet."[3]

On July 30th, the NCWO sent letters to the CEOs of the television sponsors of the Masters—Citigroup, Inc., the Coca-Cola Company, General Motors Corporation (with a separate letter addressed to the general manager of the Cadillac Motor Division) and IBM Corporation—requesting that they suspend sponsorship of the tournament, since it is owned, controlled and produced by Augusta National Incorporated, an organization that discriminates against women by excluding them from membership.[4] A letter was also sent to Tim Finchem, Commissioner of the Professional Golfers Association (PGA) asking the PGA Tour to adhere to its written policy on discrimination (the PGA will not cosponsor an event with a club having discriminatory policies) by withdrawing recognition of any kind from the Masters Golf Tournament. Curiously, the letter does acknowledge that the Masters Tournament is not an "official" part of the PGA Tour.[5]

In mid-August, Mr. Finchem replied to the NCWO, saying that they were correct in identifying the Masters as an event not co-sponsored by the Professional Golfers Association, and as such, the PGA would be unable to require Augusta National to implement the PGA's host club policy with respect to the Masters.[6]

Leah C. Johnson, Director of Public Affairs for Citigroup, also replied to the NCWO, stating that, with regard to their comments about the Masters Golf Tournament, Citigroup had communicated its views privately to the management of the club.[7] Finally, Rick Singer, Director of Worldwide Sponsorship Marketing for IBM, wrote to Ms. Burk and the NCWO, saying that IBM did not view sponsorship of the Masters as contradictory to the company's long-standing commitment to diversity and support for women in business.[8] Within days, Ms. Burk sent a follow-up letter to Samuel J. Palmisano, CEO of IBM, telling him that Mr. Singer's letter was not responsive to points raised in the NCWO's initial complaint. Specifically, the NCWO wanted answers to two specific questions:

1. *"Is IBM's policy on sex discrimination different from its policy on race discrimination?"*
2. *"How does IBM reconcile its sponsorship of the Masters with its written policies against gender discrimination, and specifically those policies against sponsoring recreational activities and organizations that discriminate on the basis of gender?"*[9]

IBM did not respond to the second letter.

On August 30th, in response to Ms. Burk's letters to the tournament's television sponsors, Mr. Johnson issued a press release, saying that the Augusta National Golf Club would not request the participation of any media sponsors for the 2003 Masters Golf Tournament. Instead, the telecast will be sponsored by the separately incorporated "Masters Tournament." In his statement, Mr. Johnson said that because the NCWO's true target is Augusta National, the sponsors should not be put in the position of having to deal with the NCWO's pressure.[10] After reading the press release, Martha Burk said, "I think they're (Augusta National) doing what they can to avoid having a woman member. They're willing to pay a lot of money to continue to discriminate. That's what it comes down to."[11]

On the following day, August 31st, the NCWO announced that it would focus its attention on the CBS Television Network and on September 18th, sent a letter to Sean McManus, the President of CBS Sports, requesting that the network suspend broadcasting the Masters Tournament. In her letter, Ms. Burk stated that if CBS Sports were to continue broadcasting the Masters Golf Tournament, it would be acting irresponsibly as a Federal Communications Commission licensee and as a corporate citizen because, she wrote, "use of the airways is not an entitlement; the FCC licenses broadcasters to operate in the public interest and broadcasters are mandated to act responsibly."[12]

On September 19th, Sean McManus responded to Ms. Burk in a letter from CBS Sports, saying that, as a sports television programmer serving millions of men and women who eagerly anticipate and avidly watch the network's Masters broadcast each year, CBS intended to cover the Masters, just as it has done for the past 46 years. To not do so, he said, would be a disservice to fans of this major championship.[13]

Augusta National Golf Club and the Masters Tournament

Located at what is now the corner of Washington and Berckmans Roads in Augusta, Georgia, Augusta National Golf Club was founded in 1932 and was designed by Bob Jones and Alister MacKenzie. Augusta's membership is limited to around 300 persons and is one of the most exclusive private clubs in the world. Play on the course is allowed only from October to May. Membership in Augusta National is by invitation only and there are currently no female members, although women played more than 1,000 rounds on the course last year, many more than were allowed at some other male-only clubs. Information about club membership is not easy to obtain, but as the controversy surrounding the club's exclusionary policies began making headlines, some details began to emerge. The average member age, according to *USA Today*, is 72 and they come mainly from old-line industries: banking and finance, oil and gas, manufacturing and distributing. New members are nominated by existing members and are determined partly by how many current members die or leave. The waiting list is said to be about 300 with the chairman having the final say on who gets invited to join. Annual membership fees are in the $25,000-to-$50,000 range, with the chairman having control of the club's purse strings.[14] Augusta National admitted its first African American member in 1990, purportedly thanks to an inside effort led by Mr. Johnson before the club could become a target of protests.

The first Masters Tournament was held at Augusta in March of 1934, and was hosted by Bob Jones and Clifford Roberts, who served as chairman of both the club and tournament for another 43 years until his death in 1977. Originally called the Augusta National Invitation Tournament, the name was changed to the Masters in 1939. Beginning in 1940, the Masters has been held during the first full week of April on an annual basis (with the exception of 1943, 1944 and 1945 because of World War II).[15] Steeped with tradition, the Masters is the first of golf's four Major Championships to be played each calendar year. The other three majors, in order of play, are the United States Open, the British Open, and the PGA Championship. The Masters is also the only Major Championship to be played at the same venue every year. In keeping with Mr. Jones' and Mr. Roberts' original concept for the tournament, the Masters is still an invitation-only event, and as such, it has the smallest playing field of any of the four Major Championships.

Each year, the winner of the Masters is presented with a green jacket. That jacket must remain at Augusta national, with the exception of the first 12 months during which the champion may take it home with him. The total purse distributed to the playing field in 2002 was $5.5 million with another $3.3 million going to charity. Award-winning columnist Ron Green Sr., who has covered golf for five decades, describes the emotional impact of the tournament on those who compete there: "The Masters has brought men to tears of joy and tears of sorrow. It has been a defining event in the lives of champions and it has scarred its victims for life."[16]

Augusta National operates the Masters independent from any golf organization. The club gets most of its money from an annual television contract with CBS Sports and sales from its souvenir store at the course. It is estimated that these "public" sources of revenue amount to about $20 million, an amount that is greater than the $15 million generated by membership dues (if the published but unconfirmed figures are accurate). Mr. Johnson has said, "Augusta National and the Masters—while happily entwined—are quite different. One is a private golf club. The other is a world-class sports event of great public interest. It is insidious to attempt to use one to alter the essence of the other."[17] Ms. Burk responded by saying, "The Masters, in my mind, is not tied at the hip to this club. An event of this profile could be held somewhere else."[18] She also adds that a private club that hosts a public event like the Masters is not really private.

The Columbia Broadcasting System

The Columbia Broadcasting System was founded in 1927, and is currently owned by Viacom, Inc. The CBS Television Network has aired the Masters Golf Tournament on a one-year contract every year since 1956. The financial agreement between the Masters and CBS Sports has been kept private, and the contract is regarded as unique in comparison both to other sporting events and to other golf tournaments. Rather than bidding on the right to broadcast the tournament and then covering their costs by selling advertising time, the Augusta National Golf Club essentially covers CBS's production costs. CBS is then permitted to show just four minutes of commercial advertisements an hour. With so little commercial time for sale, the Masters has never been a moneymaker for CBS. Analysts have estimated that, in 2002, fees paid to CBS were approximately $5 million, as compared to an average price range of $8–$20 million for other popular golf tournaments. There is some speculation that the club may be forced to lower the fee even further and make up the cost difference by raising ticket prices and selling more merchandise. However, CBS regards its broadcast of the Masters as a privilege, as it is traditionally the highest rated televised golf tournament of the year.

The Sponsors

Each of the television sponsors of the Masters Golf Tournament has a corporate policy forbidding gender discrimination. Ms. Burk and the NCWO acknowledged this fact in each of the letters sent to the companies, asking them to suspend their sponsorship of the Masters television broadcast.

Citigroup Corporation

Citigroup Corporation (originally known as The Travelers) has been a sponsor of the broadcast for many years. Ms. Burk praised Citigroup for the creation of its corporate division, Women and Company, and acknowledged that they had been chosen as one of the "100 best companies for working mothers" in 2001.[19]

The Coca-Cola Company

Coca-Cola has been a sponsor of the tournament for only one year. In her letter to Coca-Cola's chairman and chief executive, Ms. Burk applauded the company's November 2000 agreement to engage an outside panel to monitor pay and promotion of minority and women workers.[20] In a nonpublic manner, Coca-Cola's CEO Douglas Daft had tried to influence Augusta National's policy with seemingly little effect. The company's talks with both Augusta National and the NCWO were reported to be friendly and noncontentious.

IBM Corporation

IBM (formerly International Business Machines) has been a sponsor of the Masters for only one year, as well. In her letter to IBM, Ms. Burk pointed out that their decision to continue sponsoring the Masters broadcast directly contradicted their actions regarding race discrimination issues involved with the PGA Championship, held at Shoal Creek Golf Club in Alabama in 1990.[21] IBM withdrew its sponsorship when it was revealed that Shoal Creek discriminated against African Americans.

Cadillac Motor Division, General Motors Corporation

General Motors' Cadillac Division has a long history of sponsoring the Masters broadcast. A press report from Cadillac spokesman Jeff Kuhlman noted that since Cadillac is the official car of the Masters Tournament and not the Augusta National Golf Club, sponsorship would continue.[22]

The Professional Golfers Association

The Professional Golfers Association (PGA) of America was founded on April 10, 1916, in New York with 35 charter members. Since its inception, the PGA has grown into the largest sports organization in the world with more than 27,000 dedicated men and women golf professionals who promote the game of golf to everyone, everywhere. The PGA conducts some 40 tournaments a year for PGA Professionals, but the Masters Golf Tournament is not an event cosponsored by the PGA Tour. The PGA Tour does require that host clubs of their cosponsored events, with whom they have contractual relationships, maintain membership policies under which membership is not restricted on the basis of race, religion, sex or national origin.[23]

The National Council of Women's Organizations

The NCWO is the nation's oldest and largest coalition of women's groups. Its 160 member organizations represent women from all socioeconomic and demographic groups, and collectively represent more than seven million women nationwide. NCWO member organizations include grassroots, research, service, media and legal advocacy groups. They work together to advocate change on many issues of importance to women, including equal employment opportunity, economic equity, media equality, education, job training, women's health and reproductive issues, as well as the specific concerns of midlife and older women, girls and young women, women of color, business and professional women, homemakers and retired women. NCWO decisions are made by a simple majority vote at bimonthly meetings where each dues-paying organization has one vote. An eight-member Steering Committee publicizes and implements these decisions. When the Council is not in session, the Chair is authorized to speak for the Council if the policy issue is clear.[24]

New Voices Are Heard

Clifford Roberts, who ran the Augusta National Golf Club with an iron fist for 45 years, actively recruited corporate chiefs as members from the club's inception. (It is important to note that Augusta National has only individuals as members, not corporations or organizations.) The CEOs appreciated having a golf club to visit in the winter, even though many of them did not golf there frequently. The local Augusta members are said to appreciate that. Many of the prominent CEOs of large national companies are still viewed as outsiders. Confrontations are not usually welcome or well received. Prudence and discretion reign.[25]

In late September of 2002, Ms. Burk began sending letters to CEOs and other prominent members of Augusta National, asking them to explain why they belong to a club that has no female members. "We'll ask them for on-the-record statements about how they reconcile membership in the club with their corporate codes of conduct and their marketing practices to women," said Ms. Burk.[26] A few club members, speaking on the condition of anonymity, said that they had become distressed by the confrontational approach taken by Mr. Johnson. This loosely knit faction could be characterized as an outer circle that lives and works outside of Georgia, choosing to communicate with one another more frequently as the dispute escalated. Some have said they will press their case to various members privately.[27]

On October 4th, Sanford I. Weill, chairman and chief executive of Citigroup, becomes the first corporate executive to openly offer his support to the women's organization. A Citigroup statement signed by Leah C. Johnson, Director of Public Affairs, sent to the NCWO said that Mr. Weill had "expressed his views to the Augusta National Golf Club and will continue to engage in what he hopes will be a constructive dialogue on this issue, toward an objective that he believes we share with your organization. However, he respectfully intends to keep this dialogue private."[28]

Within a few days, members Lloyd Ward, the chief executive of the United States Olympic Committee, and Kenneth I. Chenault, the chief executive of American Express, also offered their support for the inclusion of women as members at Augusta. In a letter to Martha Burk, Mr. Ward said, "I am committed to breaking down barriers which exclude women from membership at Augusta in the weeks and months ahead."[29] And in a statement released through American Express, Mr. Chenault said, "I believe women should be admitted as members of the Augusta National Golf Club. I have made my views known within the club because I believe that is the most effective and appropriate way to bring about a change in membership policy."[30] Ms. Burk said in an interview that she was gratified by Mr. Ward's letter because "it's strongly worded and puts a short time frame on the issue."[31] Ms. Burk also said that she believed that the position taken by these men would lead more Augusta members to push for the admission of women. The Augusta National Golf Club offered no public announcement with regard to these latest revelations.

Will the Real "Hootie" Johnson Please Stand Up?

William "Hootie" Johnson, 71, is a native of Augusta, Georgia, who attended his first Masters when he was four and has been the chairman of the Augusta National Golf Club since 1998. His recent actions concerning female membership seem to be an enigma. Four years earlier, Mr. Johnson brokered a deal in which South Carolina became the first major college to name its business school after a woman, New York investment banker Darla Moore. He also invited the University of South Carolina women's golf team to play at Augusta. I. S. Leevy Johnson, one of three African Americans elected to the South Carolina state legislature in 1970 with Mr. Johnson's backing, speaking about female membership at Augusta said, "I think it's inevitable. If anything, I think this controversy has delayed it. In my opinion, [Mr. Johnson] was already trying to do it on the inside."[32]

Martha Burk, 61, Chair of the National Council of Women's Organizations, has made it clear that her battle with the Augusta National Golf Club is not, in any way, a legal issue. As a private club, Augusta has the legal right to set its own policies, but Ms. Burk indicated that they have the moral imperative to do better. When asked why Augusta National and why now, Ms. Burk said, "Because it's the home of the Masters, it is highly symbolic. It reminds women of the glass ceiling and unequal pay and all the reasons women are running second in America."[33] Ironically, Ms. Burk's brothers and cousins called her "Hootie" as a youngster. "It is strange how that worked out," she says.[34]

The Final Word?

On November 12, Mr. Johnson's remarks to the press were finally published. He adamantly affirmed his stance against admitting a woman to the Augusta National Golf Club anytime in the near future. In an Op-Ed article appearing in *The Wall Street Journal*, Mr. Johnson wrote, "If we wish to open all private organizations to men and women, as Ms. Burk and [the] NCWO wish to do with Augusta National, the end is near for many uncontroversial and long-standing private groups. Women's colleges like Smith and Wellesley, historically black colleges like Spelman, the Girls Scouts of America, the Junior League, fraternities and sororities would all have to be dissolved or radically changed from the single-sex profile that has become an essential part of their character and, indeed, the reason they are sought after. Do they, too, 'discriminate'?"[35] Mr. Johnson goes on to say, "Whether, or when, we have women as members is something that this club will decide alone, and in private. It is for others to decide, from where they stand, whether threat-based tactics are appropriate. But from here, it feels like some things are worth defending, and sometimes that means taking a stand. In my mind and in my heart, I know this is one of them."[36] When asked if Augusta National would try to proceed with the [Masters] tournament as usual, Mr. Johnson responded: "No, we won't try. We will proceed. And will succeed."[37]

Martha Burk reacted quickly and with dismay to Johnson's position. "If the decision stands not to admit a woman before next year's Masters, then it's a slap in the face to Augusta members who have spoken out asking for this discrimination to end."[38] Ms. Burk also said, "I hope cooler heads and rationality will prevail and they will come down on the side of fairness, regardless of what [Mr.] Johnson thinks. These guys are not Boy Scouts or Girl Scouts, they're adult human beings, many of them CEOs of the largest U.S. corporations."[39]

In a statement made several weeks earlier Ms. Burk said, "It's not our goal to aggravate Augusta National. Our goal is to get the club membership open to women—period. Some members of that community would like to characterize us as strident, which we are not. We are, however, resolved. And we all know there's only one way for this story to end. It's just a matter of time."[40]

And what of those members Ms. Burk refers to? The members who said they had expressed their views directly to Mr. Johnson or his allies at the club in recent weeks were civilly told to back off on the issue, that their opinions were out of touch with the rest of the membership. With an agreement that they not be identified, one member said, "A few of us were made to feel like we should keep to ourselves on this subject, or maybe consider whether we belonged at Augusta National."[41] Another said, "I was told that maybe I did not understand the history and tradition of Augusta National as well I should."[42] A third member observed that, "Some of us find this all needlessly embarrassing, but I believe we are a distinct minority. We are being told that maybe we don't understand the way things are done and why, that this is a thing of principles, important principles, as they see them. It's a strong, defiant attitude."[43]

When asked for his reaction to several members' saying they want to see a woman member at Augusta, Mr. Johnson would only say, "I'm not going to talk about member issues. Those are private matters to be dealt with from within."[44]

"What [Mr. Johnson] means by that," one anonymous member said, "is that those members have been or will be firmly reminded that they are violating a club policy by speaking out. They will be reminded that that is not the way things have been done around our club for decades and decades."[45]

Discussion Questions

1. What are the basic business issues in the case?
2. Should women be invited to join Augusta National Golf Club? If so, when?
3. Who are the key stakeholders in this case? Does anyone have a stake in the outcome of this dispute other than the principals whose views have been aired in the media?
4. Should the NCWO continue to press this issue? If so, how?
5. What are the implications for both Augusta National and the NCWO?
6. What problems might prominent Augusta National members (CEOs, for example) face?
7. What other courses of action could have been pursued by key individuals?

Case Study: Mothers Work Inc.

Brand Image and Accusations of Employment Discrimination

Introduction

On June 27, 2003, Rebecca Matthias, the COO of the world's largest maternity clothing company, Mothers Work, Inc., called an urgent meeting with her top executives: Dan Matthias, Mothers Work's chairman, Sheryl Roth Rogers, vice president of marketing, Mona Astra Liss, Mothers Work's publicity director and Frank Mullay, vice president of stores. The five administrative personnel were gathered to discuss how the company would address a recent lawsuit filed against Mothers Work, Inc. by a former district manager, Cynthia Papageorge. Papageorge has accused Mr. Mullay of firing her three years earlier because of her gender and pregnancy.

Mothers Work, Inc. has already settled two similar discriminatory complaints (one of which was filed by Papageorge's boss, Jane Dowe). Papageorge's case, however, has been embraced by the media and damage to Mothers Work's reputation could ensue. Women's rights groups issued statements of disapproval within days of the lawsuit's filing. For example, Serrin Foster, the president of Feminists for Life, declared, "It is mind blowing to think that a company named Mothers Work that profits from selling apparel to pregnant women would terminate [women's employment] simply because of their maternity."[46,47,48]

Rebecca Matthias is renowned for her support of women in the workplace, as her company was founded on the premise that women can be both professionals and mothers. The Mothers Work corporate officers must now determine how their $500 million maternity clothing company should react to allegations that it discriminates against pregnant women.

Matthias has earned degrees from MIT, Columbia University, and the University of Pennsylvania. She is the author of *Mothers Work: How a Young Mother Started a Business on a Shoestring and Built It into a Multi-Million Dollar Company*. Matthias serves on the Board of Trustees at Drexel University and Hahnemann MCP Medical University and is a member of the Board of Overseers of the School of Arts and Science at the University of Pennsylvania.[49] On September 16, 2003, Rebecca Matthias was recognized by the United States Small Business Administration at the National Entrepreneurial Conference in Washington, D.C., for her success with Mothers Work.[50]

Corporate Communication at Mothers Work

No Corporate Communication division exists at Mothers Work, so many of the communications tasks are undertaken by Rebecca Matthias and Publicity Director Mona Astra Liss. Liss is responsible for all of Mothers Work's fashion publicity in print and in broadcast. She organizes Mothers Work's fashion shows and other activities promoting the Mothers Work maternity lines. One of

Ms. Liss's initiatives was the creation of A Pea in a Pod's celebrity program. Famous women such as Cindy Crawford, Sarah Jessica Parker, Toni Braxton, and Claudia Schiffer showcased Mothers Work maternity wear while pregnant.

Ms. Liss has written for *The New York Times*, *The Washington Post*, *People*, and *US Weekly* and has been featured on the Today Show, Oprah and E! Entertainment. She is currently working with cable television channel, TBS Superstation, to provide maternity clothing advice to pregnant women. Ms. Liss has been a very prominent individual known for promoting Mothers Work clothing and products.[51]

Women in the Workforce

Since 1950, the increase in the percentage of working women has been overwhelming. In 1999 about 60 percent of females 16 years of age and older were in the workforce, an increase of 20 percent since the turn of the 20th century. Women also accounted for 85 percent of the total increase in the number of workers with more than one job for periods between 1989 and 1999. Labor force participation for women continues to be highest in the 35–44 age groups.[52]

Women are working harder as with all Americans. The average full time worker works about 43 hours per week. For married working women, the amount of hours increased from 41 hours in 1989 to 46 hours in 1998.[53] In addition, women also have to take care of their families and so in a way, they are working "double shift." Balancing between a career and a family can be difficult. As the number of women entering the workforce continues to rise, more businesses are offering services and information to help women find jobs or to better their understanding maternity rights. A good example of such an information source would be *"The 100 Best Companies for Working Mothers List 2003,"*[54] a magazine published by Working Mothers.

Pregnancy Discrimination

The Pregnancy Discrimination Act of 1978 was passed as an amendment to Title VII of the Civil Rights of 1964. The act states that "women affected by pregnancy, childbirth, or related medical condition shall be treated the same for all employment-related purposes, including receipt of benefits under fringe benefit programs, as other persons not affected but similar in their ability or inability to work."[55]

Despite the protection offered by the legal system against pregnancy discrimination in the workplace, the number of pregnancy-related discrimination cases is on the rise. Pregnancy discrimination complaints nationwide jumped 10 percent last year to just over 4,700 cases, according to the Equal Employment Opportunity Commission (EEOC). Such complaints have increased by approximately 40 percent since 1992.[56]

Lawyers, enforcement officials and workers' advocates believe that the increase is partly a symptom of widespread layoffs. According to Will Hannum, an Andover, Mass., attorney who represents employers in labor matters, the shaky economy has exacerbated the situation as companies try to cope with pressures that sometimes force them to choose which employees to keep on the payroll.[57]

The Family Medical Leave Act

The Family Medical Leave Act (FMLA) was passed by the Congress of the United States and signed into law in 1993. That legislation guarantees employees of companies up to 12 weeks of unpaid leave annually for certain medical reasons or for the birth or adoption of a child.

To be eligible, the employer must have 50 or more employees who have worked for the employer at least 12 months and 1,250 hours in the last year. The FMLA requires that employers reinstate employees to their former job or an equivalent job at the end of the leave, and must maintain any group health insurance coverage under the same conditions of coverage and cost-sharing arrangement as if the employee were working during the leave.[58]

Massachusetts Medical Leave Act

Besides the Family Medical Leave Act, residents of Massachusetts (the state in which Papageorge filed her lawsuit) receive additional protection from the Massachusetts Maternity Leave Act (MMLA). The MMLA requires that an employee on leave be restored to her previous or a similar position upon her return to employment following leave. That position must have the same status, pay, length of service credit, and seniority as the position the employee held prior to the leave.[59]

The MMLA also requires that a maternity leave not affect an employee's right to receive vacation time, sick leave, bonuses, advancement, seniority, length of service credit, benefits, plans or programs for which she was eligible at the date of her leave, and any other advantages or rights of her employment incident to her position. Such maternity leave, however, need not be included in the computation of such benefits, rights and advantages.[60]

An employee returning from the leave does not have greater rights in terms of benefits or work conditions over other employees who have been working while the prior employee was on leave. The employer is also not required to reinstate a returning employee to her previous position if other employees of the same caliber and length of service have been laid off during her leave period due to economic conditions or operation changes.

Nothing in the MMLA shall be construed to affect any bargaining agreement, employment agreement, or company policy providing benefits that are greater than, or in addition to, those required under the statute. An employer may grant a longer maternity leave than required under the MMLA. However, if the employer does not intend for full MMLA rights to apply to the period beyond eight weeks, the employer must communicate it clearly to the employee in writing prior to the commencement of the leave.[61]

Papageorge's "Condition"

Cynthia Papageorge began working for Mothers Work, Inc. in 1997 as a district manager for stores in Massachusetts, Connecticut, and Rhode Island.[62] In October of 1999, Papageorge was 37 weeks pregnant with her first child when Mothers Work vice president, Frank Mullay, inspected four of Papageorge's stores unannounced. Mullay found deficiencies in the stores' housekeeping, made several references to Papageorge's pregnancy and even suggested that Cynthia could not meet her job requirements as a result of her "condition."

The lawsuit claims that within several days of the random store inspection, Mullay ordered Papageorge's supervisor, Jan Dowe, to fire Papageorge on the grounds that Papageorge was pregnant. In an affidavit, Dowe stated she refused to fire Papageorge after company officials told Dowe it would be illegal to let Papageorge go. Dowe met with Mullay and informed him of the illegality of his proposal. He responded with, "There are ways of getting around the law."[63] Six months later, Papageorge was released after requesting medical leave for a shoulder injury, which was unrelated to her pregnancy. Dowe was also fired for inadequate job performance after taking maternity leave.

Mark Itzkowitz, Papageorge's lawyer, has claimed, "It seems that pregnant women are subject to termination by virtue of their pregnancy. That position was made known in meetings with managers at Mothers Work. The other women [from the other three lawsuits] were terminated for the same reason."[64]

Discussion Questions

1. What facts in this case appear to be the most important to you?
2. Who are the key stakeholders in this case? How will a verdict for or against Papageorge affect the parties?
3. What actions (if any) should Mothers Work, Inc. take? What message should the company send to the public? Who is Mothers Work's target audience?
4. What are the critical issues of this case? Which issues should Mothers Work confront first?
5. Since there is no Corporate Communications department, who should deliver Mothers Work's message? What media should Mothers Work use to convey its position?
6. This lawsuit has not received much media attention (since the original filing of the suit). Why do you think this is the case?

Appendix A

MOTHERS WORK INC.

Copyright 2003 Yahoo! Inc.   http://finance.yahoo.com/

FIGURE 4-5

Notes

1. Bill Pennington and Dave Anderson, "Some at Augusta National Quietly Seek a Compromise," *The New York Times,* September 29, 2002, Section 8, pp. 1, 6.
2. Letter from Martha Burk to William Johnson, June 12, 2002. Available from http://www.womensorganizations.org/news/augustaletter.pdf.
3. Letter from William Johnson to Martha Burk, July 8, 2002. Available from http://www.womensorganizations.org/news/augustaletter.pdf.
4. Press Release: "Statement by Hootie Johnson," *The Golf Central Newsroom*, July 9, 2002, http://www.womensorganizations.org/news/position04_press.htm.

5. Letters from Martha Burk to Sanford Weill, Douglas Daft, G. Richard Wagoner, Mark LaNeve and Samuel Palmisano, July 30, 2002. Available from http://www.womensorganizations.org/news/.

6. Letter from Martha Burk to Tim Finchem, July 30, 2002. Available from http://www.womens organizations.org/news/august%20letter.

7. Letter from Tim Finchem to Martha Burk, August 20, 2002. Available from http://www.womensorganizations.org/news/august%20letter.

8. Letter from Leah C. Johnson to Martha Burk, August 22, 2002. Available from http://www.womensorganizations.org/news/august%20letter.

9. Letter from Rick Singer to Martha Burk, August 15, 2002. Available from http://www.womensorganizations.org/news/august%20letter.

10. Letter from Martha Burk to Samuel Palmisano, August 20, 2002. Available from http://www.womensorganizations.org/news/august%20letter.

11. Press Release: "Statement by Hootie Johnson," August 30, 2002. Available from http://www.women sorganizations.org/news/augusta%20press%20.

12. Ferguson, Doug. AP Golf Writer, "Women's Group Targets CBS," *USA Today*, August 31, 2002. Available from http://www.usatoday.com/sports/golf/masters.

13. Letter from Martha Burk to Sean McManus, September 18, 2002. Available from http://www.womensorganizations.org/news/augusta_CBS.pdf.

14. Letter from Sean McManus to Martha Burk, September 19, 2002. Available from http://www.womensorganizations.org/news/augusta_CBS.pdf.

15. Michael McCarthy and Erik Brady, "Privacy Becomes Public at Augusta," *USA Today*, September 27, 2002. Available from http://www.state.ma.us/mcad/maternity2.html.

16. Ron Green, Sr., "It Is Still Augusta National Golf Club," April 8, 2002. Available from http://www.golfweb.com/u/ce/multi/0,1977,5209104,00.html.

17. Ron Green, Sr., "It Is Still Augusta National Golf Club," April 8, 2002. Available from http://www.golfweb.com/u/ce/multi/0,1977,5209104,00.html.

18. Press Release: "Statement by Hootie Johnson."

19. Doug Ferguson, Associated Press Golf Writer. "Augusta Chairman Lashes Out at Group," July 9, 2002. Available from http://www.radicus.net/news/wed/cn/Aglf-augusta-national.

20. Letter from Martha Burk to Sanford Weill, July 30, 2002. Available from http://www.womensorganizations.org/news/august.

21. Letter from Martha Burk to Douglas Daft, July 30, 2002. Available from http://www.womens organizations.org/news/august%20letter.

22. Letter from Martha Burk to Samuel Palmisano, July 30, 2002. Available from http://www.womens organizations.org/news/august%20letter_IBM.pdf.

23. Letter from Martha Burk to G. Richard Wagoner, July 30, 2002. Available from http://www.womens organizations.org/news/august%20letter.

24. http://www.pga.com.

25. http://www.womensorganizations.org.

26. Bill Pennington, "At Ever-Contrary Augusta, Even Ike Didn't Hold Sway," *The New York Times*, October 10, 2002, C21, C24.

27. Michael McCarthy, "Group Takes Augusta Golf Fight to Companies," *USA Today*, July 17, 2002. Available from http://www.usatoday.com/sports/golf/masters/2002.

28. Pennington and Anderson, "Some at Augusta National Quietly," 1, 6.

29. Geraldine Fabrikant and Richard Sandomir, "Executive Speaks Up for Women at Augusta," *The New York Times*, October 5, 2002, B1, B21.

30. Richard Sandomir, "U.S.O.C. Chief Backs Women at Augusta," *The New York Times*, October 8, 2002, C21, C25.

31. "A Welcome to the Club," *The New York Times*, October 9, 2002, C17.

32. Sandomir, "U.S.O.C. Chief Backs Women at Augusta," C21, C25.

33. Paul Newberry, Associated Press. "Hootie Johnson: Complex Man at Center of Masters Dispute." Available from http://pga.com/Newsline/Industry.

34. Harry Blauvelt, "Burk Not Afraid to Take on Status Quo," *USA Today*, October 9, 2002. Available from http://www.usatoday.com/sports/golf/masters/2002.

35. Ibid.

36. Johnson, William. "Why I'm Teed Off," *The Wall Street Journal*, November 12, 2002, A20.

37. Ibid.

38. Clifton Brown, "At Club in Augusta, Policy of Chairman Remains 'Men Only,' " *The New York Times*, November 12, 2002, A1, C24.

39. Ibid.

40. Comments made by Martha Burk to *The Washington Post*, November 12, 2002. Available from http://www.now.org/issues/wfw/111202 augusta.html.

41. Barker Davis, "Burk Keeps Swinging Away at Golf's Augusta," *The Washington Times*, October 23,

2002. Available from http://www.washtimes.com/national/20021023_13631490.thm.

42. Bill Pennington and Clifton Brown. "Members of Club Who Favor Change Told to Back Off," *The New York Times*, November 13, 2002, C19, C22.

43. Ibid.

44. Brown, "At Club in Augusta, Policy," A1, C24.

45. Pennington and Brown. "Members of Club Who Favor Change," C19, C22.

46. Steven Ertelt, "Maternity Store Sued for Pregnancy Discrimination After Employee Fired," June 30, 2003, http://www. prolifeinfo.com/nat19.html.

47. Wharton Entrepreneurial Programs, "Profiting from Pregnancy," http://www.wep.wharton.upenn.edu/maternity.html; http://www.wep.wharton.upenn.edu/maternity.html.

48. Tom Belden, "Mother Work Includes Serving as Role Model," September 18, 2003, http://www.philly.com/mld/inquirer/6797380.htm.

49. Wharton Entrepreneurship Conference, http://www.whartonentreconf.org/wec/bios.asp#matthias.

50. Mothers Work, Inc., "US Small Business Administration (SBA) Honors Rebecca Matthias, President & COO of Mothers Work," September 16, 2003, http://biz.yahoo.com/prnews/030916/phtu022_1.html (November 17, 2003).

51. http://tbssuperstation.com/hostedmovies/expert/0,14005,7721,00.html.

52. http://www.roadandtravel.com/businessandcareer/careers/dyk_womworkers.htm

53. Ibid.

54. http://www.workingmother.com/oct03/100BestList.shtml

55. http://womensissues.about.com/library/weekly/aa062901a.htm

56. http://www.reddingemployment.com/news/business/past/20031005bus075.shtml

57. Ibid.

58. http://www.people.virginia.edu/~jhv3q/EmpLaw2001/fmla_summary.htm

59. http://www.state.ma.us/mcad/maternity2.html

60. Ibid.

61. Ibid.

62. Theo Emery, "Maternity Co. Fires Pregnant Woman," June 27, 2003, http://www.cbsnews.com/stories/2003/06/27/national/printable560715.shtml (November 18, 2003).

63. Burrelle's Information Services: CBS News Transcripts, in *LexisNexis*, http://80-web.lexis-nexis.com.lib_proxy.nd.edu/universe/document?_m=e32f03b65dd39d7f69819adda18510b3&_docnum=2&wchp=dGLbVtbzSkVA&_md5=a4ecbf93dbc25c150d9cdba78c08e739.

64. Steven Ertelt, "Maternity Store Sued for Pregnancy Discrimination After Employee Fired," June 30, 2003, http://www.prolifeinfo.com/nat19.html (November 18, 2003).

CHAPTER 5

Race and National Origin

Race, as a protected class, is defined in accordance with the following categories as determined by the U.S. government: Caucasian/White, Asian, African American/Black, Pacific Islander/Native Hawaiian, and American Indian/Alaskan Native. National origin is also a protected class and is defined as a person's country of birth, ethnicity, ancestry, or culture.

Objectives

- To examine the relationship between people of different races/national origins and the workplace.
- To examine the claim that minority employees should be mentored differently than their white counterparts.
- To examine how an organization's marketing strategy led to discrimination lawsuits.
- To examine how an organizational leader responded to a diversity management crisis in an effort to protect corporate image and improve stakeholder relations.
- To examine how an organization known for its acts of discrimination can implement a comprehensive diversity management policy and become a model of effective diversity management.

Preview Questions

- Should organizational leaders modify their mentoring style when mentoring minority employees?
- How should an organization respond to a diversity crisis—should it take a short-term approach and simply settle the lawsuit, or should it take a long-term approach and make diversity systemic throughout the organization?
- How can an organization known for its mismanagement of diversity regain public trust regarding their value of diversity?

Some Important Dates

1619	First African slaves arrive in Virginia.
1789	U.S. Constitution is ratified with a clause that equates a slave to three-fifths of a white citizen and includes a provision that slave trade will end within 20 years.
1798–1808	Decade of greatest U.S. importation of African slaves, totaling approximately 200,000.

1819 U.S. law equates slave trading with piracy, punishable by death.

1857 U.S. Supreme Court rules slavery legal in the *Dred Scott* case.

1861 The Civil War begins.

1863 Emancipation Proclamation, issued in 1862 by President Lincoln to free slaves in Confederate territory, goes into effect.

1865 Thirteenth Amendment, passed and ratified in the same year, abolishes slavery; first historical black colleges and universities form.

1868 Fourteenth Amendment grants African Americans full U.S. citizenship and equal civil rights.

1870 Fifteenth Amendment grants African American men the right to vote.

1873–83 Supreme Court cases weaken key postwar civil rights laws and constitutional amendments; states can now reinstitute discriminatory laws.

1884 "Jim Crow" laws appear throughout southern and western states to segregate African Americans in education, travel, and public accommodations.

1896 Supreme Court deals a blow to integrated education in *Plessy v. Ferguson,* reinforcing the "separate but equal" concept.

1950–52 Five cases are filed in Kansas, Delaware, South Carolina, Virginia, and the District of Columbia to challenge the constitutionality of segregated education.

1952 Supreme Court consolidates five cases into *Oliver Brown et al. v. the Board of Education of Topeka, Kansas.*

1954 Supreme Court unanimously declares that separate educational facilities are "inherently unequal" and violate the Fourteenth Amendment, which guarantees all citizens "equal protection of the laws."

1963 Equal Pay Act is passed by Congress, promising equitable wages for the same work, regardless of the race, color, religion, national origin, or sex of the worker.

1964 Title VII of the Civil Rights Act passes including a prohibition against employment discrimination on the basis of race, color, religion, national origin, or sex.

NFL LOOKING TO EXPAND ROONEY RULE

FORT LAUDERDALE, Fla.—NFL teams looking to hire general managers may soon be required to interview at least one minority candidate.

Commissioner Roger Goodell said Wednesday the league's owners discussed expanding the Rooney Rule—which already applies to coaching openings—during the final session of their two-day meetings in South Florida. No vote was taken, though Goodell indicated any changes could be made soon.

"It's a judgment I will make with the diversity committee," Goodell said.

The Rooney Rule is named for Pittsburgh Steelers owner Dan Rooney, who was not at the meeting for a good reason: He's at what Goodell described as "ambassador school."

Rooney, a lifelong Republican, was picked by President Barack Obama earlier this year to be U.S. ambassador to Ireland.

"When he gets concluded with his tutoring, I will probably speak with him and we'll make a determination from there," Goodell said.

The Rooney Rule was born nearly seven years ago, when two lawyers threatened to sue the NFL if it didn't open up more opportunities for minorities. Rooney led a committee to develop a policy to stop what the league viewed as an embarrassing lack of diversity.

(continued)

Expanding that policy to GMs isn't expected to meet much resistance.

"It's a good idea," Miami Dolphins owner Stephen Ross said. "We certainly have it with the coaches and this would be expanding it to the general managers. From what I understand, we did follow that when we did hire Bill Parcells."

In other developments before the meetings closed Wednesday morning with a 2¹/₂-hour session, seeking ways to generate new revenue streams, NFL clubs can now arrange to have their logos on cards sold by their respective state lotteries.

Delaware became the only state east of the Mississippi River to allow betting on sports after new legislation was signed last week. The NFL is strongly against betting on the outcome of games but said the lottery move could generate significant money to be directed back to "many different public purposes," Goodell said.

In states where there are more than one NFL team, those clubs will be expected to negotiate how to proceed with the lottery.

Talks were held on a tougher anti-tampering stance involving free agents, although Goodell said some owners simply suggested that clubs adhere to the rules already in place.

Some teams have said clubs have illegally reached out to agents before signing periods begin, which could theoretically make it tougher for a team to re-sign its own player. The proposed change would likely install a short window of opportunity for teams to talk to free agents before the signing period begins—but with no contracts finalized.

"We're discussing it, that's all," Atlanta Falcons owner Arthur Blank said.

The issue was tabled Wednesday. Talks will continue, Goodell said, and a vote is likely in October.

More talks were held on a 17- or 18-game regular season, but once again no vote was held and the league's analysis of such a move will continue.

"We did not take any action, but it was a very good discussion," Goodell said.

The Dolphins released plans to offer a wireless video unit to its fans at the club and suite levels this season, a 4.3-inch screen that will give ticket-holders a chance to see replays and other action from around the league from their seats. Talks are planned to have the device available on some level when Miami hosts this season's Super Bowl as well.

Associated Press: "NFL Looking to Expand Rooney Rule," ESPN.com May 20, 2009.

ESSAY: THE TRUTH ABOUT MENTORING MINORITIES

Race Matters

Diversity has become a top priority in corporate America. Despite the best intentions, though, many organizations have failed to achieve racial balance within their executive teams. Some have revolving doors for talented minorities, recruiting the best and brightest only to see them leave, frustrated and even angered by the barriers they encounter. Other companies are able to retain high-potential professionals of color only to have them become mired in middle management. Still others have minorities in their executive ranks, but only in racialized positions, such as those dealing with community relations, equal employment opportunity, or ethnic markets.

In my research on the career progression of minorities at U.S. corporations, I have found that whites and minorities follow distinct patterns of advancement. Specifically, promising white professionals tend to enter a fast track early in their careers, whereas high-potential minorities take off much later, typically after they have reached middle management. I've also found that

David A. Thomas, Harvard Business School.

the people of color who advance the farthest all share one characteristic—a strong network of mentors and corporate sponsors who nurture their professional development.

Patterns of Movement

In a 3-year research project, I studied the career trajectories of minority and white professionals at three major U.S. corporations. The most striking aspect of my findings was the consistency of the data. White professionals who eventually became executives—a group I'll henceforth refer to simply as "white executives"—usually entered a fast track in Stage 1, whereas both white and minority professionals who later plateaued in middle management, and minorities who eventually became executives, all inched along during that period. In Stages 2 and 3, the careers of minorities who ultimately became executives took off, surpassing those of the plateaued managers.

This stark difference in the career trajectories of white and minority executives suggests that companies implicitly have two distinct tournaments for access to the top jobs. In the tournament for whites, contenders are sorted early on, and only those deemed most promising proceed to future competition. In the tournament for minorities, the screening process for the best jobs occurs much later. This and other differences have important implications for minority professionals—and for the people mentoring them through the different stages.

Stage 1

According to my research, a pernicious result of the two-tournament system was that many high-potential minorities became discouraged when they failed to be fast-tracked early in their careers. They became demotivated—and deskilled, especially when they saw their white colleagues receive plum assignments and promotions. As a result, their performance fell to a level that matched their modest rewards.

But some minorities—those who eventually became executives—avoided that fate. What kept them motivated and prepared to take advantage of opportunities that arrived belatedly? A common thread among them was their relationships with mentors. Even though the minority executives were not on an obvious fast track, influential mentors were investing in them as if they were, which helped prevent them from either ratcheting down their performance or simply leaving the organization.

This is not to say that the minorities in the study who became executives did not experience their share of disappointments; they did. But they evaluated themselves in terms of personal growth, not external rewards. Committed to excellence, they found the process of learning new skills rewarding. In general, minority executives made early career choices that placed them at the leading edge of the work they liked. They were more enthusiastic about the work itself and less concerned with how quickly—or slowly—they were climbing the corporate ladder. In fact, two minority executives in the study actually took demotions to transfer from staff jobs into operations, where they saw a better match for their skills and a greater opportunity for professional growth. Stage 1 was thus a time for minority executives to gain the three C's: confidence, competence, and credibility.

In contrast, minority professionals who subsequently plateaued in middle management tended to make their decisions based on perceived fast-track career opportunities, not on the actual work. They were more prone to take salary and title promotions that offered little increase in management responsibility.

Interestingly, minority executives were promoted to middle management only slightly faster than minority plateaued managers, but with much greater job continuity. They were much less likely to have changed departments, made lateral moves, or transferred away from core positions. Surprisingly, they even received, on average, fewer promotions within a given level than did minorities who failed to make it past middle management. A close inspection of the data, however, revealed that the promotions of minority managers offered little real expansion of responsibilities, as compared with the promotions of minority executives.

Minority executives attributed much of their later success to their immediate bosses, other superiors, and peers who helped them develop professionally. Of course, such developmental relationships are important for everybody climbing the corporate ladder, regardless of race, but what distinguished minority executives from white executives and plateaued managers was that they had many more such relationships and with a broader range of people, especially in the early years of their careers. Within the first three years at the organization, minority executives had established at least one developmental relationship, usually with a boss or a boss's boss. These mentors provided critical support in five ways.

First, the relationships opened the door to challenging assignments that allowed the minority executives to gain professional competence. Second, by putting the future executives in high-trust positions, the mentors sent a message to the rest of the organization that these people were high performers, thus helping them gain confidence and establish their credibility. Third, the mentors provided crucial career advice and counsel that prevented their protégés from getting sidetracked from the path leading to the executive level. Fourth, the mentors often became powerful sponsors later in the minority executives' careers, recruiting them repeatedly to new positions. Fifth, the mentors often protected their protégés by confronting subordinates or peers who leveled unfair criticism, especially if it had racial undertones. For example, a superior-performing African American in the study had a laid-back style that detractors said was an indication of his slacking off, playing on the stereotype that blacks are lazy. The mentor directly challenged the detractors by pointing out that his protégé was the leading salesperson in the division.

In summary, in Stage 1, the winners in the white tournament earned fast promotions into middle management. In the minority tournament, the signals sent to winners were more subtle, taking the form of rich mentoring relationships, challenging assignments, and expanded responsibilities, which showed the rest of the organization that these people merited future investment. (Winners of the white tournament also received those benefits, but the most obvious prizes in that contest were fast promotions.)

Stage 2

Once minority executives entered middle management, they typically had to wait another 10–15 years before reaching the executive level. But Stage 2 was usually where their careers took off. And without exception, the minority executives in the study vividly recalled that their initial middle-management jobs were critical to their eventual success. Interestingly, few of the white executives felt that way, perhaps because they did not regard their jobs in early Stage 2 as big opportunities to prove themselves in the same way that their minority counterparts did.

In Stage 2, minority executives continued to increase their functional knowledge, allowing them to deepen and broaden their foundation of the three C's. When leading others, minority executives often were able to influence subordinates who might otherwise have been resistant, owing to the sheer technical or functional competence they had acquired in Stage 1. Through that process, they were able to enhance their managerial skills and judgment. Stage 2 was also an important period for the minority executives to apply their existing skills to complex situations, which then helped them demonstrate their potential and extend their credibility within the larger organization. Thus, they were able to expand their network of relationships, including those with mentors and sponsors, beyond the boundaries of their original functional groups. By the end of Stage 2, every minority executive in the study had at least one influential executive as a mentor, and many were highly regarded by several executives who acted as sponsors.

The split between minority executives and plateaued managers became more pronounced in Stage 2. Minority executives still received fewer promotions than minority plateaued managers, but they reached upper middle management in less time because their promotions were bigger and more significant. The assignment patterns of the minority managers continued to be unfocused: They had more job changes—either by department, location, or function (especially changes from line to staff jobs)—and they tended to serve in fix-it roles involving the same kind of challenges over and over, with no opportunity to acquire new skills.

Stage 2 was also when the careers of minority and white executives began to converge—their experiences, assignments, and pace of advancement became increasingly similar. There were still, however, some notable differences. Compared with their white counterparts, minority executives were twice as likely to change functions, twice as likely to take on special projects or taskforce assignments, three times as likely to take a turnaround assignment, almost twice as likely to change locations, and four times as likely to report a big success. In many ways, these differences are a reversal of what occurred in Stage 1, in which white executives had markedly more opportunities to prove themselves than minority executives did. For that reason, Stage 2 can be thought of as a catching-up and breaking-out period for minority executives.

Interestingly, although minority and white executives had a similar number of developmental relationships in Stage 2, minority executives were far more likely to have powerful corporate-level executives as sponsors and mentors. In reviewing their careers, minority executives usually described a senior person who had been watching their progress during this period without their full awareness.

Stage 3

The climb from upper middle management to the executive level required a broad base of experience—well beyond a functional expertise. In Stage 3, people took on issues specific to working across functional boundaries, and that change encouraged them to think and act more strategically and politically.

To distinguish oneself as executive-level material in Stage 3, an individual needed highly visible successes that were directly related to the company's core strategy.

Minority executives in Stage 3 continued developing their network of highly placed mentors and sponsors. An individual's relationship with his executive boss, in particular, became crucial; it played a central role in helping each minority executive break through to the highest level. Furthermore, in Stage 3 the minority executives reported developing at least two new relationships with other executives. In contrast, most of the minority plateaued managers did not establish any new developmental relationships during that time.

The networks of minority executives were also much more diverse than those of the minority managers. For example, African American managers who plateaued relied either almost exclusively on members of their own racial group for key developmental support or predominantly on whites. In contrast, those who reached the executive level, especially the most successful among them, had built genuine, personal, long-term relationships with both whites and African Americans.

The careers of minority and white executives continued to converge in Stage 3, especially with regard to developmental relationships. Clearly, it was impossible to make it to the executive level, regardless of race, without the active advocacy of an immediate boss and at least one other key sponsor or mentor. Nevertheless, as was the case in Stage 2, minority executives tended to have a higher proportion of their developmental relationships with the corporate elite than did white executives.

In summary, during Stages 2 and 3, the careers of minority executives became clearly differentiated from those of plateaued managers, and in Stage 3, the career trajectories and experiences of minority and white executives finally converged.

Mentoring Challenges

A key finding of this research is that professionals of color who plateaued in management received mentoring that was basically instructional; it helped them develop better skills. Minority executives, by contrast, enjoyed closer, fuller developmental relationships with their mentors. This was particularly true in people's early careers, when they needed to build confidence, credibility, and competence. That is, purely instructional mentoring was not sufficient; protégés needed to feel connected to their mentors.

Specifically, a mentor must play the dual role of coach and counselor: Coaches give technical advice—explaining how to do something—whereas counselors talk about the experience of doing it and offer emotional support; both are crucial.

Many people, however, do not approach mentoring from a developmental perspective. They do not understand how to work with subordinates, especially minorities, to prepare them for future opportunities. My own experience and the findings of other studies suggest that organizations can change this situation by educating managers about their developmental role and by teaching them how to mentor effectively.

Cross-Race Issues

This education process must include an awareness of the inherent difficulties of mentoring across race. A significant amount of research shows that cross-race (as well as cross-gender) relationships can have difficulty forming, developing, and maturing. Nevertheless, the mentoring of minority professionals must often be across race, as it was for most of the minority executives in my study. And to develop the personal connections that are the foundation of a good mentoring relationship, the participants must overcome the following potential obstacles.

NEGATIVE STEREOTYPES   Mentors must be willing to give their protégés the benefit of the doubt: They invest in their protégés because they expect them to succeed. But a potential mentor who holds negative stereotypes about an individual, perhaps based on race, may withhold that support until the prospective protégé has proven herself worthy of investment. (Such subtle racism may help explain why none of the minority professionals in my study had been fast-tracked. Whites were placed on the fast track based on their perceived potential, whereas people of color had to display a proven and sustained record of solid performance—in effect, they often had to be overprepared—before they were placed on the executive track.)

Moreover, when a person of color feels that he won't be given the benefit of the doubt, he behaves in certain ways—for example, he might not take risks he should for fear that if he fails, he will be punished disproportionately.

IDENTIFICATION AND ROLE MODELING   Close mentoring relationships are much more likely to form when both parties see parts of themselves in the other person: The protégé sees someone whom he wants to be like in the future. The mentor sees someone who reminds him of himself years ago. This identification process can help the mentor see beyond a protégé's rough edges. But if the mentor has trouble identifying with her protégé—and sometimes differences in race are an obstacle—then she may not be able to see beyond the protégé's weaknesses. Furthermore, when the mentoring relationship is across race, the mentor will often have certain limitations as a role model. That is, adoption of the behavior of the mentor by the protégé may produce different results. In my study, an African American participant recounted how his white mentor encouraged him to adopt the mentor's more aggressive style. But when the protégé did so, others labeled him an "angry black man."

SKEPTICISM ABOUT INTIMACY   At companies without a solid track history of diversity, people may question whether close, high-quality relationships across race are possible. Does the mentor, for example, have an ulterior motive, or is the protégé selling out his culture?

PUBLIC SCRUTINY   Because cross-race relationships are rare in most organizations, they tend to be more noticeable, so people focus on them. The possibility of such scrutiny will often discourage people from participating in a cross-race relationship in the first place.

PEER RESENTMENT   A protégé's peers can easily become jealous, prompting them to suggest or imply that the protégé does not deserve whatever benefits she has received. Someone who fears such resentment might avoid forming a close relationship with a prospective mentor of another race. Of course, peer resentment occurs even with same-race mentorships, but it is a much greater concern in cross-race relationships because of their rarity.

Not surprisingly, many cross-race mentoring relationships suffer from "protective hesitation": Both parties refrain from raising touchy issues. Protective hesitation can become acute when the issue is race—a taboo topic for many mentors and protégées. People believe that they aren't supposed to talk about race; if they have to discuss it, then it must be a problem. But that mindset can cripple a relationship. Consider, for example, a protégé who thinks that a client is giving him a difficult time because of his race but keeps his opinion to himself for fear that his mentor will think he has a chip on his shoulder. Had the protégé raised the issue, his mentor might have been able to nip the problem early on. The mentor, for instance, might have sent the protégé to important client meetings alone, thereby signaling that the protégé has the backing of his mentor and the authority to make high-level decisions.

In other words, relationships in which protégé and mentor openly discuss racial issues generally translate into greater opportunity for the protégé. To encourage and foster that type of mentoring, organizations can teach people, especially managers, how to identify and surmount various race-related difficulties. It should be noted that when the complexities of cross-race relationships are handled well, they can strengthen a relationship. For one thing, if a mentor and protégé trust each other enough to work together in dealing with touchy race-related issues, then they will likely have a sturdy foundation to handle other problems. In fact, people have reported that race differences enabled them to explore other kinds of differences, thus broadening the perspectives of both parties. That education is invaluable because people who can fully appreciate the uniqueness of each individual are more likely to be better managers and leaders.

Network Management

As discussed earlier, one of a mentor's key tasks is to help the protégé build a large and diverse network of relationships. The network must be strong enough to withstand even the loss of the mentor.

My research has shown that the most effective network is heterogeneous along three dimensions. First, the network should have functional diversity; it should include mentors, sponsors, role models, peers, and even people toward whom the protégées themselves might be developing mentoring relationships. Second, the network should have variety with respect to position (seniors, colleagues, and juniors) as well as location (people within the immediate department, in other departments, and outside the organization). And third, the network should be demographically mixed in terms of race, gender, age, and culture.

A network of relationships becomes vulnerable when it lacks any one of the dimensions. For example, if a person's network is limited to her organization, she will find it difficult to find employment elsewhere. However, people of color have the tendency to draw on a network from primarily outside their organizations. Such support can be invaluable, but it will provide little help when that individual is being considered for a highly desirable in-house assignment. Establishing a diverse network is just the start—a person's network must be replenished and modified continually.

Creating the Environment for Success

Many mentors of minority professionals assume that their job begins and ends with the one-on-one relationships they establish with their protégées. This is hardly true. Mentors, especially those at the executive level, must do much more by actively supporting broader efforts and initiatives at their organizations to help create the conditions that foster the upward mobility of people of color.

Organizations should provide a range of career paths, all uncorrelated with race, that lead to the executive suite. Ideally, this system of movement would allow variation across all groups—people could move at their own speed through the three stages based on their individual strengths and needs, not their race. Achieving this system, however, would require integrating the principles of opportunity, development, and diversity into the fabric of the organization's management practices and human resource systems. And an important element in the process would be identifying potential mentors, training them, and ensuring that they are paired with promising professionals of color.

Discussion Questions

1. What are the differences between instructional and developmental mentoring?
2. Why might race be an obstacle to identification between mentor and protégé?
3. Why are necessary conversations about race between mentor and protégé so often difficult?
4. Why is a diverse network of supporters particularly significant for the advancement of minority executives?

Case Study: The Classic Look of Discrimination: Abercrombie & Fitch's Struggle to Manage Diversity

Who represents an "all-American" standard? For national clothing retailer Abercrombie & Fitch, a company that meticulously branded itself as having the "A&F Look"—"cool," "classic," and "all-American"[1]—the answer was simple: a young, athletic, beautiful, white male. As Abercrombie & Fitch developed their brand, they worked diligently and systematically to create their image by hiring employees and models who reflected this specific look. What began as merely a marketing strategy developed into a pattern of human resource management that ultimately led to two discrimination lawsuits in which Abercrombie & Fitch was charged with creating an "exclusively white company image used to discriminate against non-whites."[2] The purpose of this case study is to describe Abercrombie & Fitch's history, development, and current status and to consider how a successful century-old organization ended up facing class-action discrimination lawsuits, ultimately paying over $40 million to several thousand African American, Latino, Asian American, and female plaintiffs.[3]

Source: This case was written by Kathryn A. Cañas and Jacob K. Sorensen.

The History of Abercrombie & Fitch

David T. Abercrombie, a passionate outdoorsman and entrepreneur, founded Abercrombie & Co. in 1892 with the intent of providing high-end outdoor products to an elite clientele. A short time later, in 1900, Abercrombie entered into a partnership with attorney, visionary, and Abercrombie & Co. customer Ezra Fitch, and in 1904 Abercrombie & Co. was relaunched as Abercrombie & Fitch Co. From 1900 to the late 1960s, Abercrombie & Fitch sold outdoor equipment, furnishings, and clothing to wealthy, high-profile customers such as Dwight Eisenhower, Ernest Hemingway, John F. Kennedy, and Teddy Roosevelt. It was during this time that the brand first became associated with the "Classic American Image" as the company catered to an affluent, largely white male customer base.[4] A quote from Otis L. Guernsey, who was president during the 1940s, provides a sense of Abercrombie & Fitch's brand elitism: "The Abercrombie & Fitch type does not care about the cost, he wants the finest quality."[5]

In the 1960s, Abercrombie & Fitch entered a period of declining profits due largely to market changes, which eventually forced the company into bankruptcy and led to the subsequent purchase of the Abercrombie & Fitch name, trademark, and mailing list by Oshman's Sporting Goods in 1978 for $1.5 million.[6] Oshman's attempted to rebuild the company by opening a chain of 26 stores across the country that largely sold sport and fitness equipment designed specifically for the brand. The sporting goods company ultimately failed, however, to turn Abercrombie & Fitch into a successful sporting goods store.[7]

In 1988, The Limited, Inc., purchased Abercrombie & Fitch from Oshman's for $46 million in cash and repositioned the company as a clothing retailer, focusing primarily on men's clothing. In 1992, Michael Jeffries was appointed CEO, and Abercrombie & Fitch entered into a phase of intense expansion, increasing from 35 to 67 stores in just three years and ultimately to over 1,100 today in the United States, Canada, and the United Kingdom.[8] In 1996, Abercrombie & Fitch entered the New York Stock Exchange,[9] and in 1998 was spun off from The Limited, Inc.[10] Sales during this time increased from $85 million in 1992 to $165 million in 1994 and have currently reached approximately $3.5 billion in 2009.[11] It was during this period of growth that Jeffries began targeting youth with the goal of branding his product as emblematic of a culture and lifestyle within the context of Abercrombie & Fitch's "Classic American Image," or, what he described as "the embodiment of 'American cool.' "[12]

The "A&F Look"

In 2002, when on a conference call with analysts, Jeffries described Abercrombie & Fitch's target customer as an "18-to-22-year-old college guy who has a good body and is aspirational." He continued, "If I exclude people—absolutely. Delighted to do so."[13] In Jeffries' quest to market the Abercrombie & Fitch brand, he seemed to suggest that the company was willing to ignore anyone who did not fit or aspire to be part of the young, white, good-looking, athletic demographic.[14] Hiring a certain kind of employee became part of this marketing effort.

At Abercrombie & Fitch, a strong emphasis is placed on hiring the best-looking people who fit the retailer's particular brand image. Abercrombie & Fitch employees, specifically the sales people, are hired as brand representatives. According to a former assistant store manager, "If someone came in with a pretty face, we were told to approach them and ask them if they wanted a job. They thought if we had the best-looking college kids working in our store, everyone will want to shop there."[15] Abercrombie & Fitch critics argue that one only needs to walk into an

Abercrombie & Fitch store and look at the salespeople as well as the quasi-risqué posters to see the pervasiveness of the "A&F Look."[16]

The company selects models for its catalogs and overall marketing campaign from among its store personnel. In terms of the selection process, each store is required to send pictures of the brand representatives to corporate headquarters from which models are chosen. A former brand representative at the Staten Island store said, "Store managers would set up photo shoots that used brand reps as models."[17] Store managers also routinely conduct grading sessions of store employees, assigning grades based upon looks.[18] Former employee Kristen Carmichael claimed that in 2008 she was pulled from the sales floor and placed in the back room to fold clothes after managers gave her face a zero rating. She also claimed that a manager told her "that she wasn't attractive enough to work on the floor."[19]

Accounts detailing the 2007 opening of an Abercrombie & Fitch store in London reflect the retailer's obsession with the perfect look. In particular, Jeffries promised "a store full of gorgeous kids," and in order to deliver on his promise, the company reportedly hired 14 recruiters to "scour pubs, clubs, gyms, sport meetings and students' unions in search of some ripplingly healthy specimen." Jeffries also said, "These great-looking college kids exist all over the world . . . We think there are Abercrombie kids everywhere."[20] On the surface, Jeffries' intense passion for branding the perfect look does not constitute discrimination; it is perfectly legal to market aggressively to a particular audience and build your brand in a particular way. In light of this, how did Abercrombie & Fitch's actions constitute discrimination?

Discrimination at Abercrombie & Fitch

There are a number of instances in which Abercrombie & Fitch's corporate culture—including policy and product design—reflected both subtle and blatant instances of discrimination. In early 2002 the company released a line of T-shirts with what were described as demeaning racial stereotypes.[21] One T-shirt with unflattering caricatures of Asians on it read: "Wong Brothers Laundry Service: Two Wongs Can Make It White." Public objection against the company for the T-shirts resulted in Abercrombie & Fitch eliminating them from the stores and stopping production. In response, an Abercrombie & Fitch representative revealed the company's obtuseness and said, "We personally thought Asians would love this T-shirt."[22] The offensive T-shirts prompted an e-mail and phone campaign among Asian Americans in California to boycott the company.[23] Asian American student groups across the nation "held rallies . . . aimed at raising public awareness about the issue."[24]

In order to maintain the appropriate store image, each brand representative received a copy of what was known as the *Look Book*.[25] This small book was the employee's guide to adopting the image of Abercrombie & Fitch. According to a 1996 copy:

> Our people in the store are an inspiration to the customer. The customer sees the natural Abercrombie style and wants to be like the Brand Representative . . . Our Brand is natural, classic and current, with an emphasis on style. This is what a Brand Representative must be; this is what a Brand Representative must represent in order to fulfill the conditions of employment.[26]

Other guidelines that are articulated in the *Look Book* include descriptions of appropriate hair cuts and styles (they must be "natural") which prohibit a fade cut (described in the book as more scalp visible than hair), shaving of the head, and dreadlocks for men and women. Jewelry guidelines include directives that jewelry be simple and classic, no thumb rings, and no gold chains for men.[27] Many of these directives in the *Look Book* have led some to criticize the racial undertones in the described Abercrombie & Fitch image, claiming that the discouraged hair styles and jewelry guidelines specifically delineate styles and habits typical for people of color.[28]

Numerous accounts from former employees paint Abercrombie & Fitch as a company that struggled to balance their branding strategy with employee rights. According to a former Abercrombie & Fitch employee, "Ninety-nine percent of us were white." The same employee explained that "style, not skin color, would discourage stores from hiring minorities since the 'A&F Look' discounts the urban style of dress and general appearance that many black youth favor."[29] In another example, former employee Karma Miller claimed that the night crew at her store, during her shift, was composed entirely of minority employees, while the retail sales staff was composed entirely of white workers. "Something felt weird," she said. "I didn't take it as discrimination at the time, or I wouldn't have worked there."[30] Miller also indicated that the night and day crews were completely separate and the day crew ignored her when she went to the store to pick up paychecks. Another former employee claimed that the night crew was told not to come into the store until after it was closed, when all of the customers were gone. This employee stated, "Everyone who worked in the daytime was Caucasian" and that minority employees who were hired automatically received the night shift.[31]

Anthony Ocampo, a Filipino-American plaintiff in the case, said that when reapplying at a store where he had previously worked, a manager said, "We're sorry, but we can't rehire you because there's already too many Filipinos working here."[32] Another plaintiff, Jennifer Lu, who was fired after a corporate visit to the store, said, "A corporate official had pointed to an Abercrombie poster and told our management at our store, 'You need to have more staff that looks like this.' And it was a white Caucasian male on that poster."[33] Carla Grubb felt that she was scheduled for menial work, coming in "at closing time and wash[ing] the front windows and vacuum[ing] and wip[ing] off mannequins. While I was washing windows and vacuuming and dusting, my coworkers, my white coworkers, were folding the clothes, which I wanted to do, selling the clothes, which I wanted to do."[34] As suggested by the above testimony, Abercrombie & Fitch's branding strategy—trying to create the perfect look throughout every aspect of their organization—moved them away from innovative marketing into the realm of discrimination because they were treating people differently and unfairly specifically because of their race or national origin (both of which are federally protected classes).

Abercrombie & Fitch Is Sued for Discrimination

In June 2003, the clothing retailer was charged with discrimination in a class action lawsuit, *Gonzalez v. Abercrombie & Fitch*, which accused Abercrombie and Fitch of racial discrimination in hiring and employment practices. A second lawsuit filed five months later by the Equal Employment Opportunity Commission (EEOC) also accused Abercrombie & Fitch of discrimination based on charges received by the commission dating to December 21, 1999.[35] A third lawsuit filed in November 2004, *West v. Abercrombie & Fitch Stores, Inc.*, investigated gender discrimination at Abercrombie & Fitch. All three lawsuits were resolved through mediation that began in April 2004 and settled a year later in April 2005. The lawsuits received backing from national groups such as the Mexican American Legal Defense and Educational Fund, the

Asian Pacific American Legal Center, the NAACP Legal Defense and Educational Fund, Inc., and the EEOC.[36]

The class-action lawsuit, which was brought by 16 individual plaintiffs, *Gonzalez v. Abercrombie & Fitch,* alleged that the retailer illegally discriminated "against minorities on the basis of race, color, and/or national origin with respect to hiring, firing, job assignment, compensation, and other terms and conditions of employment."[37] The allegations continued that the company enforced "a nationwide corporate policy of preferring white employees for sales positions, desirable job assignments, and favorable work schedules in its stores throughout the United States."[38] This lawsuit was settled by negotiating a consent decree.

According to the consent decree documentation, the EEOC first issued a Letter of Determination "finding probable cause that the charging party was denied a permanent sales or brand representative position, denied assignments, and terminated due to his national origin."[39] The EEOC also found probable cause that Latinos and African Americans were discriminated against as a class. Additional Letters of Determination were issued in September and November of 2004, "finding probable cause that Abercrombie violated Title VII by discriminating against minority individuals on the basis of national origin, color, race, and/or gender (female including minority women) in hiring, staffing, constructive discharge, failing to promote into manager positions, steering, and discharge, on an individual basis and also on nationwide class basis."[40]

Abercrombie & Fitch denied the allegations. Jeffries said, "We have, and always have had, no tolerance for discrimination. We decided to settle this suit because we felt that a long, drawn out dispute would have been harmful to the company and distracting to management."[41] This sentiment is reflected in a Miscellaneous Provision included in the consent decree:

> Abercrombie denies that it has engaged in any policy or pattern or practice of unlawful discrimination, or that it has engaged in any other unlawful conduct as alleged in the Consolidated Litigation, and Abercrombie's entry is not and may not be used by any person in any proceeding as an admission or evidence that Abercrombie and/or its employees, managers, and/or attorneys have on any occasion engaged in discriminatory employment practices or any other unlawful conduct, such being expressly denied. Abercrombie has voluntarily entered into this Decree because it believes the actions it has agreed to undertake demonstrate its strong commitment to diversity and equal employment opportunity.[42]

Terms of the Consent Decree

Although the clothing retailer never admitted guilt in the lawsuits, it agreed to pay approximately $50 million in settlement costs.[43] The settlement included $40 million in payments to the plaintiffs and approximately $10 million to monitor compliance and pay attorney's fees. The consent decree outlines each diversity initiative agreed to by Abercrombie & Fitch. In particular, Abercrombie & Fitch agreed:

- Not to implement any policy or engage in any practice that discriminates against African Americans, Asian American, Latinos, or women.
- To retain a diversity consultant.
- To establish an Office of Diversity within the company.

- To hire a Diversity Vice President.
- To provide diversity training for all employees, especially those in management positions.
- To set up an internal complaint procedure to provide for the filing, investigation, and remedying of complaints of discrimination.
- To revise performance evaluations for all managerial positions to include measurement of diversity management performance.
- To change its job analysis and criteria to eliminate any criteria that described involvement of candidates in target colleges, sororities or fraternities, or specific athletic events.
- To develop and implement recruiting and hiring protocols that require Abercrombie & Fitch to seek out qualified minority applicants.
- To work to promote minority employees into managerial positions.
- To hire no fewer than 10 diversity recruiters to help with recruiting minority applicants.
- To attend minority recruiting events.
- To maintain proper documentation for all recruiters.
- To establish benchmarks for hiring and employment.
- To change their marketing to reflect diversity.
- To change their advertising strategy to include periodicals and media outlets that target minority audiences.
- To put in place a court-appointed monitor to supervise the company's compliance with the decree.[44]

The diversity initiatives agreed to by Abercrombie & Fitch and outlined in the consent decree represent an attempt both to create more diversity within the organization and to manage diversity more effectively. According to Kimberly West-Faulcon, Western regional counsel for the NAACP Legal Defense and Education Fund, "Abercrombie had a back-of-the-bus mentality . . . . Now instead of hiring them in the back of the store, they will have diversity recruiters. It sends a message to young people that we're moving past this kind of thing."[45]

Current Status

So what lasting change was effected by the lawsuits and the settlement? Has Abercrombie & Fitch been able to change the corporate culture that promoted and encouraged discrimination in its hiring practices? According to reports, the *Look Book* has been revised to represent a more diverse "A&F Look."[46] Store managers now take pictures of their brand representatives to send to the corporate headquarters so that it is able to list the top 25 and bottom 50 stores in terms of achieving the greatest staff diversity.[47]

In another attempt to embrace diversity, Abercrombie & Fitch teamed with the Anti-Defamation League to create and carry out diversity training on college campuses across the country. The company also designed diversity training to be carried out in high school. According to Abercrombie & Fitch's new vice president of diversity and inclusion Todd Corley, "This is an important initiative for us because it helps us support the dialogue among college students about the importance of appreciating difference."[48]

Many critics of the clothier, however, still feel that it is not living up to expectations—that any changes in the company are only superficial and not indicative of real change.[49] Many still believe that Abercrombie & Fitch is merely complying with the terms of the settlement and not utilizing the opportunity to create real change regarding the company's hiring practices. The company maintains that 35 percent of 88,000 store employees are ethnic minorities;[50] however, this claim is unsubstantiated and the court-appointed monitor has not confirmed it. The company maintains that it has not been in violation of the mandate to show "best efforts" in increasing diversity since the settlement.[51]

The company may indeed not be strictly violating the terms of the settlement. A review of Abercrombie & Fitch's Web site, which is a public representation of the company, shows a slide show of models of a variety of ethnic backgrounds. These images, however, are located only on Abercrombie & Fitch's diversity page; all other models on the Web site are white.[52] Abercrombie & Fitch's diversity page also includes statements related to diversity and the company's commitment, strategy, and internal and external initiatives to promote diversity, in addition to a "Diversity & Inclusion" statement that reads: "Diversity and inclusion are key to our organization's success. We are determined to have a diverse culture, throughout our organization, that benefits from the perspectives of each individual."[53]

Although Abercrombie & Fitch has been affected by the current downturn in the economy—it posted a 34 percent drop in same-store sales from 2008 to 2009[54]—it remains committed to protecting its image as "the essence of privilege and casual luxury."[55] Unlike other retailers who are slashing price points, Abercrombie & Fitch is not pushing promotions. Continuing to grow its brand, the company plans to expand globally into Europe and Asia[56] as well as "grab another slice of the under-30 market with a new brand known as Concept 5," a project that the retailer has "already spent up to $50 million on its development."[57]

Abercrombie and Fitch's understanding of workforce diversity is a work in progress. Problems still exist, as an employee with a disability is suing the retailer on the grounds that she was forced to work in the stockroom because of her prosthetic arm.[58] At the same time, however, there is progress. Corley, who represents the Abercrombie & Fitch voice on diversity, is in the beginning stages of clearly communicating diversity's role within Abercrombie & Fitch: "The diversity of our associates and partners is the foundation for us to better serve our diverse customers and stakeholders worldwide. Our strategy is focused on a diverse work environment that reflects the community and our valuable customers."[59]

Discussion Questions

1. How did Abercrombie & Fitch's branding strategy of the "All-American" look lead to class-action lawsuits?
2. Do you believe Abercrombie & Fitch managed their diversity crisis effectively?
3. Do you believe that Abercrombie & Fitch has made legitimate, systemic organizational changes in terms of diversity management?
4. Does the Abercrombie & Fitch Web site reflect the Company's new approach to managing diversity?

Notes

1. "The Classic Look of Discrimination: Abercrombie & Fitch Charged with Employment Discrimination in Federal Class Action Lawsuit," NAACP Legal Defense and Educational Fund, Inc., http://www.naacpldf.org/content.aspx?article=55.
2. Ibid.
3. Steven Greenhouse, "Abercrombie & Fitch Bias Case Is Settled," *New York Times* (Late Edition—Final), November 17, 2004.

4. "Abercrombie & Fitch Co.—Company History," *FundingUniverse.com*, http://www.fundingunivers. com/company-histories/Abercrombie-amp%3B-Fitch-Co-History1.html.

5. "Abercrombie & Fitch," *Answers.com*, http://www.answers.com/topic/abercrombie-fitch-co.

6. Sophia Banay, "Abercrombie & Fitch Portfolio.com Overview," *Portfolio.com*, http://www.portfolio. com/resources/company-profiles/Abercrombie—Fitch-Co-3375.

7. "Abercrombie & Fitch," *Answers.com*. See also, "Abercrombie & Fitch Company," *FashionEncyclopedia. com*, http://www.fashionencyclopedia.com/A-Az/Abercrombie-Fitch-Company.html.

8. "Abercrombie & Fitch Company," *FashionEncyclopedia.com*.

9. Shelly Branch, "Style & Substance: For a U.S. Clothier, Essence of Its Brand Has Turned Many Off," *Asian Wall Street Journal*, December 15, 2003, A8.

10. "Historical Timeline," www.limitedbrands.com/about/history.jsp.

11. "Investors," *Abercrombie.com*, http://www.abercrombie.com/anf/lifestyles/html/investorrelations. html. See Sales History 1998-2009, Store Count History, and Historical Income Statement. See also, "Abercrombie & Fitch Co.—Company History," *FundingUniverse.com*; "Abercrombie & Fitch's 2008 Annual Report," http://phx.corporate-ir.net/phoenix.zhtml?c=61701&p=irol-reportsannual.

12. Marla Matzer Rose, "A New Look for Abercrombie," *The Columbus Dispatch*, November 2008, D01, http://www.dispatch.com/live/content/business/stories/2008/11/09/abercrombie_diverse.ART_ ART_11-09-08_D1_H0BQ33U.html?type=rss&cat=&sid=101.

13. Ibid.

14. Rebecca Leung, "The Look of Abercrombie & Fitch: Retail Store Accused of Hiring Attractive, Mostly White Salespeople," *60 Minutes*, CBS News, December 2003, http://www.cbsnews.com/stories/2003/ 12/05/60minutes/main587099.shtml.

15. Steven Greenhouse, "Going for the Look, but Risking Discrimination," *The New York Times*, July 13, 2003, http://www.nytimes.com/2003/07/13/us/going-for-the-look-but-risking-discrimination.html.

16. Kevin McCullough, "Is Abercrombie & Fitch Racist?" WorldNetDaily, November 2003, http://www. worldnetdaily.com/news/article.asp?ARTICLE_ID=35860.

17. Jim Edwards, "Whitewash," *Adweek*, October 6, 2003, http://www.allbusiness.com/marketing-advertising/ 4199435-1.html.

18. Jessica Meyers, "Employees: 'Hierarchy of Hotness' Rules at Abercrombie & Fitch," *The Dallas Morning News*, August 2008, http://www.dallasnews.com/sharedcontent/dws/dn/latestnews/stories/ 082708dnmetabercrombie.4027698.html.

19. Ibid.

20. Ian Herbert and John Walsh. "Undressed for Success: The Store that Discovered Sex," *The Independent*, March 2007, http://www.independent.co.uk.

21. John M. Glionna, "Answering Protests, Retailer to Pull Line of T-Shirts That Mock Asians," *Los Angeles Times*, April 19, 2002, B1; Cecilia Kang and Donna Kato, "Clothier's New Line of Shirts Backfires," *The San Jose Mercury News*, April 17, 2002; "Shirts Depict Stereotypes of Asians," www. 10news.com; See images of the T-shirts at www.snopes.com/racial/business/tshirts.asp.

22. "Abercrombie & Fitch Asian T-shirts Trigger Boycott," *San Diego News*, 10 News, http://www. 10news.com/news/1405909/detail.html.

23. Ibid.

24. Shabina S. Khatri, "Abercrombie and Fitch Offends Asian American Community," *The Michigan Daily*, April 29, 2002, http://www.michigandaily.com/content/abercrombie-and-fitch-offends-asian-american-community.

25. Dwight A. McBride, *Why I Hate Abercrombie & Fitch: Essays on Race and Sexuality* (New York and London: New York University Press, 2005), 67.

26. Ibid., 67.

27. Ibid., 70–71.

28. Ibid., 71.

29. Edwards, "Whitewash."

30. Jessica Esemplare, "Abercrombie & Fitch Settles Racial Bias Case," *Cincinnati Herald*, http://www.blackpressusa.com/news/Article.asp?SID=3&Title=National+News&NewsID=3703.

31. Ibid.

32. Associated Press, "Abercrombie & Fitch Faces Discrimination Lawsuit," *USA Today*, June 2003, http://www.usatoday.com/money/industries/retail/2003-06-17-abercrombie_x.htm.

33. Leung, "The Look of Abercrombie & Fitch."

34. Ibid.

35. Consent Decree, *Gonzalez v. Abercrombie & Fitch Stores, Inc.*, West v. Abercrombie & Fitch Stores, Inc., EEOC v. Abercrombie & Fitch Stores, Inc. Case Nos 03-2817 SI, 04-4730, & 04-4731. Northern District of California, United States District Court, April 2005, 6.

36. "Abercrombie Discrimination Racism Lawsuit: Official Website for Class Action Suit Against Abercrombie," http://afjustice.com/.

37. Consent Decree, 4.

38. Consent Decree, 4.

39. Consent Decree, 7.

40. Ibid.

41. Leung, "The Look of Abercrombie & Fitch."

42. Consent Decree, 13–14.

43. "Abercrombie & Fitch Settles Discrimination Suit," NPR.org, http://www.npr.org/templates/story/story.php?storyId=4174147.

44. "Abercrombie Discrimination Racism Lawsuit: Official Website for Class Action Suit Against Abercrombie," http://afjustice.com/.

45. Steven Greenhouse, "Abercrombie & Fitch Bias Case Is Settled."

46. Rose, "A New Look for Abercrombie."

47. Ibid.

48. Elisha Sauers, "Abercrombie & Fitch Tries to Make Diversity Fashionable," *The Jewish Daily Forward*, http://www.forward.com/article/6371.

49. Rose, "A New Look for Abercrombie."

50. Ibid.

51. Ibid.

52. "Abercrombie & Fitch Careers/Diversity & Inclusion," http://www.abercrombie.com/anf/careers/diversity.html.

53. Ibid.

54. Thomson Reuters, "BRIEF—Abercrombie & Fitch Reports March Sales Results," http://www.forbes.com/feeds/afx/2009/04/09/afx6274404.html

55. Abercrombie & Fitch 2008 Annual Report, "Description of Operations/Brands," 2, http://phx.corporate-ir.net/phoenix.zhtml?c=61701&p=irol-reportsannual.

56. Banay, "Abercrombie & Fitch Portfolio.com Overview." See also, "10-K: Abercrombie & Fitch CO/DE/," http://www.marketwatch.com/news/story/10-k-abercrombie—fitch-co/story.aspx?guid={C09C7157-DCA8-4CC6-ABEB-0F4D04BF934C}&dist=msr_2.

57. Banay, "Abercrombie & Fitch Portfolio.com Overview."

58. Rebecca English, "I was Banished to the Stockroom, Says Disabled Shop Girl Now Suing Abercrombie & Fitch for Discrimination," *DailyMail.co.uk*, http://www.dailymail.co.uk/news/article-1192674/I-banished-stockroom-says-disabled-shop-girl-suing-Abercrombie—Fitch-discrimination.html. See also, Liam Berkowitz, "Abercrombie Sued By Former Employee," ABCNews.com, http://www.abcnews.go.com/Business/story?id=7916247&page=1.

59. Todd Corley, "Who Abercrombie and Fitch Is, Our Diversity Journey," *Affirmative Action Register: An Employment Magazine*, http://www.aarjobs.com/aarjobs/index.php?option=com_content&view=article&id=140:todd-corley&catid=52:may-2009-issue.

Case Study: Texaco, Inc.

Racial Discrimination Suit (A)

Amidst pending allegations that Texaco had consistently failed to promote blacks in certain employee groups because of their race and had "fostered a racially hostile environment,"[1] Texaco was hit with yet another allegation. As reported by *The New York Times* on November 4, 1996, Texaco executives were taped discussing a $520 million lawsuit which was filed by six employees in 1994 on behalf of almost 1,500 other minority workers at the firm. In these discussions, "senior Texaco managers made disparaging comments about minorities and discussed destroying documents related to [the] class-action discrimination suit."[2]

Texaco Chief Executive Officer, Peter I. Bijur, now faced a major corporate crisis in just his sixth month at the helm of Texaco. "The tape recording is [the latest] piece of evidence in [the] anti-discrimination lawsuit brought against the company in two years."[3] Texaco's history of hiring and promoting minorities was less than exemplary, even for the oil industry. The written transcripts of the audiotape, as provided to the courts by an ex-Texaco executive, containing racial slurs and stating intentions to destroy evidence, threatened to exacerbate Texaco's already mounting minority-related issues. The once hardly-noticed racial discrimination suit, *Roberts v. Texaco*, quickly began to attract media and public attention.

The Charge

Among the many questions immediately facing Texaco's CEO, Peter Bijur, were these: what action should he take on behalf of the company in response to the newly released tapes? What would the best approach be in managing this public-relations disaster? Should employees be addressed separately from the public sector? Is racial discrimination part of the Texaco culture? What, if any, steps can be taken to minimize future discrimination practices? Are reparations necessary? If so, how should it be addressed?

Texaco, Inc. Background

"Texaco Inc., originally known as The Texas Company, was founded in 1902 in Beaumont, Texas, by oilman 'Buckskin' Joe Cullinan and New York investor Arnold Schlaet."[4] In 1996, the time of the case, Texaco ranked #11 on the *Fortune 500* (Exhibit 1) list and employed more than 27,000 people worldwide.[5] Within the petroleum industry, Texaco ranked third behind Exxon and Mobil. At year's end in 1996, Texaco had assets of $27 billion and revenues of more than $45 billion.[6]

The company's recent employee history had been less than ideal. *The Wall Street Journal* reported that:

> Texaco had been a snakepit of disappointed middle management since the 1980s . . . It went from 11 layers of management to five, dumping tens of thousands

---

Source: This case was written by Research Assistants Tanya Goria, DeWayne Reed, and Dan Skendzel under the direction of James S. O'Rourke, Concurrent Associate Professor of Management, as the basis for class discussion rather than to illustrate either effective or ineffective handling of an administrative situation. Information was gathered from corporate as well as public sources.

of employees over the next decade. Last year [1996], in fact, was the first in a long time that Texaco's payroll grew instead of shrank.[7]

Middle management discontent may have been an issue, but Texaco claims to have been working earnestly toward a more integrated workforce, despite the layoffs. In a November 1996 interview on *Nightline,* Texaco CEO Peter Bijur offered this assessment of Texaco's employment figures: "16.6 percent of our U.S. work force of 27,426 were minorities in 1991, while as of last June, 22.3 percent of our 19,554 employees were minorities. Of those employees, the percentage of minorities in supervisory, management, and executive positions was 6.8 percent in 1989, and 9.5 percent in 1994."[8]

In early 1996, the Equal Employment Opportunity Commission (EEOC) reviewed the lawsuit against Texaco and found that black workers seeking promotion were chosen "at rates significantly below that of their nonblack counterparts."[9] The EEOC's finding also support the results of a study of one Texaco division by the Department of Labor. They discovered that minority employees took up to twice as many years as white workers to win promotions and ordered Texaco to pay compensation and revised its company-wide appraisal system.

Another survey, carried out for a rival oil company, found that the proportion of highly paid black workers at Texaco was consistently below the industry average. White senior managers at Texaco outnumbered their black counterparts by more than 80 to one.

The Meeting

During a 1994 meeting between Texaco finance department manager Richard Lundwall and other Texaco finance department managers, recordings were made by Lundwall allegedly detailing derogatory remarks being made by the department managers concerning Texaco's African-American employees. The transcript filed by Plaintiffs of the pending discrimination lawsuit against Texaco contains four instances of remarks with apparent racial connotations: (1) a statement characterizing African-Americans as "f****** n****rs"; (2) a statement, "you know how black jelly beans agree," followed by other remarks relating to jelly beans; (3) references to an event at which African-Americans allegedly sat through the playing of the United States National Anthem and then standing for a song presented as the Black National Anthem; and (4) references to Hanukkah and Kwanzaa.[10] Further comments included: "All the black jelly beans seem to be glued to the bottom of the bag."[11]

The behavior captured on tape revealed discrimination issues within the culture at Texaco. The term "black jelly beans" was used on the tape and Bob Ulrich, an attendee of the meeting and one of the individuals who used the term, through his attorney Jonathan Rosner, stated that the reference on the tape was not in any way intended to be a racial slur. Rosner pointed out that the term "jelly bean" is not, in and of itself, known to be a derogatory term, and Ulrich had no reason to think that the reference carried any such connotations.

Rosner also observed that Ulrich's reference to jelly beans was prompted by a speech given by an African-American at a conference at which the speaker, advocating integration and opposing separatist philosophies, illustrated his remarks by using jars of jelly beans as an analogy for racial integration. While Ulrich could not remember the name of the speaker to whom he referred, Dr. R. Roosevelt Thomas, Jr. was identified as the probable source of the remarks alluded to by Ulrich. Dr. Thomas is the founder and former President of the American Institute for Managing Diversity, at Morehouse College in Atlanta, Georgia.[12]

Public Outcry

The public was outraged when it received the initial reports that top executives within Texaco had made derogatory remarks about its African-American employees. Those derogatory remarks seemed to validate the public thought, feeling and insecurity surrounding Corporate America. At a time when affirmative action was being questioned, and the issues of prejudice and injustice were being debated, tangible evidence was offered that the "good ole boys" network, "glass ceilings" and many other negative Corporate America caricatures did in fact exist. This incident was specific to Texaco, but the public sentiment reflected a wider scope of discriminatory issues.

Rev. Jesse Jackson quickly became the voice of the black community, calling for a boycott of all Texaco products. The public responded by cutting up Texaco credit cards, and boycotting independent Texaco dealers. Wall Street recognized the potentially disastrous effects on business and adjusted its stock price accordingly. Texaco stock traded at $99^{5/8}$ at the opening on November 4th, 1996, and dropped to 97 by the end of trading that day.

Unresolved Issues

At the time of the case, Texaco, Inc. appeared to have disproportionately lower levels of minorities in roles of authority as compared to whites. Also it should be noted that the discrimination lawsuits that the tape supported were pending prior to the meeting in 1996. The U.S. EEOC had begun an investigation into the employment practices of Texaco prior to the taping of the conversation. These and other unresolved issues appeared to support the notion that Texaco had substantive discrimination problems that management would have to address directly.

Discussion Questions

1. What are the critical issues surrounding the newly released tapes?
2. How should Peter Bijur and Texaco respond to the allegations? How should the company respond to the publicity?
3. Should the employees be addressed separately from the general public? How can Texaco mend fences with minority employees and customers?
4. What would be an effective corporate strategy in dealing with encouraging diversity in the workplace?

EXHIBIT 1

Texaco's Initial Press Release Concerning Taped Racial Slurs

TEXACO RESPONDS TO MEDIA INQUIRIES REGARDING ALLEGATIONS IN NEW YORK TIMES ARTICLE

FOR RELEASE: MONDAY, NOVEMBER 4, 1996.

WHITE PLAINS, N.Y., Nov. 4 - Texaco was informed last week of new allegations regarding misconduct by certain current and former employees. These allegations relate to a pending employment discrimination lawsuit brought against Texaco and were reported in today's *New York Times*.

The following is a statement from Texaco:

> If these allegations are true, they represent an outrageous violation of the company's core values and principles. Any such conduct is deplorable and will never be tolerated by Texaco.
>
> Texaco has clear and vigorously-enforced policies against discrimination in the workplace. The company is committed to providing a work environment which reflects an understanding of diversity, and is free from all forms of discrimination, intimidation, and harassment. The company also prohibits conduct or language which is unwelcome, hostile, offensive, degrading, or abusive. Such conduct is unacceptable and will not be tolerated.
>
> In addition, Texaco enforces strict policies regarding the retention and production of documents. If any documents related to this lawsuit were in fact concealed or destroyed, such conduct would constitute a clear violation of these policies.
>
> Immediately upon learning of the allegations of misconduct, Texaco retained outside counsel, Michael Armstrong of Kirkpatrick and Lockhart, to conduct an extensive independent investigation to determine whether these allegations are true.
>
> If the company through its investigation determines that the alleged misconduct occurred, it will take appropriate disciplinary action against the employees, which could include termination.
>
> Texaco is determined to maintain an environment of respect for the individual and a work environment that allows every employee to develop and advance to the utmost of his or her abilities. We are dedicated to equal opportunity in all aspects of employment and will not allow any violation of law or company policies.

Source: http://www.texaco.com/compinfo/diversity/diversity_main.htm

Case Study: Texaco, Inc.

Racial Discrimination Suit (B)

Roughly one week after *The New York Times* story of Texaco's racial discrimination fiasco hit the street, the company's stock price had tumbled to $95^{3/8}$.

Texaco's reaction to the debacle was swift. On learning of the allegations of misconduct, the company hired Michael Armstrong, a Manhattan lawyer with Kirkpatrick & Lockhart. Armstrong

Source: This case was written by Research Assistants Tanya Goria, DeWayne Reed, and Dan Skendzel under the direction of James S. O'Rourke, Concurrent Associate Professor of Management, as the basis for class discussion rather than to illustrate either effective or ineffective handling of an administrative situation. Information was gathered from corporate as well as public sources.

Source: Eugene D. Fanning Center for Business Communication, Mendoza College of Business, University of Notre Dame. Copyright ©2000. Eugene D. Fanning Center for Business Communication. All rights reserved. No part of this publication may be reproduced, stored in a retrieval system, used in a spreadsheet, or transmitted in any form by any means—electronic, mechanical, photocopying, recording, or otherwise—without permission.

conducted an extensive independent investigation into the affair that included a review of Texaco's diversity and equal-opportunity policies.

On November 4, 1996, the day *The New York Times* story broke, the company issued a press release stating that "if these allegations are true, they represent an outrageous violation of the company's core values and principles. Any such conduct is deplorable and will never be tolerated by Texaco."[13] (Exhibit 1)

The company also vowed to take appropriate disciplinary action against those employees proved guilty. The two managers caught on tape, who at the time still worked for Texaco, were quickly suspended (with full pay) pending the results of the investigation. Subsequently, the two decided to leave the firm and Richard Lundwall and Bob Ulrich were stripped of benefits.[14]

Peter Bijur, Chairman and CEO since only July of 1996, personally authored a letter on November 4, 1996, addressed to Texaco employees explaining the allegations against the firm and outlining Texaco's investigation into the matter (Exhibit 2). In the letter, Bijur expressed his deep anger and sadness at the alleged incident and re-affirmed Texaco's policy toward the highest ethical and moral standards. "My personal commitment to you is to intensify our efforts to eliminate this [discriminatory] behavior from the workplace," said Bijur. He took further action by broadcasting a message to all employees via satellite on that same day. "We care about each and every employee," he said. "I care deeply."[15]

Behind the scenes, Bijur was also getting the Board of Directors involved in the process. "We had several board and executive committee meetings," said Bijur. Through these meetings, Bijur was able to express Texaco's position and listen to the board's counsel and guidance. The support of the board of directors, according to Bijur, was a crucial ingredient in moving to end the lawsuit quickly.

Additionally, Bijur began to meet with shareholder groups and influential individuals. For example, he met with the Interfaith Center on Corporate Relations (which is a group of religious shareholders), the New York State Comptroller, and the New York City Comptroller.

Over the course of the next three weeks, Bijur would make himself available for interviews with *The New York Times, Business Week,* and *NBC Nightly News,* among others. Throughout these interviews, he did not attempt to evade questions or deny the reality of the situation. His message was two-pronged: to relate the company's embarrassment about the incident; and to tell Texaco's side of the story—namely that racial discrimination was not commonplace at Texaco and that the company had been making strides to improve minority presence in past years.

"I do not think there is a culture of institutional bias within Texaco," said Bijur. "I think we've got a great many very good and decent human beings, but that unfortunately we mirror society. There is bigotry in society. There is prejudice and injustice in society. I am sorry to say that, and I am sorry to say that probably does exist within Texaco. I can't do much about society, but I certainly can do something about Texaco."[16]

In a November 6, 1996, statement, Bijur publicly outlined a six-step plan aimed at "moving quickly to right these [discriminatory] wrongs (Exhibit 3)." The CEO vowed that Texaco senior executives would visit every major company location in the U.S. to meet with employees and apologize for the embarrassing incident. He also pledged to refocus on the company's core values through the creation of a special committee of board members that would review human resource and diversity programs.

On November 12, 1996, Bijur met with Rev. Jesse Jackson and other black leaders in an effort to stave off a planned boycott of Texaco products and to reassure minorities that Texaco did not condone discrimination in any form. Rev. Jackson emerged from the meeting only to reaffirm the nationwide boycott and picketing of Texaco service stations scheduled to begin four days later, on November 16, 1996.[17]

Three days after Bijur met with Jackson, Texaco settled the *Roberts v. Texaco* lawsuit filed on behalf of 1,400+ minority employees. Under the settlement, Texaco agreed to pay $115 million in cash plus expenses and salary adjustments to the plaintiffs. In total, the settlement was valued at $176 million. In addition, the company agreed to create an Equality and Tolerance Task Force to determine potential improvements in Texaco's human resources programs, and to monitor the progress of these programs. In a company press release announcing the deal, Bijur said, "with this litigation behind us, we can now move forward on our broader, urgent mission to make Texaco a model of workplace opportunity for all men and women."[18] (Exhibit 4)

On November 15, 1996, Bijur also authored a statement for Texaco employees explaining the lawsuit settlement and the company's reasoning for reaching such an agreement. He again used this format to reassure employees of Texaco's commitment to fairness and equal opportunity (Exhibit 5). In a subsequent interview, Bijur would state, "I made the judgement that we needed to accelerate the settlement process. And those discussions on settlement commenced almost immediately."[19]

Texaco had also signed an agreement with Judge A. Leon Higginbotham Jr., chief judge emeritus of the U.S. Court of Appeals for the 3rd Circuit, to guide it through its review of human resource and diversity policies and practices.[20] The result of this review was Texaco's Workforce Diversity Plan, which it unveiled in mid-December 1996. To help achieve its goal of attracting and retaining a highly capable workforce, among other things, Texaco said it would in 1997:

- Enhance the interviewing, selection, and hiring skills of its managers;
- Expand its overall college recruitment;
- Use search firms with a record of recruiting from a wide, diverse range with key competencies for Texaco.

"Based on our review, we have set . . . initiatives that are well balanced and beneficial to all our employees and bring us a critical competitive advantage," said Bijur. "The goals of our program were set by determining what the demographics of Texaco's workforce are likely to be in the year 2000. And, to be clear, these are goals—they are not quotas."[21]

After the diversity plan was announced, Rev. Jackson declared that the boycott of Texaco should be ended. During the summer of 1997, with both Lundwall and Ulrich up on obstruction-of-justice charges, Texaco's own experts digitized the tapes and found that the word reportedly said to be "niggers" was in fact "Nicholas," a conclusion that nobody disputes.[22]

As time passes, Texaco's success at implementing and following through on its proposed initiatives will be assessed. By November 1997, all indications pointed toward the company remaining true to its agreements.

Discussion Questions

1. How would you rate the effectiveness of Texaco's response to the allegations of racial discrimination?
2. Did Texaco's response address the core problems and issues surrounding racial discrimination and prejudice at the company?
3. If you were Peter Bijur, what would you have done differently?
4. What kinds of company policies can affect long-term change in diversity in a corporate culture such as Texaco?

Notes

1. Kurt Eichenwald, *The New York Times*, "Texaco Executives, On Tape, Discussed Impeding a Bias Suit," November 4, 1996, Section A, p. 1, Column 1.
2. *Business Week*, "Texaco: Lessons from a Crisis-in-Progress," News: Analysis & Commentary, December 2, 1996.
3. Kurt Eichenwald, *The New York Times*, "Investigation Finds No Evidence of Slur on Texaco Tapes," November 11, 1996, http://www.dorsai.org/~jdadd/texaco2.html.
4. Texaco, Inc., Home Page, "A Brief History of Texaco," http://www.texaco.com/compinfo/history_d.html.
5. Bijur, Peter, I. Statement of Chairman and CEO, Texaco, Inc. to Company Employees, Friday, November 15, 1996, http://www.texaco.com/compinfo/pr/pr11_15b.html.
6. Texaco, Inc., Home Page, "A Brief History of Texaco."
7. Jenkins, Holman, W. Jr., " History of a $20 Million Lie, Business World," *The Wall Street Journal*, Tuesday, August 12, 1997, A15.
8. Fritsch, Peter, " Texaco's New Chairman Navigates PR Crisis," *The Wall Street Journal*, Friday, November 8, 1996, B1, B5.
9. *The Economist*, "Black Hole: Race in the Workplace," November 16, 1996, Vol. 341, no. 7992, p. 27.
10. Court TV Library Home Page, Report from Independent Investigator, http://205.181.114.35/library/business/texaco/report.html
11. Eichenwald, Kurt, "Investigation Finds No Evidence of Slur on Texaco Tapes," *The New York Times*, November 11, 1996.
12. Court TV Library Home Page, Report from Independent Investigator.
13. Texaco, Inc., Home Page, http://www.texaco.com/compinfo/diversity_main.htm.
14. *The Economist*, "Black Hole," 27.
15. Texaco, Inc., Home Page, http://www.texaco.com/compinfo/diversity/diversity_main.htm.
16. *Business Week*, "Texaco," 44.
17. Culbertson, Katherine, *The Oil Daily*, Independent retailers brace for boycott of Texaco stations, November 13, 1996, Vol. 46, no. 216, p. 1.
18. Texaco, Inc., Home Page, http://www.texaco.com/compinfo/diversity/diversity_main.ht.
19. *Business Week*, "Texaco," 44.
20. *The Oil Daily*, "Texaco Hires Race Adviser," December 2, 1996, Vol. 46, no. 227, p. 5.
21. *The Oil Daily*, "Texaco Calms Dispute, Setting Out Minority Employment Goals," December 19, 1996, Vol. 46, no. 240, p. 3.
22. Holman, W. Jenkins Jr., *The Wall Street Journal*, "History of a $20 Million Lie," August 12, 1997, A15.

EXHIBIT 2

Statement by Peter I. Bijur

Chairman and Chief Executive Officer, Texaco Inc.
November 6, 1996

RE: Allegations of Employee Misconduct

Good afternoon. My name is Peter Bijur, and I am chairman and chief executive officer of Texaco. I have a brief statement for you, after which I will take your questions.

You are all aware of alleged misconduct, first reported by the New York Times on Monday, which referred to statements made by several current and former Texaco employees in 1994. As soon as we heard about these allegations, we immediately hired Michael Armstrong as outside counsel to conduct an independent investigation to determine whether the allegations were true.

At the same time, I spoke and wrote to all of Texaco's employees, denouncing the alleged behavior in the strongest possible terms.

Until this morning, we did not have audible versions of the tapes. I have just today listened to them myself. I can tell you that the statements on the tapes arouse a deep sense of shock and anger among all the members of the Texaco family and decent people everywhere.

They are statements that represent attitudes we hoped and wished had long ago disappeared entirely from the landscape of our country—and certainly from our company.

They are statements that represent a profound contempt not only for the law, not only for Texaco's explicitly clear values and policies, but, even more importantly, for the most fundamental standards of fairness, of mutual respect, and of human decency.

We are now moving quickly to begin righting these wrongs.

The first step in that process is to say, on behalf of all of the people of Texaco, that we believe unequivocally it is utterly reprehensible to deny another human of his or her self-respect and dignity because of race, color, religion or sex.

And it is absolutely deplorable and intolerable to evade the laws of this land.

These beliefs go beyond an understanding of our legal obligations; they are grounded in a recognition of our moral obligations.

Texaco's statement of our core values is very clear. It says, "Each person deserves to be treated with respect and dignity in appropriate work environments without regard to race, religion, sex, national origin, disability or position in the company. Each employee has the responsibility to demonstrate respect for others."

Our corporate conduct guidelines are also clear and state that "it is the obligation of all employees to report known or suspected violations of the law or company policies to their supervisor" or other appropriate corporate officials.

These are not empty words. They enunciate the immutable principles to which we adhere . . . to which every person in our company has agreed. . . and which must form the basis of every act and utterance of all Texaco people in the course of our duties. Every employee signs our guidelines each year acknowledging that they have read them, understood them, and are in compliance with them.

Our review of the tapes has made it clear to us that these values and policies have been violated.

With regard to the four individuals involved in the allegations before us, two are active employees. They are both being suspended today pending completion of the investigation, which will be accomplished promptly.

As to the two retired employees, we believe there is sufficient cause to withdraw benefits. Pending the outcome of the independent outside investigation, further financial or other penalties may be imposed.

As I told our employees on Monday, my personal commitment is to intensify our efforts to eliminate forever this kind of behavior from our workplace. To that end, I am also announcing the following steps:

One—senior executives from Texaco will visit every major company location in the U.S. to meet with our people. Their mission will be to apologize to them for the embarrassment and humiliation this has created. We want them to understand both our personal embarrassment and our firm resolve to ensure that nothing like this ever happens again at Texaco.

Two—we will gather employees together immediately to refocus on our core values and on what we each need to do to create a workplace free of intolerance. It will be a time of reflection and a time for taking personal accountability for actions and attitudes.

Three—we are expanding our diversity learning experience to include all employees, in addition to our managers and supervisors. This two-day seminar, in which I have already participated, along with the senior officers of the company, focuses on both the intent and the impact of personal behavior on peers, teams and the organization overall.

Four—we will reemphasize the critical importance of our confidential Ethics Hotline as a vital tool for reporting any behavior—any behavior—that violates our core values, policies or the law. Calls may be made anonymously, 24 hours a day, seven days a week. We are extending this service to a broader list of countries outside of the U.S.

Fifth—I have today asked Judge A. Leon Higgenbotham of the New York law firm of Paul, Weiss, Rifkind, Wharton & Garrison to work side by side with us to assure that the company's human relationship policies and practices are consistent with the highest standards of respect for the individual and to assure that the company treats all its employees with fundamental fairness.

Judge Higgenbotham is Chief Judge Emeritus of the United States Court of Appeals for the Third Circuit and Public Service Professor of Jurisprudence at Harvard University. The Judge is the recipient of numerous honors, including the Presidential Medal of Freedom, the nation's highest civilian honor, and the National Human Relations Award of the National Conference of Christians and Jews. He is the author of IN THE MATTER OF COLOR—Race and the American Legal Process. I am grateful that he will be assisting us.

Sixth—we are also creating a special committee of our Board of Directors, to be headed by John Brademas, President Emeritus of New York University. This committee will be charged with reviewing our company's diversity programs in their entirety—at every level within our company.

Fundamentally, we don't believe the statements and actions on the tapes are representative of Texaco; but we also recognize that we have more to learn—further to go. Our goal is to become a model company in providing opportunities for women and minorities, and in ensuring respect for every individual.

Let me leave you on a personal note, but one in which I know the people of Texaco join me. I want to offer an apology . . . to our fellow employees who were rightly offended by these statements; to men and women of all races, creeds and religions in this country; and to people throughout America and elsewhere around the world: I am sorry for this incident; I pledge to you that we will do everything in our power to heal the painful wounds that the reckless behavior of those involved have inflicted on all of us; and I look forward to the day we are all striving for when the attitudes in question are consigned to a sorrowful chapter of our past—and that we have created for our future, within the very soul of Texaco, a company of limitless opportunity and utmost respect for every man and woman amongst us.

Source: http://www.texaco.com/compinfo/diversity/diversity_main.htm

EXHIBIT 3

Texaco Announces Settlement in Class Action Lawsuit

Company Moving Ahead Vigorously with Broader Actions to Promote Greater Diversity, Tolerance and Economic Opportunity

FOR IMMEDIATE RELEASE: FRIDAY, NOVEMBER 15, 1996.

WHITE PLAINS, N.Y., Nov. 15 - Texaco Inc. today announced it has reached an Agreement in Principle to settle the Roberts v. Texaco class action lawsuit, brought in 1994 on behalf of a class of approximately 1,400 individuals, comprised of all current and certain former African American employees.

Under the settlement, which was described to the Court, Texaco agreed to:

Provide a payment to the plaintiff-class in the amount of $115 million, along with a one-time salary increase of about 11 percent for current employees of the plaintiff-class, effective January 1, 1997;

Create an Equality and Tolerance Task Force which will be charged with determining potential improvements to Texaco's human resources programs, as well as helping to monitor the progress being made in those programs (three members of the Task Force to be appointed by the plaintiffs, three members by Texaco and a mutually agreed-upon chairperson); Adopt and implement company-wide diversity and sensitivity, mentoring, and ombuds programs;

Consider nationwide job posting of more senior positions than are currently posted; and Monitor its performance on the programs and initiatives provided for under the settlement agreement.

Commenting on the agreement, Texaco Chairman and Chief Executive Officer Peter I. Bijur said, "With this litigation behind us, we can now move forward on our broader, urgent mission to make Texaco a model of workplace opportunity for all men and women.

"Texaco is committed to developing and instituting specific, effective policies that will ensure that discrimination is wiped out wherever it may be, and that will expand the positive economic impact we can have in the minority community. These policies will be clearly defined and achievable—with measurable goals set out on a specific timetable.

"Today's agreement affords us a renewed opportunity to join in common purpose and unified action to achieve shared goals of greater inclusion and opportunity at Texaco—and in America," Bijur added.

Following the signing of the Agreement in Principle, all relevant legal documents will be finalized.

Source: http://www.texaco.com/compinfo/diversity/diversity_main.htm

EXHIBIT 4

Texaco Announces Comprehensive Plan to Ensure Fairness and Economic Opportunity for Employees and Business Partners

Company's Initiatives Follow Rigorous Review of Human Resources and Business Partnering Programs

Texaco Outlines Measures to Enhance Company's Performance in Increasingly Competitive and Diverse Marketplace

FOR IMMEDIATE RELEASE: WEDNESDAY, DECEMBER 18, 1996.

WHITE PLAINS, N.Y., Dec. 18 - Texaco Inc. today announced a comprehensive plan to ensure fairness and economic opportunity for its employees and business partners. The company's plan follows a rigorous review by Texaco of its human resources and business partnering programs. The review was undertaken as a result of events over the past six weeks and was conducted as part of Texaco's commitment to ensure that its employment and business partnering practices enhance its ability to compete even more successfully in the complex global market. In its plan, the company outlined detailed programs and initiatives for all employees, including minorities and women, working for and with Texaco.

Texaco Inc. Chairman and CEO Peter I. Bijur said, "Based on our review, we have set forth comprehensive employment and business partnering initiatives that are well-balanced and beneficial to all our employees and bring us a critical competitive advantage in the constantly changing and increasingly diverse environment in which we operate. Our review encompassed every aspect of employee recruitment, hiring, retention and promotion; workplace environment; and business partnering efforts. We sought input from our employees, numerous organizations and individuals, and we looked at the best practices in industry. The result is a broad program that we believe will ensure a fair and open environment in which all employees and business partners can contribute to the full measure of their abilities.

"The goals of our program," Mr. Bijur continued, "were set by determining what the demographics of Texaco's workforce are likely to be in the year 2000. And, to be clear, these are goals—they are not quotas. Goals focus and guide the efforts of a committed organization. Quotas arbitrarily impose rigid results and do not recognize fairness or judgement. We will continue to hire the best qualified candidates for all positions, based on merit and capability.

"And let me underscore another point: this plan was designed specifically to meet Texaco's unique business strategies and, as such, singularly applies to our company. This program is good business for Texaco," Mr. Bijur said.

He added, "This plan builds on a number of strong programs already in place that have yielded progress in recent years. But we are moving ahead quickly with new and enhanced efforts, because we believe that we must continue to expand our perspectives and make full use of resources that generate the creativity and innovation to meet our goals for success in today's competitive marketplace."

Texaco will track the progress of all of the new and enhanced programs outlined in this review and report on these efforts.

REVIEW ADDRESSED RECRUITMENT, HIRING AND DEVELOPMENT, ALONG WITH WORKPLACE ENVIRONMENT

Recruitment and Hiring

Texaco's global competitiveness depends, first and foremost, on its ability to attract and retain a highly capable workforce that reflects the diverse talents of its competitive marketplace throughout its organization. To help achieve this goal, Texaco will in 1997:

Enhance the interviewing, selection and hiring skills of its managers, in order to better enable them to identify and bring to Texaco the best possible and most capable candidates to help the company reach its operating goals;

Expand its overall college recruitment so that the company can draw upon a broader talent pool;

Use search firms that have a demonstrated record of recruiting from a wide, diverse range of men and women with key competencies for Texaco; and

Undertake, as previously announced, a new, nationwide scholarship and internship program in partnership with INROADS Inc. to develop minority students for management careers in disciplines important to Texaco, such as engineering, the physical sciences, information systems and international business.

Through its previous efforts to improve performance by diversifying its workforce, Texaco increased total minority employment from 16 percent in 1991 to 23 percent today. As part of its effort to enhance its marketplace competitiveness through the implementation of the above programs, the company expects that it will reach a level of 29 percent by the end of the year 2000. Also by that time, Texaco expects that its African-American employment will increase from 9 percent to 13 percent of total employment, and employment of women from 32 percent to 35 percent. These increases will take place in the context of modest overall employment growth during this period.

Retention and Career Development

Texaco believes it can continue to enhance its performance and lower its costs by strengthening career development and promoting the retention of employees. A series of enhanced and new programs will be implemented by mid-1997, under which the company will:

Develop and implement a new set of core skill and behavior standards required of managers to help ensure that leaders are able to maximize the performance of their teams over the long term;

Establish a mentoring process that will link managers and senior professionals with aspiring employees to provide them with feedback and advice on career success; and Enhance its global succession planning system to improve the identification, selection and development of individuals from all sources using a dynamic, rigorous, and disciplined approach.

These programs will provide managers and supervisors with the information and improved skills they need to ensure that promotions are fair and equitable throughout the company.

Workplace Initiatives

Texaco will launch several programs by mid-1997 that will enhance the efficiency of its team-based approach and, as a result, help reduce cycle times and improve productivity. They will do so by creating a more open and inclusive environment, which will promote better understanding, cooperation and teamwork among all employees. The company will seek to:

Implement a redesigned diversity learning experience, launched last year for Texaco managers and supervisors, to encompass all U.S.-based employees. This experience will help all employees evaluate interpersonal skills and behaviors, especially in a more diverse environment, and enable them to communicate and cooperate more effectively;

Ensure that the decisions of Human Resource Committees are aligned as closely as possible with the company's broadened business imperatives by including women and minorities on all such Committees throughout the company;

Introduce a comprehensive, core learning program to support all Texaco managers and supervisors with improved skill and knowledge in change management, selecting and developing a world class team, communicating and coaching; and

Implement an Alternative Dispute Resolution process to include mediation and arbitration, and introduce an ombuds program in which employees may also make use of a confidential outside counselor—both of which should help create a more positive, productive work environment.

Accountability and Oversight

Texaco is committed to achieving its immediate and long-term goals and will continue to hold all employees, especially managers and senior executives, responsible for the success of these programs. The company will establish rigorous reporting structures to increase accountability and also will:

Expand the company's 360-degree feedback process for 1997 to include all managers and supervisors. The employees, peers and supervisor of each manager will complete a confidential questionnaire annually to help evaluate how well that manager demonstrates expected leadership behavior;

Revise further the company's performance evaluation system to ensure alignment between individual and organizational goals, and more closely link managers' compensation to their performance in creating openness and inclusion in the workplace as a means of fostering improved team performance; and

Redesign the company's employee opinion survey, to be conducted annually beginning in 1997, to help managers and teams improve overall performance and monitor the success of Texaco's change efforts.

TEXACO TO EXPAND BUSINESS PARTNERING EFFORTS

Texaco believes that, by broadening its base of vendors and suppliers of services, it will be able to draw upon additional resources that will contribute to the company's competitive position. The company noted that the accelerated and expanded programs being implemented at this point in its review process are consistent with its existing business plans, are expected to help the company achieve or exceed its goals, and will not negatively impact profitability.

The review identified the following areas in which the company will strengthen its business partnering efforts:

Purchasing, Contracting and Services

Texaco's goal is to increase its overall purchasing activities with minority- and women-owned businesses, including providers of professional services, from $135 million in 1996 to a cumulative total of more than $1 billion over the next five years, with the expectation that it will reach at least 6 percent. The program to accelerate purchasing activities is already underway and will encompass the following areas:

> Expanding the scope and focus of programs with minority- and women-owned vendors, suppliers, engineering and construction firms, environmental remediation companies and sub-contractors; and

> Increasing the amount of work Texaco does with minority- and women-owned professional service firms in the areas of law, advertising, accounting, tax, government and public relations. Texaco also intends to increase its use of women and minority professionals at other firms. In addition, the company has already started to contract with minority-owned advertising agencies, and this program will be expanded in 1997.

Finance

In order to broaden the range of its financial relationships, the company will seek to increase financial activities with minority- and women-owned banks and money managers from $32 million to $200 million.

> Texaco is already increasing the number of women and minority banks with which it does business from 21 to 50 and increasing deposits in those banks. Texaco will work to expand its use of other banking services with minority- and women-owned financial firms in key marketplaces.

> Texaco will increase the number of women and minority fixed-income and equity managers of its pension fund from 1 to 8, and the funds under management will increase from $31 million to $186 million, or 13 percent of the fund.

> Texaco intends to increase its involvement with minority and women businesses by investing $10 million in 1997 in a minority-managed domestic emerging market fund investing in such companies.

Insurance

Texaco will increase insurance coverage from minority- and women-owned insurance companies from $25 million to $200 million. Texaco will seek women- and minority-owned companies to write property and liability coverage for contractors.

IMPROVING RETAIL PERFORMANCE IN A DIVERSE MARKETPLACE

Texaco's wholesale and retail operations must be responsive to the shifting demands of the marketplace. The company will accelerate its program to diversify wholesalers/retailers in key markets. These efforts include:

Wholesalers: Texaco's goal is to double the number of minority- and women-owned wholesaler marketers from 43 to 85 (from 5.5 percent to over 11 percent) within a five-year period. The company also plans to encourage wholesalers to maintain the number of minority and women retail operators at the current level of at least 20 percent of their more than 10,000 retail outlets and to increase the number of under-represented minority retail operators.

Independent/Lessee Retailers: Texaco will work to maintain women and minority independent retail owner and lessee operators at the current level of at least 45 percent of retail outlets in this category. Within five years, it will work to more than triple African-American-owned retail outlets from 35 to 117 (from 2 percent to 6 percent of the total).

Texaco Owned/Operated Outlets: Texaco will work to maintain its current level of at least 70 percent of minority and women managers at company-owned and -operated retail outlets, and will seek to increase its under-represented minority retail and store managers from 67 to 100 (7.4 percent to 12 percent of the total).

Lubricants: Texaco will strive to double the number of minority- and women-owned lubricant distributors from 29 to 58 (from 4.5 percent to 9 percent of the total), and to double the number of lube outlets from 52 to 104 (from 8.7 percent to 17 percent of the total).

Financing: The company will make available financing support for the development and expansion of minority and women wholesale marketers and retailers, as set forth in Texaco's goals. This financing will also support the development of Texaco-owned or Texaco-branded retail outlets in urban core areas. The company will assist minority entrepreneurs in the start up of business operations for branded outlets in these areas, which represent under-developed opportunities for business expansion.

Community Programs

Texaco has long recognized and acted upon the critical importance of local community outreach and support, and has in particular established a strong record of local volunteerism by its employees. Texaco will evaluate in the coming months its level of support for all programs, including women and minority organizations, that complement its business focus and further promote community improvements.

Source: http://www.texaco.com/compinfo/diversity/diversity_main.htm

EXHIBIT 5

Polishing the Star

As part of its settlement of a discrimination lawsuit brought by black employees, Texaco has moved on a half-dozen fronts to alter its business practices.

Hiring. Asked search firms to identify wider arrays of candidates. Expanded recruiting at historically minority colleges. Gave 50 scholarships and paid internships to minority students seeking engineering or technical degrees.

Career Advancement. Wrote objective standards for promotions. Developing training program for new managers. Developing a mentoring program.

Diversity Initiatives. Conducted two-day diversity training for more than 8,000 of 20,000 U.S. employees. Tied management bonuses to diversity goals. Developing alternative dispute resolution and ombudsman programs.

Purchasing. Nearly doubled purchases from minority- or women-owned businesses. Asking suppliers to report their purchases from such companies.

Financial Services. Substantially increased banking, investment management, and insurance business with minority- and women-owned firms. A group of such firms underwrote a $150 million public financing.

Retailing. Added three black independent retailer, 18 black managers of company-owned service stations, 12 minority or female wholesalers, 13 minority- or women-owned Xpress Lube outlets, and 6 minority- or women-owned lubricant distributions.

Source: Adam Bryant, "How Much Has Texaco Changed?" *The New York Times*, November 1997.

Case Study: *Denny's Restaurants*

Creating a Diverse Corporate Culture (A)

On the morning of February 5, 1995, Jim Adamson walked into the corporate headquarters of Flagstar Companies (renamed Advantica Restaurant Group in 1998) in Spartanburg, South Carolina. As Flagstar's newly hired CEO, he was responsible for the future of the firm—a future

Source: This case was written by Research Assistants M. Jennifer Abes, W. Brent Chism, and Thomas F. Sheeran under the direction of James S. O'Rourke, Concurrent Professor of Management, as the basis for class discussion rather than to illustrate either effective or in effective handling of an administrative situation. Information was gathered from corporate as well as public sources.

he knew would be difficult. After a series of recent events, Adamson knew that Flagstar was in need of serious change. His predecessor, Jerry Richardson, struggled to keep the company alive with $2.3 billion in debt from a series of restructuring attempts in the 1980s. Despite his attempts, the company lost money for five consecutive years from 1989 to 1994.

Adamson also had to consider the issue of discrimination. Flagstar was the parent company of Denny's restaurants, a chain that had become a symbol for racism in the United States. He also had some serious questions about the firm he had just taken charge of. Would he be able to improve the financial performance of the firm? Could he begin to change the pervasive culture throughout the firm that had allowed these events to take place? As he sat at his new desk, Adamson began reviewing the challenges he faced.

April Fool's Day

On April 1, 1993, a group of 21 uniformed United States Secret Service agents stopped at a Denny's Restaurant not far from the Andrews Air Force Base in Annapolis, Maryland. They had a free hour before their detail would assemble and had decided to stop for breakfast. Of the 21 men, seven were African-American. Six of them—Alfonso Dyson, Melvin Fowlkes, Merrill Hodge, Joseph James, Leroy Snyder, and Robin Thompson—sat at a table together. The other 15 agents sat elsewhere.

Many of the agents ordered the All-You-Can-Eat breakfast, a menu feature allowing a customer to choose five items from the menu and eat all he wanted for one price. After 30 minutes, however, the table of black officers had still not been served any food, while the other officers were already eating. Robin Thompson asked their server twice about their meals, but was told to wait. William Winans, a white officer who was sitting nearby, noticed that the server had made a face and rolled her eyes as she left the table. After 45 minutes had passed, the black officers noticed that customers who entered half an hour after they had arrived were already served their meals. Further, their fellow officers were being served second helpings. At this point, Thompson asked to see the restaurant manager.

Given that the group was on a tight schedule, James Sobers, the agents' supervisor, advised that they should file a complaint against the restaurant. When the restaurant manager approached them, the agents asked for his name and the address of the Denny's regional management office. The manager, who did not seem to understand English, only provided them with the address of the restaurant itself.

Alfonso Dyson stated later, "I didn't want to believe it was discrimination. But I couldn't think of what else it would be."[1] The six Secret Service agents, soon after the incident, filed a class action race-discrimination lawsuit against Denny's.

Events That Followed

Some three weeks later, on April 24, 1993, the company released a statement from corporate headquarters regarding the event, stating that after an on-site investigation of the incident, the manager involved was terminated. They also stated their commitment to further investigation of the incident and the elimination of any possible racial discrimination.

The incident involving the Secret Service agents was far from a one-time occurrence. Rather, discrimination against minorities was pervasive throughout the Denny's culture. Discrimination had been previously reported, even before any lawsuits were filed. This incident, however, triggered a growing number of customer complaints and subsequent lawsuits.

Denny's had become, in the words of Jim Adamson, "a poster child for racism."[2] One law firm, Saperstein Mayeda, even ran advertisements targeted at minorities, inviting those who thought they had been discriminated against at any Denny's restaurant to contact the firm for information. This led to a strong, negative public image for Denny's and more plaintiffs. Also contributing to negative publicity was the fact that another, similar class-action lawsuit had been filed by a group of young African Americans who were asked to prepay at a Denny's restaurant in California. Ironically, the lawsuit had been settled the same day that this incident had occurred.

Jerry Richardson, CEO of Flagstar companies at the time, quickly settled both lawsuits. By December 1995, Denny's had paid $54 million to 294,000 customers and their lawyers, the largest public accommodations settlement ever.[3] Denny's was forced to sign a consent decree with the U.S. Justice Department, which mandated that Denny's restaurants publicize its nondiscriminatory policies and train employees about diversity issues. Further, a civil rights monitor was assigned to keep tabs on all 1,721 existing restaurants, as well as any future restaurants, for the next seven years.

Flagstar Companies: Corporate History

In 1961, Jerry Richardson, former wide receiver for the Baltimore Colts, and Charles Bradshaw, his college football teammate, bought the first Hardee's franchise in Spartanburg, South Carolina. By 1969, they grew their franchise into Spartan Food Systems and went public. In 1979, a conglomerate, TransWorld Corporation, acquired the company. Bradshaw chose to leave the company while Richardson decided to stay on and run his division. In 1986, TransWorld spun off many of its nonfood related investments and renamed itself TW Services. The following year, TW Services purchased Denny's restaurants, along with El Pollo Loco, a chain of grilled-chicken restaurants, and Richardson became president of the food service company. (In an effort to centralize overall company operations, Denny's corporate headquarters was moved from Irvine, California, to Spartanburg in 1991.) In 1989, the company took on a huge debt as a result of a hostile takeover by the private equity firm of Gollust, Tierney, & Oliver. In 1992, Kohlberg, Kravis, Roberts & Co. (KKR), rescued the company by investing $300 million of equity to restructure its debt. This investment gave them control of the company, and a new name in 1993: Flagstar Companies.

Flagstar Companies: Key Leaders

Jerry Richardson, CEO of Flagstar, had mishandled several financial and racial issues during his tenure. In 1990, before any racial issues were publicized, Richardson had hired a consulting firm, Synetics, to help Flagstar [devise] a strategy to mold the company into a top-rank food service organization. Following a series of employee focus groups, Synetics' initial observations focused on a lack of diversity within the company. Despite being warned that the firm was in a dangerous position, Richardson saw no urgency to make any changes. His response to Synetics was, "I'm sure you're right about our being behind on diversity, but I never thought about it."[4] When racial problems first arose, Richardson and his management team wrote them off as isolated incidents.

Despite such neglect, Richardson grew Flagstar under his leadership into a $3 billion company, and made Denny's restaurants the nation's largest, best-known family restaurant chain. His goal was to make Flagstar the best food service company in the world by the year 2000. After a 33-year career in the restaurant business, however, Richardson resigned as Chairman of the Board and Director of Flagstar Companies. After relinquishing his Chief Executive title, Richardson turned his attention to the Carolina Panthers, a National Football League team that he owned. The majority owner of the Flagstar Companies, KKR, recruited Jim Adamson from Burger King to replace Richardson as CEO of Denny's parent company. Within months after the Secret Service agent incident, Adamson hired Ron Petty, former head of Burger King USA, as CEO of Denny's to manage the chain's transformation.[5]

Jim Adamson's personal history was a good fit for the job as Flagstar's new CEO. After growing up in the racially mixed environment of Army bases around the world and in the neighborhoods of Washington, D.C., and Oahu, Hawaii, Adamson was sensitive to acts of racial discrimination. Because of that background, Adamson would be certain not to tolerate them at Flagstar. He had developed a reputation as a calm and approachable leader. A former boss once noted that because of his sincerity, Adamson's team was devoted to him.

Racism within Flagstar

By the early 1990s, racial issues were still common to Flagstar. Many communities in California had already begun to complain about the treatment they had received at Denny's restaurants. Further, the U.S. Department of Justice had begun looking into charges that Denny's demonstrated a pattern of discrimination against customers who were African-American. In fact, Richardson, who was chairman of Flagstar at the time, had begun talking with local NAACP members as early as January of 1992 to find ways to respond to the challenge of diversifying the company.[6]

Although there had never been a deliberate corporate policy advocating discrimination, top executives of Flagstar did not pay much attention to what was happening in their restaurants. Their ignorance allowed many restaurant managers to set their own racist policies. Some managers asked African American diners to show identification before being served, requested that they pay before food arrived, and forced them to wait interminably for their meals.[7] Some were even known for ordering "blackouts," a situation in which employees were directed to lock patrons out of the restaurant.

Flagstar was insensitive to minority business people, as well. Samuel Maw, Flagstar's executive vice president and chief procurement officer, claimed that it was extremely difficult to find minority vendors. Minority vendors who called on Denny's, however, claimed they were ignored by the company's buyers.

Key External Factors

Because of the nature of race relations in the United States, any organization that participates or is accused of discriminatory practices will face a number of external challenges, including unwanted press attention, lawsuits, and scrutiny from organizations such as the National Association for the Advancement of Colored People (NAACP) and People United to Save Humanity (PUSH). Denny's faced such a situation on April 1, 1993. The same day that the firm settled a federal discrimination lawsuit, a Denny's restaurant in Maryland refused to serve six African-American Secret Service agents while their white counterparts were served. Because of this incident and the company's checkered past, Adamson knew that Denny's was at a crossroads. He had to fix this or risk losing the company.

During this latest crisis, Denny's endured relentless press coverage of not only the current racial incident involving the six Secret Service agents but also its history of nationwide discrimination. The media coverage included a press conference with the six agents, interviews with disgruntled employees, and other angry former customers. Closely following the media coverage was a class action lawsuit and additional scrutiny from organizations such as the NAACP, PUSH, and the Southern Christian Leadership Conference (SCLC). The class action lawsuit helped prolong damage from the racial problems at Denny's and its parent company. Additionally, these activist groups began using Denny's to help promote their own agendas and organize boycotts of the restaurants. Adamson knew those groups, well intentioned though they may have been, would have the potential to damage to the long-term growth of a firm more than any lawsuit.

Can Denny's Hit a Grand Slam?

Adamson stood up and walked to the window. It would take an enormous amount of hard work, innovation, and commitment to turn this company around. Many stakeholders were involved. Could he satisfy each of their needs? Denny's current strategy was somewhat low-key and focused principally on internal change. Would this strategy work to resurrect Denny's name?

Discussion Questions

1. As Jim Adamson, what would your managerial approach be in this sensitive situation?
2. List key issues for Jim Adamson to address at this point.
3. How does a company categorize discrimination in order to create an effective corporate policy for diversity in the workplace?
4. How can Adamson and Flagstar Companies effect change and sustain that change in the corporate culture?
5. How can they manage diversity throughout the organization?
6. Is a strong communication campaign needed to ensure the public of Denny's commitment to diversity or is a more subtle approach needed?
7. How can Flagstar Companies go about reaching the public with their message of diversity?
8. How should Adamson respond to the special interest groups?

Notes

1. Jim Adamson, *The Denny's Story* (New York, 2000), 8–9.
2. Ibid., 9.
3. Faye Rice, "Denny's Changes Its Spots," *Fortune*, 1996.
4. Ibid., 4.
5. Adamson, *The Denny's Story*, 20.
6. Ibid., 14.
7. Segal, David, "Denny's Serves Up A Sensitive Image," *Washington Post*, July 4, 1999, E1.

Case Study: *Denny's Restaurants*

Creating a Diverse Corporate Culture (B)

Diversity Initiatives

Under Jim Adamson's leadership, the new management team wasted no time re-educating the entire family of Flagstar restaurants on the importance of making the company, "a better place for women and minorities."[1] Adamson reinforced this re-education initiative in November of 1995 by promising, "If you discriminate, I'm going to fire you."[2] Under this new philosophy, nine out of the twelve top managers at Flagstar chose to leave the company. Of the nine replacements, one was an Hispanic man and the other an African-American woman.

In addition to new hiring practices, the management team devised a four-part strategy to introduce cultural diversity to the company. The new strategy included steps designed, "to loosen up the hierarchical environment; make diversity a performance criterion for all managers; require the entire staff to attend workshops on racial sensitivity; and never miss an opportunity to preach the gospel of diversity."[3] Aside from the personnel and policy changes, Adamson used other methods to symbolize the changes at Flagstar by declaring Martin Luther King's birthday a company holiday. Although this additional holiday was met with anger and resistance by some within the organization, it sent a strong message to the headquarters about diversity.[4] These new policies were constantly reinforced through open and honest communication between management and the entire organization.

To further convince the public of Denny's turnaround, top management required all Denny's locations to display a toll-free number (1-800-827-9315) so that customers could report incidents if they felt they had been discriminated against. The company also developed an image polishing campaign which included radio and TV commercials, magazine advertisements, and purchased television time for a documentary titled, "The Denny's Turnaround." The company began to sponsor minority-related events, such as the *Soul Train 25th Anniversary Special*, as well as national charities, such as Save the Children.

People

Adamson could not have implemented these policies and achieved necessary change by himself. He knew that in order to change the company's policies and culture he would have to change the

---

Source: This case was written by Research Assistants M. Jennifer Abes, W. Brent Chism, and Thomas F. Sheeran under the direction of James S. O'Rourke, Concurrent Professor of Management, as the basis for class discussion rather than to illustrate either effective or in effective handling of an administrative situation. Information was gathered from corporate as well as public sources.

leadership at the various Flagstar divisions. He also needed an internal champion to oversee the entire diversity effort and help make the changes in company policies into reality. Adamson selected a former colleague from Burger King, Ray Hood-Phillips. Based on her success in helping Burger King become a more diverse company, Adamson knew she would be well suited to the job, so he appointed her to be the company's Chief Diversity Officer. Hood-Phillips worked on diversity training, new purchasing contracts, marketing, franchising, and performance evaluations. Adamson gave credit to her dedication and tenacity in helping to implement the new policies at Flagstar, and believed it would be her continued dedication that would change the culture.

Results

The result of these internal changes at Denny's has been a drastic change in the company's image (see Exhibit 1, "Advantica Restaurant Group Under Adamson's Leadership.") Following the changes, Adamson received the 1996 CEO of the Year Award from the NAACP for his work at Flagstar. These positive results continued with a *CBS 60 Minutes* story in 1998 and Denny's being named number one on *Fortune's* "50 Best Companies for Minorities" in 2000.

Next Steps

Even after all of the praise and awards that the new Advantica Restaurant Group and Denny's had received, the management team's job was not yet done. Adamson also had to fix the firm's financial problems. Company profits had been lagging due to increased pressures in the family dining segment of the industry, arising principally from competition with traditional fast-food restaurants on one end and casual dining chains on the other.

Additionally, the firm had to contend with a large debt load, placing a severe burden on cash flow.[5] Further, the fight against racial discrimination was not over. Adamson and his management team would have to continue their work to make changes within the corporate culture permanent.

Discussion Questions

1. Has Jim Adamson been successful in changing the corporate culture at Advantica?
2. How effective is the diversity strategy Advantica has put in place?
3. Do their efforts get to the core problems at Advantica?
4. What are the other major challenges facing the financial future of Advantica?
5. What other avenues of communication could be used to demonstrate the new corporate culture of diversity?

Notes

1. Faye Rice, "Denny's Changes Its Spots," *Fortune*, 1996.
2. Del Jones, "Denny's Strives to Eliminate Racist Elements," *USA Today*, November 2, 1995, 1A.
3. Faye, "Denny's Changes Its Spots."
4. Adamson, Jim, *The Denny's Story: How a Company in Crisis Resurrected Its Good Name* (New York, NY: John Wiley & Sons, Inc., 2000).
5. Faye, "Denny's Changes Its Spots."

EXHIBIT 1

Advantica Restaurant Group Under Adamson's Leadership

- Parent company renamed to Advantica—suggested by employees—to incorporate the words "advantage" and "America."
- Of 823 Denny's franchises, 309 people of color are owners.
- Denny's does over $125 million in business with minority suppliers each year.
- Every Denny's employee, from servers to security officers to managers, receives specific sensitivity training that emphasizes respect for differences among people—all employees acknowledge in writing that they understand the discrimination policy.
- Denny's current Board of Directors is composed of 36% people of color (3 people of color and one Hispanic out of 12).
- At Senior Management level, 27% are women and people of color.
- For two consecutive years, *Fortune* magazine ranked Denny's among the top ten companies for minorities in the US. By 2000, Advantica was #1 on that list.

CHAPTER 6

Age

The focus of this chapter is the age group protected by the Age Discrimination in Employment Act of 1967 (ADEA): workers age 40 and over. Although the focus of this chapter is older workers, it is important to recognize that other people of a wide range of ages may be discriminated against because of their age, for example, younger workers or women in their childbearing years.

Objectives

- To examine the relationship between older workers and the workplace.
- To examine the impact of the baby-boomer generation on the workplace.
- To examine flexible organizational models that help keep talented older workers working productively for longer periods of time.
- To examine how age discrimination can emerge as the result of a highly aggressive diversity plan that prioritizes other primary dimensions of diversity.

Preview Questions

- Does society need to rethink the traditional notion of retirement?
- What strategies can managers implement in an effort to manage effectively their older employees?
- Can employing older workers provide a competitive advantage? Substantiate your views.

Some Important Dates

1903 The state of Colorado passes legislation specifying that no employer may discharge anyone between the ages of 18 and 60 because of his or her age.

1958 Age is added to the New York State statute barring discrimination in employment.

1967 Congress passes the Age Discrimination in Employment Act of 1967 (ADEA) protecting individuals who are between 40 and 65 years of age from discrimination in employment.

1989 Congress eliminates mandatory retirement at age 70 or any other age.

1990 Older Workers Benefit Protection Act becomes law. It bans employers from denying benefits to older employees because of age, unless the cost of providing the benefits can be shown to increase with age.

1996 In *O'Connor v. Consolidated Coin Caterers Corp.*, the U.S. Supreme Court rules that ADEA does not require a fired worker to show that he or she was replaced by someone under 40 to prove age discrimination.

2000   In *Kimel v. State of Florida Board of Regents*, the high court rules that state government agencies are protected by the Constitution from being sued for money damages under the ADEA.

Many Workers Ages 50+ Downshift in New Jobs—And Love the Work

Washington, DC—A new AARP long-term study shows that many workers ages 50 and over (26.9 percent of those surveyed) switch jobs and employers, and in the process often take pay cuts, give up pension and health care benefits, and face loss of managerial duties.

But many of the 1,705 workers surveyed over a 14 year period beginning in 1992 also said they dealt with less stress and enjoyed flexible work schedules in their new jobs.

And, apparently as a result, a staggering 91.3 percent of those surveyed said they enjoyed their work, an increase from the 79 percent who said they liked their work in their old jobs.

"Many older workers are ready to give up the long-time grind, and look for stimulating jobs with flexible schedules as they begin the process toward retirement," said Susan Reinhard, Senior Vice President of the AARP Public Policy Institute, today in releasing the new report. "The study shows dramatically that workers are putting a premium on reduced stress as they downshift a bit."

"The current downturn presents a real bump in the road," Reinhard added, "but, for the future, the findings are a welcome signal that workers 50 and over can really enjoy themselves while remaining productive in a vibrant economy."

The new study was conducted for the AARP Public Policy Institute by The Urban Institute of Washington, and is titled: "Older workers on the Move: Recareering in Later Life."

The AARP analysis is one of the most comprehensive ever undertaken on late-career change in the 50+ cohort. It also stands out in that much of the previous research done on older career change focuses on what the report refers to as "upward occupational mobility, based on the assumption that people change their line of work to move into better-paying jobs."

The study evaluates data compiled by the Health and Retirement Study (HRS) from 1992 to 2006. Designed by the University of Michigan for the National Institute on Aging, the HRS is a nationally representative long-term study that includes periodic interviews. The analysis tracks a sample of workers who were ages 51 to 55 in 1992 until 2006, when they were ages 65 to 69.

For this analysis, recareering involves a move to a new employer in a different occupation. (Terms such as "occupational change" and "career change" are used interchangeably with "recareering.") An individual who took a new job with his current employer was not then considered a recareerer.

Those who became self-employed in their new job are included in the study. And the number who did so skyrocketed, based on the sample: 23.6 percent were self-employed in their new jobs, as opposed to only 11.5 percent in their old jobs.

The study also found that 50+ career change is more common among men than women because women are less likely than men to continue working if they leave an employer at that age. The statistic for men recareering is 28.8 percent; 24.3 percent of older women made a career change, according to the survey.

Here are some other highlights of the study for both women and men:

- The median hourly wage (in 2007 dollars) fell in the new job to $10.86 from $16.86 in the old job.
- Employer-sponsored pensions covered 19.9 per cent in the new job, compared to 61.4 percent in the old job.
- Employer-sponsored health insurance covered 55.8 percent in the new job, compared to 69.6 percent in the old job.
- Pay and promotion decisions (managerial duties) were performed by 14.4 percent of the workers in the new job, contrasted with 22.3 percent in the old job.

(continued)

On the other hand, there are these findings:

- Only 36.3 percent of those surveyed reported stressful work conditions in the new job, a sharp drop from 64.7 percent in the old job.
- A large group—45.1 percent—said that they had a flexible work schedule in the new job, as opposed to 27 percent in the old job.

All in all, after outlining what some might view as positives and negatives of new jobs, the report found that an astounding 9l.3 percent said they enjoyed their work, up from 79 percent in the old job.

The report is available at www.aarp.org/ppi.

AARP is a nonprofit, nonpartisan membership organization that helps people 50+ have independence, choice and control in ways that are beneficial and affordable to them and society as a whole. AARP does not endorse candidates for public office or make contributions to either political campaigns or candidates. We produce *AARP The Magazine*, the definitive voice for 50+ Americans and the world's largest-circulation magazine with over 34.5 million readers; *AARP Bulletin*, the go-to news source for AARP's 40 million members and Americans 50+; *AARP Segunda Juventud*, the only bilingual U.S. publication dedicated exclusively to the 50+ Hispanic community; and our website, AARP.org. AARP Foundation is an affiliated charity that provides security, protection, and empowerment to older persons in need with support from thousands of volunteers, donors, and sponsors. We have staffed offices in all 50 states, the District of Columbia, Puerto Rico, and the U.S. Virgin Islands.

Source: AARP, "Many Workers Ages 50+ Downshift in New Jobs—and Love the Work," May 7, 2009, http://www.aarp.org/aarp/presscenter/pressrelease/articles/Recareering_Study.html

ESSAY: IT'S TIME TO RETIRE RETIREMENT

In the past few years, companies have been so focused on downsizing to contain costs that they've largely neglected a looming threat to their competitiveness, the likes of which they have never before experienced: a severe shortage of talented workers. The general population is aging and, with it, the labor pool. People are living longer, healthier lives, and the birthrate is at a historic low. While the ranks of the youngest workers (ages 16–24, according to Bureau of Labor

Ken Dychtwald is the founding president and CEO of Age Wave, a San Francisco–based think tank and consulting firm focused on the maturing marketplace and workforce. A psychologist, gerontologist, and adviser to business and government, he is the author of 10 books, including *Age Wave* (J. P. Tarcher, 1989) and his latest book *Age Power* (J. P. Tarcher, 1999). Tamara Erickson is an executive officer and member of the board of directors for the Concours Group, a management consulting, research, and education firm based in Kingwood, Texas. Bob Morison is an executive vice president and the director of research of the Concours Group. Dychtwald, Erickson, and Morison are coauthors of a book about the impact of demographic shifts on the workplace (Harvard Business School Press, 2005). They can be reached at kdychtwald@agewave.com, tjerickson@concoursgroup.com, and rfmorison@concoursgroup.com.

About the Research

Our yearlong research project, "Demography is Destiny," concluded in the fall of 2003 and was conducted by the Concours Group in partnership with Ken Dychtwald and Age Wave. Sponsored by 30 major public and private organizations in North America and Europe, the project explored the emerging business challenges presented by workforce aging and other profound shifts in workforce demographics. On the basis of our findings, we developed a series of management actions and pragmatic techniques for anticipating, coping with, and capitalizing on those changes. Member organizations shaped the focus and direction of the project, shared their experiences as part of the field research, and participated in a series of workshops. (For a management summary of our research findings, see http://www.concoursgroup.com/Demography/DD_MgmtSumm.pdf.)

Statistics groupings) are growing 15 percent this decade as baby boomers' children enter the workforce, the 25-to 34-year-old segment is growing at just half that rate, and the workforce population between the ages of 35 and 44—the prime executive-development years—is actually declining.

In the United States, the overall rate of workforce growth faces a sharp drop. After peaking at nearly 30 percent in the 1970s (as the baby boomers as well as unprecedented numbers of women entered the workforce), and holding relatively steady at 12 percent during the 1990s and again in the present decade, the rate is projected to drop and level off at 2 percent to 3 percent per decade thereafter. That translates into an annual growth rate of less than 1 percent today and an anemic 0.2 percent by 2020. Meanwhile, age distributions are shifting dramatically. The proportion of workers over 55 declined from 18 percent in the 1970s to under 11 percent in 2000—but it's projected to rebound to 20 percent by 2015. In other words, we've recently passed what will prove to be a historic low in the concentration of older workers. Just when we've gotten accustomed to having relatively few mature workers around, we have to start learning how to attract and retain far more of them.

During the next 15 years, 80 percent of the native-born workforce growth in North America—and even more so in much of Western Europe—is going to be in the over-50 cohort. In the next decade or so, when baby boomers—the 76 million people born between 1946 and 1964, more than one-quarter of all Americans—start hitting their sixties and contemplating retirement, there won't be nearly enough young people entering the workforce to compensate for the exodus. The Bureau of Labor Statistics projects a shortfall of 10 million workers in the United States in 2010, and in countries where the birthrate is well below the population replacement level (particularly in Western Europe), the shortage will hit sooner, be more severe, and remain chronic.

The problem won't just be a lack of bodies. Skills, knowledge, experience, and relationships walk out the door every time somebody retires—and they take time and money to replace. Given the inevitable time lag between the demand for skills and the ability of the educational system to provide them, we'll see a particularly pronounced skill shortage in fast-growing technical fields such as health care. What's more, employees are your face to the marketplace. It's good business to have employees who reflect the ethnic, gender, and, yes, age composition of your customer base—especially when those customers are well off. Baby boomers will be the most financially powerful generation of mature consumers ever; today's mature adults control more than $7 trillion in wealth in the United States—70 percent of the total. As the population at large ages, and ever-more spending power is concentrated in the hands of older customers, companies will want to show a mature face to their clientele—and yet those faces will be in high demand.

The problem is pretty clear. Workers will be harder to come by. Tacit knowledge will melt steadily away from your organization. And the most dramatic shortage of workers will hit the age group associated with leadership and key customer-facing positions. The good news is that a solution is at hand: Just as companies are learning to market to an aging population, so they can also learn to attract and employ older workers.

And yet, despite irrefutable evidence of workforce aging, many managers may be marching their companies straight off a demographic cliff. According to a recent survey from the Society for Human Resource Management, two-thirds of U.S. employers don't actively recruit older workers. Furthermore, more than half do not actively attempt to retain key ones; 80 percent do not offer any special provisions (such as flexible work arrangements) to appeal to the concerns of mature workers; and 60 percent of CEOs say their companies don't account for workforce aging in their long-term business plans. Instead, relying on the mistaken assumption that the future will be populated by a growing pool of talented and loyal young workers, companies are systemically offering older workers the "package" and skimming people out of the labor force from the top age brackets down.

Little wonder that baby boomers and "mature" workers (those 55 and above) are feeling little loyalty to their current employers. These employees are bottlenecked, with too many people competing for too few leadership positions. They're distrustful, fearful, and defensive, knowing that they're "too old" to easily find work elsewhere and likely to be pushed out before the "official" retirement age. They're struggling to update their skills, and they're feeling burned out after 30-plus years on the job. Meanwhile, they stand back and watch as recruiting, training, and leadership development dollars, as well as promotion opportunities, are overwhelmingly directed at younger employees, with little thought to the skills and experience that the over-55 crowd can bring to bear on almost any business problem.

In short, most baby boomers want to continue working—and they may need to, for financial reasons—but they may not want to work for you. Twenty percent of those collecting employer pensions are still working in some capacity, and among people under 60 who are already collecting pensions, more than 50 percent are working. Among those age 55 and older who accepted early retirement offers, one-third have gone back to work. But these working retirees are more likely to be working part-time or be self-employed than their not-yet-retired counterparts—in other words, they're working on their own terms. That's increasingly where you'll need to meet these older workers if you want to gain access to their skills. As the labor market tightens, they will have more choices, and the most capable and accomplished among them are likely to be the most mobile and financially independent; they're the ones who are most likely to move on. The challenge is to find a way to reconnect with these employees before they're ready to take a retirement package and run—perhaps to a competitor.

We recently conducted a yearlong research project in which we looked at the implications for businesses of an aging workforce. Broadly speaking, our findings suggest an urgent need to find ways to attract and retain employees of all ages. But of most concern is the potentially debilitating mass retirement that threatens to starve many businesses of key talent in the next 10–15 years. On the basis of our research, we've concluded that the concept of retirement is outdated and should be put out to pasture in favor of a more flexible approach to ongoing work, one that serves both employer and employee. In this article, we'll describe how companies can retain the skills of employees well past the traditional age of retirement by moving from a rigid model where work ceases at a certain age to a more flexible one where employees can become lifelong contributors.

Create a Culture That Honors Experience

If companies are to win back the hearts and minds of baby boomers and other generations of mature workers, they need to start with the work environment itself, which has become increasingly alienating to anyone over the age of 50. Human resource practices are often explicitly or implicitly biased against older workers, and these biases can seep into the culture in a manner that makes them feel unwelcome.

It starts with recruiting, in subtle ways such as the choice of words in a job advertisement. Even high-energy, young-in-spirit older workers, for example, may interpret an ad stressing "energy," "fast pace," and "fresh thinking" as implicitly targeting younger workers and dismiss the opportunity out of hand. Mature workers are more likely to be attracted to ads emphasizing "experience," "knowledge," and "expertise."

Traditional recruiting channels such as want ads or help wanted signs may not attract older workers either. Twelve years ago, pharmacy chain CVS looked at national demographic trends and concluded that the company needed to employ a much greater number of older workers. But managers didn't know how to find them—older people shopped in the stores but didn't apply for openings, perhaps believing they wouldn't be hired. Now the company works through the National Council on Aging, city agencies, and community organizations to find and hire productive new employees.

Interviewing techniques can be unintentionally off-putting as well. Being left alone for half an hour to build something with Legos or being asked to perform the type of verbal gymnastics Microsoft became famous for in job interviews (e.g., how are M&Ms made?) may be daunting to candidates accustomed to a more traditional approach to demonstrating their skills. One major British bank realized that its psychometric and verbal-reasoning tests were intimidating to older candidates and replaced these tests with role-playing exercises to gauge candidates' ability to handle customers. And Nationwide, Britain's largest building society, has begun short-listing job candidates by telephone to reduce the number of applicants who are rejected because they look older.

Training and development activities also tend to favor younger employees. According to the Bureau of Labor Statistics, older workers (age 55 plus) receive on average less than half the

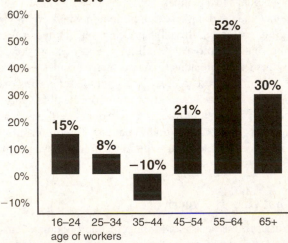

Growth in U.S. Workforce by Age 2000–2010

FIGURE 6-1   Who Will Run Your Company?
If we look at workforce growth rates by age segment, the patterns are dramatic. In the current decade, the ranks of youngest workers (ages 16–24, according to Bureau of Labor Statistics groupings) are growing by 15%, thanks to the "echo boom" as baby boomers' children enter the workforce. The 25–34-year-old segment is growing at just half that rate, and the workforce population between 35 and 44 years old is actually declining. With the baby-boom generation moving into middle age and its vanguard nearing retirement age, the fastest workforce growth rates are in the three oldest age segments.

amount of training that any of their younger cohorts receive, including workers in the 45–54 age range. One reason may be that they're reluctant to ask: As people well established in their careers and very busy on the job, they may not feel or want to admit the need for training and development. And yet many midcareer and older employees require refresher training in areas from information technology to functional disciplines to nonhierarchical management methods. The challenge is to make them feel as though it's not a sign of weakness to ask. At Dow Chemical, the companywide expectation is that employees at all levels will continue to learn and grow; as a result, employees regularly seek training and development opportunities, readying themselves for their next career moves.

Most important, mature workers will be attracted to a culture that values their experience and capabilities—an environment that can take some time and effort to build. The Aerospace Corporation is a company that has, over the years, built a reputation for valuing experience and knowledge. Nearly half of its 3,400 regular, full-time employees are over age 50—a clear signal to job candidates that experience is appreciated. CVS has made great strides in creating a company that is more welcoming to older employees, having more than doubled the percentage of employees over age 50 in the past 12 years. It has no mandatory retirement age, making it easy to join the company at an advanced age and stay indefinitely (six employees are in their nineties). The company boosts its age-friendly image through internal and external publications. Company and HR department newsletters highlight the productivity and effectiveness of older workers, and the company coproduces with a cosmetics company a senior-focused magazine that's called *In Step with Healthy Living*.

Older workers can see that CVS honors experience. A year ago, after taking a buyout package from his management job in a major drugstore chain, 59-year-old Jim Wing joined CVS as the pharmacy supervisor for the company's southern Ohio stores. What influenced his decision? "I'm too young to retire. [CVS] is willing to hire older people. They don't look at your age but your experience." Pharmacy technician Jean Penn, age 80, has worked in the business since 1942. She sold her own small pharmacy to CVS five years ago and began working in another CVS store the next day. She was recently given a 50-year pin. ("Turns out they don't make 60-year pins," she says.) By giving Penn credit for time served before she joined the company, CVS once again sent a strong signal about the value attached to experience.

Offer Flexible Work

While older employees won't sign on or stick around if the HR processes and culture aren't welcoming, the substance and arrangement of work are even more important. Companies need to design jobs such that staying on is more attractive than leaving. Many mature workers want to keep working but in a less time-consuming and pressured capacity so that they may pursue other interests. And many baby boomers have a direct and compelling need for flexibility to accommodate multiple commitments, such as caring for children and elderly parents at the same time. Flex work—flexible in both where and when work is performed, as well as flexibility in the traditional career path—can offer many attractions and rewards and appeal to employees' changing needs.

The concept of flexible work is not new, of course, and many companies offer it in some form—job sharing, telecommuting, compressed workweeks, and part-time schedules. But such programs are usually small in scale and, in practice, are often taken up by new mothers and others with consuming family commitments. What's more, the implicit bargain is often that employees who participate will see their careers suffer for it. Companies that have successful flex programs not only make these programs easily accessible to older workers but also structure them so that people who participate don't feel that they're being sidelined or overlooked for promotions—and so that participation leads to a win-win for employer and employee.

Look at ARO Incorporated, a business process outsourcer based in Kansas City, Missouri. Six years ago, its staff turnover was at 25 percent, which limited its productivity as an operator of contract call centers, back-office and forms processing, outbound customer interaction, and more. Kansas City hosts some 90 call centers, so employees had numerous other options, and the applicant pool was shallow.

Michael Amigoni, the company's chief operating officer, soon found a way to cut costs and improve service by upgrading the company's technology to allow some 100 teleworkers to remain off-site. He then actively recruited baby boomers, who were attracted to the flexibility, to fill these jobs. Employees were not permitted to do the work simultaneously with child care, elder care, or pet care, and company managers visited people's homes to make sure they had an appropriate working environment. While some younger workers signed on initially, the company found that these employees missed having an office community and largely dropped out.

Meanwhile, ARO gained access to a large pool of mature, experienced employees, who, on the whole, have stayed with the company longer than younger employees have. Turns out, they're also a much better match for the company's customer demographics. "ARO has clients in the insurance and financial services sectors, and a lot of the people we talk to are older," says Amigoni. "It helps that the people making the calls are older, because they are in similar circumstances to customers." For insurance companies, a lot of ARO's work is underwriting, which involves asking questions about health, among other things. It's useful to have workers who are facing some of the same health concerns—their own or perhaps their parents'—that their customers are. ARO has found that younger, entry-level workers cannot make these connections as easily. Turnover is now down to 7 percent, and productivity is up 15 percent, partly because the company now has more seasoned staff. To boot, the company was able to expand without having to move into a larger facility, which it didn't want to pay for.

Other companies offer flexibility in work assignments to reignite older employees who have come to find their jobs a bit stale—an approach that can be of particular value in appealing to highly paid managerial talent. For example, four years ago, Deloitte Consulting looked at the firm's demographics and realized that by 2003, 40 percent of its then 850 partners would be 50 or older and eligible to retire at 55. The firm didn't want to lose this talented group of men and women en masse, so it created what it called a Senior Leaders program, which enabled partners in their early fifties to redesign their career paths. (The program, along with a similar program at Deloitte's sister company, Deloitte & Touche, is currently on hold as the two companies reintegrate operations following last year's decision not to separate as planned.)

Here's how the Senior Leaders program worked: Each year, a 10-member global selection committee assessed candidates who had made a unique contribution to the firm and would continue to add significant value. The committee then sat down with each nominated employee to customize a second career with the firm, including flexible hours and work location, special projects, and the opportunity to engage in mentoring, research, training and development, company promotions, or global expansion. Deloitte still has about a dozen active senior leaders, most of whom opted for full-time work in their rejuvenated roles. The partner who launched the program told us: "The biggest surprise was the prestige the program gained. Being a senior leader became extremely prestigious both to the firm and to the clients."

Still other companies appeal to older workers' desire for flexibility by reducing hours in the years leading up to retirement. The reduced hours are an attractive option because it gives workers opportunities to pursue outside interests. At Varian, a leading provider of radiotherapy systems, employees age 55 and over who have a minimum of five years of service and who plan to retire within three years can negotiate a reduced work schedule. The typical arrangement is four days per week the first year and three days a week thereafter. Half-time is the minimum, and two half-timers can job share. Participants retain full medical and dental benefits and can request a return to full-time work if the new schedule results in economic hardship.

We are strong advocates of flexible work, in all the varieties described here, not only because it's a way to entice older workers to continue working but also because it forms the foundation of a flexible new approach to retirement, one that assumes people can continue to contribute in some way well into their "retirement" years.

Introduce Flexible Retirement

Flexible retirement is flexible work in the extreme—a logical extension of the flexible work models just described, where the work may continue indefinitely.

Retirement, as it's currently understood, is a recent phenomenon. For almost all of history, people worked until they dropped. It was only during the Great Depression that, desperate to make room in the workforce for young workers, governments, unions, and employers institutionalized retirement programs as we know them today, complete with social security and pension plans. When the modern notion of retirement was first articulated near the end of the nineteenth century, the designated retirement age of 65 was longer than the life expectancy at the time. Over the last 50 years, the average retirement age declined steadily; in the United States, Great Britain, and Canada, the average retirement age is currently around 62. Meanwhile, life expectancies have increased, leaving more years for leisure.

But in fact, many people don't want a life of pure leisure; half of today's retirees say they're bored and restless. A recent AARP/Roper Report survey found that 80 percent of baby boomers plan to work at least part-time during their retirement; just 16 percent say that they won't work at all. They're looking for different blends—three days a week, for example, or maybe six months a year. Many want or need the income, but that's not the only motivator. People tend to identify strongly with their work, their disciplines, and their careers. Many wish to learn, grow, try new things, and be productive indefinitely, through a combination of commercial, volunteer, and personal pursuits. They enjoy the sense of self-worth that comes with contributing to a business or other institution, and they enjoy the society of their peers. For some people, the workplace is their primary social affiliation.

For all these reasons, the notion of retirement as it is traditionally practiced—a onetime event that permanently divides work life from leisure—no longer makes sense. In its place, companies are starting to design models in which employees can continue to contribute in some fashion, to their own satisfaction and to the company's benefit. Some regulations currently restrict our vision of workers moving seamlessly in and out of flexible work arrangements without ever actually retiring. The IRS prohibits defined benefits plans from making distributions until employment ends or an employee reaches "normal" retirement age. And pension calculations often discourage people even from reducing their hours with a current employer prior to retirement because payouts are often determined by the rate of pay in the last few years of work. But a growing number of companies have found ways to call on the skills of retired employees for special purposes.

From the standpoint of the employee, these flex programs offer opportunities to mix work and other pursuits. They also offer personal fulfillment and growth, ongoing financial rewards, and continued enjoyment of the society of colleagues. For employers, the programs provide an elastic pool of staff on demand and an on-call cadre of experienced people who can work part-time as the business needs them. Recruiting and placement costs are close to zero because the business is already in contact with these workers, and training costs are minimal. They know the organization and the organization knows them; they fit in right away and are productive without ramp-up time. And they bring scarce skills and organizational knowledge that can't be matched by contractors unconnected with the organization.

Retirees can also act as leaders on demand. Corporations periodically face waves of executive retirements, and many have done a poor job of maintaining the leadership pipeline. A group of experienced executives who can step in at a moment's notice can both fill gaps and help bring the next generation of leaders up to speed.

Typically, these programs allow an employee to take regular retirement and then, sometimes after a specified break in service (typically six months), return to the employer as an independent contractor, usually for a maximum of 1,000 hours a year. (The IRS imposes the hourly restriction to discourage companies from substituting full-time employees with retirees and thus avoiding expenses such as benefits and FICA. Employees who work more than 1,000 hours per year usually need to be contracted through an agency and make their services available to other employers as well.)

While most such programs today lack sufficient scale to make a difference in a company's overall staffing, serving instead as a safety valve and a source of specific skills and experience, large corporations would do well to bring these programs up to scale as labor markets tighten. An example of a program at a scale proportional to the overall employee population is that of the Aerospace Corporation, which provides R&D and systems-engineering services to the air force. The personnel needs of this California-based company vary from year to year and contract to contract, and its Retiree Casual program helps level the staffing load.

Long-term employees can generally retire with full benefits at age 55 or older. As part of the Retiree Casual program, they can then work on a project-consulting basis for up to 1,000 hours per year at their old base salaries, sometimes less, depending on roles and responsibilities. Eighty percent of retirees sign up, and some start back the day after they retire. About 500 retiree casuals are available at any given time, while 200 are working. They work various patterns—most work two days per week, but some work six months on, six months off (the 1,000-hour limit is approximately the equivalent of half-time). A few (three to four a year) are so indispensable that they have to be dropped from the program and scontracted via an agency after they hit the 1,000-hour limit. Most participate into their midsixties, some beyond 80.

The program assures the company a degree of "corporate memory," according to George Paulikas, who retired in 1998 at age 62 as an EVP after spending his entire post-PhD career with the company. He was off only a couple of weeks before being asked back to help on a project and has worked part-time ever since—about one-quarter time last year. "You don't want people with enormous experience to just walk out the door. The Retiree Casual program keeps expertise around and helps transfer it to others. People often remark that we don't have many consultants around here. Actually, we do, but they're called retirees, and they already know the business inside out." Paulikas sticks with the program because it allows him to keep his association with the organization but on his own terms. "This program is a pleasant way to keep associated with a great organization, great people, great work. I get to work less often and with less intensity." And because he's not working full-time, Paulikas has been able to pursue other professional interests;

he works as a consultant to the Institute for Defense Analyses and is a member of the National Academy of Sciences Space Studies Board.

Monsanto has a similar program, which it calls the Resource Re-Entry Center. It's open to all employees who leave the company in good standing and want to return to a part-time position, though departing employees have to wait six months after leaving a full-time job. Managers are directed to use retirees for job sharing, for cyclical spikes, and for temporary positions in the case of unplanned leaves. They're told not to attempt a reduction in benefit costs by hiring retirees for long-term work. Participants are eligible for company savings and investment plans as well as spot bonuses (though not the normal bonus structure). Originally, participants were limited to 1,000 hours of work per year to ensure the program wouldn't interfere with pension payouts, but Monsanto recently relaxed the requirement for those people whose pensions wouldn't be affected, such as retirees who had received a lump-sum payout.

Jim Fornango, who retired from Monsanto in 1996 at the age of 53, has returned to work on a variety of projects since 1998. He likes the flexibility: "I spend the amount of time I want doing things I want. I'm not locked into a structure." And, like Paulikas, he's been able to explore other interests at the same time; he serves as a substitute teacher and as a counselor to other teachers.

. . .

It's fashionable to invest heavily in high-potential employees, creating programs that give these select (and historically young) people the leadership experiences they'll need to ascend quickly through an organization. Why not, then, develop a similar type of program aimed at older and midcareer workers with the skills, abilities, and experiences that your organization most needs? A lifelong-contributor or high-retention program could call on a variety of techniques to reengage these valuable players. Such a program might include fresh assignments or career switches, mentoring or knowledge-sharing roles, training and development, and sabbaticals—all of which have the potential to rejuvenate careers while engendering fresh accomplishments and renewed loyalty.

And yet in our research, we didn't find a single company that explicitly created such high-retention pools among over-55 workers. Some businesses are taking the first step: Sears, for example, has expanded its talent-management and retention focus to include not just highly promotable people but also solid contributors and pros with specific, tough-to-replace skills. Dow Chemical has oriented its human resource management systems toward "continuous rerecruitment" of its workforce, in part by encouraging people to move into different roles throughout their careers. And companies like Aerospace and Monsanto are using their retiree programs to retain employees with valuable skills. But by and large, in most companies, the over-55 crowd continues to get very little attention from management.

That's going to have to change. Sixty-five isn't what it used to be. In 2001, Bob Lutz, then 69, was recruited to join General Motors as vice chairman of product development, charged with rejuvenating the product line as he had done at Chrysler with the Dodge Viper, Chrysler PT Cruiser, and Dodge Ram truck line. In last fall's World Series, the winning Florida Marlins were led by 72–year-old Jack McKeon, called out of retirement early in the season to turn around the fortunes of a youthful but underperforming club. Collecting Grammy Awards in 2000 were Tony Bennett, Tito Puente, and B. B. King—combined age around 220. Al Hirschfeld's caricatures graced the print media for more than 75 years, and he was still drawing when he passed away last year, his 100th. And then there's the litany of business executives called out of already active retirement to inject stability, direction, confidence, and sometimes legitimacy into major corporations in need of leadership. Examples include 67-year-old Harry Stonecipher, who recently succeeded Phil Condit as Boeing's CEO; John Reed, named interim chairman and CEO of the New York Stock Exchange; Allan Gilmour, vice chairman of Ford, who rejoined the company after retirement; and Joseph Lelyveld, who stepped in temporarily at the *New York Times* last year.

But then, maybe 65 was never what we thought. Lee Iacocca once told *Wired,* "I've always been against automated chronological dates to farm people out. The union would always say, 'Make room for the new blood; there aren't enough jobs to go around.' Well, that's a hell of a policy to have. I had people at Chrysler who were 40 but acted 80, and I had 80-year-olds who could do everything a 40-year-old can. You have to take a different view of age now. People are living longer. Age just gives experience. Besides, it takes you until about 50 to know what the hell is going on in the world."

What Iacocca understood was that people don't suddenly lose the talent and experience gained over a lifetime at the flip of a switch. It's not good business to push people out the door just because your policies say it's time. Smart companies will find ways to persuade mature workers to delay retirement or even eschew it entirely as long as they remain productive and healthy.

Discussion Questions

1. Older workers are one group who might help companies keep their workforces at full strength; what other groups might contribute to this effort?
2. What attitudes and policies inhibit the effectiveness of companies' strategies for hiring older workers?
3. Why might older workers be particularly interested in flexible work schedules and assignments?
4. What advantages do firms obtain by creating flexible work schedules and assignments for older workers?
5. One day you will be considered an "older" worker. What strategies can you implement in the workplace to avoid being stereotyped or discriminated against.

Case Study: Asleep at the Wheel: Ford Motor Company's Exclusion of the Older Worker

Ford Motor Company—founded by Henry Ford in 1903 with 11 associates, $28,000, and the slogan "I will build a motorcar for the great multitude"—was sued for age discrimination in 2001 and again in 2003.

Jacques Nasser, who became chief executive officer of the multibillion-dollar automaker in January 1999, quickly began an aggressive crusade to infuse diversity into the tradition-based Ford. Two years later, Nasser was ousted and replaced by Henry Ford's great-grandson, Chairman William Clay Ford, Jr. One of the primary reasons for Nasser's fall from power was his well-intentioned diversity initiative that ironically became a method of exclusion of and discrimination against older workers.

In a 2000 address to top executives, Nasser complained: "I do not like the sea of white faces in the audience and Ford Motor Co. must ensure that in the future the company reflects the broad spectrum of Ford's customers."[1] These words reflected his seemingly aggressive position on

Source: This case was prepared by Dr. Kathryn A. Cañas and Dr. Harris Sondak, The University of Utah.

workplace diversity—Ford must diversify to maintain its competitive edge. Taking the conventional Ford Company on an unconventional journey, Nasser pushed his employees full speed ahead: "While we honor our traditions, we are not bound by them. The energy and ambition of the Ford team to create new ways is almost limitless. As long as they keep their eyes on the road and their hands on the wheel."[2]

Despite his efforts to increase diversity at Ford, Nasser found his company facing two class-action age-discrimination lawsuits in addition to a number of individual discrimination lawsuits. The story of how a revolutionary crusade for diversity led to serious charges of age discrimination begins with an understanding of the dynamic yet polarizing leadership style of former Ford CEO Jacques Nasser.

Jacques Nasser

Nasser's impressive career with Ford began in 1968 when, at age 20, he accepted a job as a financial analyst with Ford of Australia. Accepting international assignments—that some may have found unappealing—enabled Nasser to move up in the company as he found himself working in Thailand, Venezuela, Argentina, and the Philippines. Nasser had a reputation for being a "rising star" and "ahead of his time," for example, when he encouraged "suppliers to cooperate and piece parts together into modules before shipping them to Ford assembly plants."[3] Just as Nasser was known for his creative problem-solving skills, he was also known for his toughness. While working in Argentina in 1985, Nasser was held hostage for three days when a Ford plant was seized during a political uprising; he eventually collapsed from exhaustion.[4]

In 1990, Nasser returned to his homeland to help salvage the deteriorating Ford of Australia by cutting the 15,000-person workforce in half and improving productivity by 40 percent. In 1996 he became Ford's head of automotive operations in Detroit; he helped Ford reduce costs by $3 billion, in part by eliminating weak vehicles like the Aspire, Aerostar, and Thunderbird.[5] In 1999, when he became Ford's CEO, he was viewed as a unique leader known for his involvement with employees and direct, immediate feedback on issues ranging from employee presentation skills to car design.

Although Nasser was described by many as pioneering and charming, he was also perceived, by others, as polarizing. And while his fearless leadership style won him prestigious honors such as the 1999 Automobile Industries Man of the Year, this same quality led to the creation of his nickname, "Jac the Knife," which reflected his reputation as a "bare-knuckle" cost cutter, unafraid to eliminate superfluous workers.[6] According to David E. Cole, director of the University of Michigan's Office for the Study of Automotive Transportation, "He is a very polarizing figure . . . People have strong emotions about him one way or the other. He's a compelling guy."[7]

Nasser never tried to hide his unique style or his four-tier plan for Ford's transformation: to improve Ford's customer focus, to develop leaders at every level, to embrace the digital consumer age, and to diversify his workforce. While Ford executives and employees embraced Nasser's goals, they slowly began to question his methods for achieving them. The main concern ultimately became his aggressive campaign—what was often described as a revolution—to diversify Ford's workforce.

Nasser's Diversity Crusade

Passion was, perhaps, Nasser's most captivating quality. It was this passion—stemming from his personal experience: being born in Lebanon and then emigrating with his parents to

Australia—that functioned as the catalyst behind his diversity initiative. Nasser's history, which he openly shared with his employees, illuminated the source of his desire to make diversity thrive on a systemic level within Ford.

Telling his personal story to Wharton Business School students, Nasser said: "I didn't look Australian, and when I went to school, I was different than the kids in my class. I spoke Arabic, not English. My lunch was tabouli and flat bread, and kids would laugh at me. But I stayed with my food. The lesson I learned was, it's okay to be different. Be yourself. Be your own brand. Stand up for what you believe in."[8]

One would assume that Nasser's philosophy would not conflict with a company that has identified diversity as "one of our founding principles" since early in its history. In 1913, for example, Henry Ford's offer to pay $5 a day attracted thousands of immigrants and African Americans drawn to the prospect of earning twice the typical daily wage—a wage proudly claimed by Ford as being "credited with helping to create the black middle class."[9] By 1916, Ford employed people who represented 62 nationalities and more than 900 people with disabilities.[10] Additionally, Ford hired many disabled veterans returning from World War I in 1919, thus "making the automaker one of the first companies to hire people with disabilities and to adapt work environments to their specific needs."[11]

Nasser viewed excellence in diversity management not only as a continuation of and respect for Ford's long-standing traditions but also as a competitive advantage. Specifically, he desired the best possible reputation for diversity management so that Ford could recruit and retain the best minority employees. The value of a diverse workforce was, for Nasser, obvious: "Greater inclusion of minorities is a priority for two reasons. It's the right thing to do. It's also good business."[12] Impressively, in 1999, Ford made 30 percent of its new hires minorities and raised the percentage of minority managers to 15 percent. In its July 2000 issue, *Fortune* magazine rated Ford the country's 30th best company for minorities—no other automaker made the top 50.[13]

Ford's diversity numbers are indeed notable. According to the company's annual report, the number of women and minorities working for Ford was 47.5 percent of its workforce in 2001. African Americans accounted for 19 percent of Ford employees, and the percentage of Latinos working for Ford was 3.1. The percentage of women and people of color in management positions at Ford was 34.9 in 2001.[14]

In an effort to tap into African American, Hispanic, and Asian markets, Ford actively recruited and trained minority dealers. Under the program, the candidates completed two years of business classes, and as a way to reciprocate, Ford helped finance their dealerships.[15]

The Performance Management Process (PMP)

As Nasser pushed Ford in ambitious new directions—embracing diversity, urging employees to get closer to customers, hiring outsiders to shake up Ford's culture, expanding Ford's luxury-car portfolio, and overhauling management pay and performance practices—Ford's bottom line was taking a hit. Net losses in 2001 totaled $5.5 billion, down from earnings of $3.5 billion the previous year.[16] Of course, although it is impossible to ignore external forces such as September 11 and the Firestone tire debacle, some observers charged that Nasser simply ignored the basics, citing for example, "quality gaffes" found in vehicles such as the 2002 Explorer[17] and the misuse of the performance evaluation system he initiated.

Nasser's evaluation system was called the Performance Management Process (PMP) and was modeled after systems used by such companies as General Electric and Microsoft. Used specifically to rank Ford's 18,000 top managers, the PMP was a type of grading system that evaluated employees on a curve. More specifically, 10 percent of the employees were rated by management as "A"; 80 percent as "B"; and 10 percent as "C." "B" employees were divided into two categories, "B-1" and "B-2," with "B-2" employees considered less productive. All "A" and "B" performers were eligible for bonuses and pay increases, although lower-level "B" employees received fewer benefits than higher-rated employees and were in jeopardy of being downgraded to "C" performer status. Those who did not improve after two years could be demoted or fired.[18]

Under Nasser, part of top managers' bonuses hinged on how well they accomplished their diversity goals. Ford set specific goals for hiring and promoting minorities and women and tied executive compensation to meeting those objectives. This tie-in to promotions was one of Nasser's diversity initiatives that ultimately helped employees—mostly older white men—successfully sue Ford for age discrimination.

Older Workers Sue

At the same time that Ford was attempting to recruit, train, and retain diverse employees, it faced two class-action discrimination lawsuits: *Siegel v. Ford Motor Co.* and *Streeter v. Ford Motor Co.* Both lawsuits accused the company of age discrimination, but whereas Siegel was brought by older workers of both sexes and several ethnicities, the Streeter plaintiffs were all white men.[19] Interestingly, the Streeter plaintiffs at first claimed "reverse discrimination" but ultimately dropped the race and gender discrimination charges, thereby focusing only on age discrimination.

The Siegel suit gained national recognition because the AARP—formerly known as the American Association of Retired Persons—supported the lawsuit both financially and with staff time.[20] In the Siegel lawsuit, the plaintiffs charged that the PMP "was part of senior management's plan to eliminate older employees from Ford Motor Company's salaried workforce" in violation of the Michigan Civil Rights Act.[21] According to the lawsuit, a preliminary review of the statistics demonstrated that older workers disproportionately received "C" ratings. Plaintiffs alleged that the performance criteria were "rooted, in part, on the negative stereotypical assumptions about older employees."[22]

Further, the plaintiffs charged that Ford managers had worked aggressively to promote minorities and women while eliminating white male employees because their "compensation and upward mobility" were "contingent upon meeting diversity goals."[23] More specifically, the complaint explained how 10 percent of executives' bonuses were contingent on their reaching diversity goals, in other words, certain percentages of minorities and females at the various levels of Ford management.[24]

Fueling the discrimination lawsuit fire was the damaging testimony, as described in the complaint, from Ford executives. For example, David Murphy, Ford's former human resources vice president, said: "We are in the middle of transforming one of the biggest companies in the world. You aren't going to do that by pleasing everybody, by having some kind of consensus. We know we are going to upset some people. Maybe they shouldn't be a part of Ford Motor Co."[25]

As noted in the complaint, Richard Parry-Jones, vice president of product development and quality, said: "We are trapped in a mono-cultural environment that is dominated by old white males. We need to change. We need more employees who are more reflective of our consumer base."[26] Echoing similar sentiments was head of Ford Credit, Don Winkler, who said: "We went to headhunters who didn't find us 51-year-old white males." Regarding the replacement of white males by minorities and women, he said, "Some people had to take packages and go."[27] The combination of the Nasser-initiated PMP and bold testimony from Ford executives worked together to shape the image of Ford as a company guilty of age discrimination.

The Age Discrimination in Employment Act

The main argument in the lawsuits was that Ford violated the Age Discrimination in Employment Act (ADEA)—signed into law in 1967 by President Lyndon B. Johnson—which required Americans to refrain from the adverse treatment of older workers those over 40. The ADEA made it unlawful for an employer to refuse to hire, to fire, or to take any other adverse action against a worker because of his or her age.[28]

The language Congress used in the ADEA to define unlawful age discrimination is as follows:

It shall be unlawful for an employer:

1. to fail to hire or to discharge any individual or otherwise discriminate against any individual with respect to his compensation, terms, conditions, or privileges of employment, because of such individual's age;
2. to limit, segregate, or classify its employees in any way which would deprive or tend to deprive any individual of employment opportunities or otherwise adversely affect his status as an employee, because of such individual's age; or
3. to reduce the wage rate of any employee in order to comply with this Act.[29]

Age discrimination is gaining increased attention because of the influential baby-boomer generation. According to Raymond F. Gregory, author of *Age Discrimination in the American Workplace: Old at a Young Age,* the baby boomers account for more than 70 million workers in the U.S. workplace—just under 50 percent of the entire workforce. In 2006, the entire baby-boomer generation fell within the protections of the federal laws against acts of age discrimination. As Gregory explains: "[A] vast army of workers"—known for its education, independence, and work savvy—"stands ready to contest employer acts of age discrimination."[30]

The baby-boomer generation will be forced to confront the pervasive, damaging stereotypes of the older worker. Glen Lenhoff, a lawyer who represented the Ford plaintiffs, spoke to the issue of stereotypes: "I think there is a significant increase in the perception within many large corporations that people over 45 lack energy and aren't receptive to new ideas . . . I think some corporations feel that such a person is not consistent with a dynamic and evolving company."[31]

According to Gregory, "the sources of age discrimination are inaccurate, stereotypical conceptions of the abilities of older workers in general."[32] Older workers are often stereotyped as stubborn, inflexible, resistant to change, unproductive, slow learners, more expensive, and eager to retire at the earliest opportunity.[33] The result of such stereotyping is how the "[u]njustified views of the diminished abilities of older workers coalesce or merge into stereotypical beliefs that form the basis for employer decisions affecting older workers."[34]

Such damaging stereotypes negatively affected both men and women in the Ford workplace. Making it clear that the discrimination lawsuits were not just about men was 54-year-old Dr. Sanaa Taraman, an Egyptian-born advanced program engineer, who maintained that she was targeted primarily because of her age. "I'm only 54 and I planned to work another 10 years . . . now they are forcing us to leave."[35]

James Brazin, 55, a mechanical engineer at Ford's Livonia transmission technical center and plant, had a streak of 32 positive annual performance reviews in a row oddly broken by a "C" grade for 2000. Brazin expressed his frustration: "My work had always been exceptional and now all of a sudden I'm at the bottom." Brazin described how his supervisor explained his "C" rating by saying "you're an old guy just like me."[36]

Angelo Guido, 52, formerly a chief engineer with Ford, said the policy played a role in his decision to retire from the company after 31 years. "I didn't like it but it was a method they were going to use. It didn't seem right. Everybody felt lousy about it."[37]

Ford Settles and Looks toward the Future

In December 2001, Ford Motor Co. agreed to pay $10.5 million, including $2.6 million in attorneys' fees, to settle two class-action lawsuits alleging that Ford's performance evaluation policy discriminated against older employees;[38] the settlement benefited more than 425 managers.[39] Had the lawsuits gone to trial, plaintiffs' lawyers planned to present studies that illustrated how older Ford managers were far more likely to receive poor job evaluations in 2000 than their younger counterparts.[40]

According to AARP CEO Bill Novelli: "This is a major victory not only for the employees but for all those who are fighting against workplace age discrimination in any form, whether it involves direct layoffs or, as in this case, sham job ratings."[41] Laurie McCann, senior attorney with AARP foundation litigation, maintained: "The message here is that age discrimination will not be tolerated. Employers shouldn't balance their books on the backs of older employees and they can't try to force out older workers and get away with it."[42]

In response to the suits, Ford made changes to its evaluation policy. Spokesperson Anne Gattari backtracked from Ford's original assertions about the PMP policy. She said that Ford would now rank its employees as "top achievers," "achievers," or "improvement required" responding to the fact that "some managers expressed concern that the system has been having an adverse effect on teamwork and morale."[43] Further, Ford has abandoned forcing supervisors to rank a certain percentage of employees in the lowest tier and has initiated giving supervisors more discretion in awarding bonuses or merit raises.[44]

Joe Laymon, the new vice president of corporate human resources, said: "The new program will drop the PMP moniker and focus more on building bonds between supervisors and workers." Laymon continued: "We have a system that has objectives built in it. We have a system that has periodical reviews. We have a system that has very strong coaching and counseling features built in. We have a performance system that has a final appraisal."[45] In short, the company claims that it is making progress at diversifying the automaker's workforce but not at the expense of older employees.

Having been sued for age discrimination in 2001 and then again in 2003,[46] Ford has seemingly still not found a solution to managing its older workforce. Despite Ford's troublesome past, *DiversityInc's* 2009 Top 50 Companies for Diversity list ranked Ford the 28th U.S. company for diversity; the year prior Ford was 27th. *DiversityInc* hailed Ford as "a long-time leader in supplier diversity and continues to be innovative, with new efforts on firms owned by veterans and veterans with service-acquired disabilities."[47] In addition, *DiversityInc* ranked Ford as third in its Top 10 Companies for Supplier Diversity. Again praising Ford, the magazine highlighted how Ford "has remained a diversity leader even as its industry is in turmoil. It consistently has been the highest-ranked auto company because of its commitment to an inclusive work force and its strong community philanthropy."[48]

In addition to achieving this coveted spot in *DiversityInc's* 2008 and 2009 rankings, Ford has earned positive recognition from other minority organizations. The Michigan Minority Business Development Council named Ford one of its 2008 Corporate ONE Award winners,[49] and the Gay & Lesbian Alliance Against Defamation awarded Ford the "Fairness Award."[50] The *Hispanic Business Magazine* ranked Ford 29th in its Diversity Elite 60 Companies in 2008.[51] Responding to the need to educate its employees about diversity, Ford developed the Multicultural Alliance. According to Director of Diversity and Worklife Planning and Peer Review Rosalind Cox, the Alliance's mission is "to educate Ford's departments on the benefit multicultural markets bring the company."[52] And impressively, Ford leads all other automakers with the largest percentage of minority-owned or -operated dealerships in the United States.[53]

Ford's diversity initiatives are both innovative and laudable; however, weaknesses remain. In 2006, Ford lost one of the auto industry's most influential women leaders, Anne Stevens, who was executive vice president and COO of the Americas. Further, in the Ford Motor Company *2008 Annual Report,* there is no mention of domestic diversity as an organizational value or as a competitive advantage in the Chairman's Message from William Clay Ford and the President and CEO's Message from Alan Mulally. Mulally has yet to show whether Ford will remain as dedicated to diversity initiatives as it has been in the past.[54]

Ford Motor Co. maintains that diversity is a "distinct advantage" and that diversity is one of their "top corporate priorities."[55] With such serious claims of diversity commitment—in light of the company's historical tie to diversity and its future plans to manage diversity—comes the responsibility of valuing the knowledge and experience of the older worker.

Discussion Questions

1. Why did Nasser's progressive goal—to diversify Ford's workforce—backfire?
2. How did Nasser's personal story and work background affect his approach and philosophy on managing diversity?
3. Why was Ford's evaluation system, the PMP, the source of contention for Ford employees who felt discriminated against? In moving away from the PMP, what did Ford do to improve this evaluation system? Did these changes create a more accurate system of evaluation?
4. The number of older workers in the workforce is increasing—many people now work into their late 60s and 70s. How can businesses adapt to and benefit from this trend?

Notes

1. Mark Truby, "Age-bias Claims Jolt Ford Culture Change," *Detroit News,* April 29, 2001, http://www.zigonperf.com/resources/pmnews/grading_workers.html; Julie Foster, "Ford's Controversial Diversity Campaign: Automaker Faces Suit over Discrimination against Older White Males," WorldNetDaily.com, May 16, 2001, http://www.worldnetdaily. com/news/printer-friendly.asp?ARTICLE_ID= 22838.
2. Jacques Nasser live Web cast July 27, 2000, http://www.npr.org/programs/npc/2000/000727. jnasser.html.
3. Mark Truby and Bill Vlasic, "Bold Ford CEO Leads a Cultural Revolution: Nasser's Hard-driving Style Draws Praise, Criticism," *Detroit*

News, August 20, 2000, http://www.detnews.com/specialreports/2000/nasser/leadlead.htm.

4. Ibid.

5. Ibid.

6. Mark Truby, "Nasser's Outgoing Style Makes Him Target of Rumors," *Detroit News,* August 20, 2000, http://www.detnews.com/specialreports/2000/nasser/rumors/rumors.htm.

7. Ibid.

8. Jacques Nasser, speech delivered at Wharton Business School, October 1999, http://webi.wharton.upenn.edu/researchDocDetail.asp?intDocID=142 and http://leadership.wharton.upenn.edu/digest/10-99.shtml.

9. "Ford Centennial Marks History of Diversity," news release, http://media.ford.com/newsroom release_display_new.cfm?release=15657.

10. Ibid.

11. Ibid.

12. "Ford News Briefs Weekly News Digest: Nasser Urges More Effort to Attract Minorities as Customers," *Detroit News,* January 12, 1998, http://www.mdcbowen.org/p2/bh/ford/ford_charged.htm.

13. "New Ford Evaluation System Focuses on Coaching, Counseling," *DiversityInc,* April 23, 2002, http://www.diversityinc.com/members/2783print.cfm.

14. Ibid.

15. Mark Truby, "Diversity Gives Ford a New Look: Aggressive Recruiting of Minorities and Women Is Sweeping Away Old Guard," *Detroit News,* August, 20, 2000, http://www.detnews.com/specialreports/2000/nasser/diversity/diversity.htm.

16. Ford's Financial Health for 2003, http://www.ford.com/en/company/about/corporateCitizenship/principlesProgressPerformance/our-performance/fin-health-data.htm.

17. Joanne Muller, "Commentary: Ford: Jacques Nasser Can't Do It All," *BusinessWeek Online,* June 18, 2001, http://www.businessweek.com/print/magazine/content/01_25/b3737047.htm?mz.

18. Foster, "Ford's Controversial Diversity Campaign."

19. Linda Bean, "Ford Settles 'White Male' Lawsuit, Second Class-Action for $10.5 Million," *DiversityInc,* December 18, 2001, http://www.diversityinc.com/public/1992print.cfm.

20. Linda Bean, "Ford's 'Older Worker' Lawsuits May Be Nearing Settlement," *DiversityInc,* November 5, 2001, http://www.diversityinc.com/members/1649print.cfm.

21. "AARP Foundation Litigation Attorneys Represent Older Workers Harmed by Discriminatory Performance Appraisal System," *AARP Foundation,* September 26, 2001, http://www.aarp.org/litigation/releases/2001/siegelann.html.

22. Ibid.

23. Foster, "Ford's Controversial Diversity Campaign."

24. Ibid.

25. Ibid.

26. Ibid.

27. Ibid.

28. Raymond F. Gregory, *Age Discrimination in the American Workplace: Old at a Young Age* (New Jersey: Rutgers University Press, 2001); 29 U.S.C. Sections 621–34. For more on the issue of age discrimination, see AARP, *Employment Discrimination against Midlife and Older Women: An Analysis of Discrimination Charges Filed with the EEOC,* vol. 1 (Washington, D.C. AARP Women's Initiative, 1997); AARP, *Valuing Older Workers: A Study of Costs and Productivity* (Washington, D.C.: AARP, n.d.); Robert Coulson, *Empowered at Forty* (New York: Harper Collins, 1990); Daniel P. O'Meara, *Protecting the Growing Number of Older Workers: The Age Discrimination in Employment Act* (Philadelphia, PA: University of Pennsylvania, Wharton School, Industrial Research Unit, 1989); Richard A. Posner, *Aging and Old Age* (Chicago, IL: University of Chicago Press, 1995); Sara E. Rix, ed., *Older Workers: How Do They Measure Up? An Overview of Age Differences in Employee Costs and Performance* (Washington D.C.: Public Policy Institute of the AARP, 1994); For a complete historical account of age discrimination, see Kerry Segrave, *Age Discrimination by Employers* (North Carolina: McFarland, 2001).

29. Statistical Abstract of the United States 1998 (Washington, D.C.: U.S. Department of Commerce, 1998), 15, 21.

30. Gregory, *Age Discrimination in the American workplace,* 2.

31. Alejandro Bodipo-Memba, "Ford Sued on Diversity," *Detroit Free Press,* February 17, 2001, http://www.freep.com/money/business/age17.

32. Gregory, *Age Discrimination in the American workplace,* 21–22.

33. Ibid., 24.

34. Ibid., 22.
35. Truby, "Age-bias Claims Jolt Ford Culture Change."
36. Ibid.
37. Ibid.
38. Bean, "Ford Settles 'White Male' Lawsuit May Be Nearing Settlement."
39. "Court OKs $10.6 Million Settlement of Ford Age Bias Case," *U.S. newswire,* March 14, 2002, www.highbeam.com/doc/161=83770764.html.
40. Mark Truby, "Ford Settles Key Bias Suits," December 19, 2001, http://www.detnews.com/2001/autoinsider/0112/19/c01=370389.htm.
41. "Court OKs $10.6 Million Settlement of Ford Age Bias Case."
42. Bean, "Ford Settles 'White Male' Lawsuit May Be Nearing Settlement."
43. Linda Bean, "Ford Puts the Brakes on Controversial Evaluation System," *DiversityInc,* July 10, 2001, http://www.diversityinc.com/public/1169print.cfm.
44. Ibid.
45. "New Ford Evaluation System Focuses on Coaching, Counseling," *DiversityInc,* April 23, 2002.
46. Mark Truby, "New Bias Lawsuits Hits Ford, Visteon: Older Workers without College Degrees Claim They Get Passed Up for Promotions,"

Detroit News, April 14, 2003, http://www.detnews.com/2003.autoinsider/0304/14/a01=136079.htm.
47. DiversityInc, "The 9th Annual 2009 DiversityInc Top 50 Companies for Diversity," http://www.diversityinc.com/public/department289.cfm.
48. Ibid.
49. Michigan Minority Business Development Council, "Corporate ONE Awards," http://www.mmbdc.com/Corporate-One-Awards/.
50. The Center for Corporate Citizenship at Boston College. "Ford Holds Diversity Summit," December 5, 2003, http://www.imakenews.com/cccbc/e_article000208048.cfm.
51. Hispanic Business Magazine, "Diversity Elite 60 2008," http://www.hispanicbusiness.com/news/2008/8/27/diversity_elite_2008_1630.htm.
52. Yoji Cole, "Top 10 Companies for Diversity," *DiversityInc*, June/July 2004, p. 64.
53. Ford Motor Company, "Minority Dealer Operations," http://www.dd.ford.com/nada/about_nada.html.
54. Ford Motor Company, "2008 Annual Report: More Products People Want," http://www.ford.com.
55. Ford Motor Company, diversity statement, "On the Team," http://www.mycareer.ford.com/ONTHETEAM.ASP?CID=15.

CHAPTER 7

Religion and Spirituality

Religion, as a federally protected class, includes all aspects of religious observance and practice as well as belief. Thus, the employer must accommodate an employee's observance of his or her religious beliefs when reasonable—that is, when the accommodation does not cause undue hardship on the employer's business.

Objectives

- To examine the relationship between religion and/or spirituality and the workplace.
- To examine why employees are increasingly attempting to bring their religious beliefs into the workplace, thereby putting pressure on organizations to manage the role of religion in the workplace.
- To examine how and why an organizational leader, Tom Chappell of Tom's of Maine, makes his spiritual framework the foundation of the organizational culture.

Preview Questions

- How should management accommodate a variety of conflicting spiritual perspectives in the workplace?
- What are the potential advantages and disadvantages of an organizational leader making his or her religious perspective the philosophical framework of the organization?
- How can a manager turn the accommodation of employees' religious and/or spiritual perspectives into a competitive business advantage?

Some Important Dates

1791 The Bill of Rights of the U.S. Constitution guarantees free exercise of religion, assuring citizens that no one religious institution or perspective holds a legally preferred status.

1963 Supreme Court prohibits mandatory prayer in public schools.

1964 The Civil Rights Act, signed by President Johnson, prohibits discrimination on the basis of race, religion, ethnicity, national origin, and creed (gender was added later).

1972 Congress amends Title VII of the Civil Rights Act to make clear that it protects *all* aspects of religious observance and practice, so that employers will not pick and choose among religions or aspects of religious practice.

1976 Election of Jimmy Carter, the first U.S. president to be openly evangelical Christian.

1987   Supreme Court holds that Title VII of the Civil Rights Act of 1964 does not prohibit religious organizations from discriminating in hiring policies in favor of members of the religion.

2003   Eleventh Circuit Court of Appeals rules that Chief Justice Roy Moore of the Alabama Supreme Court must remove the monument of the Ten Commandments from the rotunda of the Alabama Supreme Court building that he had installed there.

Religion in the Workplace is Diversity Issue for U.S. Companies

Many Firms Seek Guidance in Accommodating Employees' Religious Practices

Washington—American companies are looking for ways to deal with a diversity issue they increasingly face: the need to accommodate workers' various religious beliefs and practices.

"A lot of companies haven't figured out what to do, but they know they need to do something," says David Miller, executive director of Yale University's Center for Faith and Culture.

Miller, who heads the center's Ethics and Spirituality in the Workplace program, said there is "a huge appetite" in corporate America for guidance on handling religious diversity issues.

Increased immigration by Muslims, Hindus, Buddhists and other groups is creating a more religiously diverse work force. These employees' spiritual beliefs and practices must be accommodated in the workplace—unless it would impose an undue burden on the employer—according to U.S. law. But that is not the only reason employers find themselves dealing with religious issues, Miller said.

"Faith at work is a bona fide social movement," he said. For many employees, faith is a resource for ethical guidance. It can help people find meaning and purpose in their work, or help them "stay anchored and keep their sanity" in a difficult job situation, Miller said. People want to bring their whole selves to work, and for many that includes their faith.

Furthermore, in a global marketplace, respecting religious differences helps attract and retain talented employees and enables companies to reach out to a larger customer base.

"This is a very powerful, growing trend," says Georgette Bennett, president of the Tanenbaum Center for Interreligious Understanding. "When we first started working on this issue, everybody said the religious dimension of diversity is a non-issue. But now if you go to meetings that deal with diversity, religion is a big item on the agenda."

Both Bennett and Miller advise companies on how to equitably accommodate employees' spiritual practices. "Our research found that the mere existence of a written policy [on religious expression in the workplace] can help reduce the perception of bias," Bennett said. Religion is usually cited in workplace anti-discrimination policies, but only 4 percent of companies have specific policies on religion, she said.

They both reject the term "tolerance" when discussing religion in the workplace. "It is patronizing. We're not about tolerance, we're about mutual respect and understanding," Bennett said.

"Tolerance is a word that is inadequate, it has outworn its welcome," said Miller, the author of *God at Work: The History and Promise of the Faith at Work Movement*. "Tolerance is a minimum threshold. To me, mutual respect is the name of the game."

Issues that can require accommodation, Bennett said, are the wearing of religiously significant attire such as hijabs (headscarves worn by Muslim women), crosses or yarmulkes; taking time off for religious observance; and having facilities for prayer breaks and meditation.

(continued)

Some companies hire chaplains to counsel employees facing personal or professional problems. Tyson Foods, for example, has some 120 chaplains at its food production plants and offices in Springdale, Arkansas.

Another approach is religion-based employee networking groups, also called religious affinity groups. Although many companies fear that such groups could be divisive, Bennett said, "a number of companies are doing affinity groups very successfully, such as American Express, Fannie Mae and IBM." Another is Texas Instruments, where employees started Christian and Muslim groups that have held joint panel discussions. . . .

"When it works well," said Miller, "the groups come together and share and have education seminars so other people can learn not to be afraid and learn about traditions that are different from their own."

Bennett said many companies, even those that do not sanction religious affinity groups, "are starting to do learning sessions. When you create a safe space where employees can discuss the issues, it's extraordinary what happens."

A few years ago, the Tanenbaum Center helped put together a panel at General Motors (GM) consisting of individuals who were members of different religions, she said. (GM has no religion-based affinity groups.)

Panel participants discussed what they value about their beliefs, how those beliefs have been stereotyped and how that affected them, and how their beliefs affect their work life, said Bennett.

"When that session was finished, there was such an extraordinary response from the employees," she said. "Those who were members of minority religions here [in the United States] said they were so grateful because they finally had an opportunity to explain their beliefs and their practices, and those who were members of what are majority religions here, namely Christians and Jews, were so grateful because they said, 'Finally, we understand—we just didn't know what all this was about before.' "

"And there was really tremendous good feeling in that packed room," Bennett said.

For more information, see the Web sites of the Tanenbaum Center for Interreligious Understanding and the Yale Center for Faith and Culture.

Source: Louise Fenner, "Religion in the Workplace Is Diversity Issue for U.S. Companies," *America.gov*, November 28, 2007, http://www.america.gov/st/%20washfile-english/2007/November/20071128173019xlrennef0.1781427.html

ESSAY: TAKING RELIGION TO WORK

Just a decade ago, there were only 25 religious employee-resource groups. Today, there are more than 900, according to the International Coalition of Workplace Ministries (ICWM). The faith-at-work movement is a corporate experiment that has no precedent. Just as a new medication may take years to reveal its side effects, it will take years before we know if people of different faiths, atheists and agnostics, gays and evangelical Christians, can practice their brands of morality in the workplace and work cohesively and successfully together.

This faith-at-work experiment is taking place inside many notable large corporations, including American Express, AOL, American Airlines, Continental Airlines, Texas Instruments and Ford Motor Co., all of which have religious or spiritual employee-resource groups. And the list of companies is growing.

C. Stone Brown, *Diversity Inc magazine*, November/December 2005.

What is happening in society and the personal lives of employees that has compelled them to reveal their faith and religion at work? And just as importantly, why are some companies complying with this trend, even embracing it, while others shy away from religion at work?

There certainly are cultural, social, economic and political developments that have fueled the faith-at-work movement. For one, we are in the midst of a heightened consciousness of faith and religion, much of which can be attributed to the election of self-described born-again-Christian President George W. Bush.

The residual effects of the terrorist attacks of September 11, 2001, also brought Americans closer to their respective faiths and made them more vocal about professing those faiths while bringing Islam and other eastern religions more into the mainstream consciousness.

"Most of the media after Bush's election got a wake-up call about this when they discovered that the real turning point for Bush that put him over the edge was the Christian vote," says Os Hillman, director of ICWM and author of *The 9 to 5 Window: How Faith Can Transform the Workplace.* "What Bush has shown is that all Americans should be free to express religious beliefs, including at work," says Hillman.

"Sept. 11 heightened the sense of the need for faith and something higher, to try and understand what happened," says Douglas Hicks, associate professor of leadership and religious studies at the University of Richmond and author of *Religion and the Workplace.* "It also raised an awareness of Islam in America, both in terms of hostility toward a misperception of Islam or Islamic extremist."

Although these events and political trends have influenced the faith-at-work movement, they were fueled by an era in which Americans collectively sought answers to the economic realities taking place in their lives. Indeed, how Americans view work and the role it plays in their lives has undergone a transformation in the last two decades.

There was a time when employment was one of the most stabilizing forces in our lives, says Martin Rutte, coauthor of *Chicken Soup for the Soul at Work* and a national lecturer who has addressed the Harvard Business School. "People began to say, 'If the company isn't the source of security, then what is?' And for some of these people it became the spiritual, God, religion."

The faith-at-work movement also reflects the life stage of the dominant generation in today's workforce—baby boomers, born between 1946 and 1964. They are represented by 73.2 million workers, 25 percent of the U.S. population. "Because the baby-boomer generation is so large, the spiritual issues it's facing have a major impact on what the world thinks is appropriate conversation [at work]," says Rutte.

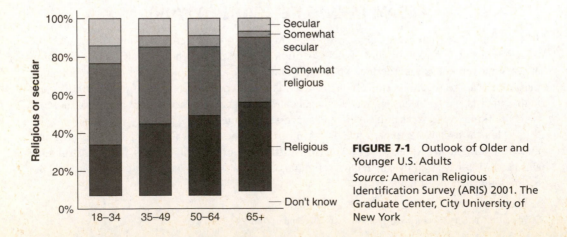

FIGURE 7-1 Outlook of Older and Younger U.S. Adults

Source: American Religious Identification Survey (ARIS) 2001. The Graduate Center, City University of New York

In addressing religious diversity as a workplace issue, there are palpable differences with other "diverse" groups. For example, traditional employee-resource groups were created for mentoring and as support networks for people who face similar challenges in a white-male-dominated corporate community. So then, what's the justification for forming a Christian employee-resource group, when Christianity is the country's dominant religion? However, for many companies that have ventured into the faith-at-work experiment, there is a business case in the faith-at-work movement.

Driving the Business Case

Ford Motor Co., No. 11 on The DiversityInc Top 50 Companies for Diversity list 2005, started Ford Interfaith Network (FIN) after September 11, 2001, at the request of a group of Christian employees. The company required the employees to come up with a business case, as well as to show how the group would be inclusive.

Ultimately, after weeks of talks, the group came back to management with representatives from eight different religions in the company, forming FIN.

FIN is a structured network that was created to avoid many of the tensions and conflicts that might arise by mixing religion and work.

"We felt that by indicating to people that this was something that our company stands behind, it would help to increase morale, employee engagement," says Rosalind Cox, manager of Diversity and Worklife Planning. "When your company gets behind you with something you value personally . . . it keeps you engaged. You want to stay and work for that employer."

Under FIN, each religion has a representative on the network's executive committee. The chairperson is voted in by members of the executive council. There is a formal way to address questions about another member's faith when they meet.

For example, if a Mormon has a question about the Quran, or a Muslim about the Torah, the individuals write questions down and present them to the other religion's representative before their meetings. The questions might be answered by the representative or by an invited religious scholar.

Dan Dunnigan, chair of FIN, is empowered by learning about the religious differences in the network.

"What I love is interacting with others with diverse doctrinal views to my own," says Dunnigan, adding that there are common bonds he finds in different religions. "Like hard work, the overall concept of things like virtuous living and high morals, importance of family, integrity . . . values that are important to me, I can find are important to people of other faiths."

FIN, though, didn't get off to a smooth start, he recalls, declining to go into specifics. "There are some places in the world where people kill each other over religious differences and nothing like that was ever threatened. But when you get together and you've got so much diversity, it takes a while to get to those common touch points," he says.

Those touch points can start with participating in each others' events, says Jordan-born Kamal Shenaq, a Ford engineer who came to the United States in 1983. "For example, celebrating Christmas, celebrating the new year for Jews, celebrating the new year for Hindus . . . Ramadan for Islam . . . we always invite each of them to attend these celebrations and we share with each other."

Shenaq, who is Muslim, represents what many would view as the business case for religious employee networks because it affords him time to pray and have a place to wash his feet. "This helps us at the work environment to be very productive because when I feel I'm at work and I'm respected and I can talk about my religion . . . I will work even more and be more loyal to Ford Motor Co," he says.

Classification	Population	Percentage
Christianity	160,000,000	77%
Denominations With More Than 1 Million Adherents		
Catholic	50,873,000	
Baptist	33,830,000	
Christian (No Denomination Supplied)	14,190,000	
Methodist	14,140,000	
Lutheran	9,580,000	
Presbyterian	5,596,000	
Pentecostal	4,467,000	
Episcopalian/Anglican	4,407,000	
Mormon	2,831,000	
Churches of Christ	2,787,000	
Non-Denominational	2,503,000	
Congregational/UCC	2,489,000	
Jehovah's Witness	1,378,000	
Assemblies of God	1,105,000	
Evangelical	1,032,000	
No Religion	29,000,000	14%
Other Religions	8,000,000	4%
Denominations With More Than 1 Million Adherents		
Judaism	3,451,000	
Islam	1,104,000	
Buddhism	1,082,000	
No Answer	11,000,000	5%
Total U.S. Adult Population	208,000,000	

FIGURE 7-2 **Self-Described Religious Identification of U.S. Adult Population (Weighted Estimate With Rounded Figures)**

Source: American Religious Identification Survey (ARIS) 2001. The Graduate Center, City University of New York.

The U.S. Census Bureau cannot legally ask questions regarding religion. Consequently, there are only a few surveys on a national level that collect such data. The 2000 Religious Congregations Membership Study (RCMS) and the 2001 American Religious Identification Survey (ARIS) are the most comprehensive.

Conducted every 10 years to parallel the U.S. census, the RCMS provides a county-by-county listing of religious congregations, memberships, and total adherents. The RCMS data are collected by the Association of Statisticians of American Religious Bodies and published jointly by the American Religion Data Archive and the Glenmary Research Center.

For statistical reasons, the RCMS data do not include millions of adherents from denominations largely associated with blacks. As a result, the data used for the charts and tables in this article are from the ARIS.

First conducted in 1990 by The Graduate Center of the City University of New York, the ARIS compiled a follow-up study in 2001 of religious identification among U.S. adults. The survey also assessed about 20 other personal characteristics to develop more inclusive profiles of religious groups.

The request for a religious network came at a time when Ford was trying to find ways to be more inclusive, says Cox. "One of the things we were really focusing on, particularly that year, was this whole concept of accepting people as 'whole' people and that your faith and your religion is a very vital part of who you are . . . we can't expect people to leave [religion] at the door of the company when they come to work," Cox says.

The verdict still is out on whether companies should expect people to leave their faith at the door. However, if it's going to be embraced, Ford's interfaith approach seems to have merit.

A strong advocate for the interfaith approach to religious understanding is the Council on American-Islamic Relations (CAIR), an Islamic civil-rights and advocacy group, based in Washington, D.C.

"Interfaith dialogue is something that we promote and encourage at the grassroots level with all of our chapters. It is the best way to get to know one another and break down these stereotypes that people have," says Rabiah Ahmed, CAIR spokesperson. "It's been our experience that when people know Muslims on a personal level, whether that be at work or school . . . they tend to have more positive attitudes toward Islam."

Texas Instruments (TI) started its Christian employee-resource group about five years ago, which was followed by the formation of the Muslim group after September 11.

It might surprise some people that there haven't been any problems, says Terry Howard, global diversity director. "Here it is, five years later, and no problems at all," says Howard, who notes that there have been business benefits that TI didn't even anticipate.

He tells the story of one of the founding members of the Christian employee-resource group, who later became chair of the TI diversity network and led TI's market-penetration initiatives in Latin America and China. "I sit back and say to myself, 'Look at what we would have lost out on had we said no,' " says Howard.

TI honored its employees' requests to express their faith at work because it made good business sense, he says. "We don't want people coming to work and masking or hiding something that is near and dear to them. We don't want someone coming to TI saying, 'I've got to hide the fact that I'm a person of faith,' " says Howard. "It's wasted time and energy—we want you to spend your time and energy focusing on helping TI get business results."

Companies can say it's all about being inclusive and building morale, which may be true. However, they have little legal recourse in putting the brakes on the faith-at-work movement,

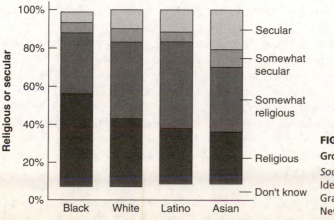

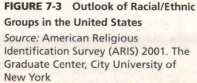

FIGURE 7-3   Outlook of Racial/Ethnic Groups in the United States
Source: American Religious Identification Survey (ARIS) 2001. The Graduate Center, City University of New York

Catholic

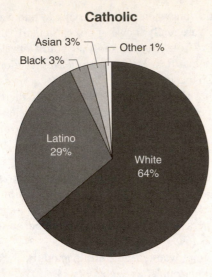

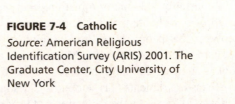

FIGURE 7-4   Catholic

Source: American Religious Identification Survey (ARIS) 2001. The Graduate Center, City University of New York

especially after opening the floodgates to nonreligious groups to form networks. Ironically, religious groups were one of the last to form, yet they have the most legal protections—an amendment to Title VII of the Civil Rights Act of 1964 prohibits workplace discrimination based on religion.

Companies really have to accommodate all groups, even the extremes of gays and lesbians to evangelical Christians, says Hicks. "They are legal and are part of the American workplace today . . . and let me add, Christian resource groups are legal, including the ones that have an evangelical bent, and are part of the American workplace."

They may be part of the American workplace, but for how long? And will companies backpedal on religious diversity when conflicts arise?

Workplace Conflicts

The most obvious opponents of the faith-at-work movement are agnostics, people who question the existence of a higher being, and atheists, who do not believe in any God. For many of them, companies are stepping out of bounds by sanctioning religious employee networks and they say the damage ultimately will affect everyone.

Bobbie Kirkhart, president of the Atheist International Alliance, argues that religious diversity isn't the same as race, gender, and ethnic diversity and, therefore, shouldn't be afforded the same status.

"All of these groups [blacks, women, gays] are groups that don't traditionally have power and they are binding together, for protection, for comfort. I think an employer would be very upset if there were a white-male networking group. And for the same reason, the religious networking group has no place, no rationale," says Kirkhart, a former self-described Christian Protestant who grew up in the Bible Belt.

If companies were consistent with the criteria to form networking groups, minority faiths, such as Muslims, Jews, Buddhists and Sikhs, would be permitted to form groups, but not a Christian group, adds Kirkhart. "I wouldn't be concerned about a Muslim group, because they are a group that doesn't have power."

"Some companies, such as Wells Fargo, No. 40 on The DiversityInc Top 50 companies for Diversity list 2005, have very strict guidelines on the creation of employee-resource groups, and religion doesn't meet the criteria," says Melissa Morey, assistant vice president, corporate communications.

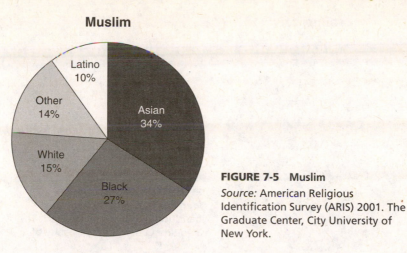

FIGURE 7-5 **Muslim**

Source: American Religious Identification Survey (ARIS) 2001. The Graduate Center, City University of New York.

"What we base this on is 'primary dimensions of diversity,' so it's things about ourselves that we can't change . . . your color or ethnicity," says Morey. "The primary reason we don't have religious groups is there are just so many different religions that we simply can't accommodate all of them."

Wells Fargo, however, does permit informal religious gatherings on site. "If there is a group of people who want to get together in a conference room to have prayer service . . . we are accommodating to that," Morey says.

Kirkhart, who says she was fired from a teaching job when her boss objected to her atheist beliefs, says everyone should fear the faith-at-work movement, not just nonbelievers. "Once the power grab starts, it's not just atheists . . . in today's climate, Muslims, then certainly Wiccans, and Hindus, and pretty soon it's going to be the wrong kind of Christian."

Hicks does agree that bringing different world views together has the potential to be very divisive. Although proselytizing isn't permissible in almost all workplaces, employees should be comfortable about inviting coworkers to off-work religious activities. But employees who do this also must be willing to accept "no" from their coworkers, Hicks says. "As soon as a coworker shows a non-interest in being invited, they have to respect that . . . just as their own views are respected."

Kirkhart, who now teaches in the Los Angeles school system, says proselytizing happens all the time, even with atheists. But it's the bullies she fears, whom she describes as people who don't care about your level of discomfort. "Then you have to go to the employer. There are laws, and atheists [and non-believers] have the same legal protections under the law as religions do. You should take action," she says.

Evangelicals Versus GLBTs

What might become a more explosive conflict than atheists conflicting with religious coworkers are the potential conflicts between Christian employee-resource groups and gay-and-lesbian groups.

Evangelical Christians, the religious group that has been right of center on issues including school prayer and anti-gay-rights legislation, are estimated to number 70 million people, according to a CBS News report.

Companies certainly are aware of the potential clash between the two groups as the faith-at-work movement continues to grow. Hicks, though, warns there shouldn't be an assumption that there always is going to be conflict or a clash between the two groups. "It's not true that 'all' evangelicals are against homosexuality or are intolerant of it. Because it's portrayed that way, it sometimes misses the quiet understanding that is happening in workplaces," he says.

Evangelical

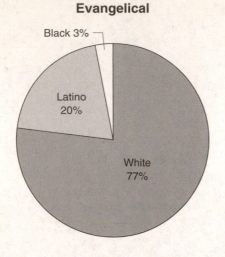

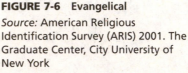

FIGURE 7-6 Evangelical

Source: American Religious Identification Survey (ARIS) 2001. The Graduate Center, City University of New York

Hicks prefers to see the networks as a vehicle for tolerance rather than conflict.

"Talking about [conflicts] and bringing them to light in the workplace through employee-resource groups on any side isn't necessarily a bad thing. It can be a way to mitigate conflict."

That was exactly the approach taken at TI, when the gay-and-lesbian network group had concerns about the formation of the Christian network. Instead of allowing a potential problem to get its footing, the company was proactive, bringing both groups together in meetings.

"It was a non-issue for us because we made it a non-issue. We got people in the room talking and it didn't take a lot of facilitation and all of that. And all of a sudden the groups came together and worked together," says Howard.

It's not always as simple as making this conflict a nonissue. All evangelical Christians may not be intolerant of GLBTs in the workplace, but it would be naive for companies not to prepare for this conflict given the track record of evangelicals' public stance against gay marriages, gay rights and active and threatened boycotts against companies that don't hold their viewpoint.

This year, Microsoft Corp. made headlines when it initially supported House Bill 1515, a Washington initiative to protect gay rights in the workplace. That made the long-time gay-friendly company a boycott target of evangelicals in Seattle. The boycott threat forced the company to change its position from public support to neutral. Although the company ultimately changed its position back to public support, the bill was defeated by one vote in the Washington Senate.

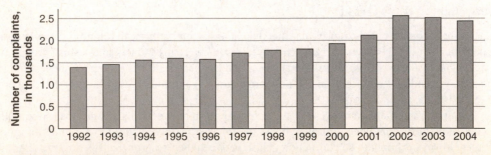

FIGURE 7-7 Religious Discrimination in the Workplace

Source: Equal Employment Opportunity Commission

Hillman, an evangelical Christian, opposes companies bringing fundamentally different employee-networking groups together. "The whole purpose of what corporations are trying to do is say, 'We acknowledge that your group exists and we are allowing this group to operate within the framework of this company.' "

Hillman, who has advised companies such as The Coca-Cola Co. and Toyota on faith-at-work issues, says companies should promote fairness for each group and leave it at that. "I don't think the corporation would want to get into a kind of a mix of how one group should mix with another as much as having fair rules for each group as they meet within the context of the corporation."

Faith Embrace or Backlash?

Even though more companies are embracing religious expression in the workplace, after the terrorist attacks of September. 11, not all groups have been accepted equally.

Since 2001, the Equal Employment Opportunity Commission reports that workplace-discrimination complaints against people of Muslim, Jewish, and "other" faiths have been on the rise.

Muslim backlash has been the most pronounced, but other groups that are perceived to have origins in the Middle East also have faced a high degree of discrimination in the workplace.

The first steps involve educating people about Islam and the Muslim community, says Ahmed of CAIR, whose organization consults with companies about understanding of the Muslim religion. "Truly, we feel that a lot of ignorance that people have about Islam is based on miseducation or lack of information."

That ignorance carries over to the hostility toward Sikhs in the United States. Sikhs, who wear beards and turbans, often are thought to be Muslims, causing them added discrimination in this post–September 11 climate.

One of the major problems of workplace discrimination facing Sikhs, who predominantly come from Northern India and now are the world's fifth-largest religion, is the prohibition against wearing beards and turbans. "Sometimes, the food industry has discriminated against Sikhs even though they were willing to put a hair net on their beard," says Rajwant Singh, president of Sikh Council on Religion and Education.

One 1988 high-profile case involved a Domino's Pizza new hire—Prabhjot Singh Kohli, who filed a complaint with the Maryland Human Relations Commission because the company

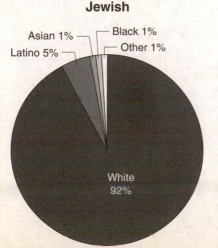

FIGURE 7-8 **Jewish**

Source: American Religious Identification Survey (ARIS) 2001. The Graduate Center, City University of New York

dress code required him to shave his beard. Ultimately, Domino's settled out of court and changed its dress code to permit beards. "We don't cut our hair in any part of the body. So we have long hair, which is tucked in under a turban or hair covering," says Singh, adding that hair for Sikhs is a symbol of spirituality and connection with humanity.

The Sikh religion also collided with the automobile industry's health and safety requirements because certain jobs require employees to wear hard hats, which would restrict the wearing of turbans.

"OSHA [Occupational Safety and Health Administration] has given an exception, and that provided an opportunity for Sikhs to be in the car industry with Chevrolet and GM, and they are doing very well . . . I would say at least 50 to 100 [Sikh] employees at each of these companies," says Singh.

The Future

Religious diversity appears to have a future in corporate America, in part because companies want to be competitive and attract the best talent available. But also, companies are recognizing that faith and religion are an important part of an employee's identity, and accommodation is no longer an option. Perhaps this marks a shift in diversity management where recognition of one's "inner self" is as important as external features, such as race, ethnicity, gender, disability, and sexual orientation.

"Companies are starting to really understand that to really affirm an employee means you should affirm them in all aspects of their lives," says Hillman. "If it's in a way that is equal to everyone, they are learning it makes a better employee and it provides a better place to work."

Discussion Questions

1. Should employees create religious employee-resource groups in the workplace? What are the pros and cons for the organization of allowing this practice?
2. Does encouraging interfaith organizations among employees provide a competitive advantage for business? If so, how?
3. What potential conflicts may arise in the workplace as a result of the formation of religious employee-resource groups and/or interfaith organizations?
4. If tolerance for and education about different religions seem to be the trend in today's workplace, why has the number of complaints filed with the EEOC risen steadily over the past 10 years?

Case Study: Purity of Spirit: Tom's of Maine

Tom's of Maine is a living, breathing—and profiting—proof that a business enterprise can be good for the earth, good for society, good for its employees, and good for its shareholders

Tom Chappell[1]

Tom's of Maine, located in Kennebunk, Maine, is a manufacturer and marketer of all-natural personal care products. The family-owned company was founded by the husband and wife team of Tom and Kate Chappell. The couple started the company because they were unable to find natural

Source: This case has been adapted by Dr. Kathryn A. Cañas and Dr. Harris Sondak from a case written by Dr. Edmund R. Gray, Department of Management, Loyola Marymount University, and Kimberly S. Petropoulos.

personal care products for their family to use and consequently believed that there must be a market for such products.

All company products are made from natural ingredients, so they are free of artificial colors, sweeteners such as saccharin, synthetic preservatives, flavors, and fragrances. Additionally, they contain no animal by-products and are not tested on animals.[2]

Sales of company products are strongest on the East and West Coasts. Target customers are active, health-conscious adults who read labels, are involved in their communities, and value education. Company sales were approximately $35 million in 2001. The company's flagship product is toothpaste, which historically has accounted for 60 percent of its revenues, with a national market share of about 1 percent. The U.S. toothpaste industry is a $1.7-billion-per-year business. Current market leaders are Procter and Gamble's Crest and Colgate-Palmolive's Colgate brands.[3]

At the beginning of 2000, Tom's had 120 employees but found itself in a self-imposed hiring freeze because of its heavy investment in a new line of alcohol-free cough, cold, and wellness products. With the introduction of the new line, the company was marketing about 150 products. In addition to toothpaste and wellness products, the company also produces deodorant, flossing ribbon, mouthwash, soap, shampoo, and shaving cream.

History

In 1968, Tom and Kate Chappell left Philadelphia and their positions in the corporate world for Kennebunk, Maine, where they "moved back to the land" and experimented with natural food and personal care items and other environmentally friendly products. Two years later, with a $5,000 loan from a friend and a single product named Clearlake, they started Tom's of Maine. Clearlake was the first nonphosphate liquid laundry detergent offered for sale in the United States. In addition to being less polluting, Clearlake came in refillable containers that were labeled with postage-paid mailers to facilitate customers returning them for reuse.[4]

The company inaugurated its signature all-natural personal care product line in 1973 with soap, shampoo, and skin lotion. Natural toothpaste was introduced in 1975. Other products followed, first baby shampoo, then deodorant, mouthwash, and shaving cream. Early on, Tom's products were distributed principally through health food stores. Moreover, from the very beginning, the company shunned the conventional practice of testing products on animals.

By 1981, sales had risen to $1.5 million. Having achieved this level, Chappell wanted to take his products into the mainstream market. To accomplish this goal, he knew that he needed to add professional talent to manage the growth of new accounts, more complex distribution channels, and a burgeoning advertising budget. Hence, he added a few new board members with business acumen and then hired several experienced marketing executives along with some young MBAs. As a result, Tom's of Maine implemented a strategy of aggressive growth by expanding beyond health food stores to big supermarkets and drugstore chains. This strategy resulted in an increase of sales to approximately $2 million in 1983.

The rapid growth strategy, however, exposed a germinating conflict between Chappell and the new professionals. For instance, the new MBAs tried to convince Chappell to add saccharin to his toothpaste to sweeten it, thus making it more palatable to the mainstream market. As Chappell perceived it, they were promoting decisions based on the numbers rather than adhering to his vision of commitment to natural products. Recalling this time in company history, Chappell noted that "our values were pushed to the margin, growth and profit dominated business planning."[5] As a consequence of these tensions, Tom Chappell found time spent at his company less and less fulfilling and began to search for inspiration elsewhere. He remembers confiding to two old friends that he was considering going to theological seminary and becoming an Episcopal minister. But one of the friends suggested that perhaps Tom's of Maine was his ministry.[6]

In 1988, Chappell enrolled on a part-time basis at Harvard Divinity School. For the next three years, he spent two and a half days a week in Kennebunk running the company and the remainder of the work week in Cambridge. At Harvard, he studied the writings of the great moral and religious philosophers, such as Immanuel Kant, Martin Buber, and Jonathan Edwards, and tried to relate their ideas to business in general and to Tom's of Maine in particular. On returning to Tom's full-time, Chappell's first priority was to codify the company's mission and values. Over an intense period of three months, first with the participation of the board of directors and later the entire company staff, two key documents—"Statement of Beliefs" and "Mission Statement"— were developed and approved (see Appendix A).[7]

Nineteen ninety-three and 1994 were trying years for Tom's of Maine. The company's newly reformulated deodorant did not perform consistently and was disliked by customers. On discovering these problems, Chappell ordered a recall at a cost of $400,000 to the company (to help cover the cost, the advertising budget was slashed 25 percent) and apologized to the company's customers. The incident came to be known throughout the company as the "deodorant debacle" and led to a significant revision of its product development process.[8]

The product recall, along with stiffer competition from the major brands (e.g., Crest and Colgate), which had introduced their own healthy baking soda toothpastes, led to the company's first loss—$400,000 in fiscal 1994. In response, Chappell hired additional salespeople with major brand experience, added a former PepsiCo executive to the board, and introduced new toothpaste flavors along with an entire line of fruity-flavored children's toothpaste. Earnings recovered to $650,000 in 1995.

Representing a sizable investment for the company, Tom's introduced a major new line of wellness products in 1999. The new line included natural echinacea tonics, nasal decongestants, Cough & Cold Rub, Natural Muscle Balm, and liquid herbal extracts. These products were developed by an interdisciplinary team of pharmacognosists (natural-medicine specialists), herbalists, and chemists put together by the company. To assure the quantity and quality of botanicals needed, the company purchased its own farm in Saxton Rivers, Vermont. Additionally, the company contracted with other organic growers for the required ingredients not produced on its farm. The new line was distributed through health food stores in the United States, Canada, and the United Kingdom.[9]

Tom and Kate Chappell seriously considered selling the company in the mid-1990s to achieve financial freedom and to pursue other interests. Working with their investment banker, they established specific criteria for the acquisition based on their company's beliefs and mission. They insisted that price not be the controlling factor in the decision but rather the dedication of the acquiring firm to the company's stated values. Six potential purchasers were identified but all found the acquisition criteria too restrictive and dropped out of the bidding. The Chappells found at that time that they could not sell their business without compromising their own values, which they were unwilling to do.[10] However, the Chappells sold an 86 percent interest in their company to Colgate-Palmolive in March 2006 for $100 million. Under the purchase agreement, the Chappells retain day-to-day management control as CEO and vice president for three years. Colgate has agreed to keep the business located in Maine and to maintain the Chappell's socially conscious management principles; in particular, Colgate has agreed to donate $125,000 annually to charity, exceeding the company's previous yearly contributions.[11]

A Spirituality-Inspired Business Philosophy

Tom Chappell grew up in western Massachusetts surrounded by farms and fields, and his family enjoyed frequent vacations in Maine. Early in life he developed a love of the land and a sensitivity to the natural environment that eventually became a vital part of his business philosophy. The fact that he was raised in the Episcopal Church and that his father was a successful entrepreneur also played a large role in the development of his personal values. Chappell has said, "When you have a family business, it becomes the DNA of every member of the family."[12]

Although Tom Chappell expressed his strongly held personal values of respect for both people and nature from the founding of the company, he was also a highly competitive businessman who wanted to grow a large and successful company. The conflicts between the company's emerging professionalism as it grew and Tom's personal values eventually led to his enrollment at Harvard Divinity School. While at Harvard he came to the conclusion, as his friend had suggested several years earlier, that the company was his true ministry, and there he developed a language that would allow him to "debate his bean-counters."[13]

Early in his academic program Chappell studied the work of Martin Buber, the twentieth-century Jewish philosopher who argued that people can have two opposite attitudes toward others, leading to two distinct types of relationships. In one, the "I-It" relationship, people treat other people as objects and expect something back from each relationship. In the other, the "I-Thou" relationship, the individual relates to others out of respect, friendship, and love. In other words, people see others either as objects to use for their own selfish purposes or honor them for their own sake. Chappell concluded that he and Kate instinctively had been doing business using the I-Thou relationship, and his professional managers were behaving in terms of the I-It model.

Chappell was also deeply influenced by the writings of the eighteenth-century American philosopher Jonathan Edwards. Edwards believed that an individual's identity comes not from being separate but from being connected or in relationship to others. Chappell began thinking of Tom's in this light, perceiving it not simply as a private entity but in relation to other entities including employees, customers, suppliers, financial partners, governments, the community, and even the earth itself. He concluded that the company had obligations to each of these that could be defined in terms of time, money, and priorities.

The ideas of Buber, Edwards, and other philosophers became the ideological underpinnings for the development of Tom's of Maine's purpose, mission, and belief statements. Once this moral foundation was in place, Chappell's next challenge was to manage the company in accordance with its stated values.

Two events illustrate the trade-offs presented by the new decision criteria. The first centered on the company's application, in the early 1990s, to the American Dental Association (ADA) to receive its Seal of Acceptance for three fluoride toothpaste flavors. The ADA required a standard efficacy protocol that is lethal to rats. Rather than compromise its values, the company worked with the ADA to develop an acceptable test that could be conducted on human subjects and in 1995 received the association's coveted seal. Because of the cumbersome process of developing a new protocol, the firm's application for acceptance took several years longer and cost approximately 10 times as much as it would have otherwise.

Interestingly, a year later the Food and Drug Administration (FDA) suggested a set of new rules for fluoride toothpaste that required testing on animals. Tom's strenuously lobbied the FDA to modify these rules and eventually identified a nonanimal protocol that was acceptable to the agency.[14]

The second event occurred during the formulation of plans for the new wellness line. It was determined that the company could save $250,000 if it located the entire production and packaging operation for the product line in Vermont as opposed to the original plan of extracting the herbs in Vermont and shipping them back to Maine for packaging. Rather than make the financially optimal decision, Chappell, adhering to the company's commitment to the Kennebunk community, split the work between the two locales.

Values-Centered Leadership

In 1999, Tom Chappell summed up his philosophy of business decision making in his book *Managing Upside Down: The Seven Intentions of Values-Centered Leadership.*[15] Here he rejects the concept of managing for maximum financial gain and instead argues for reversing the values of American business by placing social and ethical responsibilities at the apex of the business goal hierarchy. He further asserts that if a company makes people and other entities the central focus of its decision making, it will be rewarded through the marketplace with growth and profits. He underscores this assertion in the book's introduction: "I have been running our company according to a mission of respecting customers, employees, community, and the environment, and we are creating more products and making more money than I ever dreamed."

The book's title, *Managing Upside Down,* also refers to flattening the organizational hierarchy and empowering people and teams at the lower end of the structure. Indeed, Chappell credits the large expansion of the company's product line during the last three years of the 1990s to the creativity and follow-through of his newly empowered product-development teams (known in the company as Acorns).

Chappell devotes a major portion of the book to what he calls the seven intentions of values-centered leadership (see Appendix B). The intentions are guidelines that managers who desire to run profitable businesses that are also socially and morally responsible can apply. After the publication of the book, Chappell established a nonprofit educational foundation, The Salt Water Institute, founded in Boulder, Colorado, and now located in Portland, Maine, to teach these "intentions" and his overall philosophy of managing through moral values.[16]

Organizational Design and Diversity

Tom Chappell describes the organizational structure at Tom's of Maine as a triangle inside a circle. The circle represents the team, which is the basic unit of organization. Teams meet in circles (there are no elongated conference tables at Tom's) to emphasize equality and to encourage everyone to contribute ideas. Chappell credits the circle concept with the creation of many of the innovative ideas and solutions that have helped the company grow and prosper in recent years. He asserts, "the power of the circle is in its openness; it is the place where you are willing to open up and listen."[17] He also credits the circle with improving employee morale.

The triangle symbolizes the company's authority structure. As Chappell sees it, Tom's is not a consensus organization. There is a leader on each team who is accountable to a higher manager, and there is a clear chain of command. Ideally, the two systems—circle and triangle—work in harmony; The circle encourages participation and creativity, and the triangle provides an apparatus for decision making and accountability.

Tom Chappell also sees intentional diversity as a critical element of the company's organizational design. After returning from divinity school, he came to the conclusion that diversity in hiring is not simply a moral responsibility but also can lead to marketplace advantage for the firm. He explained his thinking this way:

> It was not long before I realized that the more sensitive my executives and I could become to the differences of the people we were trying to serve, and the more perspectives we could plug into our discussions about product design, business strategy, and customer service, the more broadly the company could range to meet its financial objectives. We had to listen to as many different sources as possible, both inside and outside the company.[18]

Because Tom's was a male-dominated company through most of its history, Chappell made bringing more women into the company a priority. By 1993, 40 percent of the workforce was female, and two key department managers were women. But Chappell also sees diversity as much more than simply hiring and promoting women and people of color. For Chappell, diversity encompasses factors such as age, education, experience, and background; a diversity of perspectives combined with the openness of a circle results in more innovative and effective business decisions. In support of its diversity goal, the company has a policy of open hiring for all jobs. In other words, when a job becomes open, all candidates, inside and outside, are given equal consideration. The thinking is that hiring only from within the company leads to greater homogeneity, the very opposite of what the company hopes to achieve.[19]

Empowering Employees and the Community

Chappell, since returning to the company full-time, has devoted much of his time to formulating the company's mission and beliefs and to molding a corporate culture that embodies these tenets. Commenting on one of the bigger mistakes he made, Chappell noted that simply handing down the company's mission and beliefs is not enough, that it is important for the staff to see the company mission in action and that "you have to do the training."[20] In practice this includes setting the example through his own behavior and decisions, encouraging and rewarding the people who "live the mission," and holding workshops and seminars on topics of company values and behavior.

Tom's policy on volunteerism is one prominent way the company is trying to live its mission. Under this policy, employees are encouraged to spend 5 percent of their paid work time (two hours per week or two and a half weeks per year) doing volunteer work for nonprofit organizations of their choosing. This policy was instituted in 1989 and has proved popular with employees as well as helpful to the beneficiaries. Volunteer chores have been as varied as the interests of Tom's diverse workforce. Many company employees take advantage of this opportunity by volunteering at local food shelters, The Animal Welfare Society, Big Brothers–Big Sisters, and at their children's schools. In one unique example, an employee brought her dog once a week to a nursing home to provide comfort and companionship for the residents.

In addition to promoting individual volunteerism, the company occasionally organizes day-long projects that may include as much as one-third of its workforce. In one instance,

14 employees, including Tom Chappell, drove to Rhode Island and spent the day helping clean up an oil spill. One of the participating employees commented afterward that the venture not only was helpful to the people of Rhode Island but also was a bonding and team-building experience for the participating employees.[21]

The company provides a generous benefit package to its employees, including four weeks of parental leave for both mothers and fathers, as well as offers flexible work schedules, job sharing, and work-at-home programs. Child-care and elder-care referral service is provided, and child care is partially reimbursed for employees earning less than $32,500 annually. Largely as a result of these family-friendly policies, Tom's was named in 1998, for the sixth year in a row, by *Working Mother* as one of the 100 best companies for working moms.[22]

Respecting the Individual and the Environment

Tom Chappell perceives his company as a social and moral entity as well as a business organization and has fashioned a body of policies and programs to help realize this goal. These initiatives include policies in the areas of the environment, animal rights, and consumer issues as well as community- and environmentally based giving programs.

Giving Programs

Tom's of Maine has committed to donating 10 percent of its pretax profits to nonprofit organizations. In the early years when profits were lean, the company confined most of its giving to community organizations and environmental groups in Maine and Massachusetts. As profits grew and more money became available, donations to charities widened in scope and dollar amount. The company's grant program is divided into four general areas: education, the arts, the environment, and indigenous peoples.[23]

Approximately 40–50 grants per year are awarded either in the form of one-time grants or multiyear pledges. Most are in the $500–$5,000 range, with larger amounts reserved for the multiyear pledges. Recent beneficiaries include Harvard Divinity School's Center for the Study of Values in Public Affairs, the Maine Audubon Society, and elementary education programs in Maine for teaching about the environment. An early grant from the company began the curbside recycling program in Kennebunk. Other donations have gone to the Rainforest Alliance, Maine Women's Fund, Maine Business for Social Responsibility, the National Parks and Conservation Fund, and a project in Portland, Oregon, to protect its regional watersheds.

In 1999, Tom's of Maine was the sole corporate sponsor of "Reason for Hope," a PBS documentary about the scientist-conservationist Jane Goodall. The company views this sponsorship as a natural fit because it shares common values with Dr. Goodall. Prior to sponsoring the television special, the company for two years had been contributing to the Jane Goodall Institute and the related "Roots and Shoots," an international environmental and humanitarian teaching program. In support of this program, the company included coupon inserts with its products that encouraged customers to mail back the coupons; in return, Tom's promised to donate $1 for each coupon returned. Additionally, the company offered to pay the $25 initiation fee for any school or community wishing to establish a Roots and Shoots program.

Tom's sponsors the national environmental radio program *E-Town*. The company has also made product donations to needy causes. For instance, in April 1999 it sent 50,000 bars of soap to the American Red Cross for families in war-ravaged Kosovo.

Environmental Policies

In addition to giving to environmental causes, Tom's has introduced numerous proenvironmental practices in its operations. Toothpaste is packaged in aluminum tubes that can be recycled when empty rather than in the less expensive, nonrecyclable plastic laminates used by most other manufacturers. Moreover, its toothpaste as well as some of its other products are packaged in 100 percent recycled paperboard cartons, of which 65 percent is postconsumer content.

Mouthwash and glycerin soap are packaged in natural-color HDPE (type 2) plastic bottles, which are considered better for recycling than other options. Shampoo is bottled in containers made from recycled milk jugs, and these bottles are, in turn, recyclable. All leaflets that are enclosed in the packaging are printed on dioxin-free paper using soy-based inks. All outgoing products are shipped in boxes made from 95 percent postconsumer cardboard. Also, because Tom's products are made from all-natural ingredients, they are biodegradable.

In the mid-1990s, the company installed an ecologically improved system for filtering the factory's wastewater. With this system, by the time water reaches the leaching bed in a field near the manufacturing facility, it has run through a tank containing layers of peat moss, stone, gravel, and sand that remove the majority of its pollutants.[24] Additionally, the company's farm in Vermont, where the botanical ingredients for its wellness line are grown, practices sustainable harvesting of herbs and is certified organic.

Respect for animals is an important value at Tom's. Consequently, the company does not use any animal ingredients in its products. Moreover, in 1991 the company extended its prohibition on animal testing to its suppliers, requiring them to sign a written guarantee that the ingredients supplied have not been tested on animals.[25]

Consumer Policies

Tom's of Maine's mission emphasizes full disclosure of product information and open dialogue with its customers. From the beginning, the Chappells have always listed all ingredients contained in their products on the packaging along with the source of the ingredients and an explanation of their purpose. They believe that this policy builds customer confidence and loyalty. A related trust-building measure is the signature of Kate and Tom Chappell on all company products.

Another trust-building company policy is to answer every letter from its customers with a personalized return letter. Organizationally, this is the responsibility of the company's Consumer Dialogue Team. This is no small task, since the firm receives some 10,000 letters per year (the team estimates that about 80 percent of them represent positive consumer feedback).

As another means of communicating with its customers, Tom's includes inserts with many of its products. Recently, the company teamed up with Leave No Trace, Inc. (LNT), an organization that promotes responsible outdoor skills, for an insert campaign. The inserts stressed the six principles of Leave No Trace and provided additional environmentally responsible tips for campers.

Spirituality in the Workplace

Tom's of Maine is only one example of the corporate trend in spiritually informed leadership.[26] It is indeed a difficult task for leaders who want to instill their values in the workplace to "create a complex, multivocal conversation among managers and employees about what values the company should uphold" rather than to use their power to impose their beliefs by declaring that "his or her values should apply to the company."[27] In other words, there is a difference between requiring a workforce to embrace one's religious beliefs and empowering all employees through a spiritual framework.

Associate Professor of Leadership Studies and Religion at the University of Richmond's Jepson School Dr. Douglas A. Hicks, who is an ordained minister in the Presbyterian Church and author of two books, *Inequality and Christian Ethics* and *Religion and the Workplace: Pluralism, Spirituality, and Leadership,* maintains that an important goal for leaders is to create a framework of "respectful pluralism." Respectful pluralism reflects an organization that is not "aligned with any explicitly religious, spiritual, or other comprehensive worldview" and where "organizations should allow for significant employee expression of various aspects of their identity on an equal basis."[28] He explains that when such expression occurs there is a shift from a workplace that is simply described as "diverse" to one that represents "pluralism"—"a term that reflects a positive quality of relationships among diverse people."[29]

Tom's of Maine is, perhaps, one of the few companies that reflects pluralism insofar as its spiritual philosophy is based on the interconnection among its founders, employees, management, shareholders, community, environment, and the earth.

Discussion Questions

1. How should management accommodate a variety of conflicting spiritual perspectives in the workplace?
2. Tom Chappell created a spiritual framework for Tom's of Maine, a family-owned business. Can such a framework be created for a publicly traded company? What differences might there be in its effects?
3. To what extent is Tom Chappell's spiritual perspective responsible for the company's organizational culture and the company's successes and/or failures?
4. What risks might a company encounter when encouraging the expression of spiritual values in the workplace? What advantages does it gain?

APPENDIX A

The Tom's of Maine Mission

To serve our customers by providing safe, effective, innovative natural products of high quality.

To build relationships with our customers that extend beyond product usage to include full and honest dialogue, responsiveness to feedback, and the exchange of information about products and issues.

To respect, value, and serve not only our customers but also our coworkers, owners, agents, suppliers, and community; to be concerned about and contribute to their well-being; and to operate with integrity so as to be deserving of their trust.

To provide meaningful work, fair compensation, and a safe, healthy work environment that encourages openness, creativity, self-discipline, and growth.

To contribute to and affirm a high level of commitment, skill, and effectiveness in the work community.

To recognize, encourage, and seek a diversity of gifts and perspectives in our work life.

To acknowledge the value of each person's contribution to our goals and to foster teamwork in our tasks.

To be distinctive in products and policies which honor and sustain our natural world.

To address community concerns, in Maine and around the globe, by devoting a portion of our time, talents, and resources to the environment, human needs, the arts, and education.

To work together to contribute to the long-term value and sustainability of our company.

To be a profitable and successful company while acting in a socially and environmentally responsible manner.

To create and manage a system of accountability which holds each person in the Company's employment or governance responsible for individual behavior and personal performance consistent with the Company's Beliefs, Mission, Destiny, Performance Goals, and Individual Work Plans.

STATEMENT OF BELIEFS

We believe that both human beings and nature have inherent worth and deserve our respect.

We believe in products that are safe, effective, and made of natural ingredients.

We believe that our company and our products are unique and worthwhile, and that we can sustain these genuine qualities with an ongoing commitment to innovation and creativity.

We believe that we have a responsibility to cultivate the best relationships possible with our coworkers, customers, owners, agents, suppliers, and community.

We believe that different people bring different gifts and perspectives to the team and that a strong team is founded on a variety of gifts.

We believe in providing employees with a safe and fulfilling work environment and an opportunity to grow and learn.

We believe that competence is an essential means of sustaining our values in a competitive marketplace.

We believe our company can be financially successful while behaving in a socially responsible and environmentally sensitive manner.

We believe that we have an individual and collective accountability to the Company's beliefs, mission, destiny, and performance goals.

APPENDIX B

The Seven Intentions of Values-Centered Leadership

1. **Intention #1: Connect.** Set aside your own ego, open up, and connect to an outside universal force that is bigger than you and available to everyone, the power of goodness.
2. **Intention #2: Know Thyself, Be Thyself.** Explore who you are, your gifts, and what you care most about in life; these are the clues to finding meaning in your work.
3. **Intention #3: Envision Your Destiny.** Envision your future with your head and your heart: Your values in today's world call you to serve. How? The answer is your destiny, and as soon as you hear it, this destiny makes total sense.
4. **Intention #4: Seek Advice.** Every leader makes mistakes, which is why the values-centered manager never makes a decision without using the secret weapon of Managing Upside Down—a diverse group of expert advisors.

5. **Intention #5: Venture Out.** Build a creative strategy for every dimension of your new business, make sure it is aligned with your values, and go for it—even if there is nothing like it in the world.

6. **Intention #6: Assess.** No matter how creative we might choose to be or how unique we are in the marketplace, we are still accountable to our values, visions, and goals. Managing Upside Down is a trial-and-error process, and assessment requires constant affirmation and editing.

7. **Intention #7: Pass It On.** It is our responsibility to fellow humans to be in a state of constant donation. When we receive gifts, knowledge, goodness, extra time, and profits, we are obliged to pass them along to others. In the process, we set up an exchange or experiences and a trial-and-error process that can help us all improve.

Notes

1. Tom Chappell, *The Soul of a Business: Managing for Profit and the Common Good* (New York: Bantam Books, 1993), 215.

2. Tom's of Maine Information Sheets, undated.

3. Bette Popovich, "Focus Report: Cosmetics/Personal Care 2000: Multi-Benefit Products Top Dental Care Market," *Chemical Market Reporter*.

4. Tom's of Maine Information Sheet, undated.

5. Chappell, *The Soul of a Business,* 25.

6. Ibid.

7. Ibid., 20–31.

8. J. C. McCune, "Making Lemonade: Companies Must Try and (Sometimes Fail) in Order to Succeed," *Management Review* 86 (1997): 49–54.

9. Thomas M. Chappell, "Letters to the Editor," *Harvard Business Review* 75 (1997): 194–95.

10. Tom's of Maine Information Sheet, "Tom's Takes a Natural Step to Wellness."

11. Seth Harkness, "Colgate to Buy Tom's of Maine," *Portland Press Herald,* March 22, 2006, A1.

12. Thomas Garvey May, "You Get What You Give," *Natural Foods Merchandiser's New Product Review,* Spring 2000, 1.

13. "Interview with Tom Chappell, Minister of Commerce," *Business Ethics* 8, no. 1 (1994): 16.

14. "Respect for Animals," www.tomsofmaine.com/mission.

15. Tom Chappell, *Managing Upside Down: The Seven Intentions of Values-Centered Leadership* (New York: William Morrow, 1999).

16. May, "You Get What You Give," 1, 6, 8; "New Book by Tom's of Maine CEO Proves that Doing Good Is Good for Business," Jane Wesman Public Relations, news release, 2000.

17. Chappell, *Managing Upside Down,* 119.

18. Ibid., 134.

19. Ibid., 128–51.

20. C. Adams, "Breakaway (Special Report): The Entrepreneurial Life—Upfront: Brushing Up on Values," *Wall Street Journal* 27 (1999): 6.

21. J. C. McCune, "The Corporation in the Community," *HR Focus* 74 (1997): 12–14, "Corporate Volunteerism at Tom's," www.tomsofmaine.com.

22. "Tom's Named One of 100 Best Companies for Working Mothers," www.tomsofmaine.com.

23. The Tom's of Maine Grant Program, www.tomsofmaine.com.

24. Elissa Wolfson, "Brushing Up on Business," *E: The Environmental Magazine,* July/August 1995, 10.

25. "Respect for Animals."

26. Other examples of spiritual leadership include the following: C. W. Pollard of ServiceMaster, Max De Pree of Herman Miller, and S Truett Cathy of Chick-Fil-A.

27. Douglas A. Hicks, *Religion and the Workplace: Pluralism, Spirituality, Leadership* (New York: Cambridge University Press, 2003), 191.

28. Ibid., 184.

29. Ibid.

CHAPTER 8

Sexual Orientation and Identity

There is no federal law protecting gay men and lesbians in the workplace; the decision to protect gays and lesbians is made by each state. Currently, 13 states (Minnesota, Rhode Island, New Mexico, California, Illinois, Maine, Hawaii, New Jersey, Washington, Iowa, Oregon, Vermont, and Colorado) and the District of Columbia ban discrimination based on sexual orientation and gender identity/expression. Seven states have passed laws that ban discrimination based on sexual orientation only (Wisconsin, Massachusetts, Connecticut, New Hampshire, Nevada, Maryland, and New York). Furthermore, in terms of Fortune 500 companies, nearly 90 percent prohibit discrimination on the basis of sexual orientation; over 30 percent prohibit discrimination based on gender identity; and over 50 percent provide domestic health insurance benefits to their employees.

Objectives

- To examine the relationship between members of the lesbian gay bisexual transgender (LGBT) community and the workplace.
- To examine the changing societal views of the LGBT community and the current legislation supporting LGBT rights in the workplace.
- To examine how a public organization blatantly discriminated against gays and lesbians in the workplace.
- To discuss the issue of transgender at work.

Preview Questions

- How can managers most effectively accommodate people who have conflicting opinions about homosexuality in the workplace?
- How should managers handle a situation in which disparaging remarks are made to a gay coworker?
- Can a public company openly discriminate against gays and lesbians in the workplace? What influence do shareholders have in such decisions?

Some Important Dates

1924   The Society for Human Rights in Chicago becomes the country's earliest known gay rights organization.

1962   Illinois becomes the first U.S. state to decriminalize homosexual acts between consenting adults.

1973 The American Psychiatric Association removes homosexuality from its official list of mental disorders.

1982 The *Village Voice,* a New York City weekly newspaper, becomes the first employer to offer domestic partner benefits to its lesbian and gay employees.

1982 Wisconsin becomes the first state to outlaw discrimination on the basis of sexual orientation.

1993 The "Don't Ask, Don't Tell" policy is instituted for the U.S. military, permitting gays to serve in the military but banning homosexual self-identification and activity.

1996 The city of San Francisco passes the nation's first equal benefits ordinance, which requires employers that contract with the city government to offer the same benefits to employees' domestic partners as they offer to their legal spouses.

2000 Vermont becomes the first state in the country to recognize legal civil unions between gay or lesbian couples. The law states that these "couples would be entitled to the same benefits, privileges, and responsibilities as spouses." It stops short of referring to same-sex unions as marriage, which the state continues to define as pertaining only to heterosexual couples.

2004 On May 17, same-sex marriages become legal in Massachusetts.

LGBT Equality at the Fortune 500

Fortune magazine's 500 largest publicly-traded companies, which collectively employ nearly 25 million people, have made significant strides in advancing equal protections and benefits for their lesbian, gay, bisexual, and transgender employees. The more successful the company (and the higher the rank on the *Fortune* list), the more likely the company is to have these protections and benefits in place.

Fortune 500

- **the vast majority** (85 percent) prohibit discrimination on the basis of sexual orientation,
- **more than a third** (35 percent) prohibit discrimination based on gender identity, compared to just three in 2000, and
- **the majority** (57 percent) provide domestic partner health insurance benefits to their employees.

Fortune 10

The higher a company ranks on *Fortune* magazine's list of the most successful businesses, the more likely it is to provide comprehensive protections and benefits to LGBT employees. Among *Fortune* magazine's 10 largest publicly traded companies:

- **nine** (90 percent) prohibit discrimination based on sexual orientation,
- **six** (60 percent) prohibit discrimination based on gender identity and
- **eight** (80 percent) provide partner health benefits.

The top two employers, Exxon Mobil Corp. and Wal-Mart Stores Inc., have traded the No. 1 spot on the *Fortune* list over the last several years, each with revenues around $350 billion, but neither company provides domestic partner benefits or comprehensive non-discrimination policies.

Source: The Human Rights Campaign, "LGBT Equality at the Fortune 500," February 12, 2009, http://www.hrc.org/issues/fortune500.htm

ESSAY: SELECTIONS FROM *STRAIGHT TALK ABOUT GAYS IN THE WORKPLACE: CREATING AN INCLUSIVE, PRODUCTIVE ENVIRONMENT FOR EVERYONE IN YOUR ORGANIZATION*

Liz Winfeld, a nationally recognized expert in workplace diversity education and consulting specific to sexual orientation, gender identity, employee-resource group development, and domestic partner benefits, discusses a wide range of topics in her book, *Straight Talk about Gays in the Workplace: Creating an Inclusive, Productive Environment for Everyone in Your Organization*, 3rd ed. The following essay is excerpted from upcoming revisions to that book. The goal of the various selections is to provide a basic understanding of the situation facing the lesbian, gay, bisexual, transgender (LGBT) community in the workplace.

I would like to begin by making two important points that frame my discussion. First, that sexual orientation is not code for homosexuality. Sexual orientation is an aspect of humanity that dictates our physical and emotional attractions—nothing more and nothing less. There are four orientations: heterosexuality, homosexuality, bisexuality, and asexuality. First, issues of gender identity (a person's own sense of identification as male or female) or gender identity disorder (when a person who has been assigned one gender at birth identifies as belonging to another gender) have nothing whatsoever to do with sexual orientation. For that reason, a section on what is commonly referred to as "transgender at work" has been included in this essay. Second, heterosexuality is not only a sexual orientation, but it is the orientation experienced by a vast majority of human beings. Therefore, leaving it out of this discussion as if it were irrelevant is illogical and irresponsible. All of what follows must be read with these two important caveats in mind.

The Changing Landscape[1]

Beyond the increase in the number of states or commonwealths that have laws inclusive of sexual orientation and gender identity for the purposes of employment, housing, public accommodations, access to education, and access to credit, there are other significant changes in our society on issues that involve sexual orientation and gender identity.[2]

- The 2000 U.S. Census found 16 million self-identified gay/lesbian people and about 3 million who self-identified as being part of a same-sex household, with or without children.[3]
- Because of the findings of the 2000 census, there are two significant changes to the upcoming 2010 census. First, the classifications of persons will change from "single, married, widowed, separated, divorced" to "single, *partnered,* married, etc." Also, it was announced in June 2009 that the federal government will allow/require gay and lesbian people, who have been legally married (in any of the states that have legalized same-sex marriage), to recognize their marriages by reporting as married.
- Forty percent of Americans favor full legalization of marriage for nonheterosexual people; 25 percent favor only civil unions. When the percentages for both are counted among people 35 and younger, the percentage who favor same-sex marriage is well over 60 percent.[4]
- Thirteen states (California, Colorado, Hawaii, Illinois, Iowa, Maine, Minnesota, New Jersey, New Mexico, Oregon, Rhode Island, Vermont, and Washington) and the District of Columbia, by law, prohibit employment discrimination on the basis of real or perceived

sexual orientation or gender identity. An additional seven states (Connecticut, Massachusetts, Nevada, New Hampshire, Maryland, New York, and Wisconsin), prohibit this discrimination on the basis of sexual orientation only.

- A 2007 CNN poll reports that 79 percent of all Americans believe that gay people should be allowed to serve openly in the military.[5]
- More than 8 out of 10, or over 80 percent of heterosexual adults say that employees with same-sex partners should be equally eligible for key workplace benefits available to spouses of married employees in general.[6]
- More than 10,000 organizations in the public, private, nonprofit, and university sectors offer domestic partner benefits to either same-sex only or same- and opposite-sex couples and their families. There were exactly 100 such organizations on January 1, 1992, and about 7,000 in 2004.
- The percentage of organizations that include the words "sexual orientation" in their nondiscrimination policies has increased 7 to 10 percent every year for the past 10 years. Currently, more than 300 organizations (all sectors) also include "gender identity" or "gender identity/expression" in their nondiscrimination policies. Three years ago, there were less than 20. Now this number comprises more than a quarter of the Fortune 500 alone.[7]
- Sodomy laws have been declared unconstitutional, signaling a growing awareness that sexual orientation is part of who you are and not entirely what you do. Also, perhaps, that whatever it is you "do" is private, as long as it is between consenting adults. It is interesting to note that when the sodomy laws were finally struck down by the Supreme Court in 2004, of the 20 states that still had any form of sodomy laws on their books, 13 of them specified heterosexual sodomy along with homosexual sodomy.

What is behind the trend toward expanding the classifications of people who can take advantage of the civil and workplace rights that all Americans are otherwise entitled to? I think it is this: A 2007 survey conducted by the Pew Research Center for the People & the Press found that four in ten Americans report that some of their close friends or family members are gays or lesbians.[8] According to the Gill Foundation in 2003, the percentage of straight people who say they know at least one gay person is 90 percent.[9] And findings from the Human Rights Campaign (HRC) Public Report from February 2004 show that more than 60 percent of gay/lesbian people are "out" to even their casual acquaintances and coworkers.[10]

The data support the conclusion that seizing every opportunity to be as inclusive as possible is not only good for the individual and the collective psyche, it is also arguably good for the bottom line. To this point, Professor Richard Florida, of Carnegie Mellon University, and Gary Gates, a demographer at the Urban Institute, released data from a study they did in May 2003.[11] Some of their conclusions follow:

- New ideas and cutting-edge industries that lead to sustained prosperity are more likely to exist where gay people feel welcome.
- Most centers of tech-based business growth also have the highest concentration of gay couples. Conversely, major metropolitan areas with few gay couples tend to be slow- or no-growth places.
- Innovation and economic vitality are closely associated with the presence of gay people and other overt indicators of acceptance and diversity such as a high percentage of immigrants and the level of racial and ethnic integration.
- Creative, innovative, and entrepreneurial activities tend to flourish in the same kinds of places that attract gays and others outside the norm.

According to Florida, more than a few heterosexuals look for a "visible gay community as a signal of a place that is likely to be both exciting and comfortable . . . They are looking for signs that nonstandard people, and ideas, are welcome."[12]

This is an incredibly poignant statement and set of data, specifically because they reinforce what many believe about people and how they like to be treated. We want to see signs that the places where we reside and work acknowledge us. Furthermore, people want to know that if they exhibit creativity, innovation, or thinking outside of the box, they will be embraced, not alienated. Places that exhibit an acceptance of diversity are more likely to be places that will accept innovations of thought and action. This frees people and allows them to put forth their best effort.

Strategies for Inclusion in the New World[13]

The strategies at managers' disposal to deal effectively with sexual orientation and gender identity in the workplace include:

- endorsing the nondiscrimination policies such as the proposed Employment Non-Discrimination Act (ENDA);
- implementing domestic partner benefits;
- establishing employee-resource groups with both mentoring and reverse mentoring programs; and
- understanding that sexual orientation and gender identity are not the same but closely associated.

Nondiscrimination Policies and the ENDA

In 2000, 42 percent of Americans thought that sexual orientation was protected in a federal statue, and I would guess that more than one-third of all Americans still believe this today. The fact is that neither sexual orientation nor gender identity is part of any federal statute, code, or law. In addition to the 20 states that provide workplace protections on the basis of real or perceived sexual orientation and gender identity and seven others that limit these protections to real or perceived sexual orientation, there are about 300 cities, counties, and local jurisdictions that provide such protections in the form of ordinances. An ordinance, or an executive order, is binding but does not carry the weight (or redress) of law.

What this means is that LGBT people in 30 states and the majority of all jurisdictions have no protections under the law in terms of whether they can be fired or not hired just for being gay or straight, or can be denied credit or service in a hotel or a restaurant, or access to housing or education based on real or perceived sexual orientation.

When an organization includes the words "sexual orientation" and/or "gender identity" in its nondiscrimination policies, it is indeed meaningful. These policies matter as statements of intent by the organization. They say, "This is who we are, and this is how we intend to treat people who work here or with whom we have become affiliated."

An example of a nondiscrimination policy is the ENDA. This policy, largely unknown to many, has been floating around Congress for about eight years now. It would accomplish the following:

- extend to sexual orientation federal employment discrimination protections currently provided based on race, religion, sex, national origin, age, and disability;
- block public and private employers, employment agencies, and labor unions from using an individual's sexual orientation as the basis for employment decisions, such as hiring, firing, promotion, or compensation;

- allow for the same procedures and similar, but somewhat more limited, remedies as permitted under Title VII and the Americans with Disabilities Act; and
- apply to Congress, with the same procedures as provided by the Congressional Accountability Act of 1995, and presidential employees, with the same procedures as provided under the Presidential and Executive Office Accountability Act of 1996.

An updated version of the ENDA to include gender identity (or transgendered persons) was sent to the House of Representatives in 2008 where they promptly stripped out the language concerning transgender people and passed it. The Representatives thought it would not pass if transgender people were included in the legislation because gay people had recently become palatable enough to deserve basic human rights, but not trans people (this was their reasoning). The ENDA passed the House, but the Senate did not take up the policy because President Bush made it clear he would not sign it. It is uncertain when ENDA will come up for a vote again and whether it will be redrafted to include gender identity/expression. President Obama seems certain to sign it either way if the legislation comes to him.

Domestic Partner Benefits

As of the beginning of 2009, about 11,000 organizations had domestic partner benefits in place for same-sex couples, and about two-thirds of those had domestic partner benefits for heterosexual couples. These companies were of all kinds, of all sizes, and in all market segments, which is to say, public entities, including cities and states; private companies, including an overwhelming majority of the Fortune 1000; colleges and universities, including those beholden to state legislatures for funding; and private, nonprofit organizations, unions, and associations.

The primary reason for the continued strong support of domestic partner benefits for both gay and straight couples is that almost two decades of data firmly support the notion that domestic partner benefits are a low-cost, high-return way to demonstrate inclusion that results in little or no backlash. The plain fact is that multiple studies unequivocally show that approximately 90 percent of Americans believe that if you have a family and you work to support them, you deserve the benefits of that labor.

A topic that is becoming increasingly interesting regarding these benefits is the tax ramifications of having them. For years, people like me have been advocating for passage of a law called The Health Care Equity Act (House version) that would stop the practice of unfairly taxing employer-provided health care benefits to same or opposite sex (unmarried couples). This question has become more complicated by the fact that in six U.S. states where same-sex marriage is now legal (Massachusetts, Vermont, Maine, Connecticut, Iowa, and New Hampshire), the state tax ramifications have disappeared while the federal tax ramifications have remained. And, unfortunately, none of these six states, at this point in time, know how to deal with that discrepancy.

Get Sophisticated about Gender Identity Inclusion

Many people, including gay and lesbian people, think that *all* transgender people are also gay. This is not true. Anecdotal evidence to date indicates that 33 percent of transgender people are heterosexual; 33 percent are homosexual; 33 percent are bisexual; and the remaining 1 percent is asexual. So while there is more homosexuality and bisexuality among the transgendered population than among the nontransgendered population, it is not a 100 percent nonheterosexual community.

People's propensity to confuse one's orientation with one's presentation or realization of their gender is profound, and again, this confusion is not limited to heterosexuals; gay and lesbian people by and large do not understand this either.

Although the term, "transgender," is used frequently, it is often misunderstood. I view transgender as an umbrella term that can refer to one of the following three states of gender identity expression: "drag" behaviors, cross-dressing, and transexualism (when a person identifies with a physical sex different from the one with which he or she was born). It is vital that issues of gender identity be separated from issues of sexual orientation while also acknowledging that, aside from being incorrect, there is nothing wrong with the association of the transgender community with the gay/lesbian/bisexual community. Therefore, we must also acknowledge that trans people are indeed a tiny subset of humanity who need a "club" to join. Gay people may be, by and large, ignorant of transgender reality, but they are still a far more welcoming community (where these issues are concerned) than the general population. In sum, as we look toward the future, the distinction between sexual orientation and gender identity needs to be better understood and better reflected in workplace diversity efforts.

Employee Resource Groups

Employee resource groups offer employees who are connected by a common aspect of diversity (although in many organizations this commonality is not a requirement) to come together to recognize and develop potential solutions to a wide variety of workplace challenges—often related to their identity affiliation. The goal of employee resource groups is to create relationships and networking opportunities as well as to guide and enhance overall business growth. It is vital for all employee resource groups—be they formed around gender, race, national origin, age, religion, sexual identity, or disabilities—to be seen in two ways: holistically and as a resource.

1. Holistically: Employee resource groups must be inclusive. For example, a group formed around "race" should not be limited in scope or by name or mission statement as being only for African Americans, or a group formed around "gender" should not be named the Women's Network. It is critical that men not only know they are welcome, but that they are needed in the group. By the same token, the LGBT group should not consist of only members of the LGBT community. Sexual orientation is a human thing and straight, gay, bisexual and asexual people need to be purposefully included.
2. As a resource: These groups should not be positioned as clubs for people sharing a characteristic since, at the end of the day, we all share characteristics relative to our orientation, race, gender, etc. We all encompass aspects of multiple categories; therefore, these groups need to redouble their efforts to be perceived and treated as the "go to gang" for issues, policies, and programming related to their group.

The following structure for successful employee resource groups has been implemented at a number of organizations, both large and small:

1. Identify a leadership team for the employee resource group. These people will lead the charge for the formation of the employee resource group and have likely done extensive outreach with others in the organization. The employee resource group's team will typically have four to six people in it and, thanks to technology, they do not have to be located in the same place.

2. The leadership team organizes subcommittees and appoints a person who is not on the leadership team to head up each one. These subcommittees can be in as many areas as are deemed necessary or desired; for example, budget, community outreach, internal education, internal and external policy, cooperation with other employee groups, marketing and assisting revenue generation, liaison with human resources, communications, Pride events, and growing membership activities.

3. Each member of the leadership team is also the primary liaison between the committee and leadership team. It is this person's job to know what the committee is doing, what it would like to do, and what it needs, so that he or she can present those proposals to the leadership team.

4. A member of senior management is appointed as a liaison or mentor for each person on the leadership team and, therefore, to a committee. The communication that the leadership team member shares with the team in general is also shared with his or her management liaison. In this way, an effective and orderly communication channel is created among all the committees and the organization as a whole.

What is particularly significant about this structure is that it allows for maximum participation across the organization while also providing for maximum oversight of all activities of the employee resource groups, communication of those activities, and control over who is doing what without it appearing as if the employees are being micromanaged.

This question of structure and leadership is the perfect place to raise the discussion of mentoring. I would like to present two mentoring strategies:

1. Classic top-down mentoring: It is necessary for senior management to mentor employees on a fair and equitable basis regardless of the known or perceived sexual orientation of the mentee(s). Further, it is beneficial to have openly gay, lesbian, bisexual, asexual, or transgender people in management mentor others.

2. Reverse mentoring: Employee resource groups can act as an important resource for using reverse mentoring effectively. If a leader of an organization or even just a manager, supervisor, or peer-level person wants to know about how a population—for example, the GLBT population—relates to a particular business circumstance, opportunity, or challenge, why not make it a point to find a member of that community who is willing, proactively, to mentor that leader or manager in this area? This is a perfect example of how employee resource groups can start to make substantive contributions to the organization.

Internal and External Outreach Strategies

Internal outreach means doing everything possible to encourage participation by all types of people in the organization and going out of the way, perhaps far out of the way, to provide a safe environment where closeted gay people feel comfortable "coming out" or participating in any way that feels safe to them.

Community outreach means getting involved in some of what is going on in the communities in which your organization operates. It means supporting local organizations such as Parents, Families and Friends of Lesbians and Gays (PFLAG)[14] or endorsing ENDA to Congress. It also means allowing your employees to participate in community speaking programs, to work on behalf of your company in support of Meals on Wheels programs, or to join the fight against breast and ovarian cancer. Put more than your money out there; give members of your organization the opportunity to represent your business in these causes in their community. The positive public relations that you will receive from this will be well worth the negligible expense.

Internal Resources

In terms of internal resources, it is important to have a resource room, kiosk, or person who is informed about everything related to sexual orientation in every facility affiliated with your organization. Other strategies that the organization may want to consider spearheading include the following:

- a hotline to report all forms of harassment and discrimination including, but not necessarily limited to, sexual orientation;
- a system of accountability for a nonhostile work environment by division, work group, business unit, geography, or other criteria;
- expansion of existing reward/award programs to include recognition of superior efforts to engender a safer, better working environment for all—with an emphasis, perhaps, on sexual orientation; and
- encouragement of gay employees to bring their partners to appropriate company events or to display items from their personal lives.

If some or all of these organizational strategies for inclusion are adopted within the organization, benefits will be reaped in terms of greater productivity that is the direct result of increased job satisfaction.

Tools and Techniques[15]

What follows is a summary list of tools and techniques that a manager can implement as a way to become a more effective manager and leader within his or her organization:

1. Educate yourself about sexual orientation in order to formulate, and where necessary express, a position that balances one's own opinion with the change-agent behavior encouraged by the organization.
2. Try to avoid making heterosexist assumptions; that is, do not assume that everyone you work with or come into contact with is heterosexual or is of a traditionally gender identified point of view.
3. Share anything you have learned about human sexuality and homophobia that might encourage others to adopt productive behaviors.
4. Use inclusive language whenever possible in all communications.
5. Encourage gay and transgender coworkers to be part of the social groups you form at work, including bringing their partners to functions when appropriate.
6. Take time to understand the local laws and ordinances that relate to sexual orientation and gender identity, and especially your organization's nondiscrimination policies. If you have questions about these policies, ask.
7. Display items in your workspace, such as books, magnets, and posters that demonstrate your awareness of inclusiveness.
8. If someone asks you a question or confronts you with an opinion about sexual orientation in the workplace that you feel unprepared for, feel free to say that you do not know how to respond, but that you will get back to her or him. Then reach out to the organizational resources available to you so that you can respond in a meaningful and helpful way.

9. Refuse to laugh at antigay humor.

10. Cite company policy about nondiscrimination, or simply walk away from a group that is indulging in verbal discrimination. If you feel comfortable doing so, personalize the issue by saying, for example, "What you just did/said offends me."

11. Encourage other people to read books or attend education sessions on sexual orientation in order to avail themselves of other points of view if they seem particularly troubled by the issue.

Discussion Questions

1. Why, do you think, is the number of gay residents in a community associated with the innovation and economic growth of the area?

2. Is it a good idea for businesses to offer domestic partner benefits? Who should be eligible for these benefits—just gay couples or unmarried heterosexual couples too?

3. What is the most inclusive way to invite employees regardless of orientation or gender presentation to come to company-sponsored social events?

4. How can managers accommodate people who have conflicting opinions about homosexuality? In particular, what should they do when some employees are uncomfortable with others?

5. What alternative responses can you use when coworkers are making disparaging remarks about gays?

Notes

1. The material in this section is excerpted from chapter 1, "The Changing Landscape," in *Straight Talk about Gays in the Workplace: Creating an Inclusive, Productive Environment for Everyone in Your Organization*, 3rd ed. (Brighamton, NY: Harrington Park Press, 2005).

2. Not all the laws cover the same things in the same ways in each of the states, but what they have in common is that they are all laws as opposed to executive orders, ordinances, or regulations and so carry the weight of litigation.

3. Witeck-Combs/Harris Interactive, "HRC Public Report," February 2004. Available online at www.witckcombs.com.

4. Human Rights Campaign, "Gay Families Deserve Nothing Less Than Equality under the Law," January 22, 2004. Available online at www.hrc.org.

5. "Most Americans Believe Gays Should Be Allowed to Serve Openly in Military," Palm Center: Blueprints for Sound Public Policy, June 27, 2007, http://www.palmcenter.org/press/dadt/releases/most_americans_believe_gays_should_be_allowed_to_serve_openly_in_military

6. "Domestic Partner Benefits," http://www.hrc.org/issues/workplace/benefits/domestic_partner_benefits.htm; http://www.hrc.org/issues/workplace/benefits.asp

7. "GLBT Equality at the Fortune 500," http://www.hrc.org/issues/workplace/6989.htm.

8. Shawn Neidorf and Rich Morin, "Four-in-Ten Americans Have Close Friends or Relatives Who are Gay," *Pew Research Center Publications*, May 23, 2007, http://pewresearch.org/pubs/485/friends-who-are-gay

9. Statistics available online from the Gill Foundation at www.gillfoundation.com.

10. Witeck-Combs/Harris Interactive, "HRC Public Report," 2004.

11. Richard Florida, "Gay-tolerant Societies Prosper Economically," *USA Today*, May 1, 2003, 13A.

12. Ibid.

13. The material in this section is excerpted from chapters 2, 6, 7, and 8 in Winfeld, *Straight Talk about Gays in the Workplace*.

14. Parents, Families, and Friends of Lesbians and Gays, available online at www.pflag.org.

15. The material in this section is excerpted from chapter 2, "Strategies for Inclusion in the New World," in Winfeld, *Straight Talk about Gays in the Workplace*.

Case Study: The Cracker Barrel Restaurants

Discrimination against lesbians and gays is common in the workplace. Sole proprietors, managing partners, and corporate personnel officers can and often do make hiring, promoting, and firing decisions based on an individual's real or perceived sexual orientation. Lesbian and gay job applicants are turned down, and lesbian and gay employees are passed over for promotion or even fired by employers who view homosexuality as somehow detrimental to job performance or harmful to the company's public profile. Such discrimination frequently results from the personal biases of individual decision makers. It is rarely written into company policy and thus is difficult to trace. However, in January 1991, Cracker Barrel Old Country Store, Inc., a chain of family restaurants, became the first and only major American corporation in recent memory to expressly prohibit the employment of lesbians and gays in its operating units. A nationally publicized boycott followed, with demonstrations in dozens of cities and towns.

The Company: A Brief History of Cracker Barrel

Cracker Barrel was founded in 1969 by Dan Evins in his hometown of Lebanon, Tennessee, 40 miles east of Nashville. Evins, a 34-year-old ex-Marine sergeant and oil jobber, decided to take advantage of the traffic on the nearby interstate highway and open a gas station with a restaurant and gift shop. Specializing in down-home cooking at low prices, the restaurant was immediately profitable.

Evins began building Cracker Barrel stores throughout the region, gradually phasing out gasoline sales. By 1974, he owned a dozen restaurants. Within five years of going public in 1981, Cracker Barrel doubled its number of stores and quadrupled its revenues: In 1986, there were 47 Cracker Barrel restaurants with net sales of $81 million. Continuing to expand aggressively, the chain again grew to twice its size and nearly quadrupled its revenues during the next five years.

By the end of the fiscal year, August 2, 1991, Cracker Barrel operated over 100 stores, almost all located along the interstate highways of the Southeast and, increasingly, the Midwest. Revenues exceeded $300 million. Employing roughly 10,000 nonunionized workers, Cracker Barrel ranked well behind such mammoth family chains as Denny's and Big Boy in total sales, but led all U.S. family chains in sales per operating unit for both 1990 and 1991.

As of 1991, Cracker Barrel was a well-recognized corporate success story, known for its effective, centralized, but authoritarian leadership. From its headquarters, Cracker Barrel maintained uniformity in its store designs, menu offerings, and operating procedures. Travelers and local customers dining at any Cracker Barrel restaurant knew to expect a spacious, homey atmosphere; an inexpensive, country-style meal; and a friendly, efficient staff. All were guaranteed by Dan Evins, who remained as president, chief executive officer, and chairman of the board.

Source: John Howard, University of York, United Kingdom, in Carol P. Harvey and M. June Ailard, *Understanding and Managing Diversity: Readings, Cases, and Exercises*, 3rd ed. (Englewood Cliffs, NJ: Prentice Hall, 2005), 302–10.

John Howard is lecturer in American history and associate faculty in women's studies at the University of York, United Kingdom. A native of Brandon, Mississippi, he is the author of *Men Like That: A Southern Queer History*, 1999, University of Chicago Press and the editor of *Carryin' On in the Lesbian and Gay South*, 1997, New York University Press.

The Policy: No Lesbian or Gay Employees

In early January 1991, managers in the roughly 100 Cracker Barrel operating units received a communique from the home office in Lebanon. The personnel policy memorandum from William Bridges, vice president of human resources, declared that Cracker Barrel was "founded upon a concept of traditional American values." As such, it was deemed "inconsistent with our concept and values and . . . with those of our customer base, to continue to employ individuals . . . whose sexual preferences fail to demonstrate normal heterosexual values, which have been the foundation of families in our society."

Throughout the chain, individual store managers, acting on orders of corporate officials, began conducting brief, one-on-one interviews with their employees to see if any were in violation of the new policy. Cheryl Summerville, a cook in the Douglasville, Georgia, store for $3^1/_2$ years, asked if she were a lesbian, knew she had to answer truthfully. She felt she owed that to her partner of 10 years. Despite a history of consistently high performance evaluations, Summerville was fired on the spot, without warning and without severance pay. Her official separation notice, filled out by the manager and filed with the state department of labor, clearly indicated the reason for her dismissal: "This employee is being terminated due to violation of company policy. The employee is gay." Cracker Barrel fired as many as 16 other employees across several states in the following months. These workers, mostly waiters, were left without any legal recourse. Lesbian and gay antidiscrimination statutes were in effect in Massachusetts and Wisconsin and in roughly 80 U.S. cities and counties, but none of the firings occurred in those jurisdictions. Federal civil rights laws, the employees learned, did not cover discrimination based upon sexual orientation.

Under pressure from a variety of groups, the company issued a statement in late February 1991. In it, Cracker Barrel management said, "We have revisited our thinking on the subject and feel it only makes good business sense to continue to employ those folks who will provide the quality service our customers have come to expect." The recent personnel policy had been a "well-intentioned overreaction." Cracker Barrel pledged to deal with any future disruptions in its units "on a store-by-store basis." Activists charged that the statement did not represent a retraction of the policy, as some company officials claimed. None of the fired employees had been rehired, activists noted, and none had been offered severance pay. Moreover, on February 27, just days after the statement, Dan Evins reiterated the company's antagonism toward nonheterosexual employees in a rare interview with a Nashville newspaper. Lesbians and gays, he said, would not be employed in more rural Cracker Barrel locations if their presence was viewed to cause problems in those communities.

The Boycott: Queer Nationals Versus Good Ol' Boys

The next day, when news of Cracker Barrel employment policies appeared in the *The Wall Street Journal*, *New York Times*, and *Los Angeles Times*, investment analysts expressed surprise. "I look on [Cracker Barrel executives] as pretty prudent businesspeople," said one market watcher. "These guys are not fire-breathing good ol' boys." Unconvinced, lesbian and gay activists called for a nationwide boycott of Cracker Barrel restaurants and began a series of demonstrations that attracted extensive media coverage.

The protest movement was coordinated by the Atlanta chapter of Queer Nation, which Cheryl Summerville joined as cochair with fellow cochair Lynn Cothren, an official with the Martin Luther King, Jr., Center for Non-Violent Social Change in Atlanta. Committed to nonviolent civil disobedience, lesbian and gay activists and supporters staged pickets and sit-ins at various Cracker Barrel locations, often occupying an entire restaurant during peak lunch hours, ordering only coffee.

Protesters were further angered and spurred on by news in June from Mobile, Alabama. A 16-year-old Cracker Barrel employee had been fired for effeminate mannerisms and subsequently was thrown out of his home by his father. Demonstrations continued throughout the summer of 1991, spreading from the Southeast to the Midwest stores. Arrests were made at demonstrations in the Detroit area; Cothren and Summerville were among several people arrested for criminal trespass at both the Lithonia and Union City, Georgia, stores. Reporters and politicians dubbed Summerville the "Rosa Parks of the movement," after the woman whose arrest sparked the Montgomery, Alabama, Bus Boycott of 1955–1956.

Support for the Cracker Barrel boycott grew, as organizers further charged the company with racism and sexism. Restaurant gift shops, they pointed out, sold Confederate flags, black mammy dolls, and other offensive items. The Cracker Barrel board of directors, they said, was indeed a good ol' boy network, made up exclusively of middle-aged and older white men. In addition, there was only one female in the ranks of upper management.

The Resolution: New York Attempts to Force Change

Meanwhile, New York City comptroller, Elizabeth Holtzman, and finance commissioner, Carol O'Cleiracain, at the urging of the National Gay and Lesbian Task Force, wrote a letter to Dan Evins, dated March 12, 1991. As trustees of various city pension funds, which owned about $3 million in Cracker Barrel stock, they were "concerned about the potential negative impact on the company's sales and earnings, which could result from adverse public reaction." They asked for a "clear statement" of the company's policy regarding employment and sexual orientation, as well as a description of "what remedial steps, if any, [had] been taken by the company respecting the employees dismissed."

Evins replied in a letter of March 19 that the policy had been rescinded and that there had been "no negative impact on the company's sales." Unsatisfied, the city of New York officials wrote back, again inquiring as to the status of the fired workers. They also asked that the company put forth a policy that "would provide unequivocally" that discrimination based on sexual orientation was prohibited. Evins never responded.

Shortly thereafter, Queer Nation launched a "buy one" campaign. Hoping to gain additional leverage in company decision making, activists became stockholders by purchasing single shares of Cracker Barrel common stock. At the least, they reasoned, the company would suffer from the relative expense of mailing and processing numerous one-cent quarterly dividend checks. More importantly, they could attend the annual stockholders meeting in Lebanon, Tennessee.

In November 1991, company officials successfully prevented the new shareholders from participating in the annual meeting, and they used a court injunction to block protests at the corporate complex. Nonetheless, demonstrators lined the street, while inside, a representative of the New York City comptroller's office announced the submission of a resolution "banning employment discrimination against gay and lesbian men and women," to be voted on at the next year's meeting. The resolution was endorsed by the Philadelphia Municipal Retirement System, another major stockholder. Cracker Barrel refused any further public comment on the issue.

The Effect: No Decline in Corporate Growth

The impact of the boycott on the corporate bottom line was negligible. Trade magazines reiterated the company's claim that neither sales nor stock price had been negatively affected. Indeed, net sales remained strong, up 33 percent at fiscal yearend 1992 to $400 million, owing in good part to continued expansion: There were now 127 restaurants in the chain. Though the increase in same-store sales was not as great as the previous year, Cracker Barrel at least could boast growth, while other chains blamed flat sales on the recession. Cracker Barrel stock, trading on the NASDAQ exchange, appreciated 18 percent during the first month after news of the scandal broke, and the stock remained strong throughout the next fiscal year, splitting three-for-two in the third quarter.

Dan Evins had good reason to believe that the firings and the boycott had not adversely impacted profitability. One market analyst said that "the feedback they get from their customers might be in favor of not hiring homosexuals." Another even ventured that "it's plausible . . . the majority of Cracker Barrel's local users support an explicit discriminatory policy." Such speculation was bolstered by social science surveys indicating that respondents from the South and from rural areas in particular tended to be less tolerant of homosexuality than were other Americans.

Queer Nationals looked to other measures of success, claiming at least partial victory in the battle. Many customers they met at picket lines and inside restaurants vowed to eat elsewhere. Coalitions were formed with a variety of civil rights, women's, labor, and peace and justice organizations. Most importantly, the media attention greatly heightened national awareness of the lack of protections for lesbians and gays on the job. As the boycott continued, increasing numbers of states, counties, and municipalities passed legislation designed to prevent employment discrimination based on sexual orientation.

The Outcome: Stand-Off Continues

As the November 1992 annual meeting approached, Cracker Barrel requested that the Securities and Exchange Commission make a ruling on the resolution offered by the New York pension fund administrators. The resolution, according to Cracker Barrel, amounted to shareholder intrusion into the company's ordinary business operations. As such, it should be excluded from consideration at the annual meeting and excluded from proxy ballots sent out before the meeting. The SEC agreed, despite previous rulings in which it had allowed stockholder resolutions regarding race or gender based employment bias.

Acknowledging that frivolous stockholder inquiries had to be curtailed, the dissenting SEC commissioner nonetheless expressed great dismay: "To claim that the shareholders, as owners of the corporation, do not have a legitimate interest in management-sanctioned discrimination against employees defies logic." A noted legal scholar warned of the dangerous precedent that had been set: "Ruling an entire area of corporate activity (here, employee relations) off limits to moral debate effectively disenfranchises shareholders."

Thus, the stand-off continued. Queer Nation and its supporters persisted in the boycott. The Cracker Barrel board of directors and, with one exception, upper management remained all-white, all-male bastions. Lynn Cothren, Cheryl Summerville, and the other protestors arrested in Lithonia, Georgia, were acquitted on charges of criminal trespass. Jurors ruled that the protestors' legitimate reasons for peaceably demonstrating superseded the company's rights to deny access or refuse service. Charges stemming from the Union City, Georgia, demonstrations were subsequently dropped. Meanwhile, within weeks of the original policy against lesbian and gay employees,

Cracker Barrel vice president for human resources William Bridges had left the company. Cracker Barrel declined comment on the reasons for his departure.

By 1996, Cracker Barrel annual net sales reached a billion dollars. The company still had not issued a complete retraction of its employment policy, and those employees fired were never offered their old jobs back. In contrast, for a year's work, chairman Dan Evins pulled in over a million dollars in salary, bonus, awards, and stock options; president Ronald Magruder, over 4 million.

As of Cracker Barrel's fiscal year-end, July 30, 1999, a total of 11 states and the District of Columbia offered protections for lesbians and gays on the job, both in the public and private sectors. With a total of 396 restaurants and 58 Logan's Roadhouse affiliates in 36 states, Cracker Barrel now operated in six of those states with protections: California, Connecticut, Massachusetts, Minnesota, New Jersey, and Wisconsin. (The other states with antidiscrimination statutes are Hawaii, Nevada, New Hampshire, Rhode Island, and Vermont.) Moreover, plans for expansion seemed destined to take the company into areas even less receptive to employment discrimination. As one business editor had correctly predicted, "Cracker Barrel isn't going to be in the South and Midwest forever. Eventually they will have to face the issue—like it or not."

The Proposal: Federal Legislation

In 39 states it is perfectly legal to fire workers because they are gay—or straight. For example, a Florida bar owner recently decided to target a lesbian and gay clientele and so fired the entire heterosexual staff. Queer activists boycotted, and the bar eventually was forced out of business. Still, for the vast majority of Americans, employment discrimination based on sexual orientation remains a constant threat.

The vast majority of Americans, 80 percent, tell pollsters that lesbians and gays should have equal rights in terms of job opportunities. In every region including the South, among both Democrats and Republicans, solid majorities support federal legislation to remedy the situation. Nonetheless, despite several close votes in Congress, the Employment Non-Discrimination Act, or ENDA, has yet to be passed into law.

Although there are no federal laws to prevent discrimination based on sexual orientation, protections do exist for workers on the basis of religion, gender, national origin, age, disability, and race. Citing these civil rights statutes, the NAACP is supporting a group of employees and former employees in a class-action lawsuit against Cracker Barrel. The suit alleges that the company repeatedly discriminated against African-Americans in hiring, promotions, and firing practices. Further, African-American workers are said to have received less pay, to have been given inferior terms and conditions of employment, and to have been subjected to racial epithets and racist jokes, including one told by Dan Evins.

Discussion Questions

1. How could Cracker Barrel's policy statement have been well intentioned?
2. What benefits did Cracker Barrel achieve by ridding itself of lesbian and gay employees? What were the disadvantages?
3. How should the perceived values of a customer base affect companies' personnel policies? In a large national corporation, should personnel policies be uniform across all operating units or should they be tailored by region according to local mores?

Case Study: When Steve Becomes Stephanie

Thunk! The Audi trunk slammed shut, and Eric and Henrietta Mercer carried their bags of groceries into the house. As Eric started putting away the food, Henrietta sorted through the mail. She was surprised to find a letter from Morgan, their 29-year-old daughter, a genome researcher in Boston.

"What's the special occasion?" Henrietta wondered aloud as she settled into a kitchen chair and kicked off her shoes. A moment later she exclaimed, "Jeez Louise."

Eric turned around. "What's up?"

"Morgan sent us a copy of her Massachusetts driver's license renewal form. Take a look at this: 'Complete only if something has changed—name, address, telephone number, *gender designation*.'"

Morgan's letter was eerily connected to the challenge foremost in her mother's mind. As the senior vice president for human resources at LaSalle Chemical, Henrietta knew that about 25% of the leading U.S. companies had policies in place to protect employees against discrimination based on gender identity. But she had never imagined she would actually encounter the issue, and certainly not at LaSalle, a *Fortune* 1000 company headquartered in Aurora, Illinois, that provided products and services to oil-drilling, refinery, and pollution-control businesses.

Yet that was precisely what had happened: Steve Ambler, a rising star at LaSalle, had informed senior management that he was going to become Stephanie through a process known as gender transition. Karl Diener, the CEO, had asked Henrietta for regular updates on the problems LaSalle might face as a result—and matters had taken an unsettling turn that very morning. Henrietta had the weekend to collect her thoughts for a Monday meeting with Karl and the executive committee.

"Look, why don't you work on your presentation while I get supper ready?" Eric said, shooing her out of the kitchen. "And don't get too discouraged," he said, deadpan. "Steve's transition to Stephanie will improve your affirmative-action numbers."

The Next Round of Change

Nine months earlier LaSalle had acquired CatalCon, a company in Detroit that sold fluid catalytic cracking technology to petrochemical businesses. Karl Diener had announced a major consolidation of the two sales teams: They would be integrated and streamlined so that both could sell CatalCon's and LaSalle's technology and services. CatalCon's salespeople would be relocated to Aurora. Karl had handpicked Steve to lead the change initiative and appointed him group sales director.

At 38, Steve was LaSalle's golden boy. He had overhauled the company's pollution-control sales strategy to make it customer driven rather than product based. Sales had more than doubled in that sector, and the new approach had been rolled out to the group's larger petrochemical customers. Steve was the natural candidate to lead the next round of change.

Source: Loren Gary and Brian Elliot, *Harvard Business Review* 86(12) (December 2008): 35–42.

Loren Gary (w.gary@comcast.net) is the associate director of leadership development and public affairs at the Center for Public Leadership at Harvard's Kennedy School of Government in Cambridge, Massachusetts.

Brian Elliot (brian@brianelliot.net) is a George Fellow, and a former Zuckerman Fellow, in the joint MBA and MPA program at Harvard Business School and the Kennedy School.

Then, just three weeks ago, Steve had made an appointment with Henrietta. When he showed up 20 minutes early, she suspected it was something urgent.

"Henrietta, I have something very personal to tell you," he said. "I know this is going to be surprising if not shocking." Steve sat stiffly on the brown leather couch in her office. Henrietta waited, wondering how she could talk him out of quitting.

"I've been seeing a psychologist for years to deal with how unhappy I am with my gender. I'm planning to live as a woman in the near future, and I want to make sure we can work through this together." Steve spoke slowly, giving Henrietta time to digest his news. She was stunned. Intellectually she knew that people sometimes had feelings of being trapped in a body of the opposite gender. But *Steve?* He was a guy's guy, a jock, a husband with two children.

When she tuned back in to the conversation, Steve had begun to tick off the steps in the transition process: electrolysis, voice lessons, hormone therapy, facial feminization surgery, genital surgery. Now that the gender counseling was behind him, he was ready to embark on the first three. "This isn't something I would undertake because of some adolescent fascination with alternative lifestyles," he said, looking at Henrietta directly.

"When are people going to be able to tell that you're . . . a woman?" she responded, a little more bluntly than she'd intended.

"I won't have facial hair anymore and in about six months I'll have breasts," Steve said. "My voice will continue to change as I train it. But I won't be overtly female until I've had the facial surgery and start wearing women's clothing in public."

Henrietta paused. Questions clouded her brain. What were the legal implications of changing gender? Maternity leave was considered disability. What about gender reassignment surgeries? And what would Steve's colleagues and customers think? LaSalle's clients were mostly conservative oilmen.

"Steve," she said, choosing her words carefully, "would it be easier for you to play an internal role while you're making this transition?"

He had anticipated her reaction and met it with a joke: "A demotion in exchange for becoming a woman? Just another woman you can pay less!"

A nervous silence followed as Henrietta avoided his eyes. She explained that she would have to do more research before the company could commit to anything.

"I'm not asking for more than that," Steve said. He got to his feet, relieved that the issue hadn't caused his job to blow up—at least not yet.

Simmering Resentment

Nearly three weeks after his conversation with Henrietta, Steve sat in a bar at the Houston airport, waiting for a delayed connection to Chicago. He and Alex Grant, CatalCon's top sales-man, were returning from a four-day sales trip. A master at putting the right person in the right position, Steve was ebullient. The trip had confirmed his hunch that Alex was critical to his plan for the sales integration. Alex, however, was exhausted and annoyed by Steve's high spirits.

"These trips together are invaluable," Steve said, sipping his pomegranate martini.

"I'm glad you think it's working." Alex reached for his draft ale. He didn't exactly dislike Steve, but he didn't like him, either. He understood that they had to work together to make LaSalle's new sales strategy a success, but it grated on him that Steve had been awarded the plum position of sales director.

True, the LaSalle folks had gotten most of the top positions after the acquisition, but Alex thought his 20 years' seniority and his sales record at CatalCon made him a better candidate than Steve, and part of him wondered if he'd been the victim of age discrimination. Alex was great at building relationships. When he advised customers to buy additional products and services from the company, they rarely questioned his recommendations; they trusted him implicitly. At the time of the acquisition he had been making almost as much money as CatalCon's CEO. The sales director position would have entailed a big salary cut, but Alex's wife, Mary, had recently been diagnosed with breast cancer, and he wanted to spend less time traveling. Not getting the job had made the move to Aurora that much more distasteful to him.

"I don't know if I should be so important in this sales integration," Alex said as the loud-speaker announced a further delay in their flight. "I'm on the road a lot more than I expected."

"I need you as my collaborator," Steve replied. "No one else in this company knows CatalCon's technology like you do. Having you play a major role after the acquisition reassures your clients." As he got up to go to the men's room, Steve patted Alex on the back. "We can do this together. Trust me."

Fatigue from the trip and his worry about Mary's condition made Alex uncharacteristically mean-spirited. "We can do this—trust me," he muttered, mimicking the peculiar way that Steve's voice tended to rise in pitch at the end of a long day.

A Toxic Tip

Alex was still in a foul mood when he arrived at work the next morning. He was coming in for just an hour or so before taking a couple of weeks' family leave to help Mary through her first round of chemotherapy. He had finished reading and answering his e-mails when he noticed a blank manila envelope among the papers strewn across his desk.

Inside it was a plain white envelope marked "Alex—For Your Eyes Only!" As he unfolded the contents, the header "Confidential" caught his eye. It was a one-page memo from Henrietta to the members of LaSalle's executive committee. The subject line read "Timetable for Steve Ambler's Gender Transition."

"Steve Ambler's *what?*" Alex gasped. He inspected both envelopes. Someone was tipping him off anonymously.

Alex's eyebrows shot up as he read about Steve's plan for the next six months, starting with hormone therapy. As Alex scanned the memo, he couldn't help imagining that he'd be named to replace Steve as sales director. Then an impossible idea dawned on him: They might let Steve keep the job! Having Steve shadow him on calls to some of his best clients was a nuisance, but if he had to take *Steph-a-nie* along—

"Alex?" Henrietta was at his door, asking if he could be interrupted. "How's Mary doing?"

Alex glared at her and thrust out the memo. "Do you really want to risk our customer relationships just to accommodate somebody's aberrations?" he barked.

"Alex, hold on a minute." Henrietta closed his office door and lowered her voice. "How did you get hold of this?"

He ignored her question. "Just when were you going to tell us?"

"You have to understand that this is new for all of us, and I'm not at liberty to discuss it right now. We have to respect Steve's privacy. Ultimately this is a medical issue."

"Have you thought about what's going to happen here in the office six months from now, when Steve shows up in a dress?" Alex was fuming. "Trust me, a lot of us are going to be wondering just how unstable a person must be to *choose* to have this kind of surgery. It's indecent. It's *wrong*. Don't expect me to feel otherwise."

"Alex, calm down," Henrietta said. "I'm not asking you to change your values or your beliefs. There are solutions to the problems that might be worrying you. Other companies have been through this and have worked out how to adjust."

"My God, Henrietta, listen to yourself. What's become of you?" Alex started to pace. "Don't you get it? It's not a question of adjusting. This is a *moral* issue, not a medical one. Frankly, I'd rather leave than be part of an organization that has lost its moral compass." He looked at his watch angrily. Mary was going to be late for her chemotherapy treatment.

"Isn't there something toxic about a work environment that stirs you up so much you forget your own wife's struggle with cancer?" he said, stalking out.

It was dreadful that Alex had heard about Steve this way, Henrietta thought as she walked back to her office. But at least she now had some idea of how people in the organization might react. Luckily, Alex would be away for the next couple of weeks, unlikely to cause a commotion. She could use that time to finish crafting her strategy for dealing with the issues raised by Steve's transition.

"Very Complicated"

Saturday night Henrietta and Eric sat on the living room couch and discussed her upcoming meeting with Karl and the executive committee.

"Illinois law protects employees against gender identity discrimination," she said, rehearsing the facts. "We have no option but to come up with a company policy that complies with state law." She rose to put another log on the fire. "But it's more than that," she said, poking the embers. "We want our people to be able to bring their whole selves to work. Having employees who are fully engaged is core to our culture."

"That's all well and good," Eric said, "but how are you going to let Alex bring his whole self to work?"

"Probably not through gender sensitivity training," Henrietta reflected. "But I'd like to find a mediator who can get Steve and Alex talking to each other." She stood in front of the fire, rubbing her hands together, before turning back to Eric. "The problem is, I've been checking into resources, and many of the coaches and advisers in this business are transgender themselves. That could turn Alex off completely."

"And Steve probably won't go along with your bringing in someone who has no experience with transgender issues," Eric replied. "Isn't there someone in-house who can fill the role? How about you?"

Henrietta grimaced.

The fire crackled and lit up the room. Eric spoke first. "I know you're not going to like this, but you could read Steve the riot act. Frankly, your customers will never accept him when he starts transitioning to Stephanie. Insist that he take an internal position—at least until the transition is complete."

"I don't know," Henrietta said. "Maybe people will be more tolerant than you give them credit for." She was thinking of an employee who had come back from rehab and had reintegrated into the company seamlessly. "Besides," she reminded her husband, "we need Steve engaged to make the integration process work. If I'm going to play hardball, it makes more sense to play it with Alex. He might choose to leave—though that's unlikely, given Mary's health and his need for benefits."

"But having Alex stay for those reasons alone is no solution either!" she said, throwing up her hands in frustration. "I don't just need Alex on board, I need *him* engaged, too. For heaven's sake, he's our top salesman—the main connection to our CatalCon customer base. LaSalle needs both these guys—"

"One guy, one gal," Eric said with a rueful smile, as Henrietta's cell phone rang. It was their daughter, Morgan, calling from Boston.

"What did you think of that license renewal application?" she asked.

"All roads lead to Rome," Henrietta replied. She started to unburden herself but thought better of it. "Morgan, you're the scientist here—what does your work on the human genome tell us about all this transgender stuff?"

"Very complicated," Morgan replied.

Great, Henrietta thought. *Just what Karl Diner doesn't want to hear*.

How can Henrietta help Steve transition in a company where not everybody is on board?
Three commentators offer expert advice. See *Case Commentary*

Case Commentary

by Linda E. Taylor

How can Henrietta help Steve transition in a company where not everybody is on board?

Raytheon Missile Systems (one of six business units within Raytheon) has about 12,500 employees. In my seven years here I've overseen three gender transitions. I inherited four others. (My predecessor had worked closely with one person, and the other three had progressed to various stages of transition without assistance from the company.) Our approach to gender transition has been shaped largely by my experience in managing these people.

Prior to 2005 Raytheon did not include gender identity and expression in its antidiscrimination policies, so the company was not fully prepared to deal with this issue. In one case I inherited, the employee's superior was still referring to her as "him" with external customers and at all-hands meetings *two years* after she had transitioned.

The line had to be drawn. I said to that manager, "I understand this change was difficult, but you've had two years to adjust. You can go home without pay and think about whether you want to change your behavior, or you can do what you need to do." Today I get managers involved early; by and large, they provide positive leadership to their employees.

My advice to companies is don't wait until someone walks in the door and tells you he or she is transitioning. You need to have your policies in place or you'll be wrong-footed, as Henrietta has obviously been. She considers giving Steve an internal position that will surely feel like a demotion. You should never create the impression that a person is somehow getting shortchanged because he or she made a gender identity choice. It will blow up in your face.

Henrietta worries too much about clients. Of the three people who most recently transitioned at Raytheon, two (both engineers) have had a lot of contact with both internal and external clients.

Linda E. Taylor (linda_e_taylor@raytheon.com) is the director of work life, equity, and inclusion at Raytheon Missile Systems in Tucson, Arizona.

We are a technology company that specializes in defense, homeland security, and other government markets. Not one military customer has behaved badly to our faces. I suspect this "business as usual" attitude has something to do with the fact that the military is less concerned about who makes the equipment that protects our men and women in uniform than about how the products work in the field. It's a safety issue.

For a variety of personal and religious reasons, some of our employees have opposed our policy of inclusion, so I give lots of gender identity training—another lesson I've learned over the years. When someone transitions, force the organization to do some training so that employees can work through their misperceptions, questions, and fears. If you don't provide that opportunity, it will come back to haunt you.

During our trainings I put the difficult questions on the table for us all to talk about— especially "Isn't Raytheon condoning some unhealthy or immoral lifestyle by allowing this change?" My answer is that Raytheon doesn't pass judgment on its employees' personal lives. At times we all have values that differ from the company's, and we don't need to change our values. But as a Raytheon employee, you are here eight hours a day, and during that time you agree to adhere to the company's policy of making our workplace as inclusive as it can possibly be.

We are not prepared to qualify that policy. It's the way of our company and the way of the future. We've built relationships with college LGBT (lesbian, gay, bisexual, and transgender) engineering groups, and they are a great source of talent. Many of the interns who've come from these groups have ended up staying with us. Our culture of inclusion absolutely gives us a recruiting edge.

Case Commentary

by Ronald K. Andrews

How can Henrietta help Steve transition in a company where not everybody is on board?

I've overseen only one transition in my career, back in 2003, and like Henrietta, I anticipated a great deal of organizational dysfunction. But instead I often heard people admiring the courage of the individual who transitioned, whom I'll call Debbie. How tormented she must have been all her life—and then to take such a grand, courageous step.

In situations like this it is crucial to work very closely with the person who's making the transition. The success of Debbie's transition owed a lot to Debbie herself. It certainly helped that she was a star employee who had been with the company for 14 years. And she has a great sense of humor that she has used to put people at ease.

Besides working closely with Debbie, we turned to other people with relevant experience. We talked to Debbie's therapist, to our internal medical director, to our employee assistance people, to lawyers, to an HR person in another company.

By law, in states that have gender identity protection, the person transitioning has to be the one to reveal the change to other people. We agreed that Debbie would send an e-mail to her

Ronald K. Andrews is vice president and head of human resources for Prudential's U.S. businesses and is based in Newark, New Jersey.

colleagues, in the full expectation that it would be forwarded. Then, because Debbie was a senior executive and made presentations to the board, we agreed that the president of our investment area (in which Debbie worked) would share the information with the directors.

Debbie also had a lot of client contact, because she worked with account executives, and we thought carefully about how to handle that. We ended up making a list of all the key clients that she had significant interactions with. We gathered together their account executives and educated them about the situation. They were given very specific talking points to use with clients, which were vetted by Debbie, our lawyers, and HR. The account executives all telephoned their respective clients. We thought it best that they discuss the news directly rather than sending a letter or an e-mail. We didn't lose a single client.

The greatest noticeable opposition to Debbie's transition occurred in that meeting of account executives. One person out of the 25 or so who were present was especially vocal. The idea of gender transition was outlandish to him, and he had ethical and religious concerns. More than anything, he worried that cooperation would be seen as an endorsement of Debbie's decision. But as we explained, you can hold to your beliefs while being civil to a colleague who has decided to transition. He accepted that argument grudgingly. He had to. Compliance is one of our employees' job requirements. That said, if strong opposition to Debbie's transition had continued, we were prepared to invest some time in sorting out the problem.

We also offered awareness training to Debbie's team on a voluntary basis—we thought it would give people an opportunity to ask the kinds of questions they might not be comfortable asking Debbie. You know what? They said they didn't need the training. They felt comfortable enough to go to Debbie directly with any questions.

Of course, the toilet situation is a delicate issue—even in a close group like Debbie's. We gave her a private bathroom at first, and only when we had all agreed that the time was right did she begin using the ladies' room. There was no fanfare; it just happened. Today Debbie's transition is a nonevent—which is exactly what we want it to be.

Case Commentary

by Stasha Goliaszewski

How can Henrietta help Steve transition in a company where not everybody is on board?

I started transitioning at Boeing in 2002, after four years with the company. First I came out to human resources, but we kept it quiet for a while. Then a woman working on her doctorate about transitioning interviewed me on the phone at work; someone overheard us and started a rumor that I was transsexual. Boeing has a policy to not let rumors circulate, so HR called my manager and me in for a meeting. Since the rumor was true, and I was planning to go public soon, we decided that it was time to make the announcement to the organization.

Stasha Goliaszewski (goliaszewski@gmail.com) is a scientist and engineer in integrated defense systems at Boeing in Philadelphia.

Our first step was to hold a meeting that included the head of HR, myself, the company therapist, my manager, and managers two levels up. The therapist went over the condition and explained the transition process. A week later we called a full staff meeting of about 100 people and presented them with all the facts. After that I began my hormone treatment and started to dress androgynously.

I like to think that I've contributed to Boeing's positive reputation today with the transgender community. When I first started transitioning, Boeing's policy could best be described as "plumbing to plumbing": You had to use the men's room until you'd had genital surgery. I quietly pointed out to HR that by federal law, employers aren't even allowed to ask when or if an employee has had any surgery. After some consultation with people inside and outside the company, Boeing included gender identity in its antidiscrimination policies.

On the whole, I didn't have many negative experiences. A few women objected to my using the ladies' room, but the head of HR called them in and basically told them to suck it up. I don't get any comments, because the company considers that to be harassment. Of course I do get looks, but part of that is because I am overweight and have not opted for any facial surgery.

Henrietta worries that her company's clients will react badly to Steve's transitioning. But while I was transitioning, Boeing sent me all over the country to talk to the likes of IBM, Raytheon, and the military. I never had a problem. I do remember dealing with a lieutenant colonel whose blood was obviously boiling. But he swallowed hard and called me ma'am. Clients knew I was transsexual, but they couldn't put me down because I have expertise.

In the case, Alex thinks that people who transition have psychiatric problems. I suffered from depression because I was so unhappy with my gender. It was a terrible situation: I was presented with equipment that I tried for years to live with. Today my therapist tells me I am a well-managed person—and that's the feedback I get at work. Also I have three children and I've succeeded in holding my marriage together.

Statistically, a company Boeing's size should have one or two transsexuals coming out a year. Boeing is seeing many more than that because of its reputation. My advice to companies with more than 30,000 employees is to get ready: Somebody in your organization is going to transition. Better to get your ducks in a row now than to run around as Henrietta has to do.

References to the Cracker Barrel Case Study

1. *Atlanta Journal-Constitution*, July 6, 11, 1993; April 2, 3, 1992; March 29, 1992; January 4, 18, 20, 1992; June 9, 1991; March 3, 4, 5, 1991.
2. Carlino, Bill. "Cracker Barrel Profits Surge Despite Recession," *Nation's Restaurant News*, December 16, 1991, 14.
3. ———. "Cracker Barrel Stocks, Sales Weather Gay-Rights Dispute," *Nation's Restaurant News,* 1 April 1991, 14.
4. Cheney, Karen. "Old-Fashioned Ideas Fuel Cracker Barrel's Out-of-Sight Sales Growth and Profit Increases," *Restaurants & Institutions*, July 22, 1992, 108.
5. Cracker Barrel Old Country Store, Inc. *Annual Report*, 1999.
6. ———. *Annual Report*, 1996.
7. ———. Notice of Annual Meeting of Shareholders to Be Held on Tuesday, November 26, 1996; October 25, 1996.
8. ———. *Third Quarter Report*, April 30, 1993.
9. ———. *Second Quarter Report*, January 29, 1993.
10. ———. *First Quarter Report*, October 30, 1992.

11. ———. *Annual Report*, 1992.

12. ———. Securities and Exchange Commission Form 10-K, 1992.

13. ———. *Annual Report*, 1991.

14. ———. Securities and Exchange Commission Form 10-K, 1991.

15. ———. *Annual Report*, 1990.

16. "Cracker Barrel Hit by Anti-Bias Protests," *Nation's Restaurant News*, April 13, 1992, 2.

17. "Cracker Barrel Sued for Rampant Racial Discrimination in Employment," NAACP Press Release, October 5, 1999.

18. "Cracker Barrel's Emphasis on Quality a Hit with Travelers," *Restaurants and Institutions*, April 3, 1991, 24.

19. Dahir, Mubarak S. "Coming Out at the Barrel," *The Progressive*, June 1992, 14.

20. "Documented Cases of Job Discrimination Based on Sexual Orientation," Washington, DC: Human Rights Campaign, 1995.

21. Farkas, David. "Kings of the Road," *Restaurant Hospitality*, August 1991, 118–22.

22. Galst, Liz. "Southern Activists Rise Up," *The Advocate*, May 19, 1992, 54–57.

23. Greenberg, David. *The Construction of Homosexuality*. Chicago: University of Chicago Press, 1988.

24. Gutner, Toddi. "Nostalgia Sells," *Forbes*, April 27, 1993, 102–3.

25. Harding, Rick. "Nashville NAACP Head Stung by Backlash from Boycott Support," *The Advocate*, July 16, 1991, 27.

26. ———. "Activists Still Press Tennessee Eatery Firm on Anti-Gay Job Bias," *The Advocate*, April 9, 1991, 17.

27. Hayes, Jack. "Cracker Barrel Protesters Don't Shake Loyal Patrons," *Nation's Restaurant News*, August 26, 1991, 3, 57.

28. ———. "Cracker Barrel Comes Under Fire for Ousting Gays," *Nation's Restaurant News*, March 4, 1991, 1, 79.

29. "Investors Protest Cracker Barrel Proxy Plan," *Nation's Restaurant News*, November 2, 1992, 14.

30. *Larry King Live.* CNN television, aired December 2, 1991.

31. *Oprah Winfrey Show.* Syndicated television, aired January 1992.

32. Queer Nation. Documents on the Cracker Barrel Boycott. N.p., n.d.

33. "SEC Upholds Proxy Ruling," *Pensions and Investments*, February 8, 1993, 28.

34. Star, Marlene Givant. "SEC Policy Reversal Riles Activist Groups," *Pensions and Investments*, October 26, 1992, 33.

35. *The* (Nashville) *Tennesseean*, February 27, 1991.

36. *20/20.* ABC television, aired November 29, 1991.

37. Walkup, Carolyn. "Family Chains Beat Recession Blues with Value, Service," *Nation's Restaurant News*, August 5, 1991, 100, 104.

38. *The Wall Street Journal*, March 9, 1993; February 2, 1993; January 26, 1993; February 28, 1991.

39. Wildmoon, K. C. "QN Members Allowed to Attend Cracker Barrel Stockholder's Meeting," *Southern Voice*, December 10, 1992, 3.

40. ———. "Securities and Exchange Commission Side with Cracker Barrel on Employment Discrimination," *Southern Voice*, October 22, 1992, 1.

41. ———. "DeKalb Drops Most Charges Against Queer Nation," *Southern Voice*, July 9, 1992, 3.

CHAPTER 9

Disabilities

The Americans with Disabilities Act of 1990 (ADA) includes protection from discrimination based on a disability, as well as requirements regarding access and accommodations for disabled employees, vendors, and patrons. The ADA defines a disability as a physical or mental impairment that substantially limits one or more major life activities, which include walking, talking, breathing, seeing, hearing, learning, sitting, standing, lifting, sleeping, working, and caring for oneself. The Americans with Disabilities Amendments Act of 2008 (ADAAA) expands the protections of the original ADA to include more individuals with less severe impairments and adds a new major life activity category, "major bodily functions," which includes (but is not limited to) functions of the immune system and cell growth.

Objectives

- To examine the relationship between people with disabilities and the workplace.
- To examine how to work most effectively with people with disabilities.
- To examine why people with disabilities are at a "critical disadvantage" when compared with people without disabilities.
- To examine successful programs and organizations creating accessibility for people with disabilities.

Preview Questions

- Why are people with disabilities at a critical disadvantage when compared with people without disabilities?
- How can organizations most effectively create accessibility within their companies for people with disabilities?
- Why might people with disabilities be unmotivated to apply for a job, and what disincentive might discourage employers from hiring a person with a disability?
- How can negative cultural assumptions and stereotypes of people with disabilities be managed at work?

Some Important Dates

1829   Louis Braille invents the raised-point alphabet that has come to be known as Braille.

1864   Institution for the Deaf and Dumb and Blind is authorized by the U.S. Congress to grant college degrees. It is the first college in the world established for people with disabilities.

1869   The first wheelchair patent is registered with the U.S. Patent Office.

1890–1920	Progressive activists push for the creation of state worker's compensation programs. By 1913, 21 states have established some form of worker's compensation; the figure rises to 43 by 1919.
1916	British Braille becomes the English language standard (although New York Point and American Braille are both being used in the United States) because of the wealth of code already available in the British Empire.
1921	The American Foundation for the Blind (AFB), a nonprofit organization recognized as Helen Keller's cause in the United States, is founded.
1927	The *Buck v. Bell* Supreme Court decision rules that forced sterilization of people with disabilities is not a violation of their constitutional rights. By the 1970s, over 60,000 disabled people are sterilized without their consent. Nationally, 27 states begin wholesale sterilization of "undesirables."
1935	The Social Security Act is passed. This law establishes federally funded old-age benefits and funds to states to assist blind individuals and disabled children. The act extends existing vocational rehabilitation programs.
1947	The President's Committee on National Employ the Physically Handicapped Week is held in Washington, DC. Publicity campaigns, coordinated by state and local committees, emphasize the competence of people with disabilities.
1960	Social Security amendments of 1960 eliminate the restriction that disabled workers receiving Social Security Disability Insurance (SSDI) benefits must be 50 or older.
1961	The American National Standards Institute, Inc. (ANSI) publishes American standard specifications for making buildings accessible to, and usable by, people with physical limitations.
1971	The National Center for Law and the Handicapped is founded at the University of Notre Dame, Indiana. It becomes the first legal advocacy center for people with disabilities in the United States.
1975	The Education of All Handicapped Children Act (PL 94–142) requires free, appropriate public education in the least restrictive setting. This act is later renamed The Individuals with Disabilities Education Act (IDEA).
1990	The Americans with Disabilities Act is signed into law.
2008	The Americans with Disabilities Amendments Act (ADAAA) expands the protections of the ADA.

Finding the Right Way to Disclose a Disability

Disclosing a disability is a personal decision but can be beneficial if done right. Only you can decide whether—and when—to tell your new employer about your disability. Disclosing a condition can help protect your legal rights but can also leave you open to discrimination. Still, experts say you're better off giving management a heads-up. Here are a few different approaches to disclosure:

Know the company. Before you even apply for a job, you can scope out a firm and its culture. Some companies have disability-friendly reputations, which can help qualm fears about revealing your condition. Check out NBDC (business-disability.com) and the National Organization on Disability's (nod.org) membership lists, or ask the company for a list of employee networks and scan for one related to disabilities. Those networks and groups can be critical. KPMG LLP's disabilities network, for example, offers employees resources, tools, advice and counsel for living with a disability or caring for someone who has one. You also can ask colleagues and friends or search Internet groups for insights into corporate culture.

(continued)

Choose the time. Don't reveal your disability on your resume or in a cover letter unless there is a direct relevance to the job. The best time to disclose to a hiring manager is during the first or second interview, once you have had a chance to demonstrate your skills and competency, says Lana Smart, director of corporate services for the National Business and Disability Council, a network of more than 100 U.S. companies that seeks to integrate people with disabilities into the workplace. At that point, you will be able to respond positively to specific disability issues that may be raised. "Discrimination is less likely face-to-face," Ms. Smart says.

Tell someone you trust. If you've waited until you've had a chance to prove yourself before disclosing your condition, you should seek out a trusted colleague, mentor or boss you get along well with to make the revelation. Dana Foote, an audit partner at KPMG's Omaha, Neb., office, who has multiple sclerosis, says she put off disclosure for three months until she started having symptoms. "At that point I trusted my boss, and he knew I was a good worker so it wasn't a big deal," says Ms. Foote.

Get accommodated. Your rights under the Americans with Disabilities Act to "reasonable accommodations" to perform your job aren't protected until you've disclosed your disability, says Judy Young, a vice president for Abilities Inc. "As soon as you realize you need an accommodation, you should tell someone," says Ms. Young, who has counseled Fortune 500 companies on hiring people with disabilities.

Join a network. Participating in a disability employee group lets you reap the benefits of a company's disability resources. This is a good option if you don't want to reveal the scope of a disability, but want to know your options and make connections, says Barbara Wankoff, KPMG's national director of workplace relations. A support network can help you find others facing similar situations and gain the courage to speak up—a move that may help your career in the long run, Ms. Wankoff says.

Source: Suzanne Robitaille, "Finding the Right Way to Disclose a Disability," *Wall Street Journal*, August 26, 2008, p. D4

ESSAY: COUNTING ON WORKERS WITH DISABILITIES

In November, Walgreens—one of the nation's largest drugstore retailers—will open a state-of-the-art distribution center in Windsor, Conn. It will be the company's second facility designed specifically to employ people with disabilities and is patterned after the 5,571-store group's Anderson, S.C., center that opened last summer.

Managers at both facilities share a goal of having people with disabilities fill at least one-third of the available jobs.

Many observers laud the retailer's plans as a source of meaningful jobs with equal opportunities for advancement and job mobility. And the outcomes so far suggest that the company's latest prescription for diversification works well, contends Deb Russell, Walgreens' manager of outreach and employee services, based at headquarters in Deerfield, Ill. Company leaders intend to launch similar initiatives at future distribution centers—and use the experience to provide managers in other divisions with information and guidance they expect will result in even more hiring of people with disabilities.

"We know of no other facility of its kind where such a significant portion of the workforce has disabilities," Russell says of the $175 million South Carolina location. Currently, 40 percent of the distribution center's 400 employees have disclosed physical or cognitive disabilities. Yet the facility's efficiency rose by 20 percent since opening, after technology and process changes originally intended to accommodate workers with disabilities improved everyone's jobs. At full capacity, the center will employ 800. Workers will include those challenged by cognitive disabilities and autism.

While Walgreens has always employed people with disabilities, the experience of creating a disability-friendly environment in its distribution division "is the first time we have looked at the issue in a systemic, holistic way. It has been a transforming event," Russell says, adding that it is "the best thing we've ever done."

Not every employer shares or practices Walgreens' level of long-term commitment and investment in hiring people with disabilities, but demographic trends suggest that more companies should—and ultimately will have to—as growth of the traditional labor pool slows, the workforce ages and disability rates rise.

Plus, as human resource, recruitment and diversity leaders recognize and support the abilities of this chronically underemployed group, the business benefits of tapping this talent pool becomes clear, experts say.

Tangible benefits include a larger labor pool and tax benefits for hiring workers with disabilities; intangibles include a workforce reflecting community makeup and the knowledge that the opportunities expand individuals' potential, awareness and achievement.

"The disabled population is the only minority group that anyone can join at any time," says Jonathan Kaufman, president and founder of DisabilityWorks Inc., a disability-strategy consulting firm in New York. "It's essential that employers see this issue as not just a disability issue, but as a human-capital issue that can literally impact anyone. Only then can they build a business strategy to include this group."

Big Numbers

Among people ages 21–64 in the United States, during 2006, 12.9 percent had at least one disability—22.4 million of the 173 million working-age adults.

Despite positive stories such as Walgreens' and others, the employment rate of working-age people with disabilities remains only half that of people without disabilities—37.7 percent compared with 79.7 percent in 2006, according to an annual analysis of the U.S. Census Bureau's American Community Survey data by the Rehabilitation Research and Training Center on Disability Demographics and Statistics (StatsRRTC) at Cornell University in Ithaca, NY.

Yet people with disabilities want to work: Two-thirds of unemployed people with disabilities say they would prefer to be working, Cornell and federal data show. "The long-standing employment gap between people with and without disabilities appears to be getting wider," says Andrew Houtenville, director of StatsRRTC and senior research associate at Cornell's Employment and Disability Institute. "People with disabilities are not keeping pace in this economy."

Why not?

One big barrier to employment of people with disabilities continues to be a perception problem. Employer' lack of knowledge, awareness and comfort level with workplace disability issues often makes them view workers with disabilities as having too many limitations to perform jobs. The resulting fear of the unknown stymies hiring.

In a 2006 study, the Bobby Dodd Institute (BDI) asked 200 human resource decisionmakers from companies of various sizes and industries to list reasons why employers are reluctant to hire individuals with disabilities. BDI, an Atlanta nonprofit, partners with employers to provide training and employment opportunities for people with disabilities.

Nearly 50 percent of the HR professional polled said people with disabilities could not adequately perform required work duties. Also topping the reasons identified: 25 percent cited lack of knowledge about the disabled as the primary deterrent, another 20 percent mentioned concern about cost of workplace adjustments and accommodations, and 15 percent admitted a lack of understanding about accommodations.

Human resource professionals, "by necessity and often rightly so, tend to spend a lot of time on risk aversion," says Wayne McMillan, president and chief executive officer at BDI. His organization places close to 200 people with disabilities a year in jobs in Georgia. " And many people with disabilities are still assessed in terms of what they can' do vs. What they can do "

A gap in earnings also exists: Median annual earnings for full-time, year-round workers are $30,000 for those with disabilities, compared with $37,000 for those without disabilities.

When it comes to work, some workers with disabilities fare better than others.

Among six types of disabilities identified in federal data, people with sensory disabilities—defined as blindness, deafness, or a severe hearing or vision impairment—now have the highest employment rate, at 47.5 percent. People with self-care disabilities—those that have difficulty dressing, bathing, or getting around inside the home because of a physical, mental, or emotional condition—experience the lowest employment rate, at 17.1 percent.

Other research suggests that job applicants with disabilities find it particularly difficult to enter the workforce and be accommodated, compared with current employees who become disabled, a 2006 study shows. In fact, according to the study—for which researchers at the Law, Health Policy and Disability Center at the University of Iowa, the International Center for Disability Information and Job Accommodation Network at West Virginia University and the Burton Blatt Institute at Syracuse University conducted interviews with 890 employers—employees who become disabled are most likely to receive workplace accommodations.

The reason: "The employer may more readily estimate that worker's direct benefit and value to the company and factor in the benefits associated with not having to replace that employee," researchers concluded.

Susanne Bruyere, Ph.D., an associate dean and director of Cornell's Employment and Disability Institute, points to another sure trend when analyzing and forecasting disability statistics: An aging workforce likely will result in an increasing number of workers with disabilities.

While 12.9 percent of people ages 21 to 64 have disabilities, that percentage more than doubles to 30.2 percent for people ages 65 to 74, and quadruples to 52.6 percent for those age 75 and older, according to Cornell's report.

"Successful companies will make it a priority to create a workplace culture that embraces and encourages diversity," Bruyere says. "It has been successfully done for race, sex and sexual orientation. Now age and disability must be added."

Identifying Causes

Researchers agree that the employment rate for working-age people with disabilities has, with few exceptions, declined over the last decade and for now, in fact, appears stuck. (See "Employment Rate Among People with Disabilities," [p. 212].) However, they don't always agree about the main cause for this decline. In an October 2007 report, Empowerment for Americans with Disabilities: Breaking Barriers to Careers and Full Employment, the National Council on Disability in Washington, DC, outlined challenges and barriers to employment of people with disabilities.

On the supply side, there may be costs associated with employing people with disabilities, such as remedial education or training, the need for flexible work arrangements, and disincentives from disability income and health care. On the demand side, barriers include employer discrimination and reluctance to hire, corporate cultures that aren't disability-friendly, and the need for accommodations.

In addition, current labor market and workplace trends reflect mixed messages. The bad news: Researchers say people with disabilities are currently underrepresented in occupations projected to grow fastest from 2004–14, and they're currently more likely to be in slower-growing service and blue-collar jobs.

The good news from National Council researchers:

- Growth in new information technologies help compensate for many types of disabilities and increase the chances for productive work.
- Growth in telecommuting and flexible work arrangements suit many people with disabilities.
- More attention to issues of diversity and disability by employers may combine to reverse the underemployment trend.

Advocates who help people with disabilities transition to the workforce say some reasons that contribute to the lingering employment gap outweigh others. (For examples, see "Why Not?" . . . .)

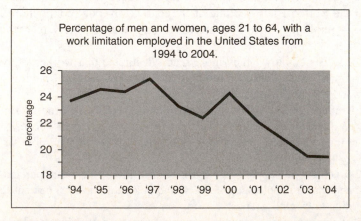

FIGURE 9-1 Employment Rate Among People with Disabilities

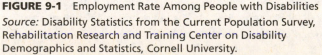

Source: Disability Statistics from the Current Population Survey, Rehabilitation Research and Training Center on Disability Demographics and Statistics, Cornell University.

A Fresh Perspective

Employers need a mind set shift when it comes to people with disabilities, says DisabilityWorks' Kaufman, who advises corporations, governments, educational institutions and nonprofits.

"The way we look at disability has become stale," he insists. "We tend to see disability based on a charitable model rather than seeing people with disabilities as valuable human capital who can have a tremendous impact on businesses.

"Rather than saying we'll give people with disabilities jobs based on good will, we need to think about the value of human capital and see people with disabilities as a critical component," he says.

To guide and plan recruitment, assessment and retention, Kaufman advises employers to view workers with disabilities as a varied group made up of five distinct "pillars": college-educated people with disabilities, aging baby boomers, seniors, disabled veterans, and people with cognitive or developmental disabilities.

Kaufman, who was born with cerebral palsy, counsels HR professionals to treat disability as a "lifespan issue," to see employees as assets and to universally respond to the needs of all.

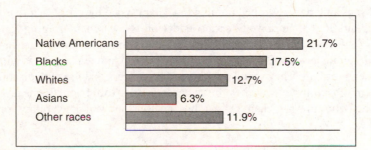

FIGURE 9-2 Prevalence of Disabilities in the United States Among Races
Source: 2006 Disability Status Report.

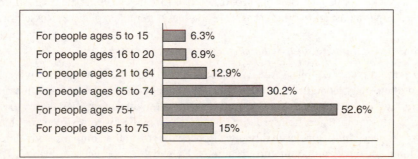

FIGURE 9-3 Prevalence of Disabilities in the United States by Age
Source: 2006 Disability Status Report.

Finding Solutions

People with disabilities vary significantly in their capabilities, strengths, limitations and personal characteristics. Based on interviews with employers, HR researchers and disability leaders, the following strategies and peer examples emerge among the best ways to advance opportunities and improve employability, no matter what the disability.

Partner with public and private disability agencies and community organizations

Walgreens, for example, works with the Disabilities and Special Needs Board in Anderson, S.C., and the South Carolina Vocational Rehabilitation Department to develop training for people with special needs at its distribution centers.

Provide information and outreach

Also at Walgreens, a specially designed web site, www.walgreensoutreach.com, provides information to help potential employees with disabilities understand what work is like at its new centers.

Mandate increased awareness and education

Current employees and managers need training too. Giant Eagle Inc., a 223-store grocer based in Pennsylvania, with 36,000 employees, sponsors disability-awareness training for its HR managers every two years. Specialists representing disability agencies participate in the sessions, which are held off-site at a YMCA camp. Attendees learn about the Americans with Disabilities Act and interviewing skills. They spend time experiencing work and life with disabilities through simulation exercises led by job coaches. In one exercise, for example, HR managers maneuver through work activities in wheelchairs, going through doors, up and down ramps, or reaching for items on shelves.

Reexamine how work, productivity and accommodation can go hand in hand

In Walgreens' case, "we didn't lower our productivity standards," Russell says. Instead, "the goal was to make work more intuitive" by using technology and redesigning jobs. For example, the company replaced keyboards with touch screens based on large pictures and icons, not words, making it easier and quicker for people with cognitive disabilities to learn and complete tasks. More-flexible, easy-to-use, height-adjustable workstations make jobs easier for all employees, Russell says.

Look at abilities first and tailor assistance and mentoring to match

At online automotive marketplace AutoTrader.com Inc. in Atlanta, a coordinator with autism—a graduate of the Bobby Dodd Institute (BDI), an Atlanta nonprofit that partners with employers to provide training and employment opportunities for people with disabilities—uses tools to help him in his work. For instance, he uses a timer at each stop along his route to ensure that he stays on pace to get everything done each day, says Rebecca Watson, the company's vice president of organizational services and community relations. He's also encouraged to bring a BDI coach with him to the office to help him understand new duties and expectations when his job expands or changes. "These things aren't that much different from the training or mentoring we would offer any employee during the course of their career here—or the daytimers and calendars everyone else uses," Watson points out.

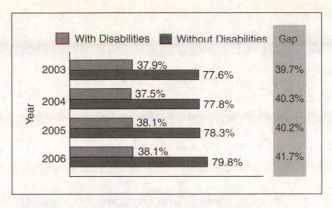

FIGURE 9-4 Disability and Employment Rates

Source: 2006 Disability Status Report, Rehabilitation Research and Training Center on Disability Demographics and Statistics, Cornell University. These data vary from U.S. Census Bureau data because of a difference in the populations sampled.

Consider "job-carving"

Wayne McMillan, president and chief executive officer at BDI, urges employers to custom tailor employment for different levels of abilities. A candidate with a developmental disability, for example, might be able to do three of the five parts of a job, he says, and that may be an acceptable level for the employer's requirements. Further, the potential employee might even be able to do everything in the job description, and more, with a small amount of assistive technology, McMillan says.

Establish pipelines to reach school-age recruits with disabilities

At an Old Navy retail store in Georgia, managers and employees work closely with high-school counselors to prepare students with learning disabilities for the workplace, according to Daphne Sorro, vice president of diversity and inclusion for parent company Gap Inc., based in San Francisco.

For two years, students with varying levels of abilities have learned to successfully complete tasks necessary to create the expected store experience for customers. (See "Gap Fills the Employment Gap," left.)

GAP FILLS THE EMPLOYMENT GAP

Like many innovations, the disability initiative by retailer Gap Inc. began with an employee's personal experience.

Tina Petallides-Markou, a Gap associate store manager in Bayside, N.Y., says she "grew up with many friends and family members who had disabilities, and I witnessed firsthand the struggles they faced when looking for jobs."

Petallides-Markou applied for and received a $50,000 grant and 80 hours of paid time off as winner of her company's Founder's Award. Her 2006–2007 proposal was to modernize a mock store operated by a nonprofit organization, Abilities Inc., where youths and adults with disabilities learn real-world retail skills.

Petallides-Markou transformed the rudimentary training site from a one-room shop with a calculator, rolling racks and donated merchandise into a fully functioning store complete with fixtures, a state-or-the-art cash register, a fitting room, and visual merchandising and marketing similar to Gap stores'.

She also helped update the curriculum for the retail training and created a job-shadowing program where participants follow Gap, Banana Republic or Old Navy employees throughout their workdays, learning firsthand about retail.

Her commitment deepened the partnership between Gap and Abilities Inc. Gap stores in the New York area now hire about one-third of the program's trainees each year.

"This is a great opportunity for students who have expressed an interest in working for us upon graduation," Sorro says. "They will have practical, on-the-job experience," an attribute often harder for entry-level people with disabilities to land on their own.

Source: Susan J. Wells, a contributing editor for HR Magazine, is based in the Washington, DC, area. SHRM, "Counting on Workers with Disabilities: The Nation's Largest Minority Remains and Underused Resource," *HR Magazine* (April 2008): 45–49.

ESSAY: SELECTIONS FROM *THE INCLUSIVE CORPORATION: A DISABILITY HANDBOOK FOR BUSINESS PROFESSIONALS*

Although most disabled people want no special treatment and greatly appreciate being treated the same as everyone else, there are occasions when it is helpful to know commonly accepted manners that promote inclusion.

The following suggestions are distilled from years of experience, many published treatments of the topic, and the suggestions of many individuals who are disabled. Please keep in mind that there are no hard and fast rules of disability etiquette, like other types of etiquette, and people frequently disagree on optimal practices. For example, one authority cautions those meeting someone with a disability: "A handshake is NOT a standard greeting for everyone." Another source lists as one of its first precepts of communicating with people who have disabilities: "Offer to shake hands when introduced." When dining some people who are blind appreciate it when sighted companions describe the location of the food they are served. ("The salmon is at 'six o'clock' on your plate; mashed potatoes are at nine.") Others consider such help to be a disability cliché. People can and do disagree on these practices. There are no universal rules.

The following are some useful tips, by no means all one could know on the subject, but some helpful information with which to start.

Excerpted from *The Inclusive Corporation: A Disability Handbook for Business Professionals* by Griff Hogan. Reprinted with the permission of Swallow Press, Ohio University Press, Athens, Ohio.

General Considerations

- Begin by imagining how you would like to be treated if you were the person with whom you are interacting.
- Interact with a person, not a disability. Do not pay more attention to the disability than is warranted.
- Do not assume anything. If you do not know, ask.
- Always speak to a disabled person directly, even if he or she is using an interpreter.
- Be patient and willing to learn. Be prepared to take a little extra time or exert a little extra effort.
- Offer assistance if it seems to be needed, and wait for your offer to be accepted before acting.
- Make effective communication a priority. Studies repeatedly show that social acceptance is the single most important factor in job success and employee satisfaction.
- Relax. A sincere commitment to including people with disabilities will compensate for most mistakes. A sense of humor should cover much of the rest.

Interacting with People Who Have Mental Health–Related Disabilities

Considerations

- There are many types of mental and emotional illnesses. Some are severe, and others are relatively mild and more easily managed.
- Mental illness can be chronic or short-term. A large proportion of the population experiences some sort of mental illness at some time.
- Mental illness can be caused by biochemical, emotional, or environmental factors.
- There are many types of medication available to assist in the treatment of mental illness.
- The presence of mental illness or the fact that a person takes a psychoactive drug does not automatically preclude his or her being able to work.
- Some medications used to treat mental illness have side effects.
- Some individuals are uncomfortable talking about their illness.
- Mental illness is an example of an "invisible disability." For this reason, it is particularly important that the confidentiality of the individual involved be preserved.
- Mental illness is the disability most frequently encountered and dealt with in employment situations.

Suggestions for Interacting with People Who Have Mental Health–Related Disabilities

- Always discuss issues related to mental illness in private. A quiet location with no distractions is generally best.
- The dignity and autonomy of people with mental illness are sometimes undermined. Treat the individual with respect, and involve him or her in problem solving.
- Do not attempt to counsel the individual or provide therapy.
- In the workplace, behavioral policies must always apply to all. If training on mental illness is provided to employees, it should be provided to all and without reference to any specific person or incident. Make sure both trainers and training participants understand the importance of confidentiality and respect for coworkers.

Interacting with People Who Have Physical Disabilities and Mobility Limitations

Considerations

- There are many reasons for a person to use a wheelchair, walker, crutches, brace, or other device. People with physical limitations have a wide range of capabilities, and may need assistance or assistive devices only at particular times, or not at all.
- Wheelchairs, walkers, canes, and other devices come in all shapes and sizes. Some wheelchairs are sleek and lightweight, others are quite heavy and cumbersome.
- Do not consider any space for which you are responsible (office, interview location, recreational area, etc.) to be physically accessible unless you know it to be the case.

Suggestions for Interacting with People Who Have Physical Disabilities and Mobility Limitations

- If you are unsure whether a person would like to shake hands, ask.
- Regard a wheelchair, cane, walker, or similar device as an extension of the person's body. Never lean on a person's wheelchair, or touch it without permission.
- If you are conversing with someone in a wheelchair for more than a few moments, use a chair so your face will be at eye level. If a chair is not available, kneel or crouch facing the person.
- When expecting someone who uses a wheelchair, see that a reasonably wide path is clear. Move aside a chair, or otherwise prepare a place for him or her to sit.
- Many people find standing for extended periods uncomfortable. When possible, provide places to sit and rest.

Interacting with People Who Have Learning Disabilities

Considerations

- Learning problems are a common disability.
- Learning disabilities affect how people process information, and may influence how they think, speak, write, read, listen, spell, or perform mathematical computations.
- There are a great number of types of learning disabilities. The stereotype of someone with a learning disability "reversing" the letters in a word is accurate for only a small minority of people.

Suggestions for Interacting with People Who Have Learning Disabilities

- If you need to know how a person with a learning disability best learns or works, begin by asking him or her.
- Be prepared to communicate in multiple formats: notes, written instructions, tape recordings, verbal directions, etc.
- Be prepared to allow a person with a learning disability to practice a new skill, or otherwise physically experience an action, rather than assuming he or she will understand just by reading or hearing about it.
- Say literally what you mean. Using subtleties such as intonation, humor, irony, or suggestion to communicate your message may be counterproductive.
- Encourage someone with a learning disability to work creatively and to develop productive nontraditional methods of working.

Interacting with People Who Have Developmental Disabilities

Considerations

- There are many levels of intellectual deficiency, and intelligence is multifaceted. Be willing to take time to understand how a person learns and prefers to communicate.
- All too often, adults with intellectual deficiencies are treated condescendingly or as children.
- Many people with developmental disabilities are extremely reluctant to discuss their learning problems. Some go to great lengths to "pass" as a person without a disability.
- Because of their previous experience, many people with intellectual limitations are particularly sensitive to signs of approval or disapproval. Your smile and undivided attention can pay great dividends.

Suggestions for Interacting with People Who Have Developmental Disabilities

- Avoid condescension and childish treatment.
- Keep your conversation simple.
- Avoid busy, noisy, or confusing environments in which to work and communicate.
- Do not hurry conversations or interactions.
- Be prepared to repeat or paraphrase, or to ask politely that a comment be repeated.
- When giving instructions, break them down into component steps.
- Encourage the use of aids that promote learning or remembering: charts, lists, colored folders, pictures, labels, etc.

Interacting with People Who Have Hearing Impairments

Considerations

- Some people, especially people born deaf, do not consider themselves to have a disability in the traditional sense. They regard deafness as a culture, and describe themselves as "Deaf" with a capital D.
- There are many different levels of hearing loss. Most people with hearing impairments have some hearing.
- Not all people who are deaf use sign language. Not all people who are deaf or hearing impaired can read lips or speak.
- Not all people with hearing impairments use hearing aids or augmentative devices. Those who do use them may not do so all the time.
- While many deaf and hearing-impaired people can read lips, the best lip readers can make out only about 35 percent of spoken words.
- Sign language has its own rules, customs, grammar, and idioms. It is not a simple translation of English.
- While a slight increase in volume may enhance your communication with some people who have hearing impairments, excessive volume is inappropriate and may cause feedback in hearing aids.

Suggestions for Interacting with People Who Have Hearing Impairments

- Find out the way in which the person prefers to communicate.
- To get a person's attention, tap him or her politely on the shoulder.
- Be prepared to use notes, or to communicate through an interpreter.

- Always look at the person with whom you are speaking, not the interpreter.
- If a person uses a hearing aid, avoid conversations in noisy, open areas. Do not shout. Speak clearly in a normal tone of voice.
- If a person reads lips, keep obstructions (smoking materials, hands, food, etc.) away from your face. Speak deliberately in short, simple sentences. Some simple gestures (nodding, shrugging shoulders) and facial expressions (furrowed brow, surprised look) may be helpful.
- Be patient and willing to repeat your message.

Interacting with People Who Have Speech Impairments

Considerations

- Many things can cause speech impairments, such as hearing loss, stroke, cerebral palsy, or traumatic head injury.
- People with speech impairments are frequently misperceived as intoxicated or mentally disabled.
- A person with a speech impairment may be easier to understand at particular times, and his or her speech may deteriorate with fatigue or in stressful situations.
- Successful communication can be a function of time: allowing time for a person to express himself or herself, allowing yourself time to understand. Eventually, you may be able to improve your receptive ability, and the speaker may be able to adjust to your listening style.

Suggestions for Interacting with People Who Have Speech Impairments

- If you do not understand what a person has said, ask politely for a repetition. Do not pretend you have understood when you haven't.
- An area with background noise or distractions may make communication more difficult. Consider moving to a quieter location.
- In meetings or group discussions, people with speech disabilities can have difficulty being heard. Help them by assuring that the group allows them an opportunity to speak.
- Do not attempt to speak for another person or finish his or her sentences.
- When necessary ask short, simple questions to confirm your understanding.
- If necessary, consider using written or some other form of communication.

Interacting with People Who Have Visual Disabilities

Considerations

- Levels of visual impairments range continuously from mild myopia to total blindness.
- Legal blindness is defined as 20/200 vision to the best correction.
- Many people who are considered blind do have some sight.
- Many people who are blind consider it to be more of an inconvenience than a disability.
- Although many blind people use Braille, most do not. Many use adaptive equipment such as text magnifiers and computers equipped with voice synthesis.

Suggestions for Interacting with People Who Have Visual Disabilities

- When you encounter a person with a visual impairment, introduce yourself or announce your presence and the names of those with you. Excuse yourself before you leave.
- Offer to describe the physical layout of a room, the position of food on a plate, and the names of other people present in a room.

- When guiding someone with a visual disability, do not grab him or her. Offer to be a "sighted guide." Let them take your arm; they will probably allow you to walk half a step ahead of them. Point out doors, curbs, stairs, and possible obstructions as you approach them.
- Don't pet or interact with a guide dog. The dog is working, and a vital part of its owner's safety and independence.
- Be aware that changing a physical environment (moving furniture, adding or deleting items, painting) can cause problems for someone with a visual disability. Inform the person of any alterations about which they should know.

Getting Started

Anyone who has ever traveled in a foreign country knows that the natives tend to appreciate any effort by a visitor to understand their culture and speak their language. People who have disabilities also appreciate those who sincerely try to understand and communicate with them. That might involve something as simple as offering someone who is tired a place to sit down, or it could be as complex as taking lessons in sign language. The important thing is to make the effort.

Discussion Questions

1. Why are there no hard-and-fast rules about how to interact politely with people with disabilities?
2. When might it be rude rather than helpful to move someone in a wheelchair?
3. How can you avoid the common tendency to treat adults with developmental disability as if they were children?
4. Is sign language universal, or are there many sign languages like spoken language? Does sign language have slang?
5. What can you do to make sure that a person with a speech impairment contributes his or her ideas in a group meeting?
6. Is it inconsiderate to use expressions like "I see what you mean" or "see you later" to someone with vision impairment?
7. How might experience traveling in a foreign country help you interact with people with disabilities?

Case Study: In the Eye of the Perfect Storm: Creating Accessibility—IBM, GM, and CISCO

A "Critical Disadvantage"

Americans with disabilities constitute an estimated 49 million people, or 20 percent of the population. In other words, one in every five people has a disability, and as some experts estimate, there is an 80 percent chance that an average person will experience some kind of disability in the course of his or her lifetime. Even with the likelihood that so many people will be in this group, Americans with disabilities are, according to the 2004 National Organization on Disability/Harris

Source: This case was written by Dr. Kathryn A. Cañas and Dr. Harris Sondak, The University of Utah

Survey, still at a "critical disadvantage" when compared with nondisabled Americans.[1] The following statistics reflect this disadvantage:

- Thirty-five percent of people with disabilities report being employed full or part time, compared with 78 percent of those who do not have disabilities.
- People with disabilities are three times as likely to live in poverty with annual household incomes below $15,000 (26 percent versus 9 percent).
- People with disabilities remain twice as likely to drop out of high school compared with people without disabilities (21 percent versus 10 percent).
- People with disabilities are twice as likely to have inadequate transportation (31 percent versus 13 percent), and a much higher percentage go without needed health care (18 percent versus 7 percent).
- People with disabilities are less likely to socialize, eat out, or attend religious services than their nondisabled counterparts.
- Life satisfaction for people with disabilities trails, with only 34 percent saying they are very satisfied compared with 61 percent of those without disabilities.
- People with disabilities are much more worried about their future health and well-being. Half are worried about not being able to care for themselves or being a burden to their families, compared with a quarter of other Americans.[2]

Alan A. Reich, former National Organization on Disability (NOD) president, expresses his concern about these findings: "Progress is too slow" and the "gaps are still too large." These statistics are important, Reich explains, because "everyone knows people with disabilities; and anyone can acquire a disability at any time. Everyone has a stake in these findings."[3]

Also contributing to this critical disadvantage is that emergency planning is insufficient for people with disabilities. According to a recent nationwide Harris Interactive survey of emergency managers in states and cities throughout the nation, 69 percent of emergency managers said that they had incorporated the needs of people with disabilities into their emergency plans. Although this percentage may seem adequate, other findings proved more troublesome: Only 54 percent of the emergency managers had plans for dealing with schools for students with disabilities; 59 percent said they did not have plans for pediatric populations with disabilities; and 76 percent said that they did not have a paid expert to deal with emergency preparedness for people with disabilities.[4]

The critical disadvantage is thus based on a number of elements: employment, transportation, health insurance, concerns about the future, general life satisfaction, and emergency planning. When people with disabilities constitute such a high percentage and when other minority groups are making significant strides toward equality, why are people with disabilities at such a critical disadvantage? Three systems of discrimination for people with disabilities come together to create a perfect storm of unemployment. The strength of the perfect storm creates a situation in which people with disabilities are, in many instances, at a disadvantage when compared with people without disabilities.

The Perfect Storm

The first of three interconnected systems of discrimination that create the perfect storm is the inadequate social structure for people with disabilities; the second is a set of pervasive cultural assumptions about hiring people with disabilities; and the third is a two-sided disincentive for both employee and employer. The power of this triple threat and the damage it leaves behind are reflected in the many lives that are diminished by it.

Inadequate Social Structure

Activism on behalf of the disabled is relatively new, and this movement's lack of historical roots contributes to its relatively weak institutional structure. Women and African Americans, by contrast, have developed protective social structures formalized by laws such as Title VII of the Civil Rights Act, affirmative action, and the Pregnancy Discrimination Act. Further, organizations such as the National Association for the Advancement of Colored People (NAACP) and the National Organization for Women (NOW) represent legitimate and powerful vehicles for social change.

People with disabilities are just beginning to experience some workplace equality since the passage of the Americans with Disabilities Act (ADA) in 1990, and educational equality with the Individuals with Disabilities Education Act Amendments of 1997 (IDEA). Without long-standing laws and experienced organizations to protect the rights of people with disabilities, the disability rights movement remains less influential than other civil rights efforts, thus making the crusade for social justice a more difficult process.

Contributing to the challenge of creating a strong social structure for people with disabilities is the extensive diversity represented among members of the disabled community. The life experiences of people with spinal cord injuries or muscular dystrophy, for example, are different from those of people with learning disabilities or who are HIV-positive. Furthermore, people who are deaf, a condition that is classified by the ADA as a disability, often do not consider themselves to be disabled.

Further complicating the situation is the confusion about what conditions are considered disabilities protected by the ADA. The ADA makes it clear that when determining whether or not a specific condition is a disability, the question is always the same: Does the diagnosable condition substantially limit one or more major life activities (i.e., walking, seeing, hearing, speaking, breathing, learning, sitting, standing, etc.)? Even with this legal standard in place, there is still debate surrounding the ADA: Do people with cancer or severe diabetes qualify under the ADA? At what point during an individual's condition do people who are addicted to alcohol or drugs, severely depressed, or HIV-positive qualify under the ADA?

Understanding and managing these issues may help people with disabilities strengthen their movement's social and institutional structure and, as a result, gain more access to and influence within the public arena. Because the disability rights movement represents a youthful, fluid, and diverse effort, gaining a legitimate voice and communicating a unified message will, of course, be difficult. Compounding the inadequate social structure for people with disabilities is a cultural mythology based on a trio of damaging assumptions about the disabled.

Cultural Assumptions about Hiring People with Disabilities

Stereotypes, attitudes that make assumptions about whole groups of people, often distort reality and disempower individuals in their daily lives. American culture and attitudes make assumptions that lead managers not to hire people with disabilities. Although each of the following assumptions—people with disabilities are unreliable, expensive, and likely to sue their company—is indeed damaging on its own, together the assumptions constitute a pervasive cultural mythology that erects barriers to employment that are likely to harm both people with disabilities and their potential employers.

ASSUMPTION 1: PEOPLE WITH DISABILITIES ARE UNRELIABLE Unsurprisingly, virtually all people with disabilities want to live as fulfilling a life as possible; for them, like for most people, a positive experience in the workplace typically translates to a more optimistic outlook on life. As Dr. Norma Carr-Ruffino, a leading expert in workplace diversity, explains: Most people with disabilities "want to work, regardless of the extent of their impairment, and see work as a major route to self-fulfillment. They want to find work that draws on their skills and talents and helps them live a more abundant life."[5] Challenging the perception that employees with disabilities are frequently sick is the fact that people who are disabled tend to have better-than-average attendance and turnover records.[6] Fraser Nelson, Executive Director of the Disability Law Center of Salt Lake City, reminds us that "being disabled is not an illness, it is a condition; understanding this distinction is important to discrediting the assumption that being disabled translates to taking more sick days."[7]

Workers with disabilities are often cast—albeit incorrectly—as less productive than their coworkers without disabilities. According to studies, employers have not only expressed more favorable attitudes toward employing persons with severe disabilities in the workplace but also viewed workers with severe disabilities as dependable, productive workers who can interact socially and foster positive attitudes on the part of their coworkers.[8] In addition, 50 percent of managers rate their employees with disabilities higher than those who are not disabled on the following dimensions: willingness to work hard, reliability, punctuality, and attendance.[9] Although the reality is that workers with disabilities are just as dependable as their coworkers, the stereotype of being unreliable is insidious and persists deep within American attitudes. This stereotype makes it easy for managers to make the next assumption—that workers with disabilities are costly—without carefully evaluating the reality.

ASSUMPTION 2: ACCOMMODATING PEOPLE WITH DISABILITIES IN THE WORKPLACE IS COSTLY Evaluating whether accommodating people with disabilities is expensive is difficult and complex. There is some evidence that accommodating those with disabilities has made them more expensive to hire, but the reliability of the data showing this trend is disputed. Moreover, there is also evidence that suggests that hiring people with disabilities not only costs relatively little but can be a savvy business decision.

According to the National Organization on Disability, a study that surveyed companies employing people with disabilities found that only 24 percent reported that any accommodations were needed. In addition, among companies that did indeed provide accommodations, "for 34 percent of businesses the average cost was $100 or less, and for 71 percent of businesses it was $500 or less. Forty-six percent of accommodations were simple things like providing a ramp or adapting a desk to fit a wheelchair." In a separate survey of employers who used the U.S. Department of Labor's Job Accommodation Network, 71 percent reported that "the cost of accommodation was $500 or less on average." This study also reflected the fact that "[a] dollar spent on accommodations leads to an estimated $35 dollars in benefits."[10]

Echoing these results is evidence reported by National Public Radio science correspondent Joseph Shapiro which indicated that 51 percent of all accommodations cost nothing; and for the other 49 percent, the average cost of an accommodation was $300. Interestingly, the study also highlighted that less than 1 percent of accommodations cost $5,000 or more.[11] To help buttress substantial costs that organizations may have to absorb, tax incentives are often available.

However, some researchers argue that employment rates among people with disabilities declined after the passage of the ADA, despite its prohibitions against discrimination in hiring, suggesting that employers are reluctant to spend even the relatively small amounts required to accommodate these potential workers.[12] Whether this decline is real or merely apparent is a controversial issue and depends on how researchers define such complicated concepts as "disability" and "employment" and how they account for the effects of disability insurance and Social Security. In any case, it may be that because many accommodations are fixed costs, the expenses associated with accommodating disabled people will decline in years to come. For example, constructing a ramp for the use of its first employee who uses a wheelchair is a cost that a firm will not have to duplicate for subsequent hires.

In light of the ambiguity about whether accommodating disabled employees is in fact costly, it is premature to assume that this is true. The negative impact of this assumption is further compounded by another, that employees with disabilities are likely to sue their employer.

ASSUMPTION 3: PEOPLE WITH DISABILITIES ARE LIKELY TO SUE THEIR EMPLOYER   When employers believe that they may be sued if they decide to fire an employee with a disability, it is not surprising that qualified, disabled job candidates do not get hired. The employers' rationale is simple: Why take the unnecessary risk of being sued? But this perceived risk begs the question whether there is in fact excessive litigation against companies for discriminating against employees with disabilities.

According to DiversityInc.com, over the past decade, employees and potential employees have "brought charges against companies citing discrimination based on disabilities associated with conditions ranging from alcoholism and epilepsy to multiple sclerosis and the HIV virus."[13] More specifically, more than $436 million has been paid in settlements to more than 31,000 people, and another $28.1 million was paid in court-ordered fines through 491 ADA cases brought by the Equal Employment Opportunity Commission (EEOC) from 1993 through 2002.[14] What are the issues underlying this litigation, and is the fear of being sued a legitimate concern for employers?

According to former Supreme Court Justice Sandra Day O'Connor, the high court's heavy load of disability-rights cases is the result of holes in the ADA. Although the original goal of the ADA was to help introduce qualified people with disabilities into the workplace, it is so complex and ambiguous that it creates uncertainty among employers about how to comply with a law with continually changing interpretation and enforcement. O'Connor explains that the ADA was written and passed hurriedly by Congress: "It's an example of what happens when . . . the sponsors are so eager to get something passed that what passes hasn't been as carefully written as a group of law professors might put together." And as a result, "it leaves lots of ambiguities and gaps and things for courts to figure out."[15]

Lawsuits brought by employees against their employers are indeed expensive for firms, but the portion of these costs attributable to the ADA is very difficult to determine. It is possible that fear of being sued for wrongful termination leads to decreased hiring of people with disabilities.[16] Research suggests, however, that even if there has been a decline in employment rates of people with disabilities since the passage of the ADA, its likely explanation is not primarily fear of litigation but rather the costs of accommodation.[17]

It is important for employers to understand that although the ADA protects people with disabilities from workplace discrimination, it also protects the employer who hires people with disabilities. First, employers do not have to hire individuals with disabilities who are not qualified for the job, nor do they have to give preference to persons with disabilities over other applicants. Second, employers are not required to make accommodations that would cause them undue hardship, in other words, when the accommodations are excessively expensive or interfere with a business imperative. Third, if a person does not identify himself or herself as having a disability, employers generally do not have to make any accommodation unless the disability is obvious. Finally, the ADA provides some subsidies for hiring disabled workers.

Disincentives

The third source of discrimination is the complexity of the American health care and insurance systems as they relate to people with disabilities. Why would a firm seek an employee whose participation in its health insurance plan will raise its costs? Conversely, why would a person with a disability assume a position in a company that may not provide affordable or adequate health insurance, or risk losing disability benefits because the salary surpasses the amount sanctioned by the federal government?

Social Security Disability Insurance (SSDI) and Supplemental Security Income (SSI) are the two options through which people with disabilities may obtain public insurance. People with general disabilities who make more than $830 per month, or $1,380 per month if they are blind, are not eligible for these public programs.[18] Employer-provided insurance is an alternative to SSDI and SSI, so in deciding whether to be employed a person with disabilities must consider the costs of health care and insurance against the benefits of working.

Furthermore, rising health care costs make it especially expensive for employers to employ people with disabilities. To contain their costs, most companies have passed on an increasing share of the costs for health insurance to employees and have selected plans with many use restrictions.[19] This situation has thus created a two-sided disincentive: First, employers may be more reluctant to hire people with high-cost medical conditions; and second, people with disabilities may not be as interested in entering the workforce if they risk losing their benefits without an adequate substitute provided by their employers.

According to Diane D. Russell, Former Director of the Governor's Committee on Employment of People with Disabilities in the state of Utah, deciding how to navigate these economic issues "can become so complicated that there are programs specifically for people who are receiving Social Security Disability Benefits and would like information on how work may affect their benefits."[20] She explains that in such a program, a benefits planner will meet people with disabilities and review their situations to help determine if and how they can go to work and not lose benefits, particularly health benefits.

Shelter From The Perfect Storm: Government Efforts

The perfect storm has created a situation in which people with disabilities who are looking to attain meaningful employment face a unique problem. To help mitigate the effects of this situation, the U.S. Department of Health and Human Services established in 2002 the Office of Disabilities. This agency serves as the focal point within the department for implementation and coordination of federal policies and programs and facilitates the interaction of the federal and state governments with community resources and private sector partners including business and nonprofit organizations.[21] The agency also plans and carries out efforts to remove barriers faced by those with disabilities, and to increase the visibility of those barriers. In addition, every state and the District of Columbia have a department that provides services to people with disabilities, including coordination of employment services. Unfortunately, state programs are often targeted for budget cuts in bad economic times, and with recently rising unemployment and escalating state budget crises, many of these agencies have been hard hit.

Shelter From The Perfect Storm: Nonprofit Efforts

Many nonprofit organizations are dedicated to the protection and advocacy of the rights of people with disabilities. For example, the National Disability Right Network provides free legal services to people with disabilities to fight violations of their civil rights in terms of accessibility, employment, schooling, housing, and similar issues.[22] Similarly, the NOD works to expand opportunities for people with disabilities so that they can fully contribute to society in all aspects of life.[23] Among its other activities, the NOD reports annually on the status of the employment opportunities for people with disabilities, emergency preparedness efforts, and changes in the accessibility of American communities and facilities for those with disabilities.

In addition, many nonprofit organizations provide education, training, and employment placement services to people with disabilities. For example, Start on Success (SOS), a program of the NOD, offers job training and internships.[24] The purpose of SOS is to prepare young people with disabilities, especially those from low-income urban families, for employment before they leave high school.

Some universities assist both employers and potential employees to understand better the issues of workplace accessibility for people with disabilities. For example, Virginia Commonwealth University's Rehabilitation Research and Training Center studies how individuals with disabilities can be supported at work and advance their careers.[25] Similarly, the School of Industrial and Labor Relations at Cornell University houses the Employment and Disability Institute, which enhances the employment opportunities for people with disabilities through research, publications, training, and technical assistance.[26] The Disability Research Institute of the University of Illinois provides resources for research on important issues of disability employment including the economics of disability, the determination of disability, transitioning people with disabilities to enter the workforce, and helping people who have developed a disability to return to work.[27]

Shelter From The Perfect Storm: Business Efforts

Many business organizations embrace accessibility. Three examples of companies with unusually innovative, sustained, and impressive models of recruiting, hiring, and retaining employees with disabilities are International Business Machines Corporation (IBM), General Motors (GM), and Cisco Systems.

IBM

IBM's history of employing people with disabilities dates to 1914, when IBM hired its first employee with a disability, 76 years before the ADA was enacted.[28] At IBM today, people with disabilities make up approximately 2 to 3 percent of the company's staff of more than 355,000. Nearly half of these employees with disabilities are working in technology positions such as electrical engineer, IT architect, or software programmer.[29]

Because IBM's model of accessibility is uniquely comprehensive, it could become a model for other companies to emulate. Indeed, IBM is DiversityInc's top-rated company for people with disabilities because of its inclusive culture, its workplace that accommodates people's needs, and its marketing that values people with disabilities as customers.[30] IBM's progressive philosophy on accessibility is to create and maintain

> a holistic, end-to-end approach to accessibility. Accessibility . . . means going beyond product compliance with regulations to include a better user experience and the vision to ultimately improve a person's total quality of life. We see this as a global journey to gain business advantage. A journey that begins with accessible technology infrastructure and ends with business transformation.[31]

On a philosophical level, IBM's mission is poignant. And when the mission is translated to a practical level—specifically in terms of internships, recruitment, accommodations, and the IBM Accessibility Center—we see that IBM is indeed enacting its vision.

An IBM internship program called Entry Point provides an opportunity for students with disabilities to get on-the-job experience in their majors and learn about the myriad of careers IBM offers nationwide. Project View and Project Able are two recruiting programs that reach outstanding college candidates of diverse backgrounds including people with disabilities. As a direct result of Project Able, which was launched in 1999, 84 college students and 139 professionals with disabilities have been hired at IBM.[32]

Internally, IBM provides a range of accommodations and assistive devices for employees who have disabilities. IBM has

- constructed ramps, power doors, parking facilities, and other accommodations to provide access for people with impaired mobility;
- captioned videotapes and provided sign language interpreters and note takers for classes and meetings for employees who are deaf or hard of hearing;
- recorded company publications on audiocassettes for employees and retirees who are visually impaired;
- provided adaptive services or modifications to enable people with disabilities to use work-related equipment (e.g., screen readers and display-screen magnifiers; keyboard guards and special switches; real-time captioning of meetings and Webcasts; telecommunications devices and telephone amplifiers);
- provided travel assistance for employees with mobility impairments.[33]

In addition to assisting their employees, 5 years ago IBM merged existing accessibility groups to form a worldwide Accessibility Center with locations in the United States, Europe, Japan, and Australia. The Center "fosters product accessibility, works toward the harmonization of worldwide standards, applies research technologies to solve problems experienced by people with disabilities, creates industry-focused solutions, and generates accessibility awareness."[34]

IBM's Director of Diversity Communications Jim Sinocchi states: "We consider diversity strategic to our organization. We don't hire people who are disabled just because it's a nice thing to do. We do it because it's the right thing to do from a business standpoint."[35] Sinocchi, who broke his neck while surfing on a vacation 20 years ago, speaks freely about his experiences as a paraplegic, "The problem is that people equate disability with stupidity. When I go out to dinner, the waiter won't ask me what I want. He'll ask the people I'm with what I want to have. This pervasive attitude must be broken for disabled workers to make a full contribution to society."[36] With its serious commitment to accessibility, IBM works daily to break this prejudice.

General Motors

Like IBM, GM understands the value of hiring people with disabilities. The GMability philosophy maintains that

> GM has long been committed throughout its global operations to hiring people with varied backgrounds. This hiring practice is the right thing to do, but just as important, it creates a competitive advantage for GM. Having a workforce that reflects the marketplace helps GM more effectively reach customers and provide products and services they want.[37]

Gary Talbot, a member of the U.S. Access Board, works as a vehicle systems engineer at the GM headquarters. According to Talbot, "With GM, if they decide that they want you as an employee, there isn't anything they won't do to help you succeed."[38] Reflecting its respect for its employees and their value to the company, GM responds expeditiously to requests and concerns and goes well beyond what is legally required or typically provided. For example, when Talbot suggested that the company replace the newly installed refrigerators in the 38 break rooms with side-by-side models so employees using wheelchairs could reach their food, GM quickly made the necessary improvements. In a second example, when Talbot's office did not fit his wheelchair, the company remodeled it twice before they reached the correct configuration.[39]

One of GM's strengths has been its open communication between employer and employee. As Talbot explains: "Workplaces need to provide cultures in which employees feel they can be honest about their needs."[40]

Many of the improvements for GM employees with disabilities came through suggestions from the company's Affinity Group for People with Disabilities. This Affinity Group—which consist of GM employees and retirees who meet once a month to discuss accessibility issues in the workplace—acts as a link between diverse employee groups and management and is formed around "employee initiatives" and is "employee-driven." The primary goal of these groups is "to create professional development opportunities for their members and to serve as an information resource to the Corporation on issues that affect that constituency."[41]

In addition, GM is reinforcing its commitment to provide transportation solutions for people with disabilities. GM's Sit-N-Lift seat—a fully motorized, rotating lift-and-lower passenger seat that makes it easier for people with disabilities to enter and exit the vehicle—has been available on Chevrolet, Pontiac, Buick, and Saturn models.[42] GM offers reimbursements to customers with disabilities for costs of installing adaptive equipment. Plus, its Web site offers helpful links to people with disabilities including evaluators who can help customers decide what adaptive modifications they need, vendors for the necessary equipment, and the licensing requirements of its state DMVs.[43]

Cisco Systems

Cisco Systems provides networking equipment for the Internet. Although founded as recently as 1984, its sales are now over $40 billion per year.[44] Cisco not only provides the means for networking, but it offers itself as an example to its customers so that they can learn from Cisco's own experiences as a company that does business over extensive networks.[45] Of particular relevance to people with disabilities is Cisco's encouragement of its employees to create innovative home networks so that they themselves can transform how they and their families live, work, and play, thus providing templates that others can use for their own telecommuting.

Cisco launched an effort in 2004 to make its facilities, products, documentation, and Web sites fully accessible to both employees and users with disabilities.[46] To accomplish this goal Cisco developed a complex initiative that included the creation of an accessibility testing and evaluation lab, the integration of accessibility teams into product development engineering, online accessibility training, and the incorporation of accessibility lessons into all business units. One result of this effort was the Cisco was awarded the 2006 Helen Keller award by the American Foundation for the Blind for making its products accessible to those with vision loss.[47] Not only does Cisco provide accessibility for its products, its products help make its customers more accessible as well.[48]

In addition, Cisco prides itself on providing an accessible environment for all its employees. In addition to facilitating telecommuting, Cisco ensures that the architecture of and equipment in its facilities meet the needs of its employees from a variety of dimensions of accessibility and helps them succeed at work in an environment that expects high levels of performance. In the words of Luís Lima, a Cisco employee with disabilities, Cisco "gives people the resources they need to do their jobs and drive their careers without pampering them."[49] Like IBM and GM, Cisco created an advisory group/support network of and for people with disabilities, the Cisco Disability Awareness Network. Finally, Cisco sponsors workshops on how employees can help each other feel more included.[50]

As illustrated here, some companies embrace accessibility in the workplace to bring qualified, motivated employees with disabilities into the workplace and to create innovative models of recruiting and retaining employees with disabilities. These companies demonstrate that it is possible to provide people with disabilities the opportunity not only to navigate the perfect storm but to conquer it by belonging to an organization that creates real opportunities and an inclusive environment.

Discussion Questions

1. According to the NOD/Harris survey, people with disabilities are at a "critical disadvantage" when compared with people without disabilities. Why, do you think, is this the case, when legislation such as the ADA was passed in 1990 in an attempt to improve the lives of people with disabilities?
2. What are the various provisions of the three most significant pieces of legislation for people with disabilities: the ADA, ADAAA, and the IDEA?
3. What can society in general and people with disabilities in particular do to change the cultural assumptions that cast people with disabilities as unreliable, expensive, and likely to sue their employer?
4. Why haven't other companies followed the lead of those organizations, like IBM, that have effectively embraced disabilities as a significant component of diversity—viewing the recruitment and the retention of people with disabilities as a competitive advantage?

Notes

1. "Landmark Disability Survey Finds Pervasive Disadvantage: 2004 N.O.D./Harris Survey Documents Trends Impacting 54 Million Americans," June 25, 2005, http://www.nod.org/content.cfm?id=1537. Other Web sites that provide insight into the situation facing Americans with Disabilities are available from http://www.adaportal.org; http://www.ilr.cornell.edu/ped/ DisabilityStatistics/; http://www.dsc.ucsf.edu/main.php; http://www.worksupport.com/Main/factsres.asp.

2. "Landmark Disability Survey Finds Pervasive Disadvantage."

3. Ibid.

4. "Survey on Emergency Preparedness for People with Disabilities: Survey Reveals Gaps

in Emergency Preparedness for People with Disabilities," November 10, 2004, http://www.nod.org/content.cfm?id=1586#episurvey.

5. Norma Carr-Ruffino, *Diversity Success Strategies* (Boston: Butterworth-Heinemann, 1999), 241. See also Norma Carr-Ruffino, *Managing Diversity: People Skills for a Multicultural Workplace* (New Jersey: Pearson Custom Publishing, 2003).

6. R. Greenwood and V. A. Johnson. "Employer Perspectives on Workers with Disabilities," *Journal of Rehabilitation* 53 (1987): 37–46 as quoted in Taylor Cox, *Cultural Diversity in Organizations* (San Francisco: Berrett-Koehler, 1993), 90.

7. Fraser Nelson, Executive Director of the Salt Lake City Disability Law Center, personal interview, 13 Oct. 2004.

8. J. M. Levy, D. J. Jessop, A. Rimmerman, F. Francis, F. and P. H. Levy. "Determinants of Attitudes of New York State Employers towards the Employment of Persons with Severe Handicaps," *Journal of Rehabilitation* 59, no. 1 (1993): 49–54, in Darlene D. Unger, "Employers' Attitudes toward Persons with Disabilities in the Workforce: Myths or Realities?" *Focus on Autism and Other Developmental Disabilities* 17, no. 1 (2002), http://www.worksupport.com/Main/proed17.asp.

9. Carr-Ruffino, *Diversity Success Strategies*, 242.

10. Seth Egert, "EEOC Forum Addresses Disability in the Workplace," March 16, 2004, http://www.nod.org/content.cfm?id=1501.

11. Joseph Shapiro, *No Pity: People with Disabilities Forging a New Civil Rights Movement* (New York: Times Books, 1993), as quoted in Carr-Ruffino, *Diversity Success Strategies*, 254.

12. Thomas DeLeire, "The Americans with Disabilities Act and the Employment of People with Disabilities," in David C. Stapleton and Richard V. Burkhauser, eds., *The Decline in Employment of People with Disabilities: A Policy Puzzle* (Kalamazoo, Michigan: W.E. Upjohn Institute for Employment Research, 2003), 259–77.

13. Angela D. Johnson, "Americans with Disabilities Act: Is Your Company Compliant?" DiversityInc.com, July 28, 2003, http://diversityinc.com/public/5343.cfm.

14. Ibid.

15. "Justice Sandra Day O'Connor Pokes Holes in Americans Disabilities Act," DiversityInc.com,

March 14, 2002, www.diversityinc.com/members/2575.com. For more information on the ADA, see: http://www.eeoc.gov/facts/adaqa1.html.

16. Burkhauser and Stapleton, "A Review of the Evidence and Its Implications for Policy Change," in *The Decline in Employment of People with Disabilities*, 369–405.

17. Daron Acemoglu and Joshua Angrist, "Consequences of Employment Protection: The Case of the Americans with Disabilities Act," *Journal of Political Economy* 109, no. 5 (2001): 915–56.

18. The Work Site—Social Security Online, http://www.socialsecurity.gov/work/ResourcesToolkit/redbook_page.html.

19. Burkhauser and Stapleton, "Introduction," in *The Decline in Employment of People with Disabilities: A Policy Puzzle*, 12–13. See also Nanette Goodman and Timothy Waidmann, "Social Security Disability Insurance and the Recent Decline in the Employment Rate of People with Disabilities," in *The Decline in Employment of People with Disabilities*.

20. Diane D. Russell, Director of the Governor's Committee on Employment of People with Disabilities in the State of Utah, personal interview, December 22, 2004.

21. "Office on Disability," http://www.hhs.gov/od/about/index.html.

22. "National Disability Rights Network: Protection and Advocacy for Individuals with Disabilities," http://www.napas.org/aboutus/default.htm.

23. "National Organization on Disability," http://www.nod.org/.

24. "Start on Success: A Program of the National Organization on Disability," http://www.startonsuccess.org/.

25. "Worksupport.com: Information, Resources, and Research about Work and Disability Issues," http://www.worksupport.com/index.cfm.

26. "Cornell University ILR School, Employment and Disability Institute: Disability Policy, Practice, and Research," http://www.ilr.cornell.edu/edi/.

27. "Disability Research Institute: University of Illinois at Urbana-Champaign," http://www.dri.uiuc.edu/default.htm.

28. "Accessibility at IBM: An Integrated Approach: Evolving from Philanthropy to Business Transformation," http://www-306.ibm.com/able/access_ibm/execbrief.html#evolving.

29. Joe Mullich, "Hiring Without Limits," *Workforce Management*, June 2004, http://www.workforce.com/section/09/feature/23/74/24/.

30. Barbara Frankel, "The DiversityInc Top 10 Companies for People with Disabilities List," *DiversityInc.com*, May 4 (2009), http://www.diversityinc.com/public/5823.cfm.

31. "Accessibility at IBM."

32. Mullich, "Hiring Without Limits."

33. "Accessibility at IBM."

34. Ibid.

35. Mullich, "Hiring Without Limits."

36. Ibid.

37. "Gmability Philosophy," http://www.gm.com/company/gmability/workplace/400_diversity/index.html.

38. Jennifer Gatewood, "Above and Beyond," *Human Resource Executive Magazine*, September 2004, http://www.hreonline.com/HRE/story1d=4222745.

39. Ibid.

40. Ibid.

41. Life@GM./Benefits. "Affinity Groups," http://www.gm.com/company/careers/life/lif_benefits_affinity.html.

42. "OnStar Improves Accessibility for People with Disabilities," *Road and Travel*, July 26, 2004, http://www.roadandtravel.com/oempages/onstar/hardofhearing.htm.

43. "GMMobility," http://www.gm.com/vehicles/services/gm_mobility/.

44. "Cisco Systems Reports Q4 and Fiscal Year 2008 Earnings," http://newsroom.cisco.com/dlls/2008/fin_080508.html.

45. "Inside Cisco IT," http://www.cisco.com/web/about/ciscoitatwork/index.html.

46. "Product Stewardship: Accessibility," http://www.cisco.com/web/about/ac227/ac222/environment/product_stewardship/accessibility.html.

47. "2006 Helen Keller Achievement Awards," http://www.afb.org/Section.asp?SectionID=28&TopicID=152&DocumentID=3080.

48. "Innovation in Accessibility," http://www.cisco.com/web/about/responsibility/accessibility/pdf/Cisco_Accessibility_Brochure.pdf.

49. "Luís Lima: A Career—and a Life—Built Upon Helping Others," http://www.cisco.com/web/about/ac49/ac55/Profile_Luis_Lima.pdf.

50. "Diversity: Diversity Education," http://www.cisco.com/web/about/ac49/ac55/diversity_inclusion_education.html.

PART THREE

Exercises: Developing Three Essential Skills

In this part, "Exercises: Developing Three Essential Skills," we include a variety of exercises and mini case studies that encourage our readers to expand their understanding of diversity as individuals and members of organizations. The purpose of the first group of exercises is to encourage self-awareness and self-assessment of one's knowledge of diversity and one's personal stereotypes and biases. The second group of exercises aims to help individuals better understand how diversity pertains to themselves, their society, and their organization. The third group of exercises provides tools that can be used to examine how diversity is understood and managed within organizations.

CHAPTER 10

Analyzing Self

EXERCISE: YOUR PIE CHART

Purpose

The purpose of this exercise is three tiered: to compare your own cultural background with that of others; to raise awareness of the importance of self-identity based on affiliations with groups; and to consider the influence of self-identity on individuals' experiences in organizational settings.

Introduction

Personal characteristics (some changeable, others not), which may influence an individual's basic self-image and sense of identity, may also influence experiences in the workplace. *Primary dimensions* of diversity are essentially unchangeable personal characteristics (e.g., gender, race, ethnicity, age, sexual orientation, and physical and mental abilities).

Secondary dimensions of diversity, however, are changeable personal characteristics that are acquired and may be modified or abandoned throughout life (e.g., education, income, marital and parental status, religion, political affiliation, and work experience). Of course, secondary characteristics are not completely self-determined; educational background, work experience, income, and marital status are affected by others' decisions. However, people generally have more control over secondary dimensions of diversity than over primary dimensions.[1]

Guidelines

1. Working individually, create a pie chart identifying group affiliations that have some importance in your self-concept. These affiliations may be based on any of the primary and secondary dimensions of diversity mentioned or on some other personal characteristic that is particularly important to you. Indicate the approximate importance of each group by the size of the slice of pie that you assign it.
2. Participate in a discussion based on the following questions:
   * What did you learn about yourself?
   * What surprised you the most?
   * What group affiliations were mentioned the most?
   * What did you learn about others that surprised you?
   * How does your self-identity influence your experiences in organizational settings?

Source: Taylor Cox and Ruby L. Beale, *Developing Competency to Manage Diversity: Readings, Cases and Activities* (San Francisco, CA: Berrett-Koehler, 1997).

EXERCISE: DIVERSITY QUESTIONNAIRE

Purpose

The purpose of this exercise is to help you gauge your openness to and awareness of diversity, as measured by your behavior and communication patterns.

Guidelines

Next to each question place the number that best describes your own actions and beliefs.

1 = almost always
2 = frequently
3 = sometimes
4 = seldom
5 = almost never

_____ **1.** Do you recognize and challenge the perceptions, assumptions, and biases that affect your thinking?

_____ **2.** Do you think about the impact of what you say or how you act before you speak or act?

_____ **3.** Do you do everything you can to prevent the reinforcement of prejudices, including avoiding using negative stereotypes when you speak?

_____ **4.** Do you encourage people who are not from the dominant culture to speak out on their concerns, and do you respect those issues?

_____ **5.** Do you speak up when someone is making racial, sexual, or other derogatory remarks, or is humiliating another person?

_____ **6.** Do you apologize when you realize you may have offended someone with inappropriate behavior or comments?

_____ **7.** Do you try to know people as individuals, not as representatives of specific groups, and welcome different types of people in your peer group?

_____ **8.** Do you do everything that you can to understand your own background and try to educate yourself about other backgrounds, including different communication styles?

Scoring: The lower your score, the better you communicate and improve the climate in your diverse organization and the community at large. To improve your communication, increase your use of the behaviors listed.

_____

Source: William Sonnenschein, *The Diversity Toolkit: How You Can Build and Benefit from a Diverse Workforce* (Chicago, IL: Contemporary Books, 1997), 47.

EXERCISE: FIRST THOUGHTS

Purpose

The purpose of this activity is to help you recognize that stereotyping is unfair and becomes a barrier to good communication and accepting people as individuals. This exercise encourages you to examine the stereotypes of the groups of people with whom you interact.

Introduction

Before you begin this exercise, you need to understand two important concepts: stereotype and prejudice.

A *stereotype* is an exaggerated belief or fixed idea about a person or group that is held by people and sustained by selective perception and selective forgetting. Stereotypes come from two sources: (1) incomplete, distorted information and limited personal experience and (2) outside sources such as others' interpretations of cultural behavior. Stereotypes are natural but often destructive because they are unfair, do not allow for individuality, and interfere with communication.

A *prejudice* is a preconceived idea or negative attitude formed before the facts are known. It is a bias without reason, resistant to all evidence. Prejudice implies inferiority, leads to suspicion, and is detrimental to communication and interpersonal relations.

Guidelines

1. Write the first two or three adjectives that come to your mind for each of the groups listed:

Persons with disabilities	Whites
New Yorkers	Asians
Californians	African Americans
Teachers	Gays and lesbians
Latinos	Managers
Women	Men

2. Working in groups of three, discuss your reactions to the exercise and to stereotyping in general. (Discuss the words used in each category, the categories that were easy and difficult, and the reasons for regarding them as such.)
3. Discuss other stereotyped groups to which members of your group may belong: blondes, farm boys, intellectuals, jocks, and the like.
4. Discuss the importance of overcoming labels and stereotypes, and offer specific ways to counteract stereotypes. For example, recognize stereotypes for what they are and where they come from; look at each person as an individual; give examples of individuals who do not fit the stereotype; remain open-minded and not influenced by opinions of others.

Source: Jonamay Lambert and Selma Myers, *50 Activities for Diversity Training* (Amherst, MA: Human Resource Development Press, 1994), 59–63.

EXERCISE: MASCULINE AND FEMININE SPEAKING STYLES

Purpose

The purpose of this exercise is to create self-awareness of how gender affects your communication style.

Introduction

According to Julia T. Woods, "Researchers report that masculine socialization teaches most men to see talk as a means of accomplishing instrumental goals. They talk when there is a problem or when there is a need to explain something, or inform or advise others. Research also indicates that masculine socialization encourages men to be assertive . . . they learn to initiate topics when they wish." Feminine talk, on the other hand, is "expressive—a means of communicating thoughts and a way to establish and sustain connections with others." And, "the content of communication doesn't need to be significant for conversation to be valuable. Talking is relating. Communication is an end in itself, regardless of what is being communicated."[2]

It is important to note, however, that these styles are not exclusive to the specific gender. In other words, some women communicate in a more "masculine" style, and some men communicate in a more "feminine" style. All of us use both types of communication at least some of the time.

Guidelines

1. With the understanding that "masculine talk" and "feminine talk" are on two ends of a continuum, locate where your own communication style fits on the continuum.
2. In what situations do you use characteristics of "masculine talk" and when do you use characteristics of "feminine talk"?
3. Is it useful to describe communication styles as "masculine" and "feminine," or is there a more representative way to describe communication styles?

Masculine Talk

1. You use talk to assert yourself and your ideas.
2. You find that personal disclosures can make you vulnerable.
3. You use talk to establish your status and power.
4. You match your experiences with those related by others as a competitive strategy to command attention.
5. To support others, you do something helpful—give advice or solve a problem for them.
6. You don't share the talk stage with others, and you interrupt them to make your point.
7. You believe that each person is on his or her own in conversations, responsible for being heard.
8. You use responses to make your own points and sometimes try to outshine others.
9. You are assertive so that others will perceive you as confident and in command.
10. You think that talking should convey information and accomplish goals; extraneous details get in the way of achieving something.

Feminine Talk

1. You use talk to build and sustain rapport with others.
2. You like to share yourself and learn about others by disclosing through communication.
3. You use talk to create symmetry/equality between people.

4. You match your experiences with those related by others to show understanding and empathy.
5. To support others, you express understanding of their feelings.
6. You include others in conversation by asking questions and encouraging them to elaborate.
7. You try to keep the conversation going by asking questions and expressing interest in others' ideas.
8. You want to be responsive to let others know you care about what they say.
9. You are reserved in a conversation so that others feel free to add their ideas.
10. You believe that talking enhances relationships; details and interesting side comments increase the depth of connection.

Source: This exercise was prepared by Kathryn A. Cañas and Harris Sondak.

EXERCISE: RELIGION AND THE WORKPLACE— A BRAINSTORMING ACTIVITY

Purpose

The purpose of this exercise is twofold: first, to gain knowledge about different religions and belief systems; and second, to gain skills on how to manage effectively organizational members who hold a variety of different religious beliefs.

Introduction

With the vast number of religions and belief systems represented in the workplace, American businesses increasingly face the need to understand and manage one of the primary dimensions of diversity: religion/spirituality. Many workers today want to bring their whole selves to work, including their religious beliefs. According to Title VII of the Civil Rights Act of 1964, employees' spiritual beliefs and practices must be accommodated in the workplace unless the accommodation would impose an undue hardship on the employer. On one hand, managing diverse religious beliefs is a legal workplace necessity; on the other hand, it is a way to empower employees, thereby enhancing the organization's overall productivity and bottom line.

Guidelines

1. Divide participants into groups of five.
2. Have groups brainstorm everything they know about major religions/belief systems—for example, Christianity, Judaism, Islam, Hinduism, Buddhism, Sikhism, Daoism, agnosticism, atheism—in which they are familiar (they may use the Internet if available). Have them organize their thoughts in terms of the following categories:

   - Name of religion
   - Values/teachings
   - Texts
   - Holy days
   - Rituals/practices
   - Important symbols
   - Place of worship
   - Branches

3. Use the white board to organize the information (with headings and columns) by writing the names of at least six major religions/belief systems that participants decide are most important to focus on.
4. To enhance the interactive quality of this exercise, have a few members from each group write their information under each heading.
5. Have each team report out loud the contributions that they have written on the board.
6. Shift focus to the workplace and have the groups grapple with questions regarding the relationship between religion and work:

   - What aspects of these religions/belief systems may come into play in the workplace?
   - As a manager, what aspects of these religions/belief systems would be helpful to know when managing a person with this particular set of beliefs?

- If an employee requests a particular religious accommodation—for example, wearing religiously significant clothing and/or jewelry, taking time to pray during the day, creating facilities for prayer, taking off a few hours during the day to celebrate a particular holy day, etc.—how would you manage this situation?

7. To end, facilitate a discussion about the role of religion in the workplace (as framed by the questions listed above).

Source: This exercise was prepared by Kathryn A. Cañas.

Notes

1. Marilyn Loden and Judy B. Rosener, "Dimensions of Diversity," *Workforce America: Managing Employee Diversity as a Vital Resource* (Homewood, IL: Business One Irwin, 1991), 17–35.

2. Julia T. Wood, "Gender, Communication, and Culture," in *Intercultural Communication: A Reader*, eds. Larry Samovar and Richard Porter, 7th ed. (New York: Wadsworth, 1994), 155–64; William Sonnenschein, *The Diversity Toolkit: How You Can Build and Benefit from a Diverse Workforce* (Chicago, IL: Contemporary Books, 1997), 71.

CHAPTER **11**

Understanding Difference

EXERCISE: ANALYSIS OF MINI DIVERSITY CASES

Purpose

The purpose of this exercise is to help you understand and manage different workplace scenarios that deal with the six primary dimensions of diversity: gender, race and national origin, age, religion and spirituality, disabilities, and LGBT issues.

Guidelines

1. Divide participants into groups of four or five. Give each group one, a few, or all of the mini diversity cases to examine.
2. Allow a few minutes for everyone to read the cases.
3. Have each group discuss and examine the situation articulated in the case(s) by answering the questions following each of the cases. Provide sufficient time for each team to grapple with these interesting, complex diversity scenarios. Have groups examine the scenarios from both legal and managerial perspective.
4. Have each team report their answers to the entire class.
5. To enhance learning, stimulate more dialogue, and make connections among cases, use the white board to guide the discussion by listing different answers and general comments.

Mini Case Study 1: Gender and the Workplace

My name is Rebecca. The first summer after receiving my MBA degree, I accepted a job offer from a reputable consulting firm for which I had previously worked as an intern. I worked extra hard during my internship because I knew I had a good chance of being offered an entry-level job after graduation.

About two years into the job, my husband and I were finally used to my hectic work schedule. Working directly with clients required a lot of traveling, but I was happy with my job and my husband did not mind my busy schedule.

After much thought we both decided that putting off having our first baby didn't make sense any longer. My husband said, "If we're going to have kids we need to adjust our schedules for it. We both need to slow down at work a bit." I agreed with him, and I was actually pretty excited about the idea of becoming a mom. I even told a few close friends at the office that I was trying to get pregnant.

A few weeks passed when I was called in for a one-on-one meeting with Tom (one of the firm's partners). He told me that the firm was very satisfied with my performance and that I was being seriously considered for the position of senior consultant. At first, I was ecstatic about the prospective offer, but then he added, "Rebecca, before we make a decision, we need to know what your plans are for the future." I proceeded to tell him my career plans when he interrupted me and said, "We see a great future for you here, but we need someone who can put in the hours. We heard rumors that you are thinking about starting a family, and we are just curious about your plans for the future."

I was shocked by that question. How did he know about my pregnancy plans? And how dare he ask me about it. Tom told me to go home and think about the possibility of becoming a senior consultant and whether I felt ready to take on such a responsibility. He also mentioned that they were considering a few others for the position and that he wanted to see me in a couple of days to talk about it again.

I left that meeting feeling frustrated. It felt like I had to choose between becoming a mom and a senior consultant. Two days had gone by when I was asked to meet Tom in his office. I was nervous as I walked to his office since I still had no idea what to say to him.

Case Questions

1. Is there anything wrong with Tom wanting to promote someone who is able to "put in the hours"? Explain.
2. How should Rebecca deal with this situation? What should she say in her meeting with Tom?

Mini Case Study 2: Race/National Origin and the Workplace

My name is Bryan. During my first two years out of college I was busy managing a small chain of fast-food restaurants in Houston. I was happy with my job, but I wanted to pursue graduate school as a way to gain more credibility in my field. I had always wanted to get an MBA, and I figured that since my grades were good, getting strong recommendations shouldn't be a big deal.

I called John, my regional manager, and asked him if we could meet to discuss some career choices I was considering. I wanted to ask him for a letter of recommendation in that meeting. "Sure Bryan, let's talk," John said and added, "There are some things I need to talk to you about anyway."

In my meeting with John he said that he would be glad to recommend me to any school of my choice. He said that he was impressed with my managerial skills and that I had a bright future ahead of me. He then shifted gears to talking about a problem that they were having with some of the restaurants in the area. He said, "Bryan, we are having issues with missing supplies and since we work with a lot of Hispanics I want you to keep an eye on them. I know we have never had theft problems with employees under your management, but you just can't trust those people."

As the husband of a Mexican wife, I felt personally offended by that comment. I didn't want to make a big deal out of it since I needed that recommendation, but I felt like I should have said something. I just didn't know how to react.

Case Questions

- What is the major problem that Bryan faces?
- If you were the regional manager—like John in this case—and you were suspicious of your employees, how could you properly handle this situation?

Mini Case Study 3: Age and the Workplace

My name is Ben. I am a senior accountant at a retail company in San Francisco. Although I am looking forward to my retirement as I am 58 years old, I still feel enthusiastic about my job and my company's internal growth goals. I particularly enjoy working with colleagues in their 20s and 30s since I believe my experience adds significant value to both my team and organization.

Although my colleagues often go out socializing, it does not bother me that I am never invited to go along. I simply figure that I am probably too old to enjoy the same kind of social activities that they enjoy.

I was sitting in my office one day when I overheard Paul, a junior accountant, complain about needing more "hands-on" time with a new software package they would soon be using in the office. Paul said, "I just need to play around with it some more . . . That little get-together we had to talk about this software was not enough." For the first time I realized that during those social gatherings the team actually discussed work issues.

I decided to talk to my manager about being left out of—what I interpreted as—an informal meeting. My manager said, "Don't worry, Ben, we were just discussing the possibility of getting a new software package. We are not even sure if we are going to implement it in our office yet. Since the software is kind of complicated and you are retiring soon, there is no need for you to learn it."

I felt left out. I confess that I am not computer savvy and learning new technology is a slow process for me, but I feel strongly that I should have been given the chance to learn it. What else was going on that I did not know about? Although I did not want to learn new complicated software packages, if I were to just keep quiet about it, I would soon be completely left out of everything because of my age.

Case Questions

- As a manager, should you exclude older workers from training that you judge unnecessary or difficult for them? Give reasons for and against your answer.
- How should Ben respond to this situation? Substantiate your answer.

Mini Case Study 4: Religion and the Workplace

My name is Rubi. Growing up a Muslim girl in the United States, I always took my religion seriously and felt very blessed because of it. My parents are hardworking immigrants and together we run a family business.

During my first year of college, our family business was not doing very well, and I wanted to be more economically independent. I decided to apply for a job and sent my résumé to different small businesses in town. I was invited for a job interview at a family-owned restaurant for the position of cashier. During my interview, I felt comfortable with my answers and made it clear that prayer service was important to me. Later I received a phone call from the manager telling me that the job was mine if I wanted it.

The following Monday, I arrived early at my job to show that I was a serious and committed employee. As usual, I was wearing an Islamic headscarf, or hijab, when the manager pulled me aside and said she needed to talk to me. "Rubi, do you wear your headscarf every day?" I told her that as part of my religious convictions I wore my hijab daily to which she responded, "You should have told me that during your interview. I am afraid you are not in compliance with the restaurant's dress code, and I am sorry but I can't allow that to happen."

Since I was wearing a headscarf during my job interview, I assumed my manager knew that I would always wear one. I didn't think that making such a small exception was too much to ask of my employers, but since they had already agreed to let me take breaks for prayer service observance, I did not know what to do.

Case Questions

- Can an employer demand the implementation of a dress code that goes against someone's religious convictions? Explain.
- How should Rubi respond to this situation? Substantiate your answer.

Mini Case Study 5: Disabilities and the Workplace

My name is Peter. After a car accident at the age of 25, getting used to using a wheelchair was no easy task for me. I went through a hard time before realizing that self-pity or pity from others would never get me anywhere.

Because of my disability I sometimes feel the need to prove my self worth so I work hard at everything I do. It makes me feel good to know that I am able to do things very well. I graduated summa cum laude from business school and accepted an amazing job offer as an analyst in a manufacturing firm.

After my first year in the office, I was getting along with everyone and felt comfortable about working there. When the time came for my first job evaluation, I felt confident that I would receive positive feedback, but I was also interested in hearing about the areas in which I could improve.

Matthew, my direct supervisor, called me to his office and started going over his evaluation of my performance. He seemed a little uncomfortable, but I figured that giving and receiving feedback can be awkward sometimes. He complimented my work and praised my professionalism and work ethic. He was about to dismiss me when I thanked him for those comments but asked, "So, what are some things I could work on?" He replied, "You know, Peter, we really appreciate your work here. I think you've done really well considering the hand you've been dealt. Just keep up the good work."

I was pretty surprised by that comment. What did he mean? That I was doing well, considering I had a disability? I know he meant well, but that final remark really bothered me. I wanted to say something, but I didn't. And the last thing I wanted to do was to put people on the defensive.

Case Questions

- Why is Matthew hesitant about giving Peter negative feedback? List at least three reasons and explain why.
- Why was Peter so offended? How should Peter respond to this situation? Substantiate your answer.

Mini Case Study 6: GLBT Issues and the Workplace

My name is Ryan. I am an associate at a marketing firm, and I am very comfortable about being "out" in the workplace. I know the news about my sexual orientation may have been surprising to some coworkers at first, but I never feel discriminated against and everyone respects my individuality.

One day, a couple of us guys were talking about how hard Mark took having his marketing campaign rejected by some top clients. "Is it true that Mark ran to the bathroom and was crying like a girl when his idea got turned down?" Fred asked. "It's true," Scott replied, "Pretty pathetic, huh?" And then Josh added, "Wow, I can't believe it! That's so gay!"

Immediately after that comment the group went silent. Josh realized what he had just said and although he didn't mean to offend me, he said nervously, "I am so sorry, Ryan. I didn't mean it that way!" He was pretty embarrassed about his comment, and I wasn't even offended by it until he added, "You are not like those people! You don't even look gay."

The way that Josh tried to fix his comment just made things worse. Now I was offended. What did he mean by saying that I didn't look gay? Although the situation was already awkward, I felt that such a stereotypical remark had to be corrected. But instead of saying something, I just smiled and walked away.

Case Questions

- Why was Ryan more offended when Josh tried to fix his initial remark? Since Josh did not mean to offend Ryan, could his comments be considered discriminatory? Substantiate your viewpoint.
- Was Ryan right about just smiling and walking away? How should Ryan respond to this situation? Substantiate your viewpoint.

Source: This case was prepared by Carlos Eduardo de Sousa.

EXERCISE: WHAT CONSTITUTES SEXUAL HARASSMENT?

Purpose

The purpose of this exercise is to help you understand what constitutes sexual harassment.

Introduction

According to the EEOC, sexual harassment is a form of sex discrimination that violates Title VII of the Civil Rights Act of 1964. Unwelcome sexual advances, requests for sexual favors, and other verbal or physical conduct of a sexual nature constitutes sexual harassment when submission to or rejection of this conduct explicitly or implicitly affects an individual's employment, unreasonably interferes with an individual's work performance, or creates an intimidating, hostile, or offensive work environment.

There are two types of sexual harassment: quid pro quo and hostile work environment. *Quid pro quo,* which means "this for that," involves a person with power over someone else who uses that power to either benefit or harm a person based on his or her willingness to participate in or tolerate some form of sexual behavior. A *hostile work environment* exists when an individual is exposed to conduct that is sexual in nature, severe and/or pervasive, and unwelcome or unwanted; a power imbalance may or may not exist.

Guidelines

Discuss each scenario and determine whether it constitutes sexual harassment.

SCENARIO ONE   Mary and Bill work in the same department and have known each other for over a year. Mary and Bill are friendly, but nothing romantic has occurred between them. One day, Mary asks Bill if he would like to go out after work.

SCENARIO TWO   Charles is attracted to his coworker, Shelly, but Shelly is unaware of the attraction. He tells her one morning, "You look really nice today."

SCENARIO THREE   At a company party, employees are called up individually to receive year-end bonuses. Susan is shocked to discover that whereas the men in her department receive cash, she and her female coworkers receive flowers.

SCENARIO FOUR   Adam and a coworker are looking at a sexually explicit Web site. Someone walks in and sees the Web site. That person is offended and reports the incident to Adam's supervisor, who never tells Adam about the complaint. The person walks into Adam's office three more times in the next several months and again sees sexually explicit material on Adam's screen. The person never tells Adam that he is offended.

Source: This exercise was prepared by Kathryn A. Cañas, P. Corper James, and Harris Sondak.

EXERCISE: RELIGION AND SPIRITUALITY: WHAT COULD BE HAPPENING HERE?

Purpose

The purpose of this exercise is to help you understand better the intersection of religion and the workplace.

Introduction

There is a strong movement toward bringing religion and spirituality into the workplace. Because so much time is spent at work, some people no longer want to separate work and religion. It is critical for business leaders to understand the role of religion in today's workforce.

Guidelines

In small groups, use the following questions as a guide to discuss each scenario:

- What are the possible explanations for this person's behavior?
- How should management respond to this situation?
- How should the employee respond to this situation?
- How should the employee's coworkers respond to this situation?

SCENARIO ONE Sonia, who was recently hired, started to wear loose-fitting clothes and a head-scarf to work. Behind her back, some coworkers responded with comments such as "Sonia is going to scare off potential clients with her crazy outfits" and "I wonder if Sonia is a part of a radical religious group." Sensing negative sentiments from her coworkers, Sonia becomes more self-conscious and less communicative.

SCENARIO TWO Harte Consulting, LLC, was thrilled to hire Jonathan onto their team. Jonathan's résumé was of the highest quality—he graduated from a top business school with honors. His coworkers are confused, however, when Jonathan seems resistant to working on Saturdays. He claims to have prior engagements and responsibilities. His coworkers begin to question his dedication to his team in particular and the company in general.

SCENARIO THREE Maya—who has just declared, "I'm really hungry"—is at a business lunch where she is served chicken, green beans, and garlic potatoes. She eats the beans, seems uninterested in the rest of her food, and then orders dessert. Her coworkers look at her strangely, and after lunch, they discuss her odd behavior.

SCENARIO FOUR The department's coed softball team has always been considered a big deal since it began 10 years ago. The softball games are played on Sunday mornings and afternoons. Jenny, who was an all-star softball pitcher in high school and college, has just been transferred into the department, and her new coworkers are thrilled that their team has just become more competitive. Jenny, however, declines to be part of the team. Jenny is now tagged as "not a team player" throughout the office.

Source: This exercise was developed by Kathryn A. Cañas and Harris Sondak.

EXERCISE: DISCRIMINATION BASED ON SEXUAL ORIENTATION: COUNTING THE COSTS

Purpose

The purpose of this exercise is to help you gain insight into the personal and organizational costs of discrimination based on sexual orientation.

Introduction

The disapproval of homosexuality causes both heterosexual and gay people to react in complex and sometimes counterproductive ways. It can force gay people into the "corporate closet"—that is, they go to great lengths to hide their sexual orientation at work. It can separate people who could work together productively and enjoy one another's company. It may cause them to avoid each other or to sabotage one another's efforts. In extreme cases, homophobia results in harassment, violence, or expensive litigation that can destroy the lives of the individuals involved and drain the organization's resources.

Guidelines

The following are examples of situations in which the costs of discrimination based on sexual orientation add up. In the space beneath each example, list what you believe would be one personal cost to the people involved and one cost to the organization to which the individuals belong. Here is an example:

Sarah is a model employee except that she never talks about herself when the others are discussing their husbands and wives. She knows that they think she is cold and reserved, but she is afraid to tell them about her life with her woman partner for fear of being rejected or even fired.

PERSONAL COST   There may be damaged relationships among coworkers; the job becomes uncomfortable for Sarah and those around her.

ORGANIZATIONAL COST   Sarah always feels on guard; she may quit for a more comfortable job; the company must spend time and money to replace her.

Now you try it. What do you think the costs are in each of the following situations?

1. When the other managers—all men—go to lunch, they gradually stop inviting Wilson, who is rumored to be gay.

Personal Cost

_____

_____

_____

Organizational Cost

_____

_____

2. Mae Linn gives preferential treatment to gay men when hiring applicants. She believes that they are more creative and sensitive and will treat women better than straight men will.

Personal Cost

_____
_____
_____

Organizational Cost

_____
_____
_____

3. Since telling others that she is a lesbian, Jayne has noticed that David, a coworker, has begun to make passes at her. She has heard via the grapevine that he has told his buddies she will be a "real challenge."

Personal Cost

_____
_____
_____

Organizational Cost

_____
_____
_____

4. Stephen has felt depressed for several weeks and has given people around the office different explanations. When his coworkers discover that he and a long-term male partner just broke up, they wonder what else Stephen is hiding.

Personal Cost

_____
_____
_____

Organizational Cost

_____
_____
_____

Source: Amy J. Zuckerman and George F. Simons, *Sexual Orientation in the Workplace: Gay Men, Lesbians, Bisexuals, and Heterosexuals Working Together* (Thousand Oaks, CA: Sage, 1996), 16–19.

EXERCISE: THE TEN COMMANDMENTS OF INTERACTING WITH PEOPLE WITH DISABILITIES

Purpose

The purpose of this exercise is to help foster more effective communication and collaboration with people with disabilities.

Introduction

The goal of the AXIS Center for Public Awareness of People with Disabilities is to create a positive public awareness of people with disabilities and to strengthen the voices of people with disabilities through advocacy. AXIS has issued a list of guidelines that offer insight into what to do when communicating with people who have disabilities.

GUIDELINES   In groups of four or five, discuss the following questions after reading the "commandments":

- Do you work with people with disabilities? If yes, what has been your experience?
- Do you follow the "commandments" when speaking with people with disabilities?
- Which "commandments" are most difficult to follow?
- Do you have friends with disabilities? If so, what is their advice on effective communication?

Ten Commandments for Communicating with Persons with Disabilities

1. When talking with a person with a disability, speak directly to that person rather than through a companion or sign-language interpreter who may be present.
2. When introduced to a person with a disability, it is appropriate to offer to shake hands. People with limited hand use or who wear an artificial limb can usually shake hands. (Shaking hands with the left hand is an acceptable greeting.)
3. When meeting a person with a visual impairment, always identify yourself and others who may be with you. When conversing in a group, remember to identify the person to whom you are speaking.
4. If you offer assistance, wait until the offer is accepted. Then listen to or ask for instructions.
5. Treat adults as adults. Address people who have disabilities by their first names only when extending that same familiarity to all others present. (Never patronize people who use a wheelchair by patting them on the head or shoulders.)
6. Leaning or hanging on a person's wheelchair is similar to leaning or hanging on a person and is generally considered annoying. The chair is part of the personal body space of the person who uses it.
7. Listen attentively when you are talking with a person who has difficulty speaking. Be patient and wait for the person to finish, rather than correcting or speaking for the person. If necessary, ask short questions that require short answers, a nod, or a shake of the head. Never pretend to understand if you are having difficulty doing so. Instead, repeat what you have understood and allow the person to respond. The response will clue you in and guide your understanding.

Source: This exercise was prepared by Kathryn A. Cañas and Harris Sondak.

8. When speaking with a person in a wheelchair or a person who uses crutches, place yourself at eye level in front of the person to facilitate the conversation.

9. To get the attention of a person who is hearing impaired, tap the person on the shoulder or wave your hand. Look directly at the person and speak clearly, slowly, and expressively to establish if the person can read your lips. Not all people with a hearing impairment can lip-read. For those who do lip-read, be sensitive to their needs by placing yourself facing the light source and keeping such objects as hands, cigarettes, and food away from your mouth when speaking.

10. Relax. Don't be embarrassed if you happen to use accepted, common expressions that seem to relate to the person's disability, such as "see you later" or "did you hear about this?"

EXERCISE: CULTURAL DIVERSITY

Purpose

The purpose of this exercise is to help you discuss culture clashes and to promote good intercultural communication practices.

Guidelines

1. Divide participants into groups of four or five. Give each group one case study.
2. Allow a few minutes for everyone to read the cases.
3. Have each group discuss what was happening in its case, how culture played a part, how the situation could have been handled, and whether the conflict could have been avoided.
4. Have each group report and discuss the different responses.

CASE 1: ETHNIC JOKE   You are in a meeting and before the boss comes in, there's a general feeling of camaraderie, with many jokes. You suddenly realize that an ethnic joke has been told, and as you look up and see the face of the person whose group has been slandered, you realize he's been hurt. There is an awkward silence for a moment, and then general sports banter takes over and the subject is changed.

Questions
- How do you feel?
- What should you do?

CASE 2: ANTICIPATION OF A NEW COLLEAGUE   One of your white male coworkers has been told he will be getting a new black colleague as his officemate. Before the white man has even met his new office mate, he is heard grumbling and groaning about all the trouble he will have and how he doesn't have time to offer the new man all the help he knows he will need. You are standing nearby when he vents his feelings.

Questions
- Why is the white employee so concerned?
- What can you do to help the situation?

CASE 3: PERFORMANCE EVALUATION GIGGLES   The "mainstream" supervisor calls in the Laotian employee for a semiannual evaluation. After the supervisor offers some positive aspects of the evaluation, she begins to discuss areas for improvement. Since the Laotian employee looks down at the floor during the entire feedback session, the supervisor concludes that the employee is hiding something. When the supervisor tries to draw it out of him, the employee begins to giggle.

Questions
- How might this behavior be explained? What do you think is taking place?
- How should the manager address this situation? What procedure should she set up?

CASE 4: THE INVISIBLE WOMAN   Ben is a successful purchasing manager with a reputation for being hardworking and fair. In his regular Monday morning buyers' meeting, the participants are Harry, Charlie, Jim, and Sally; Ben gets along with them all. After the latest meeting, Ben is surprised when Sally approaches him almost in tears, and complains, "Ben, first thing in today's meeting, I suggested we consolidate the commodity purchasing into one section. Before I was halfway through, you cut in to let Jim speak. By the end of the meeting, you agreed with my idea, but gave Jim all the credit." Sally is thinking, Nobody listens to me; is there something wrong with me? Ben doesn't know what to think, and besides, he can't even remember Sally's bringing up the idea in the first place. Is something wrong with Sally today? he wonders; why is she making a federal case out of this? He makes a joke to minimize the situation.

Questions
- What is happening here?
- If you were Ben, would you have been able to understand what was going on and avoided it?
- If you put yourself in Sally's shoes, how would you have handled the situation?

Source: Jonamay Lambert and Selma Myers, *50 Activities for Diversity Training* (Massachusetts: Human Resource Development Press, 1994), 81–83.

CHAPTER 12

Assessing Organizations

EXERCISE: EXAMINING EXEMPLARY LEADERS IN MANAGING DIVERSITY

Purpose

Your task is to locate and examine organizational leaders who embrace diversity and who manage diversity effectively.

Guidelines

1. Research any of the following organizational leaders on your own.
2. Then, in small groups, pool all your information.
3. As a group, report your findings to the class.
4. To summarize, discuss the significance of leadership support when developing and implementing diversity management initiatives.

Here are a few topic areas and questions to guide your research:

- *Background* What is the professional background of this leader? Is there any personal information or experience that led to his or her passion for managing diversity?
- *Status of Diversity within Organization* What role did diversity play before the leader became a part of the organization?
- *Philosophy* What is the leader's philosophy on diversity management?
- *Strategies* What strategies did the leader implement to transform the way in which the organization managed diversity?
- *Goals* What were the diversity-related goals implemented by the leader? What are his or her future goals related to diversity?
- *Current Status* What is the current status of the organization in terms of diversity in particular and overall success in general?

Examples of organizational leaders from whom you may choose:

- Sharon L. Allen, Deloitte and Touche
- Kenneth Chenault, American Express
- Johnnetta B. Cole, The United Way

- Louis V. Gerstner, Jr., IBM
- Andrea Jung, Avon Products, Inc.
- J. W. "Bill" Marriott, Jr., Marriott International
- Indra Nooyi, PepsiCo
- Dick Parsons, Time Warner
- Antonio Perez, Eastman Kodak
- David M. Ratcliffe, Southern Company
- Steve Reinemund, PepsiCo
- Johnathan Rodgers, TV One
- Barry Salzberg, Deloitte
- Ivan Seidenberg, Verizon Communications
- John Stumpf, Wells Fargo
- Jeff Valdez, SiTV
- William C. Weldon, Johnson & Johnson

Source: This exercise was developed by Kathryn A. Cañas and Harris Sondak.

EXERCISE: ANALYSIS OF DIVERSITY CONSULTING COMPANIES

Purpose

The purpose of this exercise is to develop your knowledge of what consulting companies are offering as diversity training. The specific objective is to get a more detailed understanding of the strategies and procedures employed by high-profile diversity consulting companies in their effort to help organizations manage diversity.

Introduction

Consulting firms can be very helpful to organizations in improving their diversity management, and diversity training has become a multi-billion-dollar industry. It is important, therefore, to be knowledgeable about what consulting companies are offering in their attempt to help organizations understand and manage diversity as a competitive advantage.

Guidelines

Research the listed companies and answer the following questions:

- How do these consulting companies define diversity? How do they define diversity management? What is their philosophy on managing diversity?
- How do they help companies manage their diverse workforce? What are their areas of specialization?
- How do these consulting companies ensure that diversity is managed systemically (on all levels) within the organization?
- How do they measure the impact of their recommendations and training?
- Where do these consulting companies fall short?

Consulting Company	Web site
1. Aequus Group LLC	http://www.aequusgroup.com
2. Diversity Training Group	http://diversitydtg.com
3. Diversity University	http://www.diversityuniversity.com
4. Elsie Y. Cross Associates	http://www.eyca.com
5. Global Lead	http://www.globallead.com
6. Jones & Associates	http://www.jandaconsult.com
7. The Kaleel Jamison Consulting Group	http://www.kjcg.com
8. Lee Gardenswartz and Anita Rowe	http://www.gardenswartzrowe.com
9. NVC Consulting	http://www.nvcconsulting.net
10. PRISM International, Inc.	http://www.prismdiversity.com
11. Tulin Diversiteam Associates	http://www.diversiteam.com
12. The Winters Group, Inc.	http://www.wintersgroup.com

Source: This exercise was prepared by Kathryn A. Cañas and Harris Sondak.

EXERCISE: ANALYZING DIVERSITY COMMITMENT ON WEB SITES

Purpose

The purpose of this exercise is to analyze the way that organizations communicate their understanding of and commitment to diversity through their Web sites.

Guidelines

Note: For this exercise to be done in-class, computer access is necessary.

1. With the entire group, describe the purpose of an organization's Web site. Why do people typically visit an organization's Web site? How important is it for an organization to have a comprehensive yet easily accessible Web site? Explain.

2. Divide participants into groups of about five people. Have each group choose five to ten organizations' Web sites to examine. Groups may choose Web sites representing organizations that interest them, or they may choose any of the organizations listed in DiversityInc's Top 50 Companies for Diversity; for example:

   - American Express Co. (http://www.americanexpress.com)
   - Cisco (http://www.cisco.com)
   - Coca-Cola Co. (http://www.coca-cola.com)
   - Ernst & Young (http://www.ey.com)
   - Ford Motor Co. (http://www.ford.com)
   - Johnson & Johnson (http://www.jnj.com/connect)
   - Marriott International (http://marriott/com)
   - MGM Mirage (http://www.mgmmirage.com)
   - PepsiCo (http://pepsico.com)
   - Verizon Communications (http://verizon.com)

3. As you examine each of the organization's Web sites, answer the following questions:

   - Is material on diversity or a link to a diversity section found on the Web site's homepage?
   - Is the organization's definition of diversity and its diversity mission statement clearly articulated on the Web site? Is it easy to locate?
   - Is the company's stance on diversity clear after reading the main diversity section?
   - Is there a statement by the CEO reflecting the organization's commitment to diversity located on the Web site?
   - Does the Web site material address diversity-related issues such as employee-resource groups, recruiting strategies, diversity training, supplier diversity, community relations, and so on?
   - Are diversity videos—in which the CEO, director of diversity, HR executive, and/or employees in general discuss the company's commitment to diversity—easily accessible?
   - Are current annual diversity reports accessible from the company's Web site?
   - Does the Web site contain current information on the company's diversity awards and any diversity-related news?
   - Are images on the Web site representative of diversity in terms of the organization's employees and customers?

4. Have each group discuss and organize analyses in their small groups.

5. To enhance the interactive quality of this exercise, use the white board as a tool to list the strengths and weaknesses of five to ten organizations' Web sites in terms of their representations and communications about diversity commitment.

Source: The exercise was prepared by Kathryn A. Cañas.

EXERCISE: DIVERSITY AND SPORTS: AN EXAMINATION OF THE NFL, NASCAR, NHL, PGA, AND NBA

Purpose

The purpose of this exercise is to help you examine the role of diversity in professional sports.

Guidelines

1. Every time you open the sports page, it seems that diversity is a topic of interest. Read the following sports snapshots that articulate the diversity management status of each of the major sports organizations, use the Internet to gather more information, and then, in groups, respond to the questions that follow each sports snapshot.

NFL

Although there is great diversity among players, following the 2008 annual diversity study performed by the University of Central Florida's Diversity Institute, the NFL received a B+ for racial diversity. Having faced criticism in the past for not considering minority candidates for coaching jobs, the NFL initiated the "Rooney Rule." The rule, implemented in 2002, requires teams to interview at least one minority candidate per head coaching vacancy. Entering into the 2008 season, the NFL had six African American coaches and five African American general managers, identical to the 2007 season. Four new head coaches were hired for the 2008 season, all of whom were white.[1] However, following continuous requests from various organizations, the NFL has extended the "Rooney Rule" to senior operations positions effective June 2009.[2] Although the NFL is taking certain measures to improve its diversity standing, its initiatives are still questioned by many parties.

Discussion Questions

1. Rate the effectiveness of the Rooney Rule in improving diversity within the NFL.
2. What impact, if any, do you think the new extension of the Rooney Rule will have on diversity within the NFL?
3. What should the NFL do to improve its diversity on all company levels?

NASCAR

With the reputation of being a sport tailored to white Southerners, NASCAR now faces great challenges in terms of its diversity initiatives. As its ratings continue to drop, NASCAR is focusing on extending its reach to a more diverse fan base by way of its "Drive for Diversity" and Diversity Internship programs. Its primary "vehicle" in reaching this goal is its "Drive for Diversity" initiative. This program seeks to develop the skills of minority and female drivers and crew members, and it offers intensive training for individuals as it prepares them for careers at NASCAR.[3] NASCAR's Diversity Internship Program provides college students of racial minority descent the opportunity to participate in a ten-week program to discover NASCAR and its career opportunities. Despite all of its efforts, NASCAR's 2007 U.S. roster consisted of 240 drivers, of which, only 9 percent were minorities.[4]

Discussion Questions

1. What is NASCAR's current public image?
2. Using its current programs, will NASCAR be able to alter its current image?
3. What other initiatives can NASCAR implement to aid in this transformation?

NHL

The NHL's lack of effective diversity management has caused it to miss out on immense potential profits and has given it an image of being a racist organization. Since 1958, the NHL roster has grown to 876 players. However, from 1958 to 2009, only 50 minority players have taken the ice.[5] The NHL's most serious problem is its lack of minority representation. Since the introduction of the first black player, there have been continuous complaints about racial remarks made by fans and other players, and the predominantly white culture of hockey has resulted in a lack of diverse players. Because the NHL seeks to expand the diversity of its fan base, it is in desperate need of minority players. The problem is that due to the NHL's fan base and image, the pool of these potential minority players is very small.

Discussion Questions

1. What actions can the NHL take in order to remedy the problems it is facing?
2. What should the NHL have done to avoid these problems?
3. What specific diversity management initiatives (both short term and long term) could the NHL implement today to manage its diversity problems?

PGA

In the 93-year history of the Professional Golf Association of America, Tiger Woods is still the only African American player on the PGA tour. In recent years, the PGA has turned its attention to diversifying the sport of golf. It has implemented programs such as the PGA Diversity Internship Program, aimed at sparking interest in the business side of golf.[6] There are also many other foundations, such as the Tiger Woods Foundation, aimed at engaging minorities' interest in the sport. These efforts have improved golf's overall popularity among minorities. However, the PGA has had particularly limited success. Much of the issue may reside in the fact that the game's corporate structure is overwhelmingly white; the PGA is governed by a committee which does not have a single African American member.[7] Following the introduction and domination of Tiger Woods, the PGA's ratings skyrocketed. Prize money for major events increased threefold, and it appeared that golf was on its way to becoming a lucrative and diverse sport. However, more than a decade after Woods' miraculous breakthrough, the PGA is still waiting for that influx of minority players.

Discussion Questions

1. What kind of message is the leadership of the PGA sending about its views of diversity?
2. How important is it for management to back up its words with actions?
3. What should the PGA do to resolve its diversity issues?

NBA

When it comes to sports diversity, the NBA is a true leader. The University of Central Florida Diversity Institute gave it the only "A" in men's professional sports. In the 2008–2009 season, African American players accounted for almost 82 percent of the NBA roster, and it boasts the highest percentage of minority head coaches at 40 percent. Furthermore, during the 2007–2008 season, there were seven African American executives among its 30 teams. Although the

(continued)

percentage of African American executives decreased during the 2008–2009 season, the percentage of female-held professional positions increased to 43 percent. There is no question that the NBA has surpassed all other sports leagues in terms of diversity. It has strong diversity not only on the court, but within the organization as a whole. Much of this success is attributed to the top executives of the NBA who have made gender and race diversity a company-wide priority.[8] The question that remains is: What can the NBA do to further improve its diversity?

Discussion Questions

1. What is the NBA doing differently than other sports organizations?
2. What can the sports associations discussed previously learn from the NBA?
3. How would you define optimal diversity with a company?

Source: This exercise was developed by Kathryn A. Cañas and Ruslan Chaplygin.

PROJECT: THE DIVERSITY CONSULTING TEAM

The final team project is a comprehensive diversity analysis of a local organization. Following the project description are research tools that will help your team craft effective survey and interview questions, thereby enhancing your ability to examine the role of diversity in your specific organization.

General Description

Your task is to write a team paper that takes the form of a "business proposal." In this paper you will examine a specific, local organization. In your teams of approximately five students, you will need to do the following:

1. Locate an organization that will allow you to perform a diversity analysis. At the beginning of the semester, teams should brainstorm possible organizations to examine for their final project. Typically, communication between students and organizational members is facilitated in an organization in which one of the team members has a connection—either a team member or perhaps a close friend or relative works there. The teams may choose an organization that currently has a clear and comprehensive diversity plan in place, or they may choose an organization that lacks any type of diversity policy.

Although the organization must be local—so the students can easily make observations, perform surveys and interviews, and so forth—the organization may also be a division of a large national company, a medium-sized company, or even a small company. It is suggested, however, that the company have at least 15 employees. The team's approach when examining a larger organization with an established diversity policy is to discover the diversity strengths and weaknesses within that organization and to improve their policy through recommendations. The team's approach when examining a smaller organization that has little—if any—policy on diversity is to build a long-term plan from the bottom up.

2. Conduct primary and secondary research. Primary research, your own assessment of the situation, is helpful when determining the organization's philosophy and approach to diversity management. After receiving permission to distribute a survey and request interviews, teams should take sufficient time to craft both. Successful surveys typically include both questions measured by a Likert scale and a few open-ended questions. Students may also want to begin their survey with a clear definition of diversity, because diversity is often defined narrowly (e.g., only the color of one's skin) instead of using more inclusive characteristics such as race, gender, religion, disabilities, sexual orientation, age, family status, and so on. Students may also want the person answering the survey to record his or her gender, age, organizational status, and the like. In terms of interviews, the students should try to interview people in leadership and supervisory positions, especially any one person in charge of diversity management within the company.

In addition to the primary research gathered by the students, secondary research, either about the organization or the context in general, is also important: Web sites; written policies; mission, vision, and value statements; diversity pamphlets or manuals; magazine or newspaper articles; and so forth.

3. **Examine the research.** Take sufficient time to examine the findings from both the surveys and interviews. After examining the surveys, students might contemplate questions including the following: Are there any trends in the findings? Are there distinct differences in how men and women responded to the questions? Do the answers to the questions reveal any diversity management strengths and weaknesses within the organization?

After examining responses to the interview questions, students might contemplate questions including the following: Do lower and middle management view diversity in the same way as upper management? Do the organizational leaders view diversity as a competitive advantage? Do the organizational leaders have an inclusive understanding of diversity? Does a disconnect exist between how the organizational leaders view diversity and how other members of the organization view it?

Your team may want to use components of a systemic model of diversity as a lens to examine the primary and secondary research:

- *Leadership commitment*: Is the CEO personally involved with the diversity management initiatives? Do the members of the board of directors reflect diversity? Is there an executive-level diversity position (e.g., vice president of diversity or chief diversity officer)? Has the organization created a diversity task force or diversity counsel? Is leadership financially committed to supporting diversity management initiatives long term?
- *Communication*: Does the organization communicate clearly about diversity, specifically in terms of a definition of diversity and diversity mission statement? Are the diversity goals articulated within a strategic context? Does the organization's Web site reflect the organization's diversity commitment?
- *Recruitment and retention*: Does the organization implement effective recruiting strategies, mentoring programs, and diversity training programs? Does the organization embrace work-life strategies and same-sex benefits?
- *Incorporation of diversity into main work of organization*: Are employee-resource groups established within the organization? Are there organizational members who reflect diversity working in decision-making and policy-making roles?
- *Ability to link diversity to outcomes*: Are the organization's diversity strategies tied to business results? Does the organization use metrics to measure the effect of diversity initiatives? Is the organization able to articulate deliverables on diversity initiatives?
- *External relationships*: Is the organization marketing to multicultural audiences? Does the organization implement supplier diversity programs? Are community outreach programs established with the purpose of reaching out to diverse groups of people? Do the organization's philanthropic contributions reflect diversity?

4. **Make organizational recommendations.** After examining all of the primary and secondary information, the students should choose either one main problem or various problems on which to focus their recommendations. The students may craft their recommendations in terms of phases (e.g., a four-phase plan to manage one serious diversity problem) or in terms of years (e.g., a five-year plan to manage three main problems). It is important to explain each recommendation in detail. For example, if a team decides that diversity training is one of the recommendations, it must also articulate details about the training—what type of training, material to be covered, and so forth. Or, if the team decides to recommend a diversity mentoring program, it must include details about the design of this program.

Specifics on Paper

In this paper, the team is to:

1. *Offer a description of the organization you researched.*
   - What is the organization's history/background?
   - How does the organization's history affect the way it perceives and manages diversity?
   - Who is the CEO? What is her/his background?

2. *Articulate your research method.*
   - How did you gather your primary and secondary information?
   - In terms of primary information, incorporate a discussion of your survey and interview results. Pie charts and other graphs are effective ways to communicate research results. You may include copies of the survey and interview questions in accompanying appendixes.
   - In terms of secondary information, be sure to reference all Web sites, material from the organization (e.g., annual report and pamphlets), books, magazine articles, newspaper articles, journal articles, and the like.

3. *Explain what type of diversity policy the organization currently has in place.*
   - What is the diversity policy?
   - What are the policy's strengths and weaknesses?
   - Are the employees, managers, and executives knowledgeable about this policy? If so, how do the employees respond to this policy?
   - Is the diversity managed sporadically or systemically within the organization?
   - If the organization does not have any diversity management policy, discuss the organization's general strengths and weaknesses in light of diversity's potential role within the organization.

4. *Focus on one or several of the organization's problems in regard to managing diversity.*
   - Explicate the problem or problems in detail. For example, after examining your research, you may see problems emerging such as lack of effective training, ineffective recruitment efforts, no supplier diversity, few women in upper management positions, lack of family-friendly policies, no clear understanding of diversity as a competitive advantage, unclear communication about diversity by leadership, or unclear communications about diversity on the company Web site.

5. *Explain what type of diversity policy the organization needs to be successful when managing diversity.*
   (In your plan, you may focus on making recommendations for what you perceive as the most serious problem, or you may focus on making recommendations for a number of problems.

There are a number of models of effective diversity management that have been implemented by organizations. If you borrow such strategies, be sure to clearly reference the sources.)

- Does the organization need both short-term and long-term diversity management recommendations? Would the organization benefit from both internal (employee focused) recommendations and external (customer and community focused) diversity management strategies?
- Would this organization benefit from a five-year plan in which the diversity plan is implemented slowly over a span of years?
- If appropriate, delineate the steps that the organization should follow to be successful in managing diversity.
- Explain how and why your recommendations would improve the organization's current situation.

Specifics on Presentation

1. Combined with this paper is a 20- to 25-minute team presentation.
2. In the presentation you should describe the organization, your research, your research methods, and your diversity plan for this company.
3. In addition to being graded on the content, you will be graded on the following:

Opening

- Effective attention-getting strategy
- Articulation of purpose and significance
- Brief discussion of team's credibility (if necessary)
- Preview of main points

Presentation style

- Used eye contact and gestures to engage audience
- Matched voice volume/inflection and facial expressions to reinforce the spoken message
- Avoided distracting mannerisms
- Used movement and varied location to reinforce key elements of the message
- Used a natural conversational delivery style—extemporaneous, not memorized
- Engaged audience interaction appropriately and made modifications based on audience reaction

Verbal presentation

- Used logical, easy-to-follow structure
- Incorporated smooth transitions between topics
- Included a combination of evidence types (e.g., facts, statistics, examples, stories, and testimony)
- Referenced sources clearly
- Spoke to audience's needs and values
- Covered company history, strengths/weaknesses, and recommendations

Graphic presentation

- Used appropriate visuals for the situation
- Visuals were simple, readable, and professional
- Visuals were presented in a skillful, nondistracting manner

Closing

- Summarized main points
- Ended with an effective concluding device that created a sense of closure
- Message was memorable (it was unique or compelling enough to cause action)
- Handled questions and challenges effectively

TOOL TO ASSIST DIVERSITY CONSULTING TEAM PROJECT: NINE SYMPTOMS THAT MAY INDICATE A NEED FOR DIVERSITY TRAINING

Purpose

The purpose of this exercise is to help you develop your skills in identifying potential diversity-related concerns and/or problems within organizations.

Guidelines

1. Organizational members respond to the checklist, checking off any symptoms they observe in the organization.
2. Checklists are then collected and results are tabulated for use by the requesting individual or group.

_____ 1. Insensitive comments or jokes told in the work unit regarding age, gender, ethnicity, sexual orientation, or physical ability.

_____ 2. Inability to retain members of diverse groups.

_____ 3. Open conflict between groups or between people from different groups.

_____ 4. Lack of diversity through all levels of the organization.

_____ 5. Cultural faux pas committed out of ignorance rather than malice.

_____ 6. Diversity-related blocks in communication that impede work flow.

_____ 7. Formal EEOC complaints.

_____ 8. Expressions of isolation from the work group.

_____ 9. Incidents that reveal that individuals are not valued for the unique contributions they can make.

Source: Lee Gardenswartz and Anita Rowe, *The Managing Diversity Survival Guide: A Complete Collection of Checklists, Activities, and Tips* (Boston, MA: McGraw-Hill, 1994), 4–5.

TOOL TO ASSIST DIVERSITY CONSULTING TEAM PROJECT: MANAGING DIVERSITY QUESTIONNAIRE

Purpose

The purpose of this exercise is to provide a method for you to assess three levels of an organization's effectiveness in managing a diverse workforce: individual attitudes, organizational values, and management practices.

Guidelines

1. Individuals respond to the questionnaire based on their perception of the organization and how it functions.

2. Questionnaires are collected and scored both for total and for individual attitudes, organizational values, and management practices separately (see scoring guide that follows). The higher the scores, the more effective the organization.

In this organization	Very true	Somewhat true	Not true
1. I am at ease with people of diverse backgrounds.	_____	_____	_____
2. There is diverse staff at all levels.	_____	_____	_____
3. Managers have a track record of hiring and promoting diverse employees.	_____	_____	_____
4. In general, I find change stimulating, exciting, and challenging.	_____	_____	_____
5. Racial, ethnic, and gender jokes are not tolerated in the informal environment.	_____	_____	_____
6. Managers hold all people equally accountable.	_____	_____	_____
7. I know about the cultural norms of different groups.	_____	_____	_____
8. The formation of ethnic and gender support groups is encouraged.	_____	_____	_____
9. Managers are flexible, structuring benefits and rules that work for everyone.	_____	_____	_____
10. I feel free to disagree with members of other groups without fear of being called prejudiced.	_____	_____	_____
11. There is a mentoring program that identifies and prepares women and people of color for promotion.	_____	_____	_____
12. Appreciation of differences can be seen in the rewards managers give.	_____	_____	_____
13. I feel there is more than one right way to do things.	_____	_____	_____
14. Members of the nondominant group feel they belong.	_____	_____	_____
15. One criterion of a manager's performance review is developing the diversity of his/her staff.	_____	_____	_____
16. I think that diverse viewpoints make for creativity.	_____	_____	_____
17. Turnover rates among women and people of color are similar to those among other groups.	_____	_____	_____
18. Managers give feedback and evaluate performance so employees don't "lose face."	_____	_____	_____
19. I am aware of my own assumptions and stereotypes.	_____	_____	_____
20. Policies are flexible enough to accommodate everyone.	_____	_____	_____
21. Managers get active participation from all employees in meetings.	_____	_____	_____
22. I think there is enough common ground to hold staff together.	_____	_____	_____
23. The speaking of other languages is welcomed.	_____	_____	_____
24. Multicultural work teams function harmoniously.	_____	_____	_____
25. Staff members spend their lunch hour and breaks in mixed groups.	_____	_____	_____

26. Money and time are spent on diversity development
    activities.   _____   _____   _____
27. Managers effectively use problem-solving skills to
    deal with language differences or other culture clashes.   _____   _____   _____
28. I feel that working in a diverse staff enriches me.   _____   _____   _____
29. Top management backs up its value on diversity
    with action.   _____   _____   _____
30. Managers have effective strategies to use when
    one group refuses to work with another.   _____   _____   _____

SCORING:

Very true = 2 points; Somewhat true = 1 point; Not true = 0 points

_____ Individual attitudes and beliefs: Items 1, 4, 7, 10, 13, 16, 19, 22, 25, 28

_____ Organizational values and norms: Items 2, 5, 8, 11, 14, 17, 20, 23, 26, 29

_____ Management practices and policies: Items 3, 6, 9, 12, 15, 18, 21, 24, 27, 30

_____ Total score

Source: Lee Gardenswartz and Anita Rowe, *The Managing Diversity Survival Guide: A Complete Collection of Checklists, Activities, and Tips* (Boston, MA: McGraw-Hill, 1994), 129–31.

TOOL TO ASSIST DIVERSITY CONSULTING TEAM PROJECT: ASKING GOOD QUESTIONS

Purpose

The purpose of this exercise is to illuminate meaningful questions that you can use to understand how diversity is seen within an organization. In diagnosing how an organization approaches diversity, it is helpful to assess the experiences and intentions of the leaders of the organization and those of members of its dominant and nondominant cultures.

Sample interview questions for leaders and policymakers

1. What have been the biggest benefits of having a multicultural workforce? What are the biggest problems and frustrations?
2. With an increasingly diverse workforce, what changes do you see in productivity, interpersonal dynamics, and bottom line (e.g., training dollars spent on education)?
3. What challenges does this present to your organization?
4. What is your organization doing to help your managers meet these challenges? What do they need to learn to do differently?
5. How do you measure and reward your managers in this area?
6. What is your organization doing to enhance the upward mobility of nondominant-group members? What obstacles prevent this mobility?
7. What processes do you have to identify and develop a diverse pool of talented employees?
8. What does your organization do that reflects how it values cultural diversity?
9. What is your organization doing to accommodate differences in values, norms, and mores?

10. What made you decide to invest your organization's resources (e.g., time, energy, and money) in making diversity development a priority? What results have you seen?
11. What organizational systems, practices, and policies present obstacles to fully developing and utilizing your diverse workforce?
12. If your organization does nothing to address the cultural diversity issue, what do you predict will happen?

Sample interview questions for employees of nondominant cultures

1. What do you like about the culture of this organization?
2. What do you find difficult about it?
3. What did you expect to find when you came to work here? What was your biggest surprise, biggest joy, and biggest disappointment?
4. What kinds of experiences made you feel welcome/unwelcome in this organization? If unwelcome, what did you do to help the situation?
5. What is your professional goal? What do you hope to achieve here?
6. How has this organization helped you toward your goal? How could it help more?
7. Have you ever felt it was a mistake to come to work here? If so, what made you feel this way?
8. How have you been treated by bosses and coworkers?
9. How do you get along with people of other groups in the workplace?
10. On a scale of 1–10, how much do you feel a part of the organization? What needs to happen to make you feel more a part of it?
11. What is the most important thing the organization can do to help you adjust? What can you do about it?

Source: Lee Gardenswartz and Anita Rowe, *The Managing Diversity Survival Guide: A Complete Collection of Checklists, Activities, and Tips* (Boston, MA: McGraw-Hill, 1994), 160–61.

Sample interview questions for employees of the dominant culture

1. What have been the biggest changes in this organization the past few years?
2. What have been the biggest benefits of being part of a multicultural workforce? What have been the biggest problems and frustrations?
3. How does diversity in the workforce affect you, your work group, and this organization?
4. What has been the biggest "culture shock" for you in working with diverse groups?
5. What kinds of experiences make you feel comfortable/uncomfortable with employees from different groups? If uncomfortable, what did you do to help the situation?
6. How have you been treated by employees of diverse groups?
7. What is the most important thing your organization can do to help members of nondominant groups adapt to this organization?
8. What is the most important thing these employees can do to help themselves adapt?

Source: This exercise was developed by Kathryn A. Cañas and Harris Sondak.

Notes

1. The Associated Press, "Study Gives NFL B+ for Diversity, Incomplete Grade on Gender Equity," *USA Today,* August 27, 2008, http://www.usatoday.com/sports/football/nfl/2008-08-27-study_N.htm.

2. The Associated Press, "Commissioner Extends Head Coach Interview Requirements to Senior Posts," *NFL.com*, June 15, 2009, http://www.nfl.com/news/story?id=09000d5d810d59db&template=without-video-with-comments&confirm=true.

3. NASCAR, "Job Opportunities Within the NASCAR Industry," *NASCAR.com*, 2009, http://www.nascar.com/2004/news/headlines/official/08/04/sport_jobs/index.html.

4. Seth Livingstone, "NASCAR Seeks Diversity But Finds the Going Slow," *USA Today* April 27, 2007, http://www.usatoday.com/sports/motor/nascar/2007-04-26-diversity-cover_N.htm.

5. NHL, Teams roster. Retrieved June 21, 2009, from *NHL.com* 2009, http://www.nhl.com/ice/teams.htm.

6. PGA Tour, "PGA Tour Diversity Internship Program," *PGATOUR.com* 2009, http://www.pgatour.com/company/internships.html.

7. Dave Seanor, "Despite the So-called Tiger Effect, Achieving Diversity in Golf Remains an Elusive Goal," *Examiner.com*, October 31, 2008, http://www.examiner.com/x-755-Golf-Examiner~y2008m10d31-Despite-the-socalled-Tiger-Effect-achieving-diversity-in-golf-remains-an-elusive-goal.

8. NBA, "NBA Gets High Marks for Diversity in New Study," *NBA.com*, June 10, 2009, http://www.nba.com/2009/news/06/10/NBA.diversity.ap/index.html?rss=true

INDEX